BLACK WORKERS REMEMBER

THE GEORGE GUND FOUNDATION
IMPRINT IN AFRICAN AMERICAN STUDIES

The George Gund Foundation has endowed
this imprint to advance understanding of
the history, culture and current issues
concerning African Americans.

BLACK WORKERS REMEMBER

AN ORAL HISTORY OF SEGREGATION, UNIONISM, AND THE FREEDOM STRUGGLE

MICHAEL KEITH HONEY

UNIVERSITY OF CALIFORNIA PRESS

berkeley / los angeles / london

THE PUBLISHER GRATEFULLY
ACKNOWLEDGES THE CONTRIBUTIONS
TO THIS BOOK PROVIDED BY THE
GEORGE GUND FOUNDATION.

University of California Press
Berkeley and Los Angeles, California

University of California Press, Ltd.
London, England

First paperback printing 2001

Library of Congress Cataloging-in-Publication Data

Honey, Michael K.
Black workers remember : an oral history of segregation,
unionism, and the freedom struggle /
Michael Keith Honey.
p.   cm.—(George Gund Foundation
imprint in African American studies)
Includes bibliographical references and index.
ISBN 0-520-23205-4 (pbk. : alk. paper).
1. Afro-Americans—Employment—History Sources.
2. Labor movement—United States—History Sources.
3. Trade-unions—Afro-American membership—History
Sources.   4. Race discrimination—United States—
History Sources.   5. Afro-Americans Interviews.
1. Title.   II. Series.
HD8081.A65H66   2000
331.6'396073—dc21   99-16357
CIP

Manufactured in the United States of America

08   07   06   05   04   03   02   01
10   9   8   7   6   5   4   3   2   1

The paper used in this publication meets the minimum
requirements of ANSI/NISO Z39.48-1992 (R 1997)
(*Permanence of Paper*). ∞

To the workers and their families
who fought for equal rights,
whose voices we will remember.

I hope I was some help to you and to younger people. As the song say, "I hope my living will not be in vain." The union is the people. You got to have your people with you. If everybody fighting for one cause, you got a strong union.

Leroy Boyd

CONTENTS

SYNOPSIS AND ACKNOWLEDGMENTS

Black Workers Remember is an oral history told in many voices. It provides both a personal account of the particular experiences of black southerners in Memphis, Tennessee, and a larger story about the experience of African Americans as workers. Its organization follows a rough chronological and thematic structure, but the narratives cross back and forth between historical and thematic frameworks. Chapter 1 provides a context for the oral histories. This chapter, unlike the rest of the book, reproduces eyewitness accounts by black workers taken at the time events occurred, allowing us to learn firsthand about the racial violence and deprivation of rights that underwrote the segregation system in the South. In chapter 2, black workers look back on the conditions they dealt with on a daily basis during the 1930s, when many of them made their transition to factory work. In chapter 3, black women describe their struggles to join the industrial labor force and to provide for their families during and after World War II. Black men in chapters 4 and 5 describe their resistance to racism and their attempts to break down Jim Crow in factories and unions during the postwar and cold war eras. Narrations in chapter 6 describe parallel civil rights and union rights struggles and relate them to the changes that began to take place in the 1960s. Chapter 7 focuses on the climactic battle of that decade during the strike of Memphis sanitation workers in 1968, which merged labor and civil rights concerns and opened a new front for organizing the working poor. In chapter 8 and the epilogue, African American workers look at the 1980s and 1990s and survey the gains and losses of six decades of their work and activism. Two "Interlude" sections underscore the theme of continuing black resistance to racism despite continual pressures to accommodate and show deference to whites.

The References and Notes section at the back of the book introduces the reader to historical background and some of my references. This book by no means provides us with a complete picture of the past, and I have tried to not burden the text with a lot of scholarly citations. I urge readers to use it as a starting place to explore the exceedingly rich literature in African American and labor history that frames this book's understandings and interpretations.

In this book, the terms "black" and "African American" are used interchangeably. I have used "black" as descriptor rather than as a term denoting nationality, hence the use of lower case. "White" denotes people of European ancestry but also does not denote specific nationality and is in lower case. In a multi-ethnic society, bi-racial terms such as "black" and "white" tell us little about a person's heritage, but in the context of this particular history these terms seem unavoidable.

It should be obvious that black workers whose accounts appear here and white workers who offered additional insights and knowledge made this book possible. I cannot thank them enough for their willingness to participate in this oral history project. But I would like to thank others as well. Ethnographers Patti J. Krueger and Janette Rawlings played crucial roles in creating most of the transcripts used in this book. Their prodigious work and their skills and ideas provided essential collaboration. Patti Krueger also read numerous drafts and helped me to pare down what seemed like an overwhelming manuscript. Kathleen Upperman and Nancy Draper did several transcriptions, and Anne Marie Cavanaugh collated census data on Memphis labor, providing timely aid near the end of this project. My thanks to Mark Allen, Joy Tremewin, Steve Lockwood, Mary Durham, and other friends in Memphis who have provided sustenance and moral support for many years.

It is my good fortune to have met numerous scholars who demonstrated to me that history is indeed a collaborative endeavor, and my debt to them is very great. Eric Arneson provided an amazingly thorough and analytically helpful review of two drafts of the text and gave me tremendous help in shaping this book. Alex Lichtenstein and Pete Daniel provided crucial readings of a first draft and offered encouragement and ideas for new directions at a time when I very much needed both. Rick Halpern gave me the sort of detailed comments one would expect from one of the most knowledgeable members of the world community of scholars concerned with labor and race. Tera Hunter, Jacquelyne Dowd Hall, and Patti Krueger all helped me to see that I did not have to explain everything and should let the workers do most of the talking. Gerald Horne asked a number of provocative questions that helped me to think again about gender and about anti-communism's impact on this history. Charles Payne and an unidentified reader for the University of California Press offered insights that helped me to shape a final text.

A number of other people helped me move this text forward at crucial moments. Kenneth Lang assisted me greatly by reading two "final" drafts and helping me improve each one of them. Paul Ortiz, Fitzhugh Brundage, and Stephanie Shaw gave me much needed encouragement by their readings of the very earliest draft of this manuscript. Paul's insights and enthusiasm, based on his work as an oral historian, provided a big boost at a time when I felt very uncertain about whether this project would work as a book. I am also very grateful to him for his guidance on research in Memphis conducted as part of the Behind the Veil Oral History Project, documenting African American life in the Jim Crow South, at Duke University's Center for Documentary Studies. Thanks to William Chafe, Robert Korstad, and Ray Gavins for allowing me to review and quote from the Memphis portion of the stunning oral histories their wonderful research group has gathered from all over the South. I also thank Laurie Green for access to several of her interviews and for her insights in papers she gave at historical conferences on the struggle of black women workers against the "plantation mentality."

These and other scholars have helped to shape my work, and acquisitions editor Monica McCormick at the University of California Press provided enthusiasm, clarity, and the support needed to make this into a publishable book. Steve Gilmartin provided excellent and much-welcomed copyediting. I have not followed all of the advice of anyone, of course, and this book's flaws and failures are mine alone.

Institutional help has also been crucial to completing this project. I would especially like to thank Ed Frank at the University of Memphis Mississippi Valley Collection for his unflagging support for this and other research related to Memphis and the South. My fellowship for one year at the National Humanities Center in North Carolina, supported by the

National Endowment for the Humanities, more than anything else made it possible to turn these oral histories into a book. I am forever indebted to all the fine people there for their gracious company and for the resources they brought to bear to enable me to do full-time research and writing. Karen Carroll played an especially invaluable role in getting transcripts and affidavits into a usable form. The University of Washington, Tacoma, provided research support and the time I needed away from teaching; students in my oral history classes strengthened my belief in the power of remembering; and my colleagues in the Interdisciplinary Arts and Sciences program have bolstered my morale and have helped to make teaching an honorable profession indeed. The Graduate School and the Center for Labor Studies of the University of Washington gave some research funds, and an early grant from the American Council of Learned Societies paid for the first transcriptions for this project nearly ten years ago. My oral history recordings and transcripts are available at the Southern Historical Collection at the University of North Carolina in Chapel Hill. Lewis Bateman, a senior editor at the University of North Carolina Press, encouraged my work on this project many years before I even began writing the text, for which I remain grateful, and I thank an unidentified reader at his press for very helpful comments. My partner and colleague, Patti Krueger, has borne with and supported this project through every stage with grace, tact, a sharp intellect, and strong commitment, for which I will always remain deeply grateful.

PREFACE

BLACK HISTORY AS LABOR HISTORY

The labor of black workers has been at the heart of U.S. history and economic development. Their labor under slavery produced the cotton and other agricultural goods that led U.S. exports into the world market, and, after slavery, undergirded industrialization as southern blacks migrated into the mines, private households, and urban economies of both the North and the South. Black migration accelerated during two world wars, and black labor became critical to the automobile, steel, meatpacking, mining, longshoring, and other basic industries, as well as to the service and household economies. Industrialization and migration produced "the long-run transformation of blacks from a predominantly rural proletariat to a predominantly urban working class," according to historian Joe Trotter.

The labor of black men and women helped build America, yet their freedom and their ability to reap the fruits of their labor always remained in question. A century of systematic racial exclusion and discrimination, and disfranchisement in the South, followed nearly 250 years of slavery. Segregation, the "separate but equal" doctrine approved by the U.S. Supreme Court in its 1896 *Plessy v. Ferguson* decision, existed not only as a set of laws in the South but also as a set of practices that applied throughout the country's work, politics, and civic life, and affected not only African Americans but other racialized minorities. In this book, black workers, many of whom grew up only one generation removed from slavery, remember how racism and segregation constrained their daily lives and how they endured and resisted. They did so, however, within work situations that required constant accommodation. Their movement from the countryside to the city and from plantation to factory did not set them free. They constantly had to resist white employers and white workers who sought to keep them from access to skilled jobs, higher wages, and citizenship rights, but not resist so overtly as to get themselves killed. Within a racial system that demanded accommodation, they, like their parents and grandparents, carved out a degree of dignity and self-respect.

Through their narratives, we see a multi-layered and multi-generational struggle in which black workers sought to deal with constraints and to change their conditions. Their personal stories, spanning the period from the 1930s through the 1990s, ask us to rethink the standard narration of the civil rights movement as one that emerged in the 1950s and 1960s led by young people and preachers. They suggest that long decades of striving by working-class people made possible the rights that so many of us take for granted today. According to these workers, not only civil rights but the right to a good job and decent wages is and always has been at the core of the African American struggle for equality.

Black workers challenged racial and economic exploitation through strikes, court suits, and courageous individual efforts to break the occupational color bar. Unions in some cases helped them to challenge racism and in others reinforced it. For black workers, unions did not confer rights so much as offer a chance to participate and exert influence in ways usually denied to them in the larger society. They seized this opportunity whenever they could. Most of those who tell their stories in this volume first gained real voting rights though National Labor Relations Board–sponsored elections at the workplace. Through factory employment and union organization, they built stable families, churches, and civic organizations and sent children to college. Black workers only rarely led the civil rights movement, but ultimately they gained a degree of political power and helped to lay a social base favorable to its emergence. And many of them participated directly in the freedom movement.

Women, as well as men, played a major role in this history. Until the 1960s and 1970s, many employers, and union leaders too, considered factories (and often unions) to be part of the white male sphere. While black men bore the brunt of racial violence and reprisals when they tried to organize, black women bore the heaviest burdens of exclusion. Faced with the triple burdens of race, class, and gender discrimination, few of them could get jobs in industrial workplaces, and when they did it took extraordinary efforts to raise their families while working in full-time factory jobs. But step by step they gained access to nondomestic work, and black women increasingly became union organizers. Unions became less of a white male space and more of a meeting place, one which included women and ethnic minorities. Through participation, black women and black men alike expanded the meaning of unionism as an instrument for social change.

The narratives in this book are tied to a particular place, located on the Mississippi River Delta in the heart of the old plantation economy. Memphis, Tennessee, represents both the high and the low points of the black experience. In Memphis, investors seeking cheap land, labor, and raw materials have long used racism in the pursuit of profit, going back to the city's first settlers, who removed the native Chickasaw and took their lands. A transportation, trade, banking, and manufacturing center for the mid-South, the city's economy always depended on the labor of black workers. Segregation tightly constrained their opportunities and drove down their wages. It split white and black workers into separate and unequal worlds. Employer discrimination, in tandem with union exclusion, white racial violence, and poor education kept blacks, and black women especially, at the bottom of the wage and job hierarchy. It is for good reason that people call Memphis "the home of the blues."

Yet the history of black workers in this place is not a depressing, hopeless one. Indeed, the creative and artistic genius of generations of workers bubbled up through the Memphis black community. It provided a way station for blues giants (W. C. Handy, Bessie Smith, Memphis Minnie, B. B. King, Muddy Waters, among others) and soul and gospel artists (such as Otis Redding, Rufus and Carla Thomas, and Al Green). It became a birthing place for the interracial fusion that became rock and roll. Music reflected the anguish and joy of black working-class culture and was an ever-present part of community life. Whether in a joint on Beale Street, a storefront church, a union hall, or at a mass labor or civil rights rally, music conveyed humor, dignity, and constant striving for a better life. Hope and an ability to endure characterized generations of people moving from slavery and sharecropping into wage labor, and their music, voluntary associations, religious activity, and, not least, civil rights and labor struggles embodied that hope and endurance.

Memphis and its black workers came dramatically to the world's attention in 1968. Black sanitation workers with their "I Am a Man" slogan and their nearly three-month strike against the city spoke for an entire community tired of being underpaid and trampled upon by a paternalistic white power structure. These strikers, supported by a strong church base and many "jack leg preachers" in their midst, fought for human dignity both as workers and as African Americans. Their struggle joined labor and civil rights issues in a new way. By winning union recognition and better conditions they raised the hopes of the black working poor all over America. The assassination of Martin Luther King, Jr., and the subsequent failure of his Poor People's Campaign, however, dashed hopes that civil rights and labor movements might join hands to uplift the poor. An era of plant closings, union decline, and widening racial and economic inequalities followed. Increasing numbers of African Americans, and white workers as well, found themselves shut out of gainful employment, as employers searched for more educated or cheaper workers in a globalized labor market.

While Memphis and the South provide the setting for these narratives of black workers, their stories concern a much larger history. In many ways, one could say that the stories told here typify the black labor experience during the industrial era. Black Firestone worker Edward Harrell pointed out to me that when he went to visit friends at the Firestone facility in Los Angeles, he discovered racial wage differentials, discriminatory seniority and job classifications systems, and tensions between white and black that he felt were in some ways worse than in Memphis or other parts of the South. Workplace apartheid operated on the waterfronts, shipyards, and in the factories of New York, Chicago, Detroit, Pittsburgh, Oakland, Los Angeles, Portland, and Seattle, as well as in Memphis, New Orleans, Birmingham, Baltimore, or Norfolk. Workplace segregation and racial subordination in fact were almost universal in the North American industrial system.

This is not a universal story, in that it concerns a particular group of black labor activists who found themselves on the cutting edge of change. Their story in some ways is not even typical, for most blacks worked not in factories but in domestic, service, and nonindustrial work. And most did not belong to unions. In other ways, however, their story is emblematic of the black labor experience. Wherever they lived and whatever they did, black workers almost universally were excluded from the better craft and factory jobs and from white-collar and managerial work. Segregation in the South and racism in the North denied them good education and housing, devalued them as workers and citizens, and consigned them to low-wage, hot, dirty employment or to no employment at all.

In the late twentieth century, while white America condemned many African Americans for their poverty and told them to pull themselves up by their own bootstraps, corporations destroyed much of the unionized factory employment that had helped them move up, and government increasingly ignored their plight. It is no exaggeration to say, as Clarence Coe does at the end of this book, that this history is one in which many whites accumulated land, education, and capital, while unfree or discriminatory conditions of work and citizenship denied these things to most African Americans and to other people of color as well. Black workers, going back to the era of slavery, built much of the American economy, in both its agricultural and industrial phases. They helped generate immense profit, but gained little of it for themselves or their families. In many ways, this historic devaluation of black labor remains deeply rooted in the American economy and social fabric.

In a sense, the story told by black factory workers in this volume is at the heart of the African American economic and racial dilemma. These stories ask us to rethink the origins and implications of the civil rights movement, and compel us to look once again at how barriers of race, class, and gender have shaped and continue to shape the American experience. They ask us to think about what it means to be poor, black, and working class, and to recognize the unfinished character of the struggle for racial and economic justice in our own time. Black history is very much about this history, which is the history of us all.

INTRODUCTION

THE POWER OF REMEMBERING

The voices of poor and working-class people are only rarely heard in the halls of government, in the media, or in the history books. Least of all do we hear from African American workers, who lived under laws and customs that sought to silence them. Yet they did make history. In this book, they break the silences imposed by segregation and gain recognition as agents of social change. Covering a period of time still within the bounds of living human memory, from the 1930s to the present, in *Black Workers Remember* they tell their story.

My search for this history in a sense came out of my own family's union, ethnic (Acadian and English), and working-class origins, which sensitized me to the economic roots of racial injustice. My work as a community and civil liberties organizer in Memphis and the South during the early 1970s also kindled a curiosity to learn, as songwriter and union organizer John Handcox put it, about "those who fought and died before." As a witness to continuing racism in my own era, I became increasingly inquisitive about its roots: how deep they went, whether they could be untangled, who had sought to do so, and to what extent they had succeeded or failed. I continue to try to unearth the roots of racism and plant other roots, and my search for these hidden narratives became part of that continuing effort.

What was the role of black workers in labor history? In my early research on southern labor, I relied heavily on union leaders and organizers, who were much more informed than the histories or newspaper accounts I had read. Yet most people in leadership positions were white. They could not tell me the inside story about the lives of African Americans, who made up some 80 percent of the unskilled labor force in Memphis and comprised anywhere from a third to a majority of the workers in many Memphis factories during the 1930s and 1940s. I soon realized I could write a well-documented and plausible history, but without black voices it could be erroneous in many ways. As I began to locate black workers I learned that, indeed, history looked very different from their perspectives. It looked different from standard American histories, most labor and civil rights histories, and even most African American histories.

Because I could not rely on written accounts, oral history provided the only available method for uncovering an active black working class in factories and other workplaces. It is the oldest form of history, in which stories are passed down from one generation to the next by word of mouth. Capturing those stories for a written culture requires the participation of a collector who breaks the usual isolation between the world of books and the lived world of communities. I played the role of collector, while black workers provided the text.

Firestone workers became the key to creating that text. They worked in one of the largest factories in Memphis (fluctuating between three thousand and seven thousand employees), a place where black workers and race issues always played a central role. What went on in that factory, one of the most prosperous in Memphis, affected the entire labor scene in the city and the economic development of the black community. Workers from Firestone, as members of the United Rubber Workers (URW), acted as the weathervane for the Congress of Industrial Organizations (CIO), the federation to which most factory unions affiliated. Firestone workers thus came to be among my most important informants about black history in the industrial unions.

Black workers, when I found them, told me a somewhat different story than had some white union officials, who tended to paint a picture of harmonious race relations. The first black worker I located, Firestone shop leader Josh Tools, spoke with me in 1983. Asked whether his union had led the way in improving race relations, as I had begun to think, he emphatically responded, "Hell no!" Some blacks at Firestone, I later discovered, regarded him as a yes-man to white union leaders, and yet even Mr. Tools still became angry when he recalled how timid those leaders had been on race relations. He felt union leaders had failed to educate white workers about racism, and despite the fact that their union constitution forbade all forms of discrimination, they had not moved to desegregate the plant. He told me that blacks at Firestone, in the wake of the Supreme Court's decision mandating integration of public schools in *Brown v. Board of Education*, had sued both the union and the company for maintaining segregation. He described how blacks struggled for years at Firestone, suggesting that black workers themselves, not white union leaders or federal officials, had led the way to desegregation. Although I had scoured many documents and had talked to many white unionists, I had found no account of this.

I soon discovered how precious the living memory of a person like Mr. Tools was: the next time I returned to Memphis to interview him, he was dead. Trying to find other informants did not prove easy. One black Firestone worker I located remained so upset about his work experiences that he refused to speak about them and angrily told me to leave him alone. Fortunately, by going to the union retiree's hall I found other black Firestone workers who were actually eager to talk. Oral history began to unlock stories and feelings long buried and events never asked about. In one session Edward Harrel, James Mitchell, Robert Matthews, Johnny Williamson, and Danny Davis told me about the workaday racism they struggled with all their lives—a conversation I have found impossible to capture on paper. Williamson, a gentle-seeming man in his eighties, remembered with some sense of amusement and irony how he worked a white man to an early death. "Hog Jowls," they called him in a matter-of-fact way, was trying to get Mr. Williamson off a machine and back into a lower-waged laboring job. Williamson, like most of the men I talked to, had worked on a farm and felt he could outwork anybody. He certainly did in the case of Hog Jowls, who had a heart problem and soon died from his exertions trying to out-produce Williamson.

As workers told me over and over, whites didn't want blacks to have "white" jobs, and in one near-riotous confrontation over this issue that this group remembered, workers, black and white alike, carried pistols to the union hall. Somewhat to my surprise, these black workers remembered their past not with bitterness, but with a sense of humor and a feeling of ultimate triumph. For these former farmhands going through what seemed to me to be the disaster of proletarianization, life had improved. They worked harder than I can imagine, but not as hard as they had worked on the farm. They no longer worked for "Mister Charlie," some white man who would steal their profits from sharecropping, and in the end they outlasted "Mister" E. H. Crump, the political boss who enforced Jim Crow in the city. At retirement, their wages were ten times higher than when they began. Through the union, they gained rights at the job that their ancestors never had, and they felt empowered by the lives they had led.

As I came to know a circle of black workers at Firestone, other kinds of testimony spurred my search for oral histories. In my archival research, I had discovered Thomas Watkins, a black longshore leader who engaged in a tumultuous, lifelong resistance to racism. He and his parents had fled sharecropping in the South, but their family disintegrated when they moved to the urban ghettos of the North. Watkins joined the army, only to be thrown in prison in Fort Leavenworth, Texas, and dishonorably discharged after he resisted abuse from a white superior. During the Depression, he rode the rails, worked in steel mills, slept in hobo camps, and ended up as a longshore worker in Memphis. In 1939 he led an extraordinary movement of solidarity on the Memphis docks during a strike in defiance of white union leaders, the city's political machine, the Mississippi River barge companies, and the police. Some forty years later, I found his affidavit in Justice Department files in the National Archives documenting the brutal post-strike attempt by police and employers to murder him.

My search for Watkins following my discovery of his affidavit soon shocked me again into realizing how precious the accounts of a dying generation of black workers were. My Freedom of Information Act request showed that FBI agents, who considered him a dangerous radical, had followed Watkins to Portland, Oregon, and last interviewed him there in 1952. I imagined that he had surely died, and did not follow these leads until after I moved to the Pacific Northwest. Late in the summer of 1989, I discovered that Watkins had died less than a year before I came to the doorstep of his old address in Portland. My chagrin turned to anguish as I tracked down some of his friends, who told me that Watkins had astonishing strength and an acute memory almost until he died. He told them stirring stories of his past, advised young black unionists, and remained widely respected among those who knew him well. This man had a story to tell.

My failure to locate such an obviously important protagonist in history prior to his death troubled me deeply. I imagined the details of Watkins's odyssey, but I could not ask him what his life had been like. Having lost one of the most important individuals I found in my research, I became desperate to locate other individuals like Watkins. My search led me to George Holloway. Numerous people in Memphis had told me he knew the "real" story of the labor movement and the black struggle for equal rights. I had reached him by phone at his home in Baltimore in 1986, but we failed to connect. I did not pursue him further until after my missed opportunity with Thomas Watkins goaded me on. When I finally found Holloway three years after first calling him, I discovered a man with a great story to tell, one which ultimately led me to write this book.

Mr. Holloway first introduced me to his kind wife, Hattie, and then we went down to his basement, not to emerge for about eight hours. He showed me his plaques, his awards, his union books, and photos. Here was a man who had met Martin Luther King, Walter Reuther, Bobby and Ted Kennedy, legendary union and civil rights leader A. Philip Randolph, and African American scientist George Washington Carver. More important, the man was a walking textbook, and he began to teach me black labor history.

Mr. Holloway had gone to college, completing several years at Booker T. Washington's Tuskegee Institute, in Alabama, where he met Carver and other important African Americans. But in Holloway's era, college education for a black man did not open the doors to skilled employment; he was forced to work as an unskilled laborer in factories, where he marshaled all his education in the union struggle. As his life unfolded, Holloway became a master at his craft of organizing and in retirement proved to be a thoughtful analyst of his eventful union career and shop experiences. He had the history and the details all in his head, ready for a grand lecture that included exact knowledge of events, work processes, conversations, and political developments. His ability to recall addresses, names, dates, and descriptions stunned me, especially as both the specific stories and the general picture he presented matched my own research. In one eight-hour interview, he gave me a dazzling view of the black union struggle in Memphis. Mr. Holloway confirmed the importance of finding individuals who could give reliable, first-hand accounts of the segregation era from the perspective of the working-class blacks who lived through it.

I had found Mr. Holloway none too soon: within months, he had died from a massive heart attack. But, as he had fervently hoped, his story has survived. For this I am extremely thankful. Over a period of years doing oral histories, the sense of loss has jolted me repeatedly. Leroy Clark, an astute organizer and political leader, also opened up new worlds to me in one short interview, but he died before I could meet with him again. As the years have passed and the lives of people I interviewed and came to know have ended, the obligation to pass on the stories of a dying generation of industrial workers has seemed ever more important.

None of those stories proved more impressive than that of Clarence Coe. Like Holloway, he had retired from factory work, yet retained a cogent and insightful knowledge of the past. His story in particular pointed me toward trying to understand the emotional and personal impact of racism and segregation. I reached Mr. Coe by phone one night while I was in Memphis, at the suggestion of one of his acquaintances. I had tried for days to find him. He did not really want to be found, I sensed. Many of his experiences in the factory had been painful. A sensitive and intelligent man, he had endured years of racial affronts from whites. He had tried to put these incidents behind him, and now here was a white stranger reopening the wounds once again by asking about the past. Yet even over the phone, once Mr. Coe started telling his story, it was as if he could not stop. He poured out his past as if it had happened yesterday.

The next day, I found him at his home and he graciously consented to continue. Although it obviously upset and pained him to do it, in about three short hours the man had hurtled us back through forty years of history. He told me of the terrors of growing up during an era of lynch law in the countryside and of the daily hardships he faced, including how white workers tried to hurt or kill him for trying to break down job segregation. In a commonsense but brilliant manner, he explained the political economy of racism, how it worked and who benefited, and summed up the lessons of the labor movement for white and black alike.

He was an extraordinary storyteller and analyst, a scholar of his own life. The power of his remembering came in part from the deep pain of his encounters with racism, and in part from the profound meaning the story held for him. Here was one of the souls who had staked his life on the chance to break down the walls of Jim Crow through the American labor movement, and the scars of his struggles remained very close to the surface of his memory.

Yet neither Mr. Holloway nor Mr. Coe stood alone in their abilities to tell history from a first-hand perspective. Over and over, I found black workers who joked, became angry, upset, or turned coolly reflective as they recounted harsh circumstances and moments of triumph. Leroy Boyd, Matthew Davis, and others I spoke with carried lifetimes of stories in their heads. Women workers Irene Branch, Evelyn Bates, Alzada Clark, Susie Wade, Rebecca McKinley, and Ida Leachman opened up yet another round of inquiry. Last hired and first fired, and for me the hardest to find, these women offered a female- and family-based perspective on the hidden history of black working-class struggle and endurance.

A Deepening Perspective

Such a history could never be recounted with such clarity by anyone who had not lived it. The power of remembering is that, instead of generalizations, we dealt in specifics. The stories in this book tell us more than a sociological survey or archival study could. Graphic details of encounters with segregation on the everyday level allow us to feel and imagine a buried part of our collective past in new ways, and reveal the subterranean history of what ordinary people did to resist racism and to build their own lives in spite of it. These work-centered accounts may be among the most reliable oral histories we can find. Black workers like Clarence Coe might wish they could forget some of the daily details of life under segregation, but these remained seared in his brain. According to oral historian Steven Caunce, the "details of everyday life [are] worn into the brain by constant repetition and are not subject to anything like the same uncertainty as memories of unusual events." Because black workers lived Jim Crow day in and day out, the oral histories of this particular group allow us, as Caunce suggests, to "examine life at a level of detail that would be quite impossible to achieve for whole populations." The combined testimonies of such "witnesses" present an indelible portrait of black life under segregation from the perspective of workers, part of a group that made up the great majority of the black community.

What it all meant in a larger sense emerged and deepened as we continued to examine the details. These oral histories not only allow us to access a hidden history, but provide a crucial element of perspective. These interviews often gave black workers their first real opportunity to recount and reevaluate their past. One black mother told interviewer Robert Coles that in the period of segregation, southern blacks normally had to hide their knowledge, "store it in the bones, way inside," and as a result, "the colored man, I think he has to hide what he really feels from himself." In these accounts, by contrast, people take their knowledge and memory out of storage and try to make sense of their lives. The opportunity to do this can provide a new way to come to terms with the terrible or sad aspects of one's life and also create a new perspective for the written record.

As Susan Tucker noted in her interviews of southern black domestic workers and their white employers, revisioning the past in this way allows people to acknowledge and incorporate its painful legacy. Instead of feeling victimized by the past, people come to see how they survived and grew. "For black women, revision made possible the discussion of 'bad times'—injustices and even cruelties—with a spirit of strength," Tucker noted. In a similar way, as Clarence Coe recollected the hurts and humiliations of Jim Crow, he also put them into a larger context and took pride in his triumphs. "I was determined to get completed what I set out to do. And I did, I did." As these workers speak to us from the present as witnesses to their own lives, their memories reinforce the truth of their experiences and deepen our understanding.

Creating a Shared Authority

Remembering in a historical sense occurs not only through the voices of history's participants but through the work of the collector of stories. To elicit, organize, and set oral testimonies in a context without interference or distortion is no small matter. How the collector gathers and then uses stories necessarily becomes crucial to how they are told. In the time available, which varied greatly and ranged anywhere from two hours to a full day, I would begin by asking my informants general questions about their lives and family backgrounds and then focus in on their experiences as workers and union members. A few leading questions in most cases elicited a great deal of testimony. Once the narrator started, I adhered largely to the "open ended" format: people chose to speak about what they thought was important and could easily recall, I followed up with questions as best I could.

The result appears in some ways to be part of an older style of labor history based on factory and union conflicts, with family, church, and community issues seeming in some cases to become secondary. But the "old" labor history might in this case be what we needed to talk about. Through this method, the experience of work and the struggle to improve conditions through unions emerged as a central theme of the narratives.

Of course, our collaboration was ho simple matter. Race shaped our interactions; how could it not? Most if not all of their encounters with white men had been far from rewarding. At the same time, they had long ago broken through racial conventions, and they all demanded respect. They sometimes commented on my "whiteness" or my outsider status as a northern academic, and they puzzled out how much I understood about racism. Yet my "outsider" status also meant I had no entangling alliances with the black community or the same prejudices one might expect of local whites. To the extent that they knew about it, my past history in Memphis as a civil liberties and civil rights organizer boded well for collaboration. Not just polite exchanges but the sense of friendly acquaintance that comes from exploring personal histories often emerged from our interactions.

Still, I wondered at their willingness to tell me about their lives. I found it remarkable, after many conversations, that black workers would open up to an outsider such as myself. In a real sense, by consenting to be interviewed these workers took a gamble, and I am eternally grateful to them for doing so. I myself did not know at the time what would become of the interviews, and we never discussed payment for their participation for the simple reason that I had none to offer (I was a graduate student or searching for a job during much of the period spanning these interviews). These workers had nothing in a material sense to gain, yet with few exceptions they welcomed the opportunity to tell me their stories. Why?

The main reason these black workers proved so willing had to do with their own objectives. This was their story, in their own words, told from their point of view. They wanted the world, or someone, to know about the struggles they had waged and the conditions they had endured. Most of them expressed surprise and pleasure that others cared to know about their lives. George Holloway told me in no uncertain terms how grateful he was that someone had recognized that he and his fellow workers had been makers of history. They could only go on faith that something good would come of our explorations, but clearly they wanted this story to be told. Without the tape recorder, they knew their stories would never go beyond close friends and family, if even that far.

After generously giving of their time, these workers even more generously gave up control over the use of their words and trusted me to find a way to use them in the best way possible. This has placed a large responsibility on me. My objective was to be faithful to what the people I talked to said and to try to make the significance of their stories as clear as possible. These two objectives have required a lot of editing and writing and taught me the great complexity of creating printed stories from the spoken word. I did not know that once stories told orally had been taped, years of work in transcribing and editing lay ahead. And trying to get these narratives into book form has been far more difficult than I would ever have imagined.

It also required other forms of collaboration. To begin with, getting the word from the tape recorder to the page required a great deal of work from skilled ethnographers and stenographers. These included primarily Patti Krueger, Janette Rawlings, and me. Each of us sought to stick to the content and speech pattern and style of the speaker, but at some point we removed the redundancies of normal speech, and in some cases merged my questions (appearing in some cases as bracketed interpolations) with the speaker's narrative. We have not tried to preserve speech patterns exactly as heard, which would have made the text difficult to read. With a few deviations from standard English, we made the speaker's meaning as clear as we could but have not imposed a uniform style for all transcriptions.

Second, to create a text that unfolds in a logical sequence required considerable reorganization of the transcription. This necessity sprang from the nature of the interviews themselves. Most people don't talk in a straight line but circle around their subject. When it comes to the printed word, however, most of us would like to speak clearly, with detail, and in a logical sequence. I tried to make this possible by merging different parts of an interview or interviews with a person and moving texts around, providing bridges (in brackets, or if not in brackets, using the speaker's own words) and deleting excess words. I have tried to make the narratives as straightforward as possible without altering meanings or dramatically changing the speaker's style or train of thought. The reader should not be under the illusion that the workers spoke these narratives exactly as printed here. Yet each interview is as true to the meaning and rhetoric of the speaker as I could make it. (Original taped interviews will be placed in a university research library for public use.)

My selection, arrangement, and commentary also strongly influence how these stories are told to the reader. In the following pages I stitch black workers' stories together into what I hope is a logical sequence. I have introduced testimonies in each chapter with some historical context while framing them in a coherent narrative structure. I could have let each account stand alone in its entirety, but this would have produced huge chapters in some cases and very small ones in others. Moreover, the narratives would have repeated topics and constantly ranged back and forth chronologically. To avoid these problems, I grouped interviews thematically and to some extent chronologically, and connected them with information and analysis intended to explain and emphasize the significance of what they are telling us. And I have not shied away from coming to some conclusions about what the narratives tell us in the larger sense. Based on the conversations I had with these workers, I feel that they would want me to do this; not to speak for them, but to speak with them about this history, and to organize the material as coherently as possible.

No doubt, this long process of transcribing, editing, reorganizing, and placing the narratives into context to some extent transforms the original interviews. The narrative presented here thus becomes a joint creation of the workers, the interviewer, the transcribers, and the historian, creating what historian Michael Frisch calls a "shared authority" over the oral history text. In fact, there is no single authority when writing history, but this method of construction makes that all the more obvious. On a practical level, good reason exists for the "shared authority" of a text such as this one. The people whose stories are collected here are retired, and some are not in good health; many have passed away before publication of the book. None of them was in a position to write his or her own story. Without shared authority, there would be no text.

Our shared authority became very real at the personal level. Limited as we were by time constraints, we searched together for the past in less-than-ideal circumstances. The clash of dishes being cleared off the table, phones ringing, grandchildren running through the house punctuate many a taped recollection. But in the comfort of someone's home, in an unheated car, or in an old union hall profoundly human exchanges occurred. Especially if the narrator was telling a story for the first time (or perhaps for the first time to a historian), it could be deeply moving for both of us. This too shaped the nature of the text we present in this book, which attempts to convey people's feelings and sense of their times as much as it tries to lay out the facts of black working-class existence.

The present deeply shaped their accounts of the past, providing the advantage of hindsight and perspective developed over lifetimes. Time dims the memory, of course, but it also allows people to select from various truths of history as they lived it. How we as individuals understand our past is influenced very much by how life has turned out, and the process of remembering also produces both new information and a new perspective. This is how we come to terms with our past. Remembering also provides some measure of healing. Although these workers looked back in horror sometimes, they were proud of what they made of their lives. They wanted the world to know how they struggled to change things and what they transcended.

The story told here is a highly personal reflection, yet it is not only personal. As testament to the hidden realities of American history, perhaps these memories will open new doors to readers not familiar with the history of black labor. By coming to know, indirectly, a few people who lived these particular experiences, readers might reconsider the broader picture of the past and think about how the past bears upon the present. These stories are as separate and distinct as the individuals who tell them. Yet they compose a collective memory, one which personalizes the tragic and heroic struggles of a larger group. It provides a "bottom-up" and working-class perspective on the many ways that African Americans in the Jim Crow era creatively shaped their environment and laid the groundwork for the advancement of their children and grandchildren.

Many know that Martin Luther King, Jr., gave his life in a battle for the dignity and rights of black workers and the poor, but few know of the struggles of black workers themselves. In this book, some of these workers stand at King's side as agents of social change. Without testimonies from ordinary people, it sometimes appears that events are directed from the top. Yet people who to others seem content may actually be resisting, and communities that appear static may be undergoing fundamental shifts. *Black Workers Remember* shows that working-class blacks were indeed a force in history. Their testimonies contradict glib assertions that the search for profit in a capitalist market economy will eliminate poverty; instead, they suggest the importance of labor organization to our collective well-being. They also show that we still have much to learn about the interconnection between racism and economics.

These workers are, as George Holloway describes himself, "witnesses" to a hidden history of struggle for freedom. It is a bitter history but one they are proud of. Far from being neutral or "objective," the history told here is a group story that allows us to feel and understand the experiences of individuals and to see how they altered their lives by taking action. The power of remembering, we might hope, is that it helps us to understand how the world in which we live came to be, and how we too might change it. It is these workers who deserve the credit for this book. For without their sometimes astonishing willingness to tell about their experiences, and without their grace, humility, and steadfastness in the struggle for a better life, there would be no story.

1 SEGREGATION, RACIAL VIOLENCE, AND BLACK WORKERS

[Jim Crow] was a man making me work to build up a country and saying don't you touch what you've built. I got no pay. We do have Jim Crow, but you don't have to accept it. See, I've never accepted it.

Arizona Marie Fort, Memphis schoolteacher,
interviewed at age 91 in 1995

Who was Jim Crow and what was his meaning? The name came from minstrel shows in the nineteenth and early twentieth centuries, in which white men in "blackface" portrayed the supposedly comic figure of "Jim Crow," a dancing, docile, and happy simpleton from the slavery era. This twisted image of the black man placed a benign facade on the ideas and practices of white supremacy, which deemed African Americans genetically and socially inferior to so-called whites. The term "Jim Crow" came to be used as slang for racial segregation, a system most whites supported. For African Americans, however, Jim Crow meant hard work at low pay, undergirded by pervasive racism and violence. Jim Crow meant keeping black people "in their place," at the bottom of society, and most black people resisted it whenever and however they could.

It took generations of struggle to finally bring down Jim Crow, and ongoing efforts to suppress that struggle created a frightening climate of repression that heavily shadowed the lives of black people in the South. Most African Americans growing up in this era could recount stories of white violence against themselves, a member of their family, or someone they knew. It could occur at any time, almost at random, yet there was nothing random or accidental about it, for racial violence had deep historical roots. For over two hundred and fifty years, slavery legitimized whipping, rape, mutilation, and even murder to control black bodies and labor. The "plantation mentality" of paternalism held that slave owners and white men, like fathers, knew what was best and demanded black deference and obedience. Defeating that mentality and its culture of violence proved no small task, for most whites, not only the upper classes but also working-class and poor whites, held strongly to the idea of white racial supremacy.

The ideas and practices of white supremacy did not begin or end in the South, and they shaped generations of white folk. Segregation actually began "north of slavery," where nominally free states imposed systematic exclusion of blacks from better housing, jobs, schools, and, very often, from voting, serving on juries, or otherwise exercising citizenship rights. Merchants and investors in the North had profited from slavery, and the federal government likewise had supported it at almost every turn. Although Euro-Americans ("whites") at times supported black struggles for freedom, racism convinced most of them that they were better than blacks. White supremacy never remained confined to elites or to the South, and was often used to undercut movements for labor solidarity.

The Jim Crow system in the South especially undermined the potential for labor solidarity. When the Civil War overturned slavery and black men gained the right to vote, new opportunities arose for black and white workers and poor people to make common cause. To some extent they did so during the turbulent eras of Reconstruction and Populism in the late nineteenth century, when bi-racial reform movements elected governments in numerous places that favored debtors over creditors, increased funds for schools, and enhanced the power and economic position of workers and farmers. Displaced elites struck back hard, using the dependable tactic of divide and rule. Aspiring Democratic Party leaders recaptured the votes of reform-minded lower- and middle-class whites with "white supremacy" election campaigns that stigmatized black men as rampaging criminals and rapists. Lynchings and race riots crescendoed as the Democrats regained power, enacting laws and constitutional amendments prohibiting African Americans from voting and creating a one-party (Democratic) "solid South" impervious to labor, civil rights, and reform movements.

Out of violent struggles for power, laws and customs created a coherent system of segregation that replaced slavery as a system of social control. It began with laws separating blacks and whites in education, with blacks paying taxes at the same rates as whites but getting almost no funding for their schools. Laws mandating separate and inferior facilities for blacks soon emerged in all other spheres, assigning African Americans a degraded status in transportation, dining, places of entertainment, and even in cemeteries. White society largely excluded blacks from sitting on juries, practicing law, or participating in government. The Supreme Court, claiming separate could be equal, upheld the right of states to impose segregation in its 1896 *Plessy v. Ferguson* decision, and allowed state miscegenation laws, prohibiting marriage between members of different "races." Segregation and the elimination of black voting rights destroyed possibilities for whites and blacks joining together at union meetings, in political reform organizations, or on a social level.

Racism rationalized the destruction of black rights. It held that evolution or God naturally placed Euro-Americans at the top and African Americans and other peoples of color at the bottom of society. It conveniently justified American imperial intervention against dark-skinned people in places like Cuba and the Philippines. Presidents (including Woodrow Wilson, who segregated federal employment), university professors, and the mass media (including motion pictures) constructed white supremacy as a good thing, and "social equality," or integration, as a dreadful evil. Lynchings of blacks by whites became widespread in the South and white race riots against blacks extended across the nation, as American racism strengthened its hold during the rapid industrialization and urbanization of the early twentieth century.

The denial of black rights and the pervasive violence of white supremacy deeply affected the lives of all those who tell their stories in this volume. As they make clear, black people faced a dual system of economic and racial exploitation. The poor wages, long hours, bad conditions, dirty work, and constricted economic opportunities they experienced were all underwritten by a racial system that prevented them from exercising citizenship rights. White employers squeezed the maximum of labor from them at the cheapest price, while the racial system stripped blacks of the legal means to challenge their conditions. This dual system enveloped the Mississippi River Delta town of Memphis. Here the ways of segregation dominated at every level, from personal relations to the allocation of jobs, capital, and political power.

Located in the heart of the plantation region, and once the slave-trading capital of the South, Memphis relied economically on black laborers, who were forced to work the hardest jobs for the least pay. After the Civil War, Memphis became a center of continuous black (and white) migration from the declining plantation economy.[1] From 1870 onward, blacks made up nearly forty percent to fifty percent of the population and constantly competed with whites for housing and jobs in a fast-growing, brawling river town. A small but influential black middle class and a large working class emerged, along with a proliferation of churches and voluntary societies, as black migrants sought to improve their lives. But whites limited black mobility in every way they could. This included one of the most violent postwar race riots, in 1866, in which Irish police and other white workers and middle-class elements killed forty-six blacks (two whites died) and burned black schools and churches down, targeting black soldiers and others who challenged the norms of white supremacy. The city passed Jim Crow laws affecting streetcars and other facilities in the 1880s. And although African Americans won seats on the Memphis city council and in the state legislature in the 1870s and early 1880s, restrictive election laws and threats of racial violence stopped them from running for office again until the 1950s. Yet they remained a potent political force (Tennessee, unlike most southern states, never completely disfranchised blacks), while building families, churches, voluntary associations, and schools. A struggle between the opposites of white supremacy and black striving and resistance became fixed in a continuing dialectic.

One man attempted to impose a synthesis, using paternalism as his method. As segregation solidified, so did the power of Edward H. Crump. Son of Mississippi slaveholders, Crump ran Memphis as a kind of plantation boss in the city from the 1910s until his death in 1954. He created his wealth through marriage, politics, and real estate, and he built his political power by controlling the vote, especially the black vote, through the poll tax, a fee intended to disfranchise blacks and poor whites. Holding elected office only sporadically, Crump paid people's poll taxes with funds collected by his political machine from vice establishments and city employees, and then he told them how to vote. The city's ruling families of cotton brokers, bankers, and real estate and commercial investors

1. The Memphis city population increased from 22,623 (17.2 percent black) in 1860 to 102,320 by 1920 (48.8 percent black) to 396,000 (37.2 percent black) by 1950. By 1990, Memphis had some 600,000 people, 55 percent of them black.

fully supported his political machine, as Crump provided efficient city services, attracted outside capital, attacked unions and reform organizations, and sought to keep blacks in their place. For good measure, Crump integrated Ku Klux Klan members into his machine and the police department.

Crump played up the supposedly benign side of paternalism, and many people, blacks as well as whites, claimed to love him. Because he ruled with almost absolute power, he could afford to dispense favors to the black community without fear of being race-baited (the operational mode of southern politics in his era). Crump valued the black vote, and black business leaders and ministers could sometimes gain his ear. Of necessity they became schooled in the art of accommodation to the racial regime and fashioned personal relations with Crump and other whites that they hoped would protect them from the worst Jim Crow had to offer. But this hope mostly proved to be illusory. Black leadership could operate only on Crump's terms, following the philosophy of Blair T. Hunt, a leading school principal and pastor, that "if you can take it, you can make it." Taking it meant following orders, and when black ministers or businesspeople refused to "go along to get along," beatings and expulsions from the city followed. Yet despite waves of terror that hit the black community, the paternalistic voting arrangement with Crump made Memphis a better place to be than some of the Jim Crow hellholes in nearby rural areas of Mississippi, Arkansas, or western Tennessee.

During the 1930s and most of the 1940s, Crump destroyed all challengers to his power and became one of America's most powerful mid-sized city bosses. To even speak of civil rights or industrial unions or to practice "social equality" in Memphis was to invite white violence, quite directly through the auspices of the police. Many white police officers came from the plantation districts and showed no mercy or restraint. They had a clear purpose, as police commissioner Joe Boyle explained during a series of particularly brutal attacks against blacks in the late 1930s. The job of the police was to keep Memphis "a white man's country," Boyle warned, and "any negro [sic] who doesn't agree to this better move on."

In the following personal accounts, Fannie Henderson, William Glover, and Thomas Watkins offer us glimpses of the daily terror experienced by African Americans living in such a city. The legal system of southern "justice" in a town like Memphis was but one of the towering barriers to change facing black people from the 1930s onward, where the narratives in this book begin.

In the testimonies that follow, I have occasionally omitted text (indicated by ellipses) and have made punctuation and spelling corrections to eliminate inconsistencies and errors resulting from the transcription process.

Fannie Henderson Witnesses Southern Lynch Law

We are going to give you a ride. It is going to be a damn long ride.

Memphis police officer

STATE OF TENNESSEE, COUNTY OF SHELBY
[A deposition made to the NAACP, c. February 1933].
FANNIE HENDERSON, being first duly sworn, states on oath as follows:

I will be fifty-nine years old on June 18. I was born on the corner of Orleans and Beale in the city of Memphis, and have lived in Memphis all my life. I have been in domestic service practically all my life.

One of my colored friends is Mary Alexander who lives at 320 South Third Street, just across the alleyway at the rear of Cordova Hotel, on the northeast corner of Vance and South Third. On last Thursday, February 23, 1933, I spent Thursday night with her. I continued all day Friday and Friday night with Mary. Mary and I were the only ones in the house. Mary has been working for Banner Laundry but they laid her off. Mary and I were at home all day Friday.

Mary and I went to bed about ten o'clock Friday night. I slept in the front bedroom and Mary slept in the rear bedroom. I went to sleep and slept until about three o'clock in the morning when I heard some loud talking in the alleyway between my room and the Cordova Hotel. The window of the room where I was sleeping looks directly down upon the concrete alleyway between the house and the hotel. The alleyway is ten or fifteen feet wide. I lay in bed for several minutes trying to hear what they were talking about. The talking continued and I got up and pulled back the window shade sligh\tly at the south window overlooking the alleyway, and peeped out to see what was going on. I saw several policemen, about four of them with a colored boy. The policemen had the boy standing up against the brick wall of the hotel with both hands raised above his head. I heard them ask him, "What in the hell are you doing out this time of the morning?" He says, "I am looking for my wife." They said, "You are telling a goddamn lie. We tried to catch you last night, but you got away. We are going to fix you tonight." He says, "Mr. Officer, if I have did anything, please ride me to the police station." They said, "We are going to give you a ride. It is going to be a damn long ride. The first one is going to be to the undertaker and the next ride will be to the goddam cemetery."

When they said this, one of the policemen went to the car, got a pair of handcuffs and put them on the boy's wrists. They took him around to Third Street in front of the stairway going into the hotel and sent for a white woman, Ruby Morris. I moved from in front of the window to the front door, which has a large glass pane. I opened the door slightly so I could hear. I could see them during all the time. They kept the boy hand-cuffed at the side entrance of the hotel while they were waiting. After a while a white woman showed up and they asked her, "Is this the one," and she bowed her head and told them "Yes."

I do not know who this white woman was, but I found out from reading the papers that it was Ruby Morris, a sporting woman who lives across the street at 251 Vance, in a sporting house. When they asked her "Is this the one" and she said "Yes," they began beating him over the head with their clubs. They beat him so they broke his neck—I tell you his neck was really broke—they took him back in the alley, hit him over the head several times; his neck shook like a chicken's neck when you break it. He wasn't saying anything because they told him, "You better not holler you son-of-a-bitch." He was handcuffed all this time. They took him back in the alley just a few feet from the Third Street sidewalk and commenced shooting him while he was down. His body was on the right side. His face was turned south and his hands still handcuffed, and he was near the hotel wall. There were four or five shots fired into his body while he was down handcuffed and after his neck was broken. The boy was unable to say anything. Before they put the handcuffs on him he cried and begged them not to kill him, but after beating him over the head with their billies and breaking his neck he said nothing more and didn't cry anymore. When the police shot him they were standing over him in the alleyway. I saw three or four flashlights. There were four shots in rapid succession. Several pistols were firing.

There were at least four officers. I did not know the names of any of the officers and would not know them if I saw them. Everyone had on uniforms. After they had fired four times he was lying there breathing heavily in death. One of the officers flashed his light on him to see his condition and said, "Why that son-of-a-bitch ain't dead yet," and pulled his pistol out and shot him again in the left side of his head and the bullet came out on the other side of his head and was found in the alleyway. I saw the bullet Saturday morning. I also [saw] his blood and brains which had oozed out on the pavement. There was a drizzling rain Saturday and [it] washed the blood down the sidewalk into the gutter.

The white woman, Ruby Morris, was sitting in the police car beside the curb while the policemen were beating the Negro boy over the head with their billies and while they were shooting him in the alleyway. After the boy had been shot the last time the S. W. Qualls ambulance came in five or ten minutes, put on the stretchers, and carried him away. They backed right up against the curb in front of Mary's house. When they carried him away some of the policemen got in the car with the white woman, Ruby Morris, and went up town. In about twenty minutes they brought her back, let her out of the police car on Third Street right across from the side entrance of Cordova Hotel. She got out and went on upstairs. This woman evidently lived over Belt Cafe at the northwest corner of Third and Vance, directly across Third Street and Vance, from the Cordova Hotel. They put her out of the police car at the stairway leading to the apartment above the Belt Cafe. She got out of the car and went upstairs. If she lives at 251 Vance she certainly was not there that night because they sure got her from upstairs over Belt Cafe.

Mary Alexander saw only part of what I told above. When they had the boy backed up against the hotel with his hand over his head, I went to Mary's room and told her to get up that they had a nigger out there backed up against the hotel wall. Mary got up and came to the window with me, looked out, stood there a few minutes and said, "Hell, I'm going back to bed; they're just after that nigger for some devilment he's done." Mary then went back to bed. She didn't see the policemen beat and shoot the Negro. Mary is awfully scary. She didn't come back to the window until after the shooting was over. Mary saw the dead boy lying in the alleyway before the ambulance drove up. When the ambulance came we went out on the porch, and the people next door came out. Before the shooting, nobody came out. After the ambulance took the body away, and after the police had driven away in the car, we turned on all the lights in the house, built a fire, and never went back to bed anymore.

There wasn't a big crowd around. I don't think nobody saw the ambulance drive up and take away the body, except me and Mary and the people next door; and of course the policemen and Ruby who were still there. There were no passer-by along the street. I do not know the Negro boy, nor did Mary. On Saturday morning I went out to try to find out who the boy was and who his people were so I could tell them just how he met his death. Somebody said that the policemen had killed the night porter at Cordova Hotel. When they described the porter, I told them the boy killed was not the one they thought it was. The boy they killed was about nineteen years old, average height and weight and had on a dark pair of trousers, a light shirt, and was bareheaded. He did not have on a coat or hat when they stood him up against the wall.

I called Thomas Hayes Company to see if they had picked up a body at Third and Vance and they said "No." I then called up S. W. Qualls and they told me they had picked up the body. I then went out to Qualls's place to see the body but they wouldn't let me see it. I found out where he lived and I went on South Second Street to his home. His wife was in bed when I got there. She had already heard about his death from Qualls. His name was Levon Carlock. I had never met his wife[,] not any of his folks before. I went into the house and found his wife, Eula May Carlock, in bed. I told her and her husband's cousin, who was there, just how the police had killed him. I stayed at Eula's house all day Saturday and Sunday and did not leave there until Sunday evening just before dark and I then went to where I live. . . .

William Glover Recounts His Frame-up by the Memphis Police

If I didn't have this star on I would kill you myself.

Memphis police officer

STATEMENT OF WILLIAM GLOVER, Made at CAIRO, ILL., Sunday, Jan. 23rd, 1938, to F. C. BATEMAN & J. T. SETTLE

My name is WILLIAM GLOVER and I will be fifty-six years old on Feb. 27, 1938. I was born at Hazelhurst, Miss., in 1882 and I lived there until I was about six months old, and my family moved to Dermott, Arkansas, and I lived there until I was nine years old. At that time I was going to school and only got to the seventh grade, when my father who was a lawyer was killed. His name was William Glover and he was killed when I was fourteen years old.[2] When I finished that term in school I went to work to support my mother, three sisters and my brother and self. . . .

[In a section of the affidavit not reprinted here, Glover recounts his eight years as a farm tenant in Arkansas, as a worker in a sawmill and as a watchman, fire builder, boiler washer, blacksmith's helper, and brakeman for various railroads in Arkansas and Memphis. He married and divorced, remarried, and joined a union of black railroad brakemen in Memphis in 1918. As chairman of its grievance committee, he became a target for an employer-instigated police frame-up in 1921. Schoolteachers and lawyers came to his defense, but his wife urged him to "resign, while you are alive." White railroad workers during this period ran an intense campaign to force blacks out of such occupations and, in the rural areas, assassinated a number of black firemen and brakemen. Hence, white terror forced Glover, like many other blacks, out of work as a brakeman. He subsequently gave the Pullman Company seventeen years of service as a porter.]

November 3, 1921, the Pullman Company called me and ordered me to go to St. Louis that night and take training for a position as porter. Since entering service I have a good record—several letters for finding and turning in money and lost articles—haven't had any trouble with the Pullman employees—always courteous—and meet every one with a smile . . . I joined the Brotherhood of Sleeping Car Porters on September 17, 1937. I lived in Memphis, continuously all this time and worked for eight straight and consecutive years without losing a day. I own my home and borrowed from the homeowner's loan company to make repairs. I have a charge account at Goldsmith's department store—a furniture account at Graves and Graves, I have had account with the Memphis Electric Company on Madison Avenue for twenty-one years. . . . I have an insurance

---

2. Glover's father was one of only a few black lawyers in the South. Although Glover does not elaborate on his father's death, his testimony suggests that his father may have been killed for becoming too prosperous and too assertive.

policy with the Metropolitan Life Insurance Company, in the sum of one thousand dollars. My immediate superior in the Pullman Company is Mr. W. H. Bucher. . . .

On Saturday morning, January 15th, 1937 . . . about 2:30 A.M. I was awakened by an officer, tall, heavy set, clean shaven, and wearing gray civilian clothes. He said, "Glover get up—put on your clothes—Chief Lee wants to talk with you." I said, "What does he want?" My wife asked him, "Have you a warrant?" He said, "No, the chief wants to talk with you and that's all." My wife said, "Glover is due out tonight and hasn't had any sleep." The officer said, "Oh well, he will get plenty of sleep tonight." While I was upstairs and dressing, the other officer came upstairs, he was also tall, clean shaven and wore gray plainclothes and he said, "What's holding you all so long." The other officer answered, "We are waiting for Glover to dress." I then went and got into their car and went to the police station, uptown. On arriving at the station, some uniformed officer, tall, red face and wrinkled, said, "That's the son-of-a-bitch." The officer that brought me in asked for a ticket, it was given to him, he wrote out the ticket and I then [went] across to the east side of the building to a captain's desk, I think, three uniformed men were there.

The man that I talked to, a heavy set man in uniform with a clean face, he said, "Have you been visiting a doctor's office?" I said, "No sir." He said, "Wasn't you injured last year and went to Dr. Stanfield's office for treatment? Do you know [the] office girl?" I said, "Yes sir." He said, "Didn't you tell her that you were keeping an eighteen-year-old white girl here, and that some colored men prefer white women because they are more affectionate? Weren't you up there this morning and sat down, and seemingly you got mad because some patient was up there in the office and you could not make a date with the girl? [A]nd you rushed to the elevator and she saw you and asked the patient not to leave, because you wanted to make a date with her?" [Glover reports that the officer continued to claim that the white girl became hysterical and went to Dr. Stanfield, and that a white mob began to form until Stanfield took the story to the police.]

I said, "No sir, I haven't been in Dr. Stanfield's office since last July, and I talked with him then." The officer said, "You remember that nigger George Brooks that was killed, you may join him before the day is over." He said to a plainclothes man, "Take him away, lock him up in a cell by himself." This was about 3:00 or 3:30 P.M., they took me away and locked me up in [a] cell to myself. Later, about first dark, they had passed the "pan" around and I had eaten one sweet potato, they came and got me and carried me to Chief Lee's office. . . . Chief Lee then went over the same thing that the officer had questioned me about, and when he had finished he said, "Mr. W. H. Bucher had been down to my office and said, 'Go out and get that black son-of-a-bitch and do what you want with him, I wish I could kill him. I have two complaints about him, but I can't fire him . . .'" Chief Lee then struck me with his fist on my right jaw about my right ear and said, "Take off them glasses—you black son-of-a-bitch."

He then rushed over to his drawer, an officer assisted him . . . and opened the drawer. Then he got his blackjack, stood me up with the black-jack in my left forehead. He then hit me again with the blackjack on the left top part of my head. By that time my face was covered with blood. I fell over, he struck me again in the back of my head with the blackjack. I threw my hand over my head for protection. Chief Lee said, "Take your goddamn black hand down, I want to beat your head." By that time I was bleeding very bad—blood was running down all over my face. Chief Lee then said, "Now, what are your going to do, resign?" I said, "Yes, anything you say." Chief Lee said, "You [go] down to the Pullman office and resign, as Mr. Bucher can't fire you, and leave Memphis, never to return. Have you got a home here?" I said, "Yes sir and a wife and four children." Chief Lee said, "Well, you will have to leave all that here in Memphis—take your handkerchief and stop that blood from running on the floor of my office—well, take him away and lock him up."

They took me to the cell and locked me up. I was hit on the head from four to six times with a blackjack by Chief Lee. A hole was knocked [in] the left forehead, a hole in the top of my head. I didn't receive any medical attention in the police station. I asked the use of the phone. The turnkey said, "Chief Lee said I can't let you use the phone." By that time I was very bloody. The turnkey told the helper to give me some clean rags and to clean the blood off the floor in my cell and this was done. Some time later Chief Lee came to my cell with someone and said, "This is the city attor-ney." (It was Mr. Bateman, assistant city attorney, but I didn't know then who it was.) Chief Lee said, "That is the black son-of-a-bitch; son-of-a-bitch ought to be killed." Chief Lee said to me then, "I will be back down here tonight, I don't know what is going to happen to you."

Between 9:30 and 10:00 P.M. I was sent for and carried to Chief Lee's office by an officer. . . . Chief Lee said, "I was trying to get Mr. Bucher, I can't get him no place. You will have to stay here until tomorrow morning, as tomorrow is Sunday and we don't do nothing on Sunday. You can phone your family and tell them you are at the police station and will be safe and well taken care of." . . . Chief Lee further said, "You can go home tonight, if you want to, but you may be dead before morning and you might cause some of your family to get killed." I said that I would stay there until Monday.

I had a conversation with Chief Lee then, the gist of it was about a mass meeting of some 1,400 negroes [sic] that was held on Friday night, January 14, 1938, at the Centenary Church on Mississippi Avenue.[3] He condemned the holding of the meeting, saying it made bad matters worse, and that he wasn't going to let anyone hurt me and that he was going to protect me, for if I was killed there would be a race riot. And if a race riot came, the niggers would get the worst of it, and he didn't want any riot and such sons of bitches as me causes such trouble. He didn't hit me any more and his attitude changed completely when I agreed to resign my job at the Pullman Company. I was taken back to my cell and stayed until Monday. No one came to me or did anything for me Sunday. I asked the use of the phone and the turnkey refused, I asked him to phone for a doctor or wife to do something for me and was refused.

Monday morning all except me were taken out for the lineup. . . . I was taken to the show-up room and in there were a lot of officers and plain-clothes men. Chief Lee did the talking. They were behind a blue screen and they put me on a spotlight. Chief Lee then went over the entire charge that he had made to me in his office. He was asked what charge was against me. Chief Lee said, "None, he is leaving the city tonight and I am going to have two officers take him to the Pullman office this morning, and he is going to resign his job, leave Memphis, and never return." As I walked out that room, one of the officers said, I didn't see who it was, "If I didn't have this star on I would kill you myself." They then took me to a room,

3. Centenary was a Methodist church later pastored by Rev. James Lawson, a leading civil rights activist and the minister who invited Martin Luther King to Memphis in support of the sanitation strikers thirty years after this incident.

fingerprinted me, photographed me, hat on and off, front and side views, weighed and measured me. Then two officers, one being an elderly Christian-hearted gentlemen, took me to the Pullman office. They were plainclothes men and the younger of the two went with me into the Pullman offices. I asked the clerk, a Mr. Stawyer, for Mr. Bucher and was told that he was in St. Louis. The officer said, "I brought Glover down here to resign." The clerk said Mr. Bucher told him that Glover would be down here to resign, and the clerk made out the resignation, which under these conditions I signed.

[Glover tells how the police took him to his home, where he retrieved clothes and money, then returned him to the jail.] I talked with the turnkey and asked him for a bath as I still had on the bloody clothes and had since Saturday night. . . . I told him that I was expecting my wife to come and bring me money and as soon as she came I would take the bath. She came with my sister in about an hour and it was the first time that I seen her or talked with her. . . .

I then bathed and was taken about 6:20 P.M. to the Grand Central Station by one of the same officers that had taken me out and around that day, the elderly one, and put out in front of the Grand Central Station. . . . I talked with him a few minutes and when I left he said "May God go with you." I then went into the Grand Central Station where I met [a] friend and about one dozen Pullman porters and we talked. Later my wife, her sisters Blanch and Edna and my niece Ruth Henry came, and we left Memphis Monday night 7:40 on Illinois Central Railroad train 4, for Cairo, and my niece Ruth Henry came with me and I am now staying with my brother Dave Gloster, at 408 Commercial Street, in Cairo, Illinois.

I hereby declare that I have never made any advances or any statements to Miss Duke, the nurse in Dr. Stanfield's office, nor did I have any conversation with her about any eighteen-year-old white girl, nor to any other white man or woman or to anyone, nor is such a fact.

While I was running between Memphis and Nashville on the North Carolina and St. Louis Railroad, I had to have examinations made for social diseases every ninety days and these were made by Dr. Stanfield. But when I got on a sleeping-car run, I had to have only annual examinations. I had an ankle sprained in February 1937, and was treated every other day

for about two weeks by Dr. Stanfield, and the last time I was in his office
was in July 1937.

(Signed)
William Glover

Longshore Leader Thomas Watkins Escapes Assassination

The real reason for those trumped-up charges is the result of the
militant way in which I conducted the affairs of the longshoremen
in Memphis.

AN AFFIDAVIT, May 26, 1939

Here are some of the facts regarding how I was kidnapped along with
my wife in Memphis, Tennessee, on Friday morning, May 26, 1939, at 2:30
as told to the Federal Bureau of Investigation. I am telling this story because I want the people of Memphis and the nation to know the truth
in the matter.

At 2:30 Friday morning, May 26, 1939, Captain John B. Cross, Lieutenant A. C. Clark, and Sergeant Crumby came to my house and knocked.
Upon getting up and looking through the door to see who was there, I recognized Captain John B. Cross. I asked who was there and they stated the
police. I opened the door and Cross and Clark came in and asked me if
anyone was living with me. I told them there wasn't anyone but my wife
and two children. They went through the house to the back door and
opened it; Sergeant Crumby entered from the back door. I was then told
that some people wanted to "look at me." I told the officers that it was
OK by me.

I got up, dressed, and Captain Cross said, "We want your wife too."
I told them that she could not hear him; she has been deaf for three years.
Lieutenant Clark told me that was all right. "You'll be back in thirty minutes." After my wife dressed, I was handcuffed and told not to disturb anyone as it would not be necessary. I was not even allowed to lock the house
where my two children aged eighteen months and five and one-half years
were left alone without any protection whatsoever.

I was then placed in the back seat of the auto between Captain Cross
and Lieutenant Clark, while my wife was ushered into the front seat with

Sergeant Crumby. The car then started west on Desoto, north on Kansas, west on Iowa, finally turning north on Pennsylvania, leading around River Drive. On the way to the station to which I thought I was being taken, I commenced talking to Captain Cross about fishing conditions on Horse-Shoe Lake, having formerly served as cook and guide at Horse-Shoe Lake during the fishing season of 1935. I did not give any thought to where I was actually going. Upon reaching the intersection of Beal Avenue and River Drive, about eleven blocks from my home, the car turned left toward the levee at the foot of Beale Street. I then began to feel suspicious about the car going over the levee. . . .

The car was stopped midway on the wharf boat of the Wolf River Transportation Company, which is about 220 feet long, having entered through its main gate. Captain Russell Warner, secretary-treasurer of the Wolf River Transportation Company, and Frank Tamble, chief mechanic and purchasing agent of said company, greeted us.[4] My wife was ejected from the front seat and led north on the wharf boat. They said while leaving the car, "We'll take care of the Nigger woman later and will take care of this bastard first."[5]

They took my wife north on the wharf boat and stashed her between two piles of lumber. Then the two officers returned to the car. I was ordered by the officers to get out and walk around behind it—a distance of twelve feet. Then Captain Cross told Russell Warner, "There he is, see if you can recognize him." Warner shined a flashlight in my right eye. I turned my head left to avoid the glare and tilted my head back slightly in order that he could get a plain view of my face.

At this point, I was temporarily dazed as the result of a heavy blow which landed on the back of my skull, cutting my scalp to the bone through the hat. I took one step forward, turned, and fell on my back. From this position I could see Frank Tamble standing over me with a full-sized capstan bar (a hard wooden bar that is made from oak timber, being 4½ inches in diameter at one end and 2½ inches at the working end,

4. Warner and Tamble carried on the strongest anti-union campaign of all the boat owners, carrying shotguns on board to use against strikers. They had a reputation for killing anyone who crossed them.

5. The Memphis news media and courts in the 1930s refused to capitalize "Negro" but, ironically, in this case did capitalize "nigger."

weighing approximately 31 pounds and in some instances 38. These bars are used to draw floating barges tied against their moorings).

Upon recognizing Frank Tamble, I asked him what was his object, "To murder me, beat me, or what?" He stated that my time had come to an end, and commenced delivering the second blow, which was also leveled at my head. But by a quick move on my part, the blow landed on my right shoulder. Whereupon I quickly sprang up, and in the process caught him in his pants leg, hoisted him above my head about eight feet, and ran under him.[6] Then I ran into a door which I could not see, because of being dazed. It was a steel door, and the impact of this collision dashed me back approximately ten feet. Captain Cross fired the first shot at me; it went wild. I then jumped up from where I fell and ran back toward them as they were standing in front of the only door out. In doing so I ran over Frank Tamble, who was getting up, struck Russell Warner, and collided with Lieutenant Clark, who was standing near him. Then I started through the doors looking back in time to see Captain Cross and Sergeant Crumby level their guns again. The bullets went astray.

I then coursed my way around the wharf boat to the south end, from which I jumped on the side of the first barge, then to the second. I missed the third barge, a distance of about nine feet. My right hand slid over the top, but my left careened down the outside. The impact knocked the right handcuff off. Somersaulting over in the barge I went, on my feet again, then over the side into the river's edge. From the time I left the door of the wharf boat to this point more than twenty-five shots were fired at me, one grazing the cuff on my right leg.

I continued on the levee following the same course we entered to Beale Street, where the I. C. Railroad crossed, and ventured up under the bridge where I could get a good view of the riverfront. [Watkins tried to get help from a black watchman named Leland Rivers, but Rivers refused to get involved when he saw the police cars circling the area.]

Weak from the loss of blood, and exhausted from the run, I laid down for approximately forty-five minutes. I arose and continued on down the

6. While this feat sounds unlikely, according to his acquaintances Watkins had tremendous physical strength. In another version of this affidavit, he said that he raised Tamble four or five feet off the floor.

I. C. track; but a sudden siege of fear came over me, which caused me to strike up a faster pace (dog-trot) toward a place of safety. But this was not fast enough, so I stopped again, took off my shoes so that I could run faster. I proceeded on down the railroad two blocks. A police squad car passed in front of me about one-half block away. Two officers got out of the car, walked back to where I formerly was, then went around the block to Front Street. I followed the railroad track on to Butler Street and over Butler to a friend's house.[7]

After gaining admission to this person's house, I sent for two of my staunch friends who came within an hour. I told my story and directed them to go straight to the Federal Bureau of Investigation, call for Mr. Wright and Mr. Vincent, and bring them to me immediately. At approximately 10:15 or 10:30 the next morning the government agents arrived, but I had moved from the first place to another place, where they questioned me. To their offices on the twenty-fourth floor of the Sterick Building we went.

After arriving at their offices, I proceeded to tell the two agents of the events that occurred during the night. They listened intently but were unable to remove the handcuff from my left wrist. They departed and within about one and one-half hour later returned with Police Inspector Clagg Richards, who sat in front of me and raised the question, "Do you know me?" I replied, "I do," and he proceeded to tell me why I was arrested.

Inspector Richards stated that I was being questioned in connection with the cutting loose of several barges during the strike. I stated that I knew nothing of the barges, their arrival, their being cut loose, nor the parties involved. He said I was "lying." I told him that I did not have to lie to him, as I knew nothing of the barges, had no way of getting over where the barges were moored, for I could not swim and would not take the chance because that would be a violation of the Merchant Marine Law. Inspector Richards further stated, "We do not know who cut the barges loose, but we are going to investigate for ten years if necessary." I told him as far as I was implicated in the matter, he could investigate for twenty years. . . .

7. Annie Anderson on 491 South Front Street, with whom Watkins had previously boarded, gave him refuge. Fellow unionists John Wells and George Henry Miles eventually got him safely to the FBI.

After making the above statement, Inspector Richards removed the handcuff from my left wrist. I then learned that the handcuffs were his. He explained, "We have no charges against you, not even resisting arrest or fleeing from an officer." I was left in the custody of the Department of Justice.

I asked for medical treatment, which was made possible. When I reached the physician's office, blood was still slowly seeping from my scalp wound. The physician remarked that the wound had been inflicted with a round or blunt instrument; that the wound on my shoulder came from the same type of instrument, and that none of the wounds were received by falling from a moving conveyance, as there were no signs of struggles, bruises, or contusions actually received in such cases.[8]

From the physician's office I went to a friend's house, not deeming it wise to return to my own home. This friend went to my home to locate my wife and to get some clean clothing for me. As the friend approached my house, he observed that the police were apparently still looking for me. He returned as he was afraid to enter my house. The patrolling continued for two days. Rather than take a chance I remained at my friend's house. Other friends and visitors going to my house to see me learned what was going on; they took notice of the police who were about in the neighborhood in great numbers.

Because of the unusualness of this situation, I was advised by my friend to remain where I was or leave town. After two days, I sent two of my friends to get me a ticket. On reaching the station they were asked my whereabouts, by some Negro men unknown to me or to them. My friends declined getting the ticket, and returned telling me of their experiences. I instructed them to go to the Greyhound bus station for the ticket; they were met by the same men at the bus station. Memphis, like all southern cities, has a corps of Negro informants who keep their oppressors up-to-date on what is being said or thought in the Negro community.[9]

8. Police officers had claimed that Watkins escaped their custody when a car door swung open and he rolled into the street. They claimed this was the cause of all his wounds.

9. The police and Boss Crump had a wide variety of black informants, some off the street, others the leaders of churches and schools, who some called the "brown screws" in the Crump machine.

I sent for a friend of mine who had an automobile, and told him of my difficulty in obtaining a ticket without it becoming the knowledge of the authorities or my enemies. It was thought by some of my friends that the officers did not want me to leave Memphis for fear I would tell the story of what had happened to me, not only to the people of Memphis, but to all people who are concerned with Justice.

A friend who owned a car drove it up to the side of the house in which I was hiding, and at 7:30 P.M. I came down, entered the car, and picked up four women in order to allay suspicion while getting out of town.[10] I directed the driver to go to the left where we counted seven or eight police cars cruising around in the neighborhood. We proceeded to Osceola, Arkansas, where I purchased a ticket to St. Louis, Missouri.

During the two days I was in hiding, the police department in Memphis issued two statements to the press. In the first, they said that I had jumped from a running auto from two officers, fled under gunfire, and was last seen running around the riverfront and had possibly escaped through Arkansas. The other statement, issued later, said that I had escaped from a moving auto, in which I was seated beside two officers, using my elbow to knock open the car door, fled under gunfire, and later surrendered to the Department of Justice.

Neither of these statements is true for in neither of them was mentioned the fact that they carried my wife with me, came into my house, and took my two children to the juvenile court. My wife was released at 7:00 Friday morning. Through seeking around she was able to learn that the children had been taken to the juvenile court.

Previous to this trouble, I was arrested on the complaint of Lev G. Loring, about a letter that I wrote to Mr. William Green, president of the AF of L, in which I complained about the twenty-five-cent-per-capita tax leveled against the AF of L members in Memphis. This is the highest rate charged by any council in the United States. Mr. Green sent Paul Amont to Memphis to check into the situation, but before he could reach me, Mr. Loring succeeded in having me arrested, charging me with assault and battery, disturbing the peace, breach of peace, and resisting arrest.

10. The longshore industry did not employ women, but Watkins and his male counterparts obviously got considerable support from them. In this case, the owner of a boardinghouse who sheltered him, the driver of the car, and the women who helped him escape Memphis together probably saved his life.

Mr. Loring's dislike for me, which is the real reason for those trumped-up charges, is the result of the militant way in which I conducted the affairs of the longshoremen in Memphis and the stand I took against the oppressive discrimination against Negro electricians, painters, rodmen, and carpenters, who were and still are kept out of jobs because they cannot join the existing white locals or . . . organize their own under the AF of L [American Federation of Labor].[11]

I have been advised from time to time during this period of two years by Loring, who is president of the Central Trades and Labor Council, that my policy of unionism was detrimental to the best interest of labor around Memphis. In pointing to the detrimental factors, he stated it wasn't the policy of the Central Trades and Labor Council to strike without giving them notice. I well knew the policy of the Central Trades and Labor Council and avoided contacts with it as much as possible because I knew the council was not sympathetic toward the organization and advancement of Negro workers.

Proof of this can be found during a recent strike. [Watkins relates that predominantly black longshoremen's locals in Memphis, Cairo, St. Louis, East St. Louis, Rock Island, Peoria, Omaha, and Kansas City had all been involved in an eighteen-day general strike under the direction of the Chicago-based R. A. Walton, vice president of the AFL's International Longshoremen's Association (ILA). The ILA undertook its strike in tandem with a strike by white river workers in the Congress of Industrial Organizations' (CIO) Inland Boatmen's Division of the National Maritime Union. Loring claimed that Watkins had conspired to work in concert with the CIO, which the AFL had sworn to destroy. Although all the ILA locals in the district had voted to strike, Loring called the strike illegal according to the AFL guidelines.]

Thirty days prior to this strike, Local 1490 of Memphis and its members were expelled from the Central Trades and Labor Council because I was considered by the said council as a dangerous agitator and very destructive to the cause of labor. In view of this action, I told Loring I could not see why he should attempt to advise us any further. Mr. Loring then stated to

11. Watkins and others attempted to form an organization to break down the color barriers in Memphis skilled trades, another reason white labor leaders in the AFL wanted him removed. "Rodmen" carried iron rods used in construction projects.

me, "Since you all are out, there will be no getting back, so start hunting for other jobs."

The following night I was called to St. Louis for a conference with the management of the company. While [I was] out of town, Loring took his car, carried men there [in Memphis] to work. These men were given the assurance that the jobs would be permanent. These men I later learned were taxed one dollar a week, for what no one knows. Incidentally, the regular dues of longshoremen is one dollar a month. From St. Louis I sent word to the Memphis strike committee of Local 1490 not to picket the job because we were assured a contract. The strike committee replied that Mr. Loring had placed in the job other AF of L union men. They asked what should be done? From St. Louis I wired Memphis to do nothing, as I would be returning in three days with a signed contract. Before leaving St. Louis I succeeded in getting the company to discharge the other men placed on the job by Loring.

After the contracts were agreed and signed and all was considered final, I returned to Memphis. The contract, however, was rejected by the operators in Memphis. [This refusal to settle in Memphis held up settlement of the entire strike for two more days.] But two days later we returned to work under the terms of the contract signed in St. Louis. All the strike breakers placed on the job by Loring were discharged. At this point Loring advised me that he would dig my grave and see me in it. To which I gave no reply. He almost dug it with the aid of the Memphis police department.

signed
THOMAS WATKINZ [sic]

The lived experiences of racial segregation are painful to recount, even on the printed page. Domestic worker Fannie Henderson's chilling witness to the horrifying murder of Levon Carlock suggests the dehumanizing power of the plantation mentality and exemplifies how quickly and with what few repercussions a black person's life could be snuffed out. In this case and so many others, including William Glover's, white men's sexual fantasies, desires, and fears intermingled to bring about particularly bloody violence against black men. According to secondary accounts, six Memphis police officers arrested Carlock for assault and claimed that they killed him when he tried to escape. But according to Henderson's eyewitness account, they murdered him in cold blood because Ruby Morris, a white "sporting woman," intimated that Carlock had a sexual relationship with her. As Leroy Boyd later explains in chapter 5, white men feared black male sexual involvement with white women, "sporting" or not, above all else, and easily rationalized lynching as protection of white "womanhood." As in the later case of Willie McGee, the Carlock murder was only one of many legalized lynchings carried out by the representatives of the state.[12]

Murderous violence against Carlock, McGee, Emmett Till, and others was rooted in a deadly southern tradition. Ida B. Wells, the famous black journalist from Memphis, had long since documented how whites justified lynchings by charging their black male victims with rape of a white woman, even when no rape had occurred.[13] Her crusade against lynching had caused the authorities to mute such activities in Memphis, but had not stopped one of the most atrocious spectacles of the era when thousands of white men, women, and children attended the festive hanging and burning of young Ell Persons in 1917, throwing his charred remains out amongst a group of blacks on Beale Street.[14] The Carlock case, unlike that of Glover and Thomas Watkins, did not have anything to do with labor organizing. But like many others, it did display the raw naked power of white supremacy and stood as a warning to other black men not to cross the color line in any way.

The Carlock case also happened, however, in the context of efforts by radicals and labor organizers in the 1930s to challenge Jim Crow and expose southern "lynch law" to the world. In 1931, whites in Scottsboro, Alabama, had sentenced nine young black men to death based on fabricated charges that they raped two white women, and the Communist-led

12. Henderson's testimony also seems to imply the police took Ruby Morris away to have sex with them after they murdered Carlock. Some white women did challenge such degrading white male "protection." See Jacquelyn Dowd Hall, *Revolt against Chivalry: Jessie Daniel Ames and the Women's Campaign against Lynching*, rev. ed. (New York: Columbia University Press, 1993).

13. According to Wells (later, Wells-Barnett), everyone in the South knew that some black men and white women often found each other attractive sexual partners. For stating this heresy in print, the town's newspaper encouraged a mob to destroy her business. Whites put a price on her head and forced her into exile in 1894, after which she became one of the great anti-lynching crusaders of the segregation era.

14. Although the daily newspapers announced the lynching in advance and its perpetrators made no attempt to conceal their identities, no one went to jail for the crime.

International Labor Defense had turned the case into a worldwide campaign to stop such legal atrocities. ILD organizers also came to Memphis and tried to get the local branch of the National Association for the Advancement of Colored People (NAACP) to take up the Carlock case. The NAACP was too weak and too frightened of Communists to do so (although it did give a small donation to Carlock's widow). But in these and numerous other less publicized cases, people in the 1930s increasingly decried the use of police as judge, jury, and executioner. Leftists and labor organizers put their campaigns in the context of breaking down racism and police terror in the South so that workers might join in organizing together.

However, although both the ILD and the Workers Defense League (under Socialist Party auspices) tried to create labor-based civil rights organizations in the South, police and vigilantes repeatedly beat up, kidnapped, and expelled their organizers. Hence, black people in Memphis and elsewhere could not count on these groups or on any other protest organizations in the Jim Crow era. Founded as an underground organization in the wake of the Ell Persons lynching, the Memphis NAACP had dissipated by the late 1920s. Factionalized and barely existing in the 1930s, it was "like a lot of the [NAACP] branches in the South—they were very quiet and people hid their memberships," recalled Leroy Clark, a witness in this volume (see chapter 6) and president of the organization in the late 1960s. "They didn't do too much, and people who were members didn't let it be known." As in many other places, the NAACP did not seriously expand in Memphis until the waning days of World War II, when unionized black factory workers joined and industrial unions began to loosen the hold of the Crump regime. Rather conservative leaders still dominated the city's NAACP until the early 1960s, when a more educated and energetic group led demonstrations and boycotts that eventually ended segregation in downtown stores and public facilities.

In the absence of a strong protest organization in the African American community, the police in the 1930s and 1940s were happy to demonstrate their power by victimizing many hapless individuals. And yet individuals did resist. Ms. Henderson, for example, acted against her powerlessness to stop a grisly lynching by becoming an official witness to it. Her friend Mary Alexander made the choice that many people would: she hid herself from direct knowledge of police crime and thus from responsibility to tell about it. Henderson not only took careful note of the crime but located Carlock's wife and stayed with her to offer emotional support. What became of Henderson we do not know, but the testimony of the other witnesses in this book suggests that many such humble and unheralded people in their own way tried to resist the bloody repressiveness of Jim Crow.

Knowing that black people did resist, white supremacists treated black men as a special threat, and one could hardly be more threatening to the status quo than to be both black and a union activist. This was the crime of both William Glover and Thomas Watkins. Grim realities confronted any black worker who sought union organization. Glover struggled for years to work on the railroads but was forced out by whites who wanted positions as brakemen and other well-paying railroad jobs for themselves. As a porter, a job no white man wanted, Glover joined the Brotherhood of Sleeping Car Porters and became a family man and Baptist church elder with savings and charge accounts (usually denied to African Americans) in major Memphis stores. Who could be more respectable? But, perhaps like his father before him, Glover's prosperity and his unionism singled him out for attack. And his respectability meant nothing when his employer concocted a fantastic charge that Glover had bragged to the secretary of the company's white medical doctor of having an affair with a white teenager. The charge of sexual bragging, a "crime" that violated no law, appears utterly transparent. Yet, like waving a red flag in front of a bull, this absurd charge was enough to send the police into a frenzy of violence.

Glover's plight appears to have had nothing to do with sexual bragging and everything to do with his employer's desire to eliminate an active union member from a job protected by union contract. His arrest and beating may have been precipitated by the mass meeting of 1,400 union and community people the night before his return on a train run to Memphis, or perhaps this show of community and labor strength saved his life. Whatever the case (I have not been able to find more details), Police Chief Will Lee's objective was to force him to leave town and quit his job, since he had no evidence of a crime. Like numerous others who fell into disfavor with the police in Crump's town, Glover had little choice but to comply.

The police did not require sexual innuendo to justify such attacks;

refusal to show deference to whites could be enough, as in the case of Thomas Watkins. His treatment shows how white officials, including white trade unionists, disposed of black men who stood up for their rights. Watkins had an unusually determined and assertive demeanor, according to white riverboat worker W. E. Davis, who knew Watkins and likened him to Denmark Vesey, the fearless leader of a slave revolt in the antebellum era. Employers and the police jointly targeted Watkins for one very obvious reason: he was an independent black labor leader, the most important in Memphis at the time of his arrest. He worked on the waterfront, the city's major source of commerce, and served as president of several amalgamated black longshore unions. Watkins helped to lead a perilous one-month strike against the barge lines on the Mississippi River in the spring of 1939. In this strike, blacks in the AFL's International Longshoremen's Association and whites in the CIO's Inland Boatmen's Division united to defeat some of the roughest employers in the Mississippi valley. The victory allowed the National Maritime Union to open the first CIO hall in Memphis, cracked the Crump machine's stone wall of opposition to CIO interracial unions, and opened the way to more widespread union organization.

Even before the strike, Watkins had challenged the union color bar by writing letters to the AFL regional representative claiming that the Memphis Trades and Labor Council overcharged dues to the few segregated black union locals that existed and also kept blacks out of the skilled trades by excluding them from various craft locals. Watkins made his own decisions and had practically absolute backing from the black members of his union, and during the strike he ignored orders from Memphis Trades and Labor Council President Lev Loring to go back to work. For these reasons, Loring, Watkins's employers, and Police Chief Lee all had targeted him. Prior to the attempt on Watkins's life recounted here, he explained in another affidavit, Lee had summoned him to the police station and threatened that "I'll get you if it takes me 20 years you son-of-a-bitch." Police had also previously waylaid and beaten Watkins, and, in yet another incident, Loring had threatened to kill him. By the time of his arrest, employers, the police, and the white trade union establishment were all in collusion to remove him from the labor movement.

Loring and other AFL unions worked with the Crump machine, which controlled federal appointments in Memphis. Not surprisingly then, the local U.S. attorney declined to prosecute the police, sided with the AFL's version of events, and concluded that Watkins was a dangerous radical not deserving of any consideration. The FBI continued to follow Watkins into the 1950s, while Warner and Tamble went about their business. But at least Watkins left Memphis alive; Watkins's employers reportedly had black longshoreman Robert Cotton taken across the Mississippi River, weighted down, and thrown overboard. Several workers saw what looked like Cotton's body floating in the river the next day, but their ship's captain would not let them stop to pull the body out. Cotton had tried to sue Tamble and Warner for back wages.

Like so many of those who resisted the racial order, Watkins lost the struggle to bring about change and never returned to take up his role as a black working-class leader. And like Glover and Henderson, he could not expect to protect his rights through the legal system; indeed, each of them took a brave step merely to swear out official affidavits against the police. Henderson and Glover at least had the sympathetic support of NAACP officials in giving their affidavits, whereas one can only imagine the difficulty Watkins must have had trying to present a candid account to white FBI agents, who worked hand in glove with the police. But he had nowhere else to turn. In 1938, attorneys defending blacks or union organizers frequently were beaten up or had their law licenses revoked. Even Governor Gordon Browning was not secure when he came into conflict with Crump in that year's election, as Crump machine thugs beat up his election workers and police arrested his poll watchers. Crump-sponsored repression peaked during an upsurge of black independent political activity and labor organizing in the 1940s, particularly when A. Philip Randolph tried to speak in Memphis in 1944, and again in 1948, when civil rights seemed to be on the agenda in national and local elections. Nobody's civil liberties were secure in Memphis but least of all those of black workers.

The testimonies in these three cases, corroborated by many other sources, suggest the unremitting, unreasoning character of the violence unleashed by a society that denied blacks citizenship rights and looked down upon them as inferior. However, if the police succeeded in forcing Glover and Watkins from Memphis, others survived to fight another day. Black resistance continued through the cruel era of segregation, and during the 1930s industrial labor organizing started to open new possibilities for change. Many of the black factory workers whose views and experiences are detailed in the coming chapters hoped that labor organization would begin to make a difference, and that the day would come when white workers would join them and stop taking the side of racism. As Clarence Coe tells us in this book's epilogue, segregation did little to advance the material conditions of most white workers; indeed, it undercut their ability to organize and improve their conditions. In reality, "white supremacy" mostly protected the wealth and power of the South's upper classes to the disadvantage of almost everyone else. Black labor activists hoped that white workers eventually would see this and rebel.

Such hopes for change fueled their daily endurance contest with Jim Crow. But they faced enormous obstacles. Long-lived traditions of racism enabled employers and political leaders to create powerful barriers to labor unity, not only in the South but across the United States. As George Holloway explains in the next chapter, black workers joined the unions not merely for economic gain but to "change all that." Whether white workers would join with them or stand against them, black workers had little choice but to take whatever steps they could to resist white supremacy and feed themselves and their families. In the context of the violence and history of racial division that undergirded daily life under segregation, what the people who tell their stories in this book accomplished in their lifetimes seems all the more remarkable.

2   FROM COUNTRY TO CITY

JIM CROW AT WORK

Me and a man was working side by side, this is what it meant,
They was paying him a dollar an hour, and they was payin' me fifty
cents.

I went to the employment office, got a number and I got in line,
They called everybody's number, but they never did call mine.

They say if you's white, you's alright, if you's brown, stick around,
But if you're black, mmm brother, get back, get back, get back.

Bill Broonzy, "Black, Brown, and White Blues"

Racial violence enforced white supremacy with the immediate strength of a policeman's club, but segregation as a system gained its staying power from its rootedness in the social relations of daily economic life. In this respect, segregation was not merely a southern phenomenon. White control over the economic fate and the opportunities of African Americans had long been an axiom in American life by the 1930s. African Americans by the millions fled the South for jobs in the industrial urban centers of the North during the various waves of the Great Migration, and while many of them attained a better standard of living, the color line trapped them in old and inadequate housing and at the bottom of the job ladder. Jim Crow at work created an impenetrable maze of discrimination; regardless of ability, blacks were banned from most skilled and white collar employment. As Clarence Coe puts it, "If you were black, you were just black." Or, as blues artist Big Bill Broonzy adroitly summarized the situation, "if you're black, mmm brother, get back." This seemed to characterize the experience of black workers not just in the 1930s but for much of the twentieth century.

Nevertheless, for most of the people who tell their stories in this book, work in the cities appeared to be a step up, compared to the mostly abysmal conditions of rural life in the cotton economy. Willie Harrell, a former sharecropper and day laborer born in 1929, told an interviewer in Memphis that life in rural Mississippi as late as the 1950s and 1960s "was just all slavery times." Plantation life divided and isolated black people, he recalled; "I couldn't get nowhere. Just like I'm in prison or something." He vividly remembered the 1955 lynching of Emmett Till in Money, Mississippi, considering himself blessed to have escaped the state with his life. In the city, he ended up doing wretched jobs like stacking furniture at Memphis Furniture Company for twenty-five cents an hour. Likewise, Robert Spencer, born in 1913 of an older generation, remembered how riding-bosses in the plantation districts rounded up everyone for work at planting and harvest time, so that children rarely got more than two to three months of schooling per year. Spencer came to Memphis in 1930 and got a job delivering goods for a packinghouse to surrounding areas, where whites cheated him out of his pay and forced him to buy his meals in the back of restaurants and eat his food in the street. Both men felt themselves lucky to have left Mississippi.

For these refugees from rural areas, the dreadful conditions on plantations provided a benchmark by which they measured their life's progress. They typically belonged to the second generation in their families free from slavery, and they knew how bad conditions could be. Their slave grandparents had sought land after emancipation, but the federal government dashed their hopes for economic independence by returning lands confiscated from slaveholders during the Civil War. Although postwar plantation owners failed to completely reimpose an unfree labor system, the new system resembled slavery nonetheless. In the aftermath of the war, former slaves became day laborers on plantations, rented land as tenants, or became sharecroppers, perpetually in debt to white merchants and landlords who furnished them with tools, seed, and food at exorbitant prices. Sharecroppers turned a fourth, a third, and even half or more of their crop over to their creditors at the end of the harvest. Some black families, like those of Clarence Coe and Matthew Davis, obtained their own land and did much better. But they exercised personal attributes of independence, a violation of Jim Crow's mores, only at their peril. Under the reign of white supremacy, former sharecropper John Handcox recalled, black people "became everybody's slave."

For black people moving to the city, what they left behind was as important as what they hoped to gain. Coe, as he tells us, was in a better position than most. His slave grandparents had bought land after emancipation, and his parents became self-sufficient farmers. Unlike most children of sharecroppers, Coe finished high school and had the means to start a farm of his own. But the sickening sight of a lynched black body and of white men kicking black men in the seat of their pants for the fun of it proved more than his spirit could bear. "I wanted to get away from this environment," Coe said. Like others whose relatives or acquaintances found jobs elsewhere, he followed the lead of a friend and joined the chain of migration from the countryside to the city.

Clarence Coe came to Memphis largely to escape the so-called paternalism of the rural areas, yet he found the "same damn things" in the city. The plantation mentality's pervasive racial etiquette still required blacks to call whites "mister" or "sir," while whites used blacks' first names, called men "boys," and referred to complete strangers as "auntie" or "uncle" or, more simply, "nigger." Racial etiquette dictated that whites should never shake hands with blacks or sit with them in a mixed group (unless blacks sat behind or opposite them) and that blacks should be served at restaurants and stores in the back or the basement and should bow and scrape to whites. In both country and city, whenever African Americans owned homes, land, good tools, or a new car, held good jobs, ran businesses, or behaved "above themselves," white landlords, police, factory supervisors, guards, and workers put them back "in their place." For simply driving a new car onto his employer's parking lot, for example, Coe found his tires slashed by the company's security guard. Whites insisted that blacks should grin and bear such indignities with good cheer.

Living in more concentrated numbers, blacks found a little more anonymity or personal freedom in the city than in the country. Yet, as George Holloway tells us, urban Jim Crow could be equally irksome and degrading. Though a native to the city, he never got used to the indignities: harassed by police as a child for walking through "white" neighborhoods; forced by theater owners to sit in the balcony with litter and rats; barred from the city zoo save for one day a week; and forced to attend underfunded city schools lacking sports programs and using old, defaced textbooks passed down from whites. He hated the fact that his wife had to buy her clothes in the basement of department stores and resented the various indignities he and his friends suffered on segregated streetcars and buses. Blacks could not sit on juries, act as judges or elected leaders, or vote freely, leaving few means to redress their many grievances. The superior-subordinate race relations of Jim Crow left a burning imprint on his memory, one which fueled Holloway's lifelong struggle to change things.

In the pages that follow, Holloway, Coe, and other African American workers explain how white supremacy dogged their work life and made it impossible for them to relate to whites as equals. Under Jim Crow, factory environments were particularly hard, especially where whites and blacks worked together; the separate and unequal rule extended not only to bathrooms, locker rooms, and water fountains but also to time clocks and parking lots. Violence as the ultimate sanction always remained a possibility at work or anywhere else where blacks and whites mingled, Coe recalls. Whether altercations with whites developed or not, the fact that "you always had to be ready for them to happen" made work life tense at best.

Even more pointedly, as in the countryside, urban whites had structured the labor market so that blacks could not get ahead. The depressed cotton economy surrounding places like Memphis devalued the price of labor, while Jim Crow made it difficult for blacks to make demands on white employers. Expected to take low wages, they had few rights with which to dispute this or anything else. Consequently, the industries that used blacks the most—cottonseed oil and compress industries, food processing, and wood-based industries—paid some of the lowest wages in the United States. In these industries that relied on cheap black labor rather than mechanization to push costs down, blacks did hot, heavy, unrewarding work. Black workers made up some 80 percent of the unskilled factory labor force in Memphis, and domestic workers, the single largest occupational grouping of blacks, earned next to nothing in white folks' homes. Blacks filled the ranks of other low-wage service jobs as janitors, waiters, and servants, or worked as day laborers. This blacks-as-servants model, a component of the plantation mentality, influenced the attitudes of white employers and workers well into the twentieth century.

Whites, by contrast, monopolized work in industry as overseers, checkers and weighers, machinists, foremen, and other higher-paying skilled and semi-skilled positions. No matter how much seniority or skill they might actually have, black men were still called "boy" and classified as helpers, and virtually all black workers came under intense white supervision. In the unionized crafts, whites who controlled much of the hiring inflicted tremendous damage by freezing blacks out of skilled trades, such as plumbing, electrical work, and carpentry, thus forcing them into jobs as laborers, plasterers, painters, and hod carriers. On docks, boats, and other places where unions had some power, support or rejection by the union often sealed the fate of blacks. Squeezed on all sides, African Americans only rarely found middle-class jobs as schoolteachers, preachers, or entrepreneurs, and these jobs were within the framework of a segregated black community. This color-coded labor market existed in every region of the United States and could not be avoided.

The testimony of Hillie and Laura Pride clearly reveals the painful effects of this segregated labor market based on low wages. They left cotton picking in the fields for factory work in Memphis, but Hillie's meager wages at the Fisher automobile body factory required Laura to shuttle back and forth to work in Arkansas cotton fields to supplement their income. Thousands of other city workers made the barest wages doing miserable, hot work in the cotton fields, where planter, police, and vigilante violence crushed Southern Tenant Farmers Union organizing in the mid- and late 1930s. Fisher Body shop, which hired large numbers of blacks, provided alternative work, but it did so at ten to fifteen cents an hour. When Hillie Pride says conditions there were "fine," he means that it was "about the only place around here to work in at the time that paid enough to do any good." He appreciated that he made a steady wage during the Depression, when others had nothing at all or worked in the cotton fields. But Fisher factory workers, he notes, barely made ends meet; they went to get their pay singing "the Lord will make a way somehow."

No matter how poorly it paid in the city, factory work represented a step up for former rural workers. But as well-muscled ex-farmworkers joined the ranks of the urban industrial labor force, they faced a predicament. Miserly public appropriations for black schools meant that black children could not gain the skills needed to advance in the job market. And even if they did somehow gain higher skills, whites would not employ them except in menial jobs. Holloway, for example, could find nothing better than factory work despite several years of college.

Employment in northern-based industries did not improve the situation. When Firestone Tire and Rubber Company moved South it set up a racially discriminatory system that in every way took advantage of the legalized segregation around them. Firestone arrived in 1937, hiring over two thousand workers, some eight hundred of them black. Its "ABC" wage system in the factory's early years classified white adult males at the "A" rate of thirty-two cents an hour, with boys under eighteen ("B") and "coloreds" ("C") earning 28 cents an hour. "B" workers could move up to higher pay at age twenty-one, while those in the "C" classification stayed at the bottom rate, with no ladder to higher wages. Even though black men used to hard toil in the fields could often outwork white men, they were always paid at a lower rate. Like Firestone, other northern-based companies accepted, indeed relished, the local wage system. Most of the companies that migrated to Memphis did so seeking non-union, racially divided, and cheap labor markets, and most of them only reinforced the city's poverty.

The key to gaining employment in urban factories, as in rural cotton fields, was the ability to work extremely hard and put up with bad conditions. Matthew Davis had worked hard on the farm and was a husky young man. But when he began work at Firestone, he experienced an extraordinary regime of brutal labor, surrounded by noise and tire pigment that permeated his skin and filled his lungs, as he and his youthful cohort of fellow black workers took on the worst occupations at the plant. While onerous conditions affected both black and white, the racial system ensured inequality of suffering. Over the course of their lifetimes these workers suffered hearing and vision loss from factory work that began in environments totally unregulated by unions or the state. Many former black Firestone workers ended their days with cancer and other diseases induced by working with tire pigment and other toxic materials.

Unionization provided the only available means of changing such harsh conditions. But, as former workers at the Memphis Firestone plant tell us in this chapter, the racial system defeated early industrial organizing efforts. The Congress of Industrial Organizations, which arose in the mid-1930s as a challenge to the craft unions, accepted all workers regardless of race. The CIO's United Rubber Workers' promise of racial equality spurred black workers to join it, but this in turn caused many whites, with a perceived stake in discriminatory wage scales and job assignments, to reject it. In reality, such white "privileges" kept the workers at odds and enabled employers to disable unions and drive down wages. Firestone's southern plant in Memphis, as one example, paid about half of what its unionized plant paid in Akron. In 1940, whites at Memphis Firestone did decide they needed a union, but they voted for a racially exclusive AFL craft union, which placed whites in one unit and blacks in another. The AFL's craft-oriented local did little to change things, and whites finally switched to the CIO in 1942. But the racial system kept workers at odds at Firestone for the next thirty years.

The black workers who lived with Jim Crow in urban factories had to find their own methods of fighting discrimination. They joined the CIO almost everywhere it appeared, based on its promise of equal rights. Yet they could not rely on the industrial unions to enforce those rights or on white workers to accept them as equals. Moreover, they got little help from black ministers or the middle class, whose ability to fight for civil rights was severely limited by the white power structure. The Crump machine, for example, could have ministers' electricity cut off or their church buildings condemned, could cause teachers to be fired, could have the police frighten customers away from the shops of black entrepreneurs, or more simply, could have people beaten up. Black preachers potentially had some independence because African Americans paid their salaries, but they frequently became tools of Crump. Blacks defined as leaders by the Crump machine and the newspapers counseled caution and conformity, not resistance to Jim Crow. Conditions were similar in most southern cities, where in the 1930s the NAACP barely existed.

Without a robust civil rights movement or aggressive trade unions to support them, most working-class blacks did what they could to survive on an individual basis. Those who underwent the transition from rural to urban and from agricultural to industrial work in the 1930s Depression era expressed some satisfaction at what they accomplished. Yet, as witnesses to this dark period tell us, when looking back on factory work and city life their sense of pride mingles with pain and anger.

Hillie and Laura Pride Move to Memphis

You were just like mules and hogs, you weren't hardly counted.

Hillie and Laura Pride lived in a small wooden house on the north side of Memphis in a neighborhood on the edge of factories and vacant lots. When I interviewed them in 1989, conditions were sliding rapidly downhill after a series of factory closures. Trying to find better-paying work, the Prides escaped from the cotton fields to the city in the 1930's Depression but found that city life and factory work had their own hardships.

LAURA PRIDE

I was born in Lucy, Tennessee. We came to the city because we wasn't makin' nothin' in the country! People don't even want to talk about it; it was just hard, hard work, with no end to it, pickin' cotton.

I was going to the field to pick cotton. I did pretty well, because I didn't get killed! You know how it is with a truck load of folks out on the road. They paid a dollar per hundred pounds of cotton picked.

[Union organizers] never made it down there.[1] It was hard work, the heat would burn you up. People *worked* in them days! We'd go to work about 7:00 A.M., get up at 5:00 A.M.

You'd get an hour off for lunch, time enough to wipe off the sweat. Cotton-chopping season was April, we'd start picking in August and on into the winter. Sometimes when people were done picking cotton in winter, they were idle until the next year. Then people would hunt for rabbits, coons, squirrels, quail, deer, or anything out in the country. Sure, it was rough work.

We were better off than some, since the factory job paid a bit. Farming was the best then, you could be a day worker. We felt lucky compared to a lot of people. Those times were hard. You know that saying, "Mr. Crump don't allow"? There's not much you can do about it, not a thing. Nothing you can do!

HILLIE PRIDE

I was born in Huntsville, Alabama. I was about four years old when I came from Alabama. My parents, nine brothers, and two sisters all came together in 1910. We were plantation farmers, came to Arkansas to sharecrop and rent, five dollars a week, one dollar a day. There was a lot of money I made that never came my way. I wish I could dig some of it up now!

---

1. Unions of day laborers and sharecroppers did emerge in parts of Arkansas and Alabama but were suppressed.

We moved here [from the country]. I was working at Fisher body, over there on Second Street in Memphis. I worked there for five years, working on the pillow line [putting seats into cars]. I can't remember how much they paid, but it was piecework. I worked there from 1932 to 1938. There were two shifts, about two thousand people worked there. Most were black.

There were just a few white supervisors there, in the glue room and on the assembly line. The whites were supervisors, there were no black supervisors. There wasn't a union then. Rip saw, finishing mills, shapers, the glue room, and on the assembly line, roof mill, were all black workers. We made maybe ten or fifteen cents an hour, doing piecework.

Conditions were fine. It was a good place to work, as long as you did your work. That's about the only place around here to work in at the time that paid enough to do any good. Murray body plant was there, where Firestone is now. Those were the only factory jobs. Other black people would pick cotton over in Arkansas, but there weren't really any other jobs around. People would go to the cotton fields from here by the busload, or in an old truck.

I know back at Fisher we got two bonuses, thirty-five dollars and twenty-five dollars. That was in about 1936, and all of the employees in the line going to get the money sang, "The Lord will make a way somehow." All of them were singin' it. And then they went on in to the factory and went back to work. When the plant went down, a lot of them made good, if they'd been there a long time. I'd been there only five years so I didn't get much, but a lot of them got two or three thousand dollars if they'd been there a long time. Colored people!

[Then, when I worked at Firestone], that lampblack got all in my skin, in my hands and arms and legs. That lampblack goes in your skin and gets in your bloodstream. You can't get rid of it. When you sweat, it comes out black. It killed a lot of people.[2] I've got white spots all over. I got chemicals in my eyes. One eye doesn't work now, my right eye. And I had one ma-

2. Lampblack was a pigment powder used to color the rubber in the process of tire manufacturing, and handling it was a job reserved for blacks. A carcinogen, the lampblack got in people's pores and still washed out in the bath tub days after exposure. Many complained of its deadly after-effects.

chine roaring on each side of my head, so my hearing is gone. Only missed a few days in thirty-five years and nine months, and I was in good shape when I went there.

Firestone owes me some money right now. We had money coming from some investors, people who had been working there a long time had invested some. Some of them got $1,600. I worked there thirty-five years and nine months, and I didn't get nothing! They owe it to me, but I don't get it. I'm going to see if I can get my money back, just like the rest of them. Some of them got two checks, some for $1,600. They owe us compensation.

The work there was hard. We didn't have no union, no help, no nothing! You had to do what they said or you were out the door. Nobody said nothing for you at all, until the union got there. You were just like mules and hogs, you weren't hardly counted. You had no choice. You had twenty minutes for lunch time, and you had to be back in them twenty minutes every day or you would be fired, and nothing was done about it.

It started out at thirty-two cent an hour in 1938. We'd get a two-cent raise at a time. And it drug on until the union came along. You'd work next to a white man doing the same job, but you didn't make what he made, oh no! Not until the union got there. Before the union, there were two different wage rates, one for colored, one for whites. The union got rid of separate wage rates. Then, when the union got in, there was piecework. You did the work, you made the money. You made the same as the white man. If you'd run the mill, you'd make the same as the white man running the mill. The more he made, the more you made. When the plant went down, they were making $106 a day, the same job I done. Some were making $300 to $400 a week. They broke up that mess [racial wage differentials].[3]

[At first] the whites had all the supervision over you. You had to do what the white people told you. After the union took over, we got colored supervisors and white supervisors both.

Lots of strikes on account of white and colored, where the people could

3. Mr. Pride is referring here to a process that took years. The United Rubber Workers Local 186 did not achieve bargaining rights until 1942, and racial wage differentials continued for some time after that. Once discriminatory wage rates ended, however, blacks still got locked into the dirtiest departments, which had the lowest wage rates in the plant.

eat, and restrooms, and all of that. They [whites] wanted the union segregated, and they'd have strikes every two days over some racial issue. If the blacks didn't do exactly what the whites wanted them to do, the whites would go on strike. They'd walk out saying they weren't going to work next to "no colored," or share a watercooler or something. That was a terrible time. Mr. [Paul] Borda was the supervisor over the plant, and he broke up those strikes. He said, "When you go out on strike, you leave your badge in that barrel there, and you won't get back in." That broke up the strike.[4]

The union was a real good thing 'cause it broke up that mess. What would you think if there was a fountain here, and one over there, and the same water come up here as there, what would be the difference if you drank over there? The union tore them both down and put up a fountain there for everyone to use. It was just a bunch of foolishness, and they broke it up.[5]

When it all boiled down, the union made the changes. The union did it. Before the union, you couldn't look at whites, especially white women. I know all about it. I stayed around there long enough to learn something. I've been through every bit of it. There were hard times until the union started working it out.

I was one of the best mill men in there, and I wanted to be. They got a record of it in there, too. They hated it when I retired. A mill man makes rubber, puts rubber in a vat, warms it up until it's hot, and works it until it gets soft. Then it goes up a line and they cut it. That's what they make tires out of. I did that most of the time there. I learned how to do it myself, and other jobs, too. By me showing the people how to do those jobs, I would help the new men on the job. The supervisors didn't know how. I did. They didn't classify me as nothing, just a worker. But they'd leave all the new workers to me to train.

When I retired, I was honored by all the workers. They gave me a little slip with all the people I'd helped on it. And when I went up there, every pocket I had they put money in. There were lots of people who wanted to

4. This incident, from what I can gather, occurred in the late 1950s or early 1960s.

5. Desegregation of the plant occurred after the 1954 *Brown v. Board of Education* Supreme Court case, and is discussed in subsequent comments by Clarence Coe, Lonnie Rowland, and Lawrence Garrison. They stress that management and the union made changes in the racial system only under pressure.

quit because they couldn't do the work, and I helped a lot of people keep their jobs by showing them how. Some of them got mad, and said they couldn't do it, but I just said to do what you can. A lot of people wouldn't have no jobs or benefits today if I hadn't talked to 'em. Colored and white.

When I retired, the man told me I'd worked good and had a good record, I'd have enough to live on. Since I've been out, I've been a security guard at the union hall, but that's all.

Matthew Davis Describes Heavy Industrial Work

They wanted healthy lookin' men and I had that appearance.

Matthew R. Davis, like most of the workers I met, was friendly and seemingly carried little bitterness when I spoke with him in 1984. Because we could not find a quiet place to talk, we conducted the interview in his car. He told about the conditions he worked under in a matter-of-fact, nothing-special tone, but like other Firestone workers, he remembered the stress of doing the hottest, dirtiest, most dangerous work for less pay than whites, while denied access to the better jobs.

I came from a rural background. My father rented them farms from them big, rich white folks and a lot of the ordinary white guys, they got mad with him because we was livin' in a big house just as nice as any house you could find in the country. He was livin' in the house that white men used to live in, you see. And then he had three or four sharecroppers. They'd be rentin' from him and he rented the farm from somebody else. I think a third of what they made would go to him, my daddy, and he just paid so much for the whole rent of the farm.

But later, after so many children got away from home we moved over on this farm that was from my mother's father, which was my grandfather, Joe Williams, out there in west Tennessee. That was 199 acres of land. Her brother was working half of it and we had half of it. That farm is still out there. It's been divided up but part belongs to us. So, I come from a rural life. My wife come from New Albany, Mississippi.

Some people who are much younger than I am, livin' right here in town had a harder time than we did out on the farm, 'cause we raised plenty of food. My daddy had a sorghum mill. Everybody from ten to twelve miles around bring his sorghum to his mill. You know, cook molasses. He would do all that kind of stuff. And he was a carpenter. You know, we made it, we made it. I've heard a lot of people talkin' about how they didn't have food to eat or clothes to wear. But as far as that's concerned, my daddy provided for us and I tried to provide for my children just like he did.

I used to watch my daddy. He grew up in the little town of Collierville, Tennessee. Every white man or woman in that town knew Matthew Davis. He had a knack when he meet them, he'd do that to black women too, he'd just tip his hat to them. In those days they didn't allow no black to sit out in the little park in Collierville. But my daddy would sit down and cross his legs and smoke his pipe, 'cause wasn't none of them goin' to bother.

He would take milk up to the cheese factory uptown. You know, you have your wagon or your truck. You'd be in line. You had to wait till the other fella get out of your way, you carry your milk in there and they pour it up. So, the white guy come up there and was goin' to cut in the front of 'em. I wasn't with him that day but they said, oh man, daddy got his knife. All the big folks in town come down there and told him stay where he was, he was right. But didn't nobody never bother our family. And so, a lot of times it's the way you carry yourself.

I was thinking about when them guys [older black workers at Firestone] started back in '39 and '37. Murray's Body Shop had it and then Firestone come and take it over. I started working for Firestone in 1940, that's after I got out of high school. It didn't go no higher than the tenth grade at that time and you couldn't go to the white school, [even though it was] right there in town. At that time I wasn't married. But when I got out of high school I decided then that I didn't want to be a farmer. I was kind of slow on learnin'. I went through high school, but if I had been a real sharp dude, I had the opportunity to go to college. But I didn't go. My people could have put me through college very easy. See, I was the youngest out of nine children and all of them had gotten jobs and they was willin' to help me go to college.

[But I moved to Memphis and] the first little job I got was at Walgreen Drug Store, and then from there to Virginia Bridge, across from Firestone, and then I worked out at Dupont, out there at Millington, and from there to Firestone. I started at Firestone December 2, 1940. I stayed at Firestone until I retired. My parents stayed on in the rural area, till both of them passed away. One thing I did [was] sending money back out there to help them.

The way I got started at Firestone, Mr. Hayes was the principal at Manassas school. Most of the fellows back in those days, especially blacks, had to have the recommendation of the principal. I walked up to that gate [at Firestone] and I asked the guard were they hiring and could I get an application, and he said, "No they ain't hiring nobody." Mr. Reynolds was sittin' there looking right out the window, and I had started walking on back, and the little children going to school they said, "Mister, that man called you." I look back at the guard was back there. "Mr. Reynolds say you come on in, he want to talk to you." I went on in there and he talked to me and he said, "You look too healthy, you come on back tonight." [laughs] I started work that night.

Yeah, that's how I got on, two places like this. Now I was at Millington Dupont, I walked out there one day. I bet you there was two thousand folk just standin' outside waitin', tryin' to get a job. And the foreman say, "Hey you!" Everybody goes "Me?" And he say "No, that big healthy lookin' dude." I went out there and got right on. I was about as tall as I am now, about five eleven. I think being around twenty-two or twenty-three years old and weighin' about 220 or 230, I just looked healthy. Yeah, I imagine I just looked healthy to them. But he wanted to put me in a ditch and I told him no, I wasn't goin' into no ditch, I just come out of high school, I didn't need no shovel in my hand or nothin' like that. When it got cold I quit. I just didn't want to be exposin' myself out there in that cold weather. I wasn't married then, see.

Back then, the big, healthy, strong lookin' men, they hired them. I enjoyed the work over there. [But] it was a struggle, you know. Conditions was pretty bad. They started me out back then on what you call the washline. Well, that washline, that's where your crude rubber come in. They used to ship it in there as raw rubber, you know, the rubber that's baled in here from Africa. They come in here in great big bales that weigh about three hundred pounds and have a band around them. That's what you call the natural rubber. Well, we had to break the band from around it and send that rubber through what you call a cracker. You'd put that whole bale in a bale splitter, and it had some sharp knives that would cut it about ten different ways. It would go through something like a compressor and then when it cut it, it would go through a cracker to soften it up. And, when it would go through that cracker, then it would come to us on the washline. We had to dip it in water, put it on a mill, and it would be crumbling and falling all apart, and then we put it on a rack.

And from there they go through a hot kiln, to kind of dry it out. [They] run it through that hot kiln and then they'd put it on a line and just let it go way on through the plant. That would give it a chance to dry out. It would just be a long belt and you would see the rubber going on through the plant. Now that was in the olden days. That was what the washline had to do.

You had to have on a rubber apron, rubber boots and water just be all over you. We was right out of a big old door, and most times you'd get a breeze comin' in that door, but it was cold in the wintertime, with that cold water! You know, a guy had to open the door to take a load out on the dock, maybe to load a train up or something. And man, when you take that load out, they wouldn't close that door back up. They're goin' to leave the door open till they come back in. In the wintertime was your tough time, 'cause that cold air be blowin' in and it would be down on freezin' temperature and then you workin' in water too, rubber gloves, rubber apron, and rubber boots. That's pretty cold. You catch cold sometime, you expose yourself. I sometime say that may be why I suffer arthritis so bad, my joints were kind of exposed.

The thing that was so bad, I didn't mind the water so much, but the noise. If we was right together, like you and me now, you couldn't hear what I was sayin' unless I get right up in your ear and just go to hollerin' at you, it was just that noisy. That's why so many Firestone guys, they're hard of hearing. In later years if there was too much noise you wear some kind of hearin' thing over your ears, or something over your eyes that keep the dust out of your eyes, or a mask over your nose. But back in them days we didn't have nothin' like that. [I worked] a couple of years, I think it was, on that job.

Then I went to the compound room. That's where I really remained most of the time there, in the compound area. That's where you mixed the rubber, the pigment. You had to weigh up all the pigment, you know, brown, black, white, green, you know, all colors. Then you'd push it on around to the banbury [machine], you know, then you mixed your pig-ment. After you get it all mixed, they had what they called a bucket. It would come down a line, it had wheels on a track. I'd put my batch in there and I'd push a bucket on down to the next man, he puts his batch in. Then a guy had to put a certain amount of rubber in there. Then it gets to the master scale and the checker weighed it.

The compound room at that time would be all black. Whites had a job and blacks had a job. The compound room mostly was black, and of course on the banbury operation there was white and black. Sometimes a white was up there on the banbury, sometimes that thing would be cluckin' and shoot that lampblack back out on his face. You couldn't tell the white man from the black man with all that lampblack all over his face. But we [always] had a white supervisor. Now whites worked on the banbury 'cause that was a good payin' job. But as soon as the rates went out on the banbury, they went off.[6]

Later I got to be checker. When you go on that master scale, all of that together is supposed to weigh, say, five hundred pounds. [But] if it's four or five pounds heavy, you'd have the tear the whole bucket down to see what went wrong. Because it had to weigh exactly right. And from there, after working at the master scale, checking it, we would push it on out the ban-bury. Then it was mixed up, for maybe five or ten minutes. That's when they would drop it on down. It would go downstairs. We was upstairs. Send it on from there until it was made into a tire. It goes through a lot of different processes.

On that washline I think there was five or six fellas on the line. But in that compound room, sometimes you'd be workin' with twelve, fourteen people up there. Everybody had something to do. Now, I didn't have to weigh that lampblack but a little while. I just hated to weigh that lamp-black, that stuff. I had a friend could weigh that lampblack, he had long arms, and when he picked that bag up he could hold it off from him and pour it on out, but I put it right up on my stomach and that stuff just get all over me. I weighed it for a short while. But most of my time was cuttin' rubber. And then after they started the whitewall, I think I was the first one that started weighin' the whitewall out there. That's what I enjoyed doin'. I worked in the whitewall department until I retired, just about. About a year before I retired I finally got a job, maybe two years, drivin' a forklift,

6. In chapter 4, Clarence Coe corroborates Davis, explaining that initially whites monopolized the banbury jobs mixing tire pigment, but once blacks broke into those jobs management downgraded them and made the whole department "black," at lower rates of pay.

just drivin' around pickin' a little load and set it down. That was about the easiest job that I've had.

On the average, [blacks made thirty-two cents an hour]. A few jobs paid maybe five or ten cents more an hour. But in those days you had to take one load of rubber, stacked this high, maybe weighin' about three thousand pounds, on a dolly. You didn't have nothing but a jack to pull it with it. One man be [pulling] at one end. The floor would be so messed up with oil and stuff on it. One man would be pulling that heavy load, until later years when we started gettin' forklifts in there to lift a load and carry it. But blacks really suffered out there with that kind of work. All kinds of injuries, that's right. You had people come on those jobs, they'd work two, three days, [and] it was too tough for them.

At that time it wasn't like where you had to have a high school education. They was not looking for so much as a high school education because blacks wasn't going have no pencil in their hand too much. They wanted healthy lookin' men and I had that appearance. But some of them little guys in there was much better than I was.

I started at Firestone in 1940. The army got me though, in July of '42. I put three years and seven months in the army. Seven months of that time was over in the Philippines, but the other three years was here in the United States. I was a quartermaster in the army. I came out of the army, I had been in the Philippines. At the train station, a man said, "All you blacks over here, all the whites come over here." And I'm just comin' out the army. To hear some remark like that, it really gets under your skin.

[When I came back], the conditions didn't change very much. Everything was segregated, the water fountains, restrooms, lunchrooms. My wife had an uncle come down here from Cleveland, Ohio. You know, you could show your guests through the plant. So he went there and drank out of the white fountain. [laughs] And folks looked at him so strange, you know.

George Holloway Remembers the Crump Era

We knew all of this was wrong . . . but there was nothing we could do about it.

George Holloway, in a 1990 interview at his home in Baltimore, Maryland, told me that he gained a civil rights consciousness at an early age, as he confronted the various dimensions of inequality and saw his father struggle with racism as a Pullman porter. He learned the value of organization through his father's union efforts, and one can see in his case how generations of experience came into play when blacks began to organize. Young Holloway became a pioneer himself, breaking down factory segregation and racism within his union. The desire for both racial and economic justice stayed with him throughout his adult life.

I was born in Memphis, Tennessee, on June 8, 1915. My daddy's parents were slaves in Tennessee. Grandaddy died on a day farm in Somerville, Tennessee, when I was one or two years old. Daddy took me to the funeral. My grandma died two or three years later. Daddy was a child of slaves, he wasn't a slave though. Daddy said that his parents were allowed to stay on the big farm, when they were free, as sharecroppers. Grandad handled a two-mule plow and scraped cotton. You make the row clean by knocking the dirt off of the cotton with a plow, that was called scraping cotton. Dad didn't want to work on a farm, so he went to Memphis and worked in the clothes-pressing shops, maybe on Beale Street. Then, he went to the Pullman Company as a way to travel.

My daddy was a Pullman porter and the second vice president, and then president of the [Memphis chapter of the] Pullman porters union [Brotherhood of Sleeping Car Porters (BSCP)]. They were part of the AF of L. He brought me my first union experiences. My daddy used to run [on the train] from Memphis to New York. I'll never forget, when I was nine years old, my daddy came home one night singing. When people [passengers] would steal things off the train, such as towels, pillowcases, and water pitchers, my daddy would have to pay for it if he hadn't noticed. My sister, Amelia, and I heard him singing one night for the first time in fifteen years since he had begun working there. Because they had formed the union, he would no longer have to deduct stolen and broken items from his paycheck. That was my first notion and recollection of the unions.

A. Philip Randolph was run out of Memphis by Crump in the 1920s when I was about eleven or twelve years old. My daddy and I saw him run from Beale Street Church at the time. He was speaking at a rally to organize the Pullman porters union. I saw Randolph up on the stage, and the policemen walked straight to the stage where Randolph was and told him to leave immediately. They didn't beat him, but I saw the policemen carry him out the side door. They put him on the train and sent him to New York.[7]

I'd say the Pullman porters union had about one hundred members [in Memphis] in the '20s. They had a band and would have parades and picnics. My daddy played in the band. Pullman porters union was one of the first to accept blacks. Most of the AFL was skilled white people, and laborers couldn't join. The only other AFL unions that had blacks at that time were the carpenters and bricklayers unions.

They [the AFL] had a separate hall for blacks. Blacks and whites couldn't go to meetings together. They actually belonged to two different unions. The AFL trades building was right on Beale Street, and the black one was behind it on Linden and Lauderdale. It was a big brick building for the white union, and a separate little wooden building in the back, at one time a servants' quarters, for the black union. The AFL machinists and electricians were all in the white union. The blacks met in that little tiny hall in the back. The whites didn't want the blacks in the union, and they weren't going to have them.[8]

When Dad was forming the union, they couldn't meet at people's houses openly. They had to sneak people in different doors in secret, so no one would notice. Mr. Crump said there wouldn't be any black union at that time, in the '20s. That went on for a year or so before they were recognized by the [labor] board in 1925 or 1926.

In Memphis, on the other hand, Mr. Bucher, who was the superintendent of the Pullman Company there, didn't fight the union. My daddy knew him, and the NLRB [National Labor Relations Board] recognized the union. The Pullman Company had a harder time in Chicago, where the headquarters were located.[9]

7. Randolph and others organized the Brotherhood of Sleeping Car Porters in 1925. He continued to lead the union and became a renowned black labor and civil rights leader, and the titular head of the mass march on Washington, D.C. in 1963. The Crump machine expelled Randolph from Memphis in the 1920s and again when he came to speak in 1943. As the result of much protest, he finally spoke in a Memphis church in 1944.

8. The AFL unions often simply excluded blacks, or when they did organize them, put them in separate locals from whites. Blacks often ended up in "federal unions," administered through the national and local AFL, with little decision-making power.

9. A 1926 federal railway law recognized railway workers' right to bargain, but the federal mediation board had little power to enforce that right. The Pullman Company did not officially recognize the BSCP until 1937.

Once the union came in, porters made more than a letter carrier, and they were looked up to in the community. They made good money, enough to buy beautiful houses or cars. Back in the '20s, black people rarely owned cars, unless they were doctors or something like that.

My daddy owned a Packard, and Mr. Bucher bought it for him. Mr. Bucher lived on Stonewall and Watkins. We went to his house one day, and gave two to three thousand dollars to buy a new car. Mr. Bucher drove the car for two months, and then he turned it over to Dad for a dollar. This was because the car salesman wouldn't sell a new car to a black man. So, Mr. Bucher bought it for him, and sold it to him.[10]

Once in a while blacks would own a business or be a doctor or lawyer, but if you were black and didn't own a business, you could only trade in the basements of the stores. Blacks could only go upstairs in the stores if they had cash. But, you couldn't try on hats or clothes, and you couldn't buy on credit.[11]

It happened like that in the South until 1948. The UAW [United Automobile Workers] broke that up after 1948. Andy Brown came in as the community service person for the UAW, and he demanded service for blacks. Goldsmith's [department store] and Black and White was the first stores that blacks could buy equally in. I still have a 1948 credit card from Goldsmith's. UAW broke this up, [and] this meant we didn't have to go to Beale Street to shop. Before then, you had to sign up as to where you worked and they wouldn't trust factory workers or anyone other than black businessmen to pay the bill. [But] most blacks weren't allowed in businesses!

I grew up in the Depression. There were two black high schools in Memphis then, Manassas and Booker T. Washington. The white kids had nine high schools, although blacks were 42 percent of the population. They really didn't build any new high schools for blacks until after World War II. We didn't get books at school until we went to high school. Our parents

10. Holloway's remembrance of a relatively benign Bucher is jarringly at odds with the story told by Pullman porter William Glover (see chapter 1). Glover was a friend of his father's, and Holloway later wrote me a note saying that police had stopped Glover one night after he left the Holloway home after speaking with his father about the union. "I heard about the Glover case, but I don't know the details," Holloway told me. "I was too young to know the true story" about what happened to him.

11. William Glover's ability to buy on credit as early as the 1930s proved an exception to the rule.

had to buy our books until high school. I went to high school in 1930, and we got the used books of the white kids. White kids all knew this, and they'd write degrading remarks all over them. The school I went to had outside toilets, no cafeteria, and it was years before they fixed up Booker T. Washington or Manassas.

We couldn't go to any swimming pools, either. There was only one place for blacks to swim, at Tabernacle Baptist Church on the corner of Lauderdale and Georgia. There were amusement parks, but blacks couldn't go in the parks. The police would kick the black kids out of the wading pool in Nathan Bedford Forrest Park, named after the Confederate general. We couldn't walk through Forrest Park.[12]

We couldn't go to any of the theaters, either, unless you'd go in the side door and sit way up in the rafters in the balcony. We had Warner Brothers, Daisy, and the Palace Theaters on Beale Street, but most of the theaters were out in the white neighborhoods where blacks couldn't go. You'd buy your ticket in the front, but then you'd have to go around to the side door if you were black.

There were times in the theater when blacks would be laughing at the film and having a lot of fun, and someone would call the police. The policemen might ask someone why they were laughing, and hit them and make them leave, or arrest them. A lot of youngsters protested it at that time, but to no avail. You'd just get a fine to pay and a mark on your record.

I also remember experiences on streetcars as a child. The blacks had to sit in the back, of course, and that was a hardship, because they'd have it blocked off. The more white people that got on, the further back you had to go. Eventually the whites would get all of the seats, and we'd have to stand up. There was more resentment there between whites and blacks than almost anywhere else that I recall. Being forced to move up and back was a point of friction constantly. There were only streetcars at that time, buses came in after the war. Protesting didn't happen until after World War II, either. Then, people began to fight for change.[13]

12. During the Civil War, Forrest had led the massacre of Union troops, black and white, at Fort Pillow, Tennessee, and later helped organize the Ku Klux Klan. A monument to him still exists in the park Holloway describes.

13. Alzada Clark and Leroy Boyd comment that bus segregation was one of the most unpopular features of segregation with blacks, and a frequent source of altercations between white and black (see "Interlude: Not What We Seem").

There was a place called a workhouse, that was actually a penal farm.
That was where they sent people they'd arrested who couldn't pay their
fine. Ninety percent of the inmates were black. I never saw this place until
much later.

There was a general fear of the police by blacks in the 1930s. If a policeman saw you on a corner, he'd almost always anticipate that you were
stealing or up to no good. If you walked through a white neighborhood,
they'd drive you out or arrest you, saying you were trying to steal or something. A lot of times, someone like my wife going to school had to walk,
since there was no transportation.

Coming from Booker Washington, you'd have to walk through white
neighborhoods to get all the way to north Memphis. The police would
always be on call to make sure the black high school students kept on
strolling. I had to walk to Manassas through a number of white neighborhoods. They kept an eye on us, and we couldn't stop at that Guthrie School
on Valentine. We couldn't even go across the yard back in those days.[14]

There was really a lot of brutality done to blacks by the police, based
on stories that were false. But the four newspapers, the *Commercial Appeal*,
the *Press*, the *Scimitar*, and another would always make the black wrong.
The only black paper was the *Memphis World*. Once in a while the *Press*
and *Scimitar* combined write-ups, and you'd get better and more fair treatment. The *Scimitar* [later] did the piece about me being mistreated at
[International] Harvester and about the workers there.[15]

We could not play football at any of the local stadiums. There were
four or five stadiums, but we could only get a group together and play at
Hodges field, somewhere between Poplar and Union streets. They finally
opened the way for us at Hodges field when I was in high school. At Manassas, we had nothing. We couldn't go in the stadium. Booker Washington
had a little fence we could play inside. I finished high school in '34, and

14. Memphis neighborhood segregation proceeded in a "patchwork quilt" fashion, as Lanetha Jewel Branch explained it: "One quilt would be black and the other
would be white." Rarely did blacks and whites live on the same block. Branch interviewed by Doris Dixon, on June 16, 1995, for the Behind the Veil Oral History
Project.

15. The *Commercial Appeal* published in the morning, and the *Press* and the *Scimitar*, which consolidated into the *Press-Scimitar*, published in the afternoon. African
Americans repeatedly protested the racist cartoons and biased reporting of both. The
black-run *Memphis World* published weekly throughout the 1930s.

blacks were just starting to play football at Hodges Stadium. We couldn't play in Crump, Messick, or Southside stadiums, or any others.

Same thing with baseball. The Memphis Chicks would play, and we could only sit at the far end. You couldn't buy a hot dog or any refreshments, because all of the food was sold on the other side of the field, where we couldn't go. We could go to the Memphis Red Sox Park, on Crump and Wellington. The Red Sox were a black team in the 1920s and 1930s. They were a good team, and many of them were from Memphis. I was a catcher on the Klondike Black Devils, but we weren't a big team, just a local team. The Red Sox would go to Chicago and all over.

We knew all of this was wrong as youngsters, and we didn't enjoy it, but there was nothing we could do about it. We had no clout because of the poll tax. In the 1930s if you didn't pay the poll tax, you didn't vote. If you got some white person to pay your poll tax, you could vote, but you had to vote the way Crump wanted you to. Not many blacks could afford to pay the poll tax on their own.

People were only making fourteen to seventeen cents an hour, until FDR brought in the minimum wage of thirty-five cents an hour. They only had paper ballots then, they didn't have any voting machines. Someone would watch you fill the ballots out and keep track of them. A lot of blacks were paid to get receipts, and since they didn't have jobs, they'd mark the ballot the way they were told, to earn some money. Someone would watch them at the polls to make sure it happened that way. Blacks couldn't work in the polling places until the 1950s.

Bob Church opposed Crump from the black community. He was a Republican. Lieutenant Lee with the Elks protested Crump, but he had only a few Republicans in Memphis. Crump ran Bob Church out of Memphis, to Chicago. Lt. Lee was accepted as token opposition.[16] Around 1940, Crump did away with houses of prostitution on Gayoso Street. People were wising up and speaking out, and the newspapers were writing it up. They were meeting in black neighborhoods around where the Martins lived. They were teaming up against Crump, so he shut it all down and ran

16. Robert Church, Sr., became one of the first black millionaires in the South, and a major leader of the Memphis black community. Crump ran his son Robert Church, Jr., out of town in 1939, as part of the wave of repression against black leaders and union organizers that also forced out Thomas Watkins and William Glover.

them out of town.[17] Beale Street was really booming then, with bootlegger whiskey and all. We had nine big bootleggers who practically ran the city. Beale Street used to have about ten joints, like Will's Barbeque. It was a big restaurant. All of the white people went in the back, and all of the black people went in the front, because we couldn't be in the same place as the whites. We were sort of a "front" for them. That was a switch! That's where they sold bootleg whiskey.

Crump controlled whatever business the black man was in. Somebody snitched to him all of the time about everything. Black people didn't have anything, only a few blacks were of independent means. They used to just have shacks for blacks. Crump controlled all of the gambling joints as well as the upper Tennessee bootleggers. He would loan money to people he could control, and this was how he ran everything. Ninety percent of the people in Memphis came from Mississippi, so Memphis was a step up for them. That's partly why all of this started. People had to borrow money to start anything, and they'd borrow it from Crump. Crump pretended to be everyone's friend, but in reality he was an enemy.

The Crump machine would get people [labor organizers] kicked out of their apartments, too, if you were late on your payments. Van Court Rental Company would move people out. So people couldn't afford to lose their jobs. A lot of black preachers went along with Crump. They would persuade people to do what Crump asked. The church was the big philosopher who told people what to do. If a minister was in with Crump, he could borrow money to build his church. Until people like me came back from college to take positions, that's just how it worked.[18] I joined the union and all to help change these things.

In the late 1930s, the barge line people [unionists] were really terrific. They had a hall on Front Street [and] a lot of people from Memphis got jobs at the barge line.[19] They made a great contribution to the unions here.

17. Memphis police ran black druggist and Republican leader J. B. Martin out of town on the pretext that he sold drugs to young people in his store, helping to destroy the tiny opposition to Crump in black business circles at that time.

18. A few college-educated people took leadership roles in the CIO unions, and college-educated preachers and professionals began to move the civil rights agenda in the black community from the mid-1940s onward, but especially in the 1950s and 1960s.

19. Holloway is referring to the local of the National Maritime Union (CIO), established during the 1939 strike discussed by Thomas Watkins in chapter 1.

I knew Thomas Watkins, [and] it made an impression to see a black stand up as a leader. People began to recognize that they needed the union as a way of fighting back. When I first came into the UAW, we had to meet over at the maritime union, because they wouldn't let us in the regular hall. Even after World War II, in '46, the AF of L wouldn't rent us a thing, but the maritime union offered us their hall. They were one of the inspirations of us organizing. They gave us money and everything in those days, the same as the coal miners union [had done for other CIO unions].

I was interested in the union at that time [during the 1939 barge strike], but I had just been to college and wasn't involved yet. I was unusually lucky to go to college at that time. My daddy made nice money, so I was able to go to Tuskegee.[20] I wanted to be a lawyer, so I majored in history. He wanted me to be a plumber, and he wanted me to go to Tuskegee. I could have gone to Tennessee State on a football scholarship and could have done all four years and gone on to law school. Back in them days, I weighed about two hundred pounds.

But things got so tight with Daddy that I could only go for three years at Tuskegee. Daddy decided Tuskegee would lead me into a plumbing apprenticeship. I did some of that in the summers. He took for granted that would be a good job for me. There was only one black licensed plumber, named Brody Reed. Dad was going to make me the second. I tried to tell my daddy that the trade unions would freeze me out, but he thought I could cut through.

I learned civics in high school, and they taught that it wasn't but one flag in America, the U.S. flag, and they taught us why the flag was honored. I never saw the Confederate flag until I went to Montgomery, on my way by train back to Tuskegee, and I saw some kids with a Confederate flag on top of the American flag. When a professor asked me back in college if there was something I wanted to do, I told him about that flag. He said, "You're gonna have to change that!" I decided to major in history. Bill Davis, the first black general in the army, taught at Tuskegee. He told me what a rough time he had at West Point and said that it could be changed. I told him about that flag, too.[21]

20. Tuskegee Institute, in Alabama, was founded by Booker T. Washington, who had emphasized hard work and social uplift as opposed to civil rights activism. Tuskegee provided one of the few colleges open to blacks in the 1930s.

21. In 1940, B. O. Davis became the first African American promoted to the rank of brigadier general.

I stayed in Rockefeller Hall with Dr. Washington Carver at Tuskegee, so I got to know him quite well.[22] He lived on the floor below me. Tuskegee instilled in us a notion of achieving against the odds. Booker T. Washington was an inspiration that put the leadership into Tuskegee. Dr. [Robert R.] Moton followed in Washington's steps as a leader. We always had a session with all of the students, and the professors would speak about achievement and how it could be accomplished. They would talk about those who had struggled and accomplished so much. I never remember any discipline problems in the dormitories the entire time I was in school at Tuskegee. We all felt pretty lucky to be there.

I wish we'd had the libraries that the kids have access to today. The libraries that our schools had, both my wife's and mine, had less than a couple hundred books in them. We had no place to go for books to do research with. When I went to Tuskegee, I had never seen such a big library in my life! It was the most wonderful sight I'd ever seen. I'd go in there and read book after book after book. I still read every night, now. That's one of the greatest things you can do for yourself, to read.

I was never raised with a lot of religion, but my family believed in justice and equality. I got a lot of education from my father being a Pullman porter. My mother disciplined us mostly, because my daddy was traveling a lot. I learned discipline at school, too. My parents would always make us study at home every night.

I really only had three jobs in my life. Professor Hayes at Manassas wrote me a recommendation, and then I got in at Firestone after college, worked at Pullman Company until I was laid off, and then I was hired at Harvester in a few days.[23]

John L. Lewis and Walter Reuther started the CIO. They moved in to organize Firestone, which was the first plant to be organized in Memphis by the CIO.[24] Crump didn't want the unions, he kept fighting back and

22. George Washington Carver became famous for his inventions and agricultural studies, which, among other things, led to numerous ways to convert peanuts into various products.

23. Holloway worked at Firestone until 1940, and for the Pullman Company until 1946 when he was hired at Harvester.

24. Lewis headed the United Mine Workers of America, which provided the dues base for the early formation for the Congress of Industrial Organizations. Reuther played an important role in organizing the United Automobile Workers in the 1930s

saying there wouldn't be any. He didn't want the professionals like machinists and electricians to be involved, either. John L. Lewis was a leader being followed, but the coal miners were at the other end of the state [east Tennessee]. But the CIO was getting stronger, which was why Crump was cracking down.

[In 1940], I was one of the leaders at Firestone. I was working in the compound room, where they put the ingredients into the rubber. When the bucket came by, I had to put in the right amounts. Most of the other blacks were cutting and carrying. The company had separate departments for blacks and whites at that time. The heat jobs were all for blacks. Firestone only hired blacks to do the heavy, hot work that was done by hand. On the mill, you had to work that rubber by hand. Those big heavy truck and tractor tires were moved by the blacks, but they wouldn't let them build them. They knew how, but they weren't allowed to except to replace a white now and then.

They used to hire by hiring whites one day, blacks the next day, saying, "Oh, we only are hiring whites today." This was at the employment office. Another day, they might be hiring blacks, but they'd only want big tall men, weighing 180 pounds or more. They picked employees by race and by stature. The white tire builders, mechanics, and all at Firestone didn't want to be in a union with us. They were the ones who voted against the [CIO] union. They were afraid they would lose some status. They wanted to stay with the divisions of the AF of L. A few around me changed their minds and went on with me.

At Firestone, the whites and blacks got along OK. We were about one-third black and two-thirds white at Firestone. We didn't have any eating places or dining rooms inside the plant. We went outside to buy stuff off of a wagon, and the whites and blacks would talk then, but otherwise, we'd sit in different places. We had separate locker rooms for white and black.

The CIO was talking about seniority rights, and moving around in departments, because blacks were stuck. Firestone at that time had departmental seniority, they could lay you off in one department and you couldn't

---

and became its president in 1946. The United Rubber Workers organized Memphis Firestone with support from the CIO.

go to another. George Bass came in and began to talk about some of these things, that we should have these opportunities, too. So whites were afraid they'd lose privilege. If they opened up those departments to us, they were afraid they'd get bumped.[25] At that time, we could only work over in a white department if someone was absent or sick or if a black was training someone.

I met George Bass, and he asked me if I would organize. He'd heard about me through my daddy at the Pullman porters' union. He knew I had contact with A. Philip Randolph through my father. Bass would call me by phone, sometimes from Akron, and told me what to do and how to do it. I would call blacks on the phone or meet them. They wouldn't go to any place but black places. Bass would give me money, and we'd bring liquor or meals, and we'd go to people's homes. We had to sneak in and out. At that time, I was the plant chairman of the organizing at Firestone, George had made me the leader of the blacks. And I took a few whites with me.

The whites [CIO supporters] met at the Claridge Hotel. I couldn't go in, it was whites only. But after the meeting H. B. Griffin[26] and Bass told me to set up a march. I led the march out of the locker room—that was a march to vote for the union. We had big buttons saying "vote for the union." I had a big white CIO button, and every black person who came out of the locker room wore one, too. Everyone met at the plant at 6:30, work starts at 7:00. We marched through the black departments, and about 90 percent of the blacks joined. The industrial relations man at Firestone told me blacks could march through the plant, as long as we didn't stop anyone from working, and told that to the supervisors. Griffin had hoped whites would join, but maybe 10 percent of the whites joined in.

George Bass was having a lot of incidents of violence against him. Crump got involved in it, too; there was so much money being passed around that we knew Crump was involved. George came out to speak to us at the plant, and these big huge men just came in with billy sticks and

25. Under seniority, the worker with the longest time at the plant could move, or bump, someone with lesser seniority out of a particular job. Holloway seems to suggest that Firestone accepted some type of departmental seniority even before unionization. However, only if blacks were allowed to move freely between departments, which had been segregated by color, would this threaten whites.

26. Griffin much later became a president of the Firestone CIO local.

beat him like hell outside the gate. The police just stood by and watched, some of them even jumped in to help beat him up with their billy sticks.[27]

I would have gotten involved in it, but the people who were with George didn't want me involved because they were afraid there would be a race riot. They wouldn't let me in it, someone held me back. I just cried. There was nothing I could do. The blacks were angry, and a few of the whites. We could see there was going to be trouble when we got there. It got so rough I really couldn't see who all was involved. It wasn't my supervisor, though. I never did leave that gate until the ambulance came to pick George up.[28] It just broke my heart to see that, and there was nothing I could do.

George Bass came in with the understanding that we would unite. George used to tell everyone that the CIO believed in justice for all, and the right to a job. That's what the CIO was built on. Blacks should have as much right to a good job as anyone else, and the company shouldn't be making color division.

You can see why we lost the CIO at first. All of the black voted for the CIO, but some were discouraged [and didn't vote]. The whites didn't buy it, but they ended up finding out. When the AFL came in, Crump sent a paper congratulating the workers for voting AFL. [But] the workers found out that the company was using them. Blacks became less cooperative when the CIO lost. They would slow work down so the whites couldn't make any money. The blacks put pressure on the whites by not cooperating, until the whites realized they needed the blacks to cooperate to make changes in the plant. They needed us. They were only under the AF of L for a year (they had actually two years before the change was official).

27. Bass had three deep gashes on his head that required eighty-five stitches to close. Noel Bedgood, his assistant, required seventeen stitches. According to W. E. Davis, a young labor organizer who became Bass's bodyguard, Firestone paid thugs to beat the men up. This incident followed another one in which thugs beat United Auto Workers union organizer Norman Smith nearly to death in two separate incidents, after Memphis Mayor Walter Chandler denounced the CIO unions. No one was ever arrested for these beatings, while the city police arrested the CIO organizers numerous times.

28. Actually, a Firestone worker braved the hostile mob, put Bass in his car, and drove him to the hospital. The police chief blamed Bass for provoking the incident and did nothing to protect him.

But when the CIO came back in [in 1942], I was a [poll] watcher for the National Labor Relations Board [overseeing the election], and I bet 99 percent voted CIO.[29]

I left about a month before the [first] election, because I knew they were going to fire me. I knew Firestone would fire me, because of the march. But do you know what they put on my papers when I quit? They said I argued about my money. That's all they put on there. They thought blacks didn't know enough to keep track when they were cheating you out of your money. They might give a dollar or two dollars less a day than you were supposed to get if you were black. All we could do was argue, you had no clout without the union. I argued, and they were afraid to fire me until after the election. I quit first.

My cousin replaced me as a leader to campaign for the CIO at Firestone. He worked where they dropped the hot rubber down, near the compound room. The blacks were unified with the CIO as far as I remember. Blacks got elected as stewards all over the plant, as well as committee men. That's why the whites were against the CIO at first. They didn't want black officers in the union.

Clarence Coe Recalls the Pressures of White Supremacy

There was just so much pressure to bear on you.

I interviewed Clarence Coe in 1989, first on the phone and then at his home. I had a hard time tracking him down, because most of the time he was out working for his church or taking part in other community activities. As during his work career, service to others was his trademark. Telling his story brought back many unpleasant memories; when he first began recalling the tension and conflict of the past it practically made him ill. He recounted a story that for me opened a new line of inquiry into labor history: the untold story of black workers who risked their lives and their jobs to resist Jim Crow at work. For him, the union movement

29. Under the terms of the New Deal's Wagner Act, passed in 1935, workers who petitioned for unions had the right to a fair and impartial election under supervision of the NLRB.

was always a civil rights struggle. He tells more of this story in chapters 4, 7, and 8.

There was just so much pressure to bear on you everywhere you went as a black person, a black intelligent person, and I give myself credit for being pretty damn bright when I was young. Some guys just couldn't handle that stuff, and I was one who just couldn't handle it, see.

[My civil rights awareness started], I guess, from my ancestors. Back during slavery, right here at Madison, Tennessee, they called it the Magden Quarters, that's the neighborhood where my foreparents came from when they were in slavery. When they were freed, they allowed each slave to buy a tract of land, and my grandparents bought land there. Right up there in west Tennessee.

My grandparents got this land. And their parents had been slaves, my grandparents and great-grandparents were slaves. I just grew up in that environment, and my parents taught me some things. They taught me. And then, when you grow up and you see this is the way it really is, you just kind of start fighting back. I just couldn't buy it.

There was one white family that lived in the neighborhood, three brothers and their sisters. Otherwise, the only time I saw a white person was on the road. We had no dealings with them, no nothing. Then, after I grew up and started going to town, I saw some things I didn't like. Saw the results of a lynching or two. I didn't see it happen, but I saw the dead body after.

Have you ever thought about why it was so common for a white man to kick a black man back then? If you were in your neighborhood and you saw a dog come down the street, you wouldn't push him aside, would you? [If you didn't want the dog around, you'd kick him.] I mean you watch those things.

I have seen it around on the job and in small country towns. I remember one morning when I was in high school, went down to the country store to get overalls to wear to school. One of the black guys who worked there at the gin, sawmill, and the blacksmith shop, named A. D. Tucker, was leaning over the counter to get him some chewing tobacco before he went to work. And one of the McCraw brothers, the millionaires, kicked him in the behind. And A. D. didn't even look back to see who kicked him, he was so used to it. Didn't even look back.

I was told twenty or thirty years later, McCraw kicked a black guy up in the second floor of the gin, and the black guy threw him out. That's the way those kind of things had to be stopped. You had to stay ready to put up a fight all the time.

For that reason, whenever a white person came toward me and raised his voice, I was ready for him. I just couldn't handle it. I think that had something to do with my attitude, and not having grown up around whites on a plantation. I came to Memphis partly to get away from that plantation scene. When I finished high school, I could have gotten a farm through the FCA [Farm Credit Administration], all the equipment I needed, and everything. I wouldn't have to pay a note on anything. I'd had five years of agriculture. But I wanted to get away from this environment. And then you come here, and you run into the same damn things.

There are two incidents I had. I was at Main and Beale one night, for the Thanksgiving weekend and parade. I was on the other side of the street, looking at the parade. I was pissed off about that, because that's the time they'd have the Negro with the wide grinning mouth and the mismatched shoes on those floats. The next thing I knew I was knocked into the street. I thought somebody would have a good fight on their hands. And I looked back, and there were probably fifteen white boys, just laughing at what they'd done. I thought, well I can't fight that. And they went on to another part of the parade.

I liked Elvis [Presley] because he was a poor white boy who didn't spend his time trying to keep me down. Many mornings I would see him out on the road when I'd be going out to work. But the regular old bunch, oh man, you could never forget it. When they'd see somebody black, their countenance would change, they'd put that cheap dirty snarl on their face. I can't describe it, but I know it when I see it. They made darn sure that you never got the impression you were an equal.

There's two things I carried with me. If anyone ever called me nigger personally on the job, that was it. I would fight. You know I worked at Firestone thirty-nine years and seven months and it never happened. But when you are living under conditions when it can happen anytime, you never know if it will happen. Maybe that's why I took early retirement. It kept the pressure on you.

When I first came to the city, a guy who used to clean my clothes in school had a brother with a pressing shop here, and he knew I could press clothes. I started coming during the summer months. So I worked in a pressing shop. I started work full-time in '39, coming from Jackson, Tennessee, place I went to school.

I began working in schools with the NAACP, we started collecting nickels and dimes. That was after the Scottsboro case. I had known about Scottsboro through the papers and news media, what little there was at that point. You knew that was a frame-up.[30] Utilus Phillips was probably the first president of the NAACP, or first I knew of. And when I came to Memphis I found the organization and started working with him. I wrote one daily column in the *Memphis World*.

I came in contact with the NAACP through my church. I joined a church, and they have an enrollment campaign each year. I found out the campaign was on and who the people were in the church, and I just made myself available to raise money for the NAACP.

And we were trying to organize. I had gotten run off of another job trying to organize a union, at a mattress company. The fellows who worked there said they didn't want a union and I was a troublemaker, and I got cut up.

U.S. Bedding Company made the Sealy mattress. I tried to organize. I was twenty-three, young and brash. Some of the older guys called old man Harris, who owned the company. They always said he would take care of us, because he had done that with some of the older workers. But I knew that he couldn't do that with 250–300 people. We needed a pension plan.

One day I went in there just shucking with an older guy who I normally was talking with all the time. I was standing up against the wall, and he hit his pocket and pulled a knife. I got a timber and got it up to defend myself. That guy hit me with that knife and stabbed me three of four times, just that quick. He had done all that [revealing a long X-shaped scar across his abdomen] before I could get down with the timber.

I went to the locker and discovered how bad I had been cut. I went back out to the factory, and they were hauling him out. I thought he was dead. I brought that timber down and caved his head in. I always could fight well.

30. As mentioned in chapter 1, in 1931 police had arrested nine black youths in Scottsboro, Alabama, and charged them with raping white women they had been riding with in a railroad boxcar. An all-white jury convicted and sentenced the men to death. Although one of the women later attested to their innocence, only long years and a worldwide campaign of protest freed them.

He fell into me, and someone had pushed a wheelbarrow behind me, so I would fall. Just that quick I knew it wasn't just him, it was a conspiracy. I tore up a few people that day. They knew I was trying to organize. They intended to kill me. This was some of the older black guys who just believed in their company. They didn't want anything done, they didn't believe in anything being done.

I stood there and looked at him, went on back, changed my clothes, went out there on Florida Street waiting on a streetcar. Jake Harris came along and told me to go to the doctor to get me fixed up. If the police or anybody else had come, that would have been the end of me in Memphis, cause that just made me so doggone hot! They'd of probably killed me, cause I'd have took off on them.

One night while I was off, I was at the post office at night, and old man Harris came down. He looked at me, said, "When are you coming back to work?" I said I didn't know I could come back. He said yeah, but I got [hired] on at Firestone, and I never would go back. He knew I was right, in a way. But, man, a labor union at that time in Memphis was, oh my God. . . .

And then that's when I went to Firestone [in 1941]. The whites had the AFL at the plant, but we [blacks] never would join it. But when we started talking about it, there was so much resentment to it. The AFL was in there before the CIO. Most of the Jim Crow whites was in it, but we wouldn't join the AFL. You still had some of these soreheads and they didn't join with the CIO until about 1955.

The Crump organization and some of the whites had really given the CIO a bad name. He said the CIO would never come to Memphis. Back in '39, '40, '41 when labor unions first tried to move in here, old man E. H. Crump, Boss Crump, vowed that the CIO union would never come to Memphis. He just wasn't going to have it. And he kept it out, for a time.

Memphis never has been a labor town. It's just never been a labor town. When we used to go on strike at the plant, they would holler, they would yell. I mean, this is just not a labor town. But in spite of that, I was right into it. And they were telling me not to do it, stay away from it. But it just so happens that my wife and I were childless. And I could stick my neck out in areas where some people were afraid to tread. And that's why today, when you visit my home and other homes [of black Firestone workers] you find a vast difference in the surroundings. Because a lot of the workers were moving far, economically. But I devoted all of my young life to betterment of the race and NAACP, and this thing and the other thing.

Be that as it may, I kept after it, I just kept after it. I just did not give up. I went to NAACP meetings, tried to enlist their support, tried to get the first five hundred members in the Memphis area. We had a terrible time trying to get the first five hundred members. About four or five of us worked at the plant to do it. Back in those days, when people didn't know what it was all about, we even signed up some white folks. [chuckles] So you got some support there, when most of the people at the plant were afraid to wear CIO buttons. It was almost suicide. They tried everything in the world to stop us.

When the organizers came in, back in those days, they would try to meet us on the riverbank, which was technically federal property. The goons were sent down there and met some of our organizers. My brother Lint was down there [on the riverfront] that day, but I wasn't there. The goons, the police, and everybody else just went down there and beat the living daylights out of them. Black and white. They beat the white harder than the blacks, 'cause they didn't think too much of the whites trying to help the Negro into organizing the CIO union. That could really get you in trouble. Yeah, they really came down on them. A lot of people trying to organize Firestone got beaten up by Crump goons and left for dead by the riverfront.[31]

After that we started meeting in groups. Albert Coleman had a group, Josh Tools had a group. George Holloway [had] worked there too. We'd meet and never congregate in the same place. But when we came out with our CIO buttons on, we had a majority of people in the plant. We identified ourselves. They didn't fire us. They saw there were too many of us to run away.

But that was one man, that his legacy, his strength, his political viewpoint still has a lot of impact on this city. And he's been dead for a long time now. Crump. In those days, whatever he said was law. If he said somebody couldn't come in here, he couldn't come.

And what happens in Memphis is this certain group of families, old

31. Ed McCrea, a white organizer, spoke to this group on the riverfront but left before the beatings began. He and George Holloway and Clarence Coe remembered this incident, but it is unclear when it happened and I have never been able to verify it in written records.

families, and so forth, succeeds each other. When you go out in the rural area, the same families that live in this area for four or five decades, it doesn't change. Memphis doesn't change much, its values, family relatives, and so forth, and then mayor, and mayor, and mayor, and top city officials. It's not going to change.

What we did when Crump was so tough on us—I remember the first union meeting I attended was in some guy's garage on Thomas Street. We had a union agent or whatever you want to call, and a secretary and somebody taking dues. But on Sunday morning at 8:00 or 10:00 we knew the eight or ten or fifteen to twenty places that a little band of people were going to meet, and we would meet and somebody would funnel the information back to the agent. And that's the way we got started. We couldn't meet publicly. And we couldn't meet in no single place together. They would kick all our asses.

[These meetings weren't blacks and whites together.] No, no. They met and we met [separately], and that created a lot of distrust, and it always existed. You couldn't hardly trust a guy that you couldn't meet with. Twenty years after we had the union, you couldn't trust certain people.

So if you supported the CIO, you just couldn't meet nowhere as a group. So we would have certain area people as our leaders, and eight or ten of us would meet at this house or somewhere else. And then we would compile our information and our dues. We had a guy named Stacy Wilson—who was the first white man who stuck his neck out—a little short guy. And then came Routon and Allen and Griffin [as union presidents]. Stacy would slip around, but then he disappeared and I still don't know today what became of him. Long before I left the plant he disappeared.[32]

When I went there in '41, the plant had been running about four and a half years. I think I largely got hired because I was able to write a very good resume. I was never large enough to get hired from the gate. When they came to the gate, they'd hire the big robust guys. But every job I've ever had, I've written my own resume and gotten inside. I even worked for the post office, but I got laid off three days before Pearl Harbor and stayed off until March. You could make more money then at Firestone

32. Richard Routon became the first CIO union president at Firestone, and was followed by, among other people, Ray Allen and H. B. Griffin. I have not found any trace of Stacy Wilson.

than you could at the post office. You were making about $1,200 a year at either one, but at Firestone I could get a lot of overtime.

The AFL was mostly a craft union—electricians, pipe fitters, mechanics, or whatever. It was good for them. But the CIO promised us [blacks] justice, and they [AFL supporters] just wouldn't have it. But we just kept closing in, and some of the AFL group came over with us, and right after the war, we began to build a strong union, a strong union. We got dues checkoff, for one thing, once we signed up a person.[33] When we negotiated dues checkoff, then we were headed for a strong union. And [after the war], it seemed like we stayed on strike all the time, people accused us of that, but we began to make progress. And then we had good contact with Akron. They had had some of these benefits. And then in negotiation, you would try to correlate with Akron-Firestone, Akron-Goodyear, U.S. Rubber in Detroit. I mean some of the things they wanted when we combined their delegation with our delegation, you had to do a lot of swappin' out. If we go with you on this, you go with us on that. That's how you develop a national contract.

When I was hired in '41, we had three divisions. Number one was black, two was predominately tire room, three was curing and shipping. But number one was predominately start, preparation, receiving, etcetera, the dirty work. What so many people are dying with now.

Memphis was about 65–35 [percent] white to black, until the whites started running from Memphis. The way they hired at the plants they'd always hire 65–35 [white to black ratio]. [But] you could not pay me what they paid the white man, it was against the law.[34] You could not do that.

When I got into the Firestone plant, having been to school a little, having read my storybooks where John came to work early and on time every morning, he kept himself neat, he kept his shoes shined, he kept his hair trimmed, and one day Mr. Jones called him into the office—and I found that [he] was a white boy! [laughs] And that irked the hell out of me! I felt whatever I had enough intelligence to do, I ought to have a chance to do it. That was a white boy that got that promotion!

It took me a while to find out that was a white boy. Didn't matter what you knew, if you were black, you were just black. You weren't going to get

33. The checkoff meant the company deducted dues from workers' paychecks on behalf of the union.

34. It was not literally against the law to give equal pay to blacks, but in practice it was not allowed, and there is no evidence that anyone did it.

anything out there at Firestone but a hard way to go. And the more intelligence you had, the harder your lot was going to be. If you were one of them simple, grinning kind of guys, you got along all right. But if you were sharp, they'd spend a lifetime trying to get you out, you've got to believe that! And that was my predicament all of the time.

I found out after I retired that a fellow in my church denomination, he's a licensed electrician now, but he couldn't get a license then. He had to do his work under a white person. He once did some electrical work out on the road by Firestone. And it was so neatly done, Raymond Firestone [chief executive at the Memphis plant] praised his work and everything, and he said, "Yes Sir, you know I would like to come out to that plant, I wish I could work out to that plant." Firestone said, "I'll give you my card. You can start work in the morning, but I can't hire you as an electrician." The Firestone Company had to put it in writing when they came here that we would be relegated to a certain status and a certain salary. They had to put it in writing to the city.[35]

Northern companies could not go against it. I'm told by good authority that when Bond Clothing Company came to Memphis they had to actually lower wages. A worldwide clothing store. They had to lower wages. I mean the blacks were being paid above the scale, and they just had to conform or they would keep you out.

They got something out of it. You take right here we have a few unions here in town that are pretty strong, but right across the line into Mississippi counties they are not. In fact, everybody comes from northeast or west to avoid the union. They come down here and get their labor cheap and we had to fight it. I started working for thirty-two cents an hour.

At Firestone, you had a separate locker room. Now the cafeteria was divided, they gave you access to your side of it, but you couldn't go up the other side. You had to come up your side. You couldn't go up the one designated for whites. You couldn't go up there.

At the main gate they had turnstiles, you know. You go through them,

---

35. There is no doubt that Firestone made some kind of an agreement with Mr. Crump. Numerous workers, white and black, told me that Crump told Firestone they had to hire a percentage of blacks, and follow the codes of segregation. Others said he also guaranteed there would be no union in the plant for at least five years. Written records do document that before it set up shop in Memphis, the Firestone company negotiated with Mr. Crump and that he gave them generous tax breaks and city services.

but it was understood you didn't go through the one on the south side because whites park up on this end, closest to the gate. We had to park on a certain area north of the gate back to what we called the river. If you parked up here, either you were going to be made to move or when you came out your tires were going to be cut. Even after we were allowed to park up there we couldn't park because your tires would be cut. I had my tires cut.

Yeah, even after the plant was integrated. I mean it was an unwritten law that you just didn't do certain things. And they held onto it. I had my tires cut once on a car I had five thousand miles on. Came in one Sunday night and a few people were working. I thought, well, no one's parking across from the gate tonight, so I parked. When I walked over to the gate the first thing the guard asked me, "Whose car is this you're driving, boy?" I say, "It could be mine. I've been working here thirteen years." And he said, "Well, you better not leave it there, we'll have it pulled in." I said, "That white guy with that old Hudson, he parks there every night but he's not here tonight." And he said, "You better not leave yours there. If you do, I'm going to have it pulled in."

So I moved it and backed it on the parking lot. And the next morning I came out and all four of my tires were slashed. I mean just for that little exchange. He did it himself. And that was a step up, that I could drive a new car on the parking lot. When I [first] went to Firestone, a Negro who had a new car, he had to park it down across the railroad track. If you drove a new car, you'd be run out. You couldn't get along with the whites if you did. You'd be likely to get three tickets on the way to work.

Oh, you just didn't drive a new car on the job. Not only Firestone, any-where. You take where you ate your lunch. They had black and white and you might have to walk as far as from here to Elvis Presley's to eat. But you didn't stop where the whites eat.

And you spent all of your good life fooling with petty stuff like this. That's what hurts me. Just nonsensical things. It didn't make no sense at all but you had to live with it.

Oh, you would get in trouble. Big trouble. And whatever a white person said, that was it. And if he fabricated something when you get to the office, "Mr. Smith said that you said so and so and so," you say, "No, I didn't." "You calling Mr. Smith a liar?" I mean that sort of a thing. Oh, no. You don't call a white man a liar, even when it's true. Whatever he said, that's it. And some of them brothers and sisters, they didn't support you.

To tell you the truth, we had our representative in our division, and for a long time our division representative couldn't meet in the personnel office with the whites. I don't think that the company resented it. But our own white CIO members wouldn't let our representative come in. Mose Lewis would hide around and come back and give us some kind of messed-up report. Finally, a year or two later, we got another person, and we just got on his butt and told him he had to go meet with the whites. We got rid of Mose and elected another guy named Josh Tools. He just reared up one day and said, "I gotta go! If [whites] goin' to meet with the company, I'm going to meet with the company, and represent my people. I'm not going to lie to my members and tell them this is the information that transpired, when I wasn't there. I'm going to have to go." And the whites accepted that.

I don't think Josh was as positive as he could have been, [although] he was fairer than most was. Because that was a period of time, during the war years and immediately after, when he was the most powerful [black] man at that plant. He really could have done things. But, you know, they kind of have a way of getting to weak junior leaders, givin' 'em the day off to go fishin', all of that sort of thing. He'd sell you out. Mess you up. He could have done a lot more during the war years. But the fact was [as a union committee man], he could walk around and shoot the bull all day, not a lot to him. Someone would clap him on the back, "What're you gripin' about, them guys are doin' all right. You seem to be doing all right, you don't look like you've worked in a day."

Later on, Matthew Davis had three kids in college, but he would always go with me to the office about discriminatory practices. He just had enough faith to do it. But the average guy wouldn't risk butting their head against the wall, their family suffering. Most people wouldn't go with me. A lot of people would walk around you. We had some educators, too, who wouldn't sign a petition, afraid they'd lose their job.

And a crazy guy like myself, they offered me supervision, and everything else to get me off of their backs. One reason I didn't take it, I was determined to get completed what I'd set out to do. And I did. I did.

Black workers took generations of day-to-day resistance to white supremacy and an ethos of hard work and persistence with them into factories and workplaces. Their grandparents had survived slavery, and their parents had fought sharecropping and racial repression. Like George Holloway, with his union father, or Ida Leachman, descendant and name-sake of the renowned civil rights leader Ida B. Wells-Barnett, almost every worker interviewed in this book could recall some person in their life who inspired them to fight back against Jim Crow.

Yet while conditions in the city were an improvement over sharecropping or day labor in the countryside, Jim Crow at work and in the society around them limited the progress of black workers in a multitude of ways. During the height of segregation, as Holloway observes, despite blacks' hatred of white supremacy, they could not confront it directly. Most of the time they adopted a pragmatic and realistic recognition of their situation: they had to accommodate whites to survive. For the early generation of factory workers, as Irene Branch and Evelyn Bates explain in the next chapter, that primarily meant cultivating the ability to "take it." To work harder than whites, to bear the pain and strain of inequality and backbreaking labor largely in silence, to look down, if you were a black man, when a white woman approached, to say "yes sir" to any white who thought he was in a position of authority, to do as told even when you knew it was wrong—these were the daily costs of bending to Jim Crow. Subtle distinctions of behavior mattered a great deal. For instance, as Matthew Davis, Clarence Coe, Leroy Boyd, and others emphasize, how you "carried yourself" made a difference. If you walked and stood with assurance, holding an even but unthreatening gaze, whites in the factory were less likely to insult or assault you. On the other hand, if you seemed too assertive or proud, trouble could follow.

A fine line existed between resistance and abject accommodation, and black workers in interracial factory settings walked that fine line every day. Recognizing the dominance of white supremacy did not mean that black workers acquiesced to it. Some younger black workers thought older people like Hillie Pride had become too adept at "taking it." Yet from Pride's perspective, you could lead by the example of work well done and gain the respect of white and black alike. Conscientiousness in your work meant something even under Jim Crow. Often coming from desperate conditions, black workers like Pride appreciated the economic benefits of a factory job. The older generation, in fact, felt good about what they had accomplished as factory workers. Pride's name symbolized his own identity as a worker.

Still, as Coe recalls, many blacks crossed too far over the line between pragmatic accommodation and utter capitulation to white supremacy. He could not trust many blacks, either at his first job, where several of them tried to kill him for union agitation, or at Firestone, where whites played blacks off against each other. "Union" remained a dirty and fearful word in Memphis, and when it came to those willing to stand up and be counted, Coe often lacked allies, either white or black. Those few union supporters who could be trusted met secretly in garages and churches, but in racially separate groups. Under the terms of segregation, it was generally understood that blacks and whites could not meet together, at least not on any sort of equal basis. And if you could not meet with a white man, Coe asks, how could you ever trust him? Interracial alliances remained fleeting and tenuous.

The system of white supremacy remained all-encompassing, affecting both black and white behavior and consciousness. But the racialized consciousness of white workers, many of them coming from rural plantation districts, remained the biggest problem. As Holloway tells us, when George Bass stressed the CIO's message of equality through seniority and contract rights, the Firestone Company easily used this to stir up fears of "nigger unionism" among white workers. Most of them stood by and watched while company supervisors led a mob, including white workers, that nearly beat Bass to death. White workers only came to see their enlightened self-interest after an AFL craft union led them down the primrose path to a weak organization and stagnant wages.

White workers in many cases did finally accept the necessity of biracial organization for industrial unions to be successful, especially when conditions for unionization became ripe during World War II. But most of them did not support racial equality on the job, in the union hall, or anywhere else. Racial division and discord dogged the labor movement, and black and white workers would continue to struggle over the racial terms of unionization at places like Firestone for decades to come. Black workers always fought on two fronts, battling both white employers and white workers.

If white supremacy naturally thwarted the formation of interracial CIO unions, it did not kill them. In a difficult situation, the witnesses in this book seized the union movement when it came along, hoping to change the equations of power. As their narratives show, the changes they made did not come all of a sudden but through lifetimes of persistent action. In places where large numbers of African Americans worked in industry, they often became the core constituency of CIO unions. In both the urban North and South, where black labor filled the mass-production meatpacking, tobacco, steel, rubber, and furniture industries, blacks became a force to be reckoned with. This reality, more than any other, forced the CIO to adopt policies of racial equality.

Those policies drew people like Pride, Davis, Holloway, and Coe strongly into the labor movement, at a time when few other organizations provided a base for real change. Step by step, from the late 1930s onward, workers in many basic industries gained collective bargaining rights, improved their wages and work conditions, and achieved some degree of dignity and security. During this process, the weight of discrimination bore down heavily on the early generations of urbanized and proletarianized black men. But although black men generally played the major role in factories and in unions, in the 1940s and beyond black women increasingly became a significant part of the industrial union struggle as well.

Prior to World War II, manufacturers practically banned black women from factory employment, and the chances of organizing seemed remote throughout the more informal service and household economies that employed black women in huge numbers. Black women, mired for generations in jobs as domestic workers, servants, cleaning and washer women, waitresses and maids, knew better than anyone the American axiom of last hired, first fired, and worst paid. When World War II took both white and black men from the factories, many black women eagerly moved into the industrial proletariat. As we witness in the next chapter, their struggles took on a distinctly family-centered cast as they sought to "make a way out of no way." These black women joined the black men already in the factories in the fight to build up family and community resources, and to continue the daily resistance to racism established by the generations that had come before them.

3 MAKING A WAY OUT OF NO WAY

BLACK WOMEN FACTORY WORKERS

> You just didn't have a privilege. . . . You had a white woman over
> you *always*, and she gonna see that you work. . . . Before they got
> that union, we black folks had a hard time, a real hard time. . . .
> We didn't see freedom until we got that union in!
>
> Irene Branch

In a society that devalued the work of African Americans, the survival of
black families depended to a great extent on the labor of black women.
Not only did they bear primary responsibility for raising children, they
also worked outside of the home in far higher proportions than did white
women; going back to slavery, they had no choice. By excluding black
men from decent jobs and holding their wages below subsistence levels,
segregation forced black women into the waged economy, at even lower
wages, in order to support their families. A brilliant cadre of "middle
class" (and usually far from wealthy) black women teachers, entrepreneurs, journalists, and women's club leaders (including women like Julia
Hooks and Mary Church in Memphis) developed organizations to lift
black families and communities out of the mire imposed by white supremacy. The working-class majority of black women played an equally
important role in raising children, bringing wages into black households
and holding families, churches, and community organizations together.

They had few employment options, especially during the Depression. Until the 1940s, manufacturers mostly refused to hire black women,
and until the 1970s, most clerical, sales, secretarial, telephone, and other

"pink-collar" jobs remained closed to them as well.[1] For much of the twentieth century, housework, laundering, waitressing, and cleaning jobs trapped them in occupations with little upward mobility. Those black women who did get factory jobs bore all the stigma attached to their skin color and their gender, and worked not as machine operators but as floor sweepers, cleaners, and in other unskilled positions. In an interlocking system of class, race, and gender oppression, they experienced even worse wage and occupational discrimination than black men.

Society held that women should remain in the household or at least work in paid occupations defined as women's work, which ruled them out of many factory jobs as well as managerial and better-paid occupations. At least white women could get "pink-collar" jobs, however. Black women, as Irene Branch tells us, just "didn't have the privilege."[2] The pattern of black female exclusion was most entrenched at the beginning of the Great Depression, when over 80 percent of black women in Memphis worked in domestic and personal service, usually earning so little that even many working-class white families could afford to hire them. Black women also worked as laundresses, nurses without training, waitresses, hairdressers, boardinghouse owners, and "cleaning women" in hotels and other public places. Nearly as many black women in Memphis worked for wages as did black men, yet they made up a mere 5 percent of the city's

1. The U.S. census found only 7 percent of black women workers in manufacturing in 1920, 5.5 percent in 1930, and 6 percent in 1940. In that year, only 1.3 percent worked in clerical jobs (where one third of all white wage-earning women worked), while 60 percent of black women toiled as domestic workers (where only 10 percent of white women wage earners worked).

2. Black women in Memphis always did most of the domestic work, while nearly all the "pink collar" jobs and most of the assembly line operative jobs available to women went to whites. As late as 1950, white women held nearly 30 percent of sales jobs (black women 2 percent), more than 60 percent of clerical jobs (black women about 2 percent), and 36 percent of professional and technical jobs (black women about 7 percent, mostly in black institutions). Black women made up 93 percent of household workers (white women 3.4 percent) and 32 percent of non-household service workers (white women nearly 18 percent). By 1960, these dichotomies had changed very little. Figures compiled by Anne Marie Cavanaugh from *Seventeenth Decennial Census of the United States* (Washington, D.C.: U.S. Government Printing Office, 1952), vol. 2, pt. 4, pp. 57, 61. *Eighteenth Decennial Census of the United States* (Washington, D.C.: U.S. Government Printing Office, 1962), vol. 2 pt. 4, pp. 199, 423–28.

factory workers, while black men constituted about 40 percent of the factory workforce in the 1930s. In an economy organized in a hierarchy of race, class, and gender, most black women ended up on the very bottom.[3]

They had few opportunities to work in industry, for whites sought to keep the wages of domestic workers down by limiting their employment in any other areas. The "bottom" did also include a few factory jobs; black and white women each made up about 5 percent of the total manufacturing labor force in Memphis in 1930. But black women were denied better-paying positions and ended up with some 70 percent of the female factory laborer jobs.[4] The pervasive master-servant framework of race and gender relations undercut their ability to bargain with employers over wages or to assert their rights on the job. In addition, the color bar sharply separated them from white women, who in many cases were their overseers or worked separately from them and under better conditions. In the factories, as Irene Branch relates, whites only accepted black women in the first place because they considered sweeping and restroom cleaning "a black woman's job." Most whites obstructed black efforts to qualify for higher-wage work, and when black women finally broke into such occupations they usually did substantially more work at half the pay of whites. The blacks-as-servants mentality remained, and the possibility of interracial working-class sisterhood remained remote until the civil rights revolution of the 1960s. White women did not provide any greater allies for black women than white male workers did for black men.[5]

The labor shortages and industrial expansion resulting from World War II weakened the barriers to black women's industrial employment. Manufacturers first hired white women to replace white men who went

3. In 1930, 17,349 black women (and 5,511 black men) worked in domestic and personal service in Memphis, a larger group than the 10,588 black men who worked in factories. Some 5,000 black women also labored in the hottest and most miserable of conditions in steam laundries.

4. Of 1,600 black women listed in manufacturing by the census in 1930, mostly in clothing, chemical, food, and agriculturally related industries, some 600 of them worked as factory laborers, while another 400 worked in poorly paid and unhealthy garment work in their homes or in small shops.

5. Historian Susan Tucker aptly observed that "most white women did not wish to change a system in which their own standards of living rested upon the cheap labor of all blacks, male and female." *Telling Memories among Southern Women: Domestic Workers and Their Employers in the Segregated South* (Baton Rouge: Louisiana State University Press, 1988), 32.

off to war, often choosing them over black men or black women; mean-time, black women took up many of the less desirable jobs in restau-rant and custodial services that white women left. When manufacturers grew more desperate for labor, they started hiring larger numbers of black women for the hottest, hardest, dirtiest jobs. These women ended up in industries that traditionally employed African American men. (Black women constituted 61 percent of the workers in lumber in 1943, for ex-ample.) The hold of these women on even unskilled and low-paid jobs re-mained very weak, their wages remaining well below those of white men, white women, and black men. Often supervised by white women, black women got little aid from federal agencies supposedly enforcing equal ac-cess to jobs and job training in defense industries.

Even so, as the women in this chapter recall, factory work opened up new vistas. During the war, white women and black women combined made up nearly 60 percent of the workers (some seven thousand of them) at Firestone Tire and Rubber Company, a former male preserve. Such jobs provided far higher pay than household, servant, and field labor. The trick was to hold onto these jobs. After the war, employers dumped black women even faster than they laid off white women, who began shift-ing increasingly back into "pink collar" and service economy jobs. Black women still did the worst jobs, involving hand labor, sweeping, and cleaning, mostly in the largely unmechanized industries such as furniture. Within an economy that placed all women in the lower paid, less presti-gious jobs, black women suffered the most extreme disadvantages.

The following narratives suggest how black women factory workers, in this world of constricted opportunities, made "a way out of no way." Tera Hunter and other scholars have shown how black working-class women built up communities and families through their associational life and daily consumption and production strategies. According to Elizabeth Clark-Lewis, they drew on a core of traditional values in which "church, home, and family came before personal ambition." In Memphis, the lucky ones got hired at Firestone and the luckiest of those managed to keep their jobs after the war. With the help of Clarence Coe, I found some of these women, who emphasized not just the disabilities they faced but also their pride in what their work had meant for them and, most especially, for their ability to advance the education and independence of their children.

Irene Branch, Evelyn Bates, and Susie Wade all accentuated the financial gains of employment in a unionized and prosperous industry. All three women eventually became the main providers in their families. After Wade fled from an abusive husband in Mississippi, her work at Firestone for thirty-five and a half years gave her independence from men (she apparently never remarried) and enabled her to raise four children who developed secure occupations as an attorney, a nurse, an assistant principal, and an accountant. Similarly, Branch emphasized that her work at Firestone enabled her to raise her first husband's two children to be successful adults after he died, and to send one of them to college. Her work became so important to her that when her second husband tried to make her quit her job, "I told him he had to get going," for she preferred her financial independence and security at work to her marriage. Bates, whose husband died when her second child was in the eighth grade, similarly raised three children on Firestone wages and with the help of her sister and stepmother. She never remarried and sent two of her children to college, one of them to the elite University of Chicago.

However, like those of black men, their stories are hardly a hymn of praise to employers and supervisors, from whom some of them received great abuse. Like the first cohort of black men who took jobs at Firestone in the 1930s, black women in the 1940s had no choice but to hold on to their jobs tightly, doing whatever they had to do. Branch and Bates hated their first jobs, starting out with the same kinds of work assigned to black women (and men) in the larger society: sweeping, cleaning restrooms, working in the cafeteria, or doing heavy labor that no white woman wanted. Like the first cohort of black men there, they survived primarily by their ability to "take it," that is, to continue working despite miserable conditions and abuse from whites. Because of their precarious position in the labor market, Branch concluded, "you couldn't do nothing else but take it or get going on." For a black woman, "one place was as bad as the next; there was no use, if they didn't have a union." Only Susie Wade, one of the very first black women hired at Firestone, felt that her work life had gone smoothly. Her work as a cleaner in the main office was less physically demanding than that of the other Firestone women, and, according to her account, she always managed to assert herself with white overseers.

The stories of Branch and Bates in particular demonstrate how hard and incessant work shaped the lives of these women as they sought to sustain their families. Branch started nursing white children and cleaning a white household at age eighteen, and felt compelled to continue working there even after getting a job at Firestone. She spent nearly twenty-nine years taking care of the white family part of the day, her own part of the day, and working eight to ten hours at the factory at night. Bates began at Firestone sorting tires in the boiling southern sun amidst snakes and insects, too tired to even walk home at the end of the day, and likewise became the sole breadwinner in her family. For a long time, color-coded departmental seniority and white resistance to every effort blacks made to get training and to break out of "black" and into "white" jobs kept these women in the worst jobs at the lowest pay.

Although most factories laid off their black women workers after the war, some of the black women working at Firestone managed to hold on and prosper when their union, pressured by black men, took action to preserve their jobs (see Lonnie Roland interview, chapter 4). However, most of the black women working in the non-unionized and mostly locally owned woodworking, cotton, and food processing companies did much less well. Rebecca McKinley's story, in contrast to those of the Firestone women, suggests how unrewarding factory work could be in such companies. Memphis Furniture, always one of the city's most intractable anti-union employers, was a bastion of low wages and poor working conditions. Its owners had defeated the organizing efforts of a racially divided AFL union in the 1930s by firing its leaders. During World War II it hired a majority of black women to replace men who went into the military or found better-paying jobs in other factories. But perhaps to the company's surprise, these black women overwhelmingly supported the CIO's United Furniture Workers of America (UFWA), which won representation rights by 379 votes to the AFL Upholsterer's International Union's 31, in September 1943. According to an FBI report, not a single white joined the CIO, and the company continued to stall all union initiatives for the next six years.

Memphis Furniture, like Firestone, segregated work by gender and race, with white women running sewing machines in the upholstery department and black women and men working on the production line. The major difference between the two companies was that the northern-based Firestone finally accepted unionization, and the family wages paid there made the north Memphis communities around the plant prosper.

Memphis Furniture never did accept unionization and stonewalled all efforts to improve wages and conditions, forcing the black women at the plant into a fierce strike for some eight months in 1949. They sought deduction of union dues from their paychecks, a necessity to stabilize membership in a low-wage industry where workers often failed to pay their dues.

This strike, as Rebecca McKinley tells us, became a classic union battle with an intransigent employer. The women workers barely survived during the strike. Some of them wrapped burlap bags around their shoes to protect their feet from frostbite during bitter winter weather, and strike supporters from other unions had a hard time raising enough funds to keep them from being thrown out of their homes. The company, assisted by the Memphis police, hauled strikebreakers into the plant in trucks decorated in red, white, and blue and made special clubs for the police. Numerous conflicts broke out on picket lines, and the police arrested many union supporters. In the same period, a massive red scare in and out of the labor movement, with United Furniture Workers one of its targets, polarized the CIO and undercut its support for strikes and union civil rights activities.

The black women at Memphis Furniture held out against privations and intimidation. Beginning in the dead of winter and proceeding throughout the sweltering heat of a Mississippi Delta summer, these poorly paid women demonstrated their capacity for union activism on the picket lines, in meetings, and in confrontations with strikebreakers. But in the end they lost the strike and their jobs and were blacklisted at Memphis Furniture. Their strike loss and the related allegations of Communist infiltration of the labor movement had a devastating effect on organizing in the Memphis furniture industry for years to come. Anyone identified as a union or civil rights militant came under attack, and this included McKinley. White Communist Party activists gave the strongest support to the strikers at Memphis Furniture, and she wanted to work with these people who were "ahead of their time" on race issues. But when she and local black UFWA leader James White attended civil rights gatherings organized by the National Negro Congress in Chicago and New York, local newspapers identified her as a possible "red," a charge that at the time put anyone, much less a black woman, in serious jeopardy.

In the aftermath of the strike and the red-baiting associated with it, McKinley, never particularly sympathetic to "communism," survived and moved on to another job. Her union local did not do as well. Black women working at Memphis Furniture remained non-union until the late 1970s, when, as Ida Leachman relates in chapter 8, a renewed organizing campaign, followed by another strike in 1980, finally created a strong local—only to have the company close down in retaliation. Memphis Furniture wanted production at low wages or no production at all. Years of hard labor left black women in this anti-union bastion, unlike those at Firestone, without pensions, health care, or any other provision for the future. These were among the hardships common to black women working in a factory system shaped by generations of low wages and Jim Crow.

Irene Branch Does Double Duty as a Domestic and Factory Worker

You couldn't do nothing else but take it or get going on.

I interviewed Irene Branch in 1989 at her home in a declining neighborhood under assault from the inner-city neglect of the 1980s. Branch told me that she spent nearly her entire life working two jobs, one in the home of a white family and the other in the Firestone factory. Her life of unremitting toil aptly illustrates the saying "a woman's work is never done." She gave me a photo of herself taken in 1948, which showed a nicely dressed, beautiful young woman. I wondered who had admired her beauty and grace as she worked her life away for others.

I was raised in Athens, Georgia. My dad got his eye knocked out in that railroad strike, somebody beat him up, around 1924. He had a brother here, and my parents moved to Memphis in '24. I was a little girl then, and I went to school here. But I left when I was eighteen, because I had a mean stepmother. Then I married at nineteen, been workin' ever since. I didn't go around these honky tonks, just went to church and worked all the time. They called me a workhorse.

So when I got grown and I married, then my husband died. I worked practically all my life from eighteen years old, nursing white children and cooking for white people, 'til I got the Firestone job. I had to do the cooking, and I had to go to the back door. I was cooking most all the time. You nursed those children and everything, and then you'd eat after they got through eating. Where I worked, the white people were really good and nice to me. I just didn't have the privilege. I was working seven days a week in the white folks' kitchen, making two dollars and fifty cents a week! You could go to the grocery store with five dollars, and you couldn't bring many groceries back. When you were working in private homes, if the white person didn't pay you the salary, you'd just have to quit.

I have two boys, adopted children. They weren't my real children, they were my husband's. But I raised my husband's children from five years old, when their mama left them. I raised them up to be good children. I just managed, and I had to do it. That's a reason I worked at night, when I'd get off from work they'd be at home. I raised them both, and they were good children. I didn't have no trouble. They finished school. Both boys finished school, and one went to college. My oldest boy is fifty-eight, and my next one is forty-three years old.

It was bad working for other folks, but not bad like at Firestone. I had two jobs at once. I worked at Firestone at night, and I'd come home every morning at 7:15. I'd take me a little nap, and at 9 A.M., I went to my other job and worked until 4 P.M. And I'd come home and go to bed. At 10 they'd pick me up to take me to Firestone at night. That's the reason I worked there at night all the time, 'cause I had two jobs. I didn't get much sleep. It was a long time after I retired at Firestone that I could sleep at night, 'cause I was always awake all night. I had to take sleeping pills to make me go to sleep when I retired from Firestone.

My husband was working at the Buckeye. He was making eight dollars a week at the Buckeye.[6] It was tough because my husband used to get the rawhide, you know how they'd rawhide 'em.[7] But once they got the union in there, then they raised the salaries. Whatever job you wanted you could get if you qualified, don't care what they was paying.

I was in the Firestone union, the rubber workers union, starting around World War II, in 1944. It was a hard time, and we weren't treated right. I started to quit a couple of times, but I'm glad I didn't. Before we got the

6. Buckeye Cellulose was a cottonseed oil plant that employed both blacks and whites, later organized into Local 19 of the Food, Tobacco, and Agricultural Workers Union (FTA), of which Leroy Boyd tells us more in chapter 5.

7. Branch, using "rawhide" as a verb, meant that supervisors pushed the workers hard to get maximum output.

union, they'd do you any kind of way. So, many people quit, but I just stuck on in there, and took what they put on me. It was better when we got the union, 'cause when they didn't treat you right, you could go to the union.[8] Then we had a right and somebody to protect us. I stayed on that job twenty-eight years and nine months, but it was really hard.

I wasn't supposed to get that job at Firestone, you were supposed to weigh 150 pounds to get that job. I didn't weigh but 145, but the woman at the employment office let that 5 pounds go.

I worked in the receiving office. I kept the office clean. I was hired on the other side of the plant. We had bicycles then, and we were making tires for bicycles. And then I made patches to patch the tires. Then, I was transferred over in the big plant and worked in the big shop. I worked all over the place.

I started at twenty-five cents an hour. Of course, I got a raise in two months. I made the regular piece and wage rate. So, you know I liked that, and I didn't want to come out. I really liked it after we got that union. But I got to that age, you get sixty-five, and I had to come out. The whole twenty-eight years, I only missed two days. I worked twenty-five years at night, and the other three years I worked in the daytime. I came out in '73.

I worked in the lampblack. There's a suit against Firestone over that lampblack 'cause so many people's died when it settled on them. I swept a lot of that lampblack that gets into your lungs. Anytime you pick up the paper, you see where two or three Firestone workers died, both white and black, from that lampblack. I got sick a couple of times, yes I did. I went in the hospital for a week.

When I first went in, they'd give the hardest jobs they could to the blacks. They'd give you the jobs a white person wouldn't want and you'd be making less money. It was really tough. You could be working side by side with a white person, and they'd get double the money that you got. You'd get less money, but you were doing the work, they weren't doing the work. But you had to take it, see! You couldn't do nothing else but take it or get going on, go somewhere else and get another job. One place was as

8. The CIO had gained bargaining rights in 1942. But the poor work conditions described here remained in force for a number of years. Ms. Branch tells us later she was unaware of the union when she first began working, and she associates "the union" with a later period in which it began to improve conditions.

bad as the next, there was no use, if they didn't have a union. It was just rough.

Before the union, those supervisors would curse you, call you names, do you any kind of way. They'd call you "nigger" and everything else, and spit on you. Do *anything* to you. Blacks was really treated bad. And they'd fire you in a minute. I know a lot of men—women too—quit out there. But I didn't quit. I had a hard time, but I stuck on in there.

We worked seven days a week during the war. After the war was declared, they had a big contract with motor companies. They made rubber for cars, boats, and they had good production. They made rubber boats, too, but I didn't work in the boat department. The war was going on and there wasn't hardly anyone working in there but womens.[9]

It was tough, but it was a good place to work if you knew how to take things. If they did me wrong, and I was working, I would just take it, you know, to stay there. We made all kinds of tires, and I'd lift those tires, even ones for busses. Big tires. All you could do was look to keep from getting killed. I didn't get hurt, but you were lucky if you didn't get your arm cut off. I worked where you made the rubber to make the tires. It was really tough. I worked at night, and I never went to sleep on the job. You had a ten-minute break, and a fifteen-minute break, and a thirty-minute lunch. You couldn't break until somebody else came to relieve you.

I swept out there. Day and night I swept, all through the year. I worked first shift, second shift, and mostly the third shift. In the first and second shift, they'd stand over you. But at night, they don't rawhide you so much, 'cause they'd be somewhere in a hole trying to sleep. Every once in a while, they'd come out and see if you're doing your work and everything.

You had a white woman over you *always*, and she gonna see that you work. You had no time to stay in the bathroom, and if you did, she'd come in there and get you. They always had a white woman over the black womens. All white supervisors, no black supervisors.

Those supervisors worked you like a dog. You had to work, I mean you *worked*. You had to lift all them tires. You had to lift everything. When we got the union in there, they had [mechanical] lifters then, you didn't have

9. Some departments were predominantly female, and at one point women composed nearly 60 percent of the whole plant, which employed up to seven thousand workers during the war.

to lift nothing. And then later there were pull carts, I pulled them. They'd be full of tires, but it wouldn't be heavy, 'cause it got a button on there, and you'd push that button. You just had to guide it, that's all. You would hardly know you was pulling it, 'cause it pulled its own self, once we got the union. Before that, everything was by hand.[10]

Before they got that union, we black folks had a hard time, a real hard time. I started to quit several times, 'cause I wasn't treated right. But I just prayed and prayed and stayed on in there 'til things got better. Wasn't for that union, I wouldn't have been in there. Then, it was a good place to work.

I remember a black woman was beat up right at the bus stop outside of the plant, around 1944. A supervisor hit her, and the blacks walked out of the plant.[11] Blacks had a hard time, they'd beat you up anytime. A white supervisor would hit a black. I didn't get hit, but several other blacks did, mens and womens. It didn't happen to me, 'cause I always took things, see. I knew that I had to work 'cause I didn't have no husband. My sister worked there too, but she got laid off and never did get called back.

I ain't married no more. My husband died in '47. I did marry again, but he didn't stay long 'cause I couldn't put up with him. He didn't want me to work at Firestone, he thought I'd be going with other men in there. So I told him he had to get going. So, I've been a widow [single] ever since. I get a good pension every month, my house bill is paid, and I pay one dollar every month for my medicine. I've got good benefits coming in. The longer you work, the more pension you got. Firestone takes care of you when you're living, and buries you when you're dead! So I don't need no husband, no how. Firestone takes care of me.

There are still a lot of black women working in private homes now. I was working for a woman for twenty years while I was working at Firestone, and I'm still working for her. I stick with her 'cause she don't want

10. Ms. Branch tends to equate the period of "the union" with the postwar era, when the United Rubber Workers gained considerable power at Memphis Firestone.

11. In this incident, in March 1945, a white guard at the factory slugged a black woman in the mouth when she ignored the rules of segregation and tried to board the bus ahead of whites. Black workers walked out of the plant in protest. Police leveled shotguns and arrested the white union president, Richard Routon, when he tried to calm the situation. The woman was fired, even though the black workers struck for three days. Clarence Coe comments on this incident in chapter 4.

nobody but me. I raised up her girl that's twenty-two now, and a boy that's twenty. I raised those kids. I did cookin' for white people, nursing children and things. Both of my sons have jobs, one of them is a policeman in Chicago. The other one is working, but he ain't got no good job, 'cause all the good jobs have left here. Ain't no factory jobs here now, but one or two. All the leading plants left.

But, you know, it's called racism. The blacks just weren't treated right, until they got that union. We didn't see freedom until we got that union in! We had to pay union dues, they'd take so much out of your salary, and that was OK. We had protection then, they didn't mistreat you. If they cursed you, you'd go to the union and they'd get on the supervisors about cursing. They were really nice after we got the union in, you was treated right then.

When they got the union in there, you could get any job that you wanted, if you qualified. If a white woman had a job but you had more seniority, you could bump her. I bumped a lot of them, and they bumped me. When you had more seniority than that person, you could bump that person and get their job.[12]

I didn't know nothing about the unions when I started at Firestone. Then we had to go to union meetings to discuss how they was treating you and everything. If you weren't treated right, you'd tell the union steward, and they'd get on the supervisors. If it wasn't for that union, there wouldn't be nobody at Firestone, 'cause they'd all quit. It was a good while before they got the union. You was treated right when you got that union.

Once the union came in, it changed things. If you qualified to be a supervisor, you could be a supervisor. They had plenty of black supervisors after a while. They had black womens and black mens as supervisors after the union come in. It was really good. Hadn't been for the union, it wouldn't have been nothing like that. Edward Harrel, he was a union steward. We had black union stewards out there, and then they had black supervisors. You was treated right then. Oh, that was a big change!

12. Early union contracts allowed seniority to accrue by department, so that workers who transferred out of their departments lost all seniority. This kept blacks in the worst jobs. In chapter 4, Lonnie Roland describes how black workers challenged this system and obtained plant-wide seniority, according to which whoever had the highest seniority won the bid for a job (bumping someone else out of line) when it was vacated. Ms. Bates, in the next interview, clarifies that integration of jobs was not simultaneous with unionization and resulted in part from the rise of the civil rights movement.

A black woman couldn't get a good job before the union. The white women could get good jobs, but a black woman couldn't get it. When we got the union, see, you could tell your steward what was going on, and how they treated you, and the union would make them be better to you. You had a right 'cause of the union.

Evelyn Bates Reflects on Her Lifetime of Factory Work

Factory employment was the best thing around.

I interviewed Evelyn Bates in her home in north Memphis in 1989. Beautifully furnished, it reflected her early training as an interior decorator. At the time, I thought it was surprising that a factory worker would have lifelong aspirations to be an interior decorator, but I later realized how much sense it made.

I went to the employment office about five or six times before I got on at Firestone, 'cause they told me I was too young, too little, and didn't weigh enough. Actually, I didn't weigh but 100 pounds when I went to Firestone. You were supposed to weigh 150 pounds. On the phone, the lady told me, she say, "You're too young and you don't weigh enough, but if you can pass the test, I'm gonna send you on over there." So we had to go down there on Second Street [the unemployment office], and they gave us a written test. I passed the written test and I passed the physical. I got by with a big dress, and I was wearing those hoop slips. They didn't weigh me, they just judged our weight by how we looked. I was hired by the time they weighed me during my physical. That's how I got on.

I grew up in New Chicago and finished high school at Manassas [neighborhoods in Memphis].[13] My first job was working in the cafeteria at Brithin's [a small local cafe]. I got on at Firestone June 1 of '44. I had married and I had two children, and my husband was working at Bruce Lumber for ten dollars a week. I felt like we needed some help, so I got a job.

My sister was living with me at that time, so when I worked at night,

13. Manassas High School provided the educational core for the industrial center of heavily black north Memphis, and a teacher there named Hayes routed numerous blacks to employment at Firestone, as mentioned by Matthew Davis and George Holloway in chapter 2.

she would be at home. She worked in the daytime, and I was at home in the day. When I worked during the day, my stepmother would keep the children. My sister didn't have any kids. My husband worked eight hours a day, he always worked in the daytime. He passed in '73. My baby was in the eighth grade when my husband died, and my brother had taken my oldest and raised him and sent him to school in Chicago. So, I just had two at home.

While I was working at Firestone, I went to college. I went to LeMoyne for a year while I was working, and I taken up interior decorating. After I went onto the night shift at Firestone, I couldn't go to school, so I just would work at home to make money on the side.

The first job that I worked on at Firestone, I was making patches, that was the first department I was in. After they closed that department down, they sent us out on the yard, separating and cutting tires. That sun was hot, and we was out there in the bare hot sun!

That was during the war. I got hired in '44. There were all black womens in the field, forty or fifty. We sorted all different sorts of tires out there in that big open field. They had water, snakes, wasps, and everything in them. They had a lot of ladies working out there in that open field, in the hot sun, sorting out those old, bad tires. You'd take a knife and cut the bad rubber off, and then they'd pick up the better rubber and do them over. These were old worn out tires, they would cure them and put them out in the field, if they were no good, for us to cut up. That was for twenty-five dollars a week, eight hours a day, seven days a week.

When they cut that job out, we went to the solos plant,[14] some of us, and some of us went to the big plant. At the solos plant, they had a big thing they called a "hog" that would grind up all of those tires and send that rubber over to the big plant. I didn't like the work, but I didn't have any choice, because I wanted to work. That was the first job that I had that had paid that much, even though we was working seven days. We were just glad to be at a factory. Factory employment was the best thing around.

In the solos plant, they waited until it got cold, and then they would transfer us outside in the yard. They had me sweeping water on the dock, and man, it was cold! In that factory, the attitude was bad. I worked two days, and then I quit.

14. A unit for recycling old rubber for recapping tires and other uses.

When I walked out because of sweeping that cold water, I went to the office the next day. I asked Mr. Lola for my money, and he told me he wasn't going to give it to me, and I should come back that Friday. I went back that Friday, and he gave me a letter to take over to the front office. They transferred me to the big plant, and I went to the thread ply.

At the thread ply, they grind the rubber up, and it comes out in great big slabs on a belt. There would be two womens on each side of a tray, and we had to throw the shorter slabs of 50 to 60 pounds off by ourselves. The longer slabs weighed 75 to 125 pounds, and we'd each grab an end and throw them in the tray. The tray would hold forty-eight slabs of rubber. It was very heavy work. They had mens doing it before they hired black womens. Didn't any women do it but black womens.

This was a long belt that kept rolling all the time. They called the mens truckers, they was the ones that trucked those trays. As soon as we would load one tray, there was another one right there for us to start back loading.

It was lots hotter inside the plant than outside, because of all of the steam from the pipes. So, if it was ninety degrees outside, it would be maybe ten degrees hotter in the plant, and you'd be wringing wet. There was one fan on the end of the line, and that was it. People would get sick and fall out from the heat.

It was fast work, you did fast work. You'd be sweating all day, and you'd be too tired sometimes to even walk to the gate to go home.

They had salt pills at the fountain. They had a black fountain and a white fountain, practically everywhere in the plant. Problem was, you couldn't go get a drink until someone came to relieve you. The supervisor would be there standing over you. He'd be standing there all the time. Some of 'em was hard on us, and some of 'em wasn't, according to how they felt, that was their attitude. It was rougher in the daytime than it was on the night shift, because there would be so many different supervisors in the day. I never did work the second shift too much.

The only time we'd get some rest was if the belt would break down, and they had to come fix it. Then they'd put you to doing something else, sweeping or something like that.

On that job, if your relief team didn't come in, you had to work on. Until someone came from somewhere to relieve you, you couldn't go any-place, not even to the restroom. It was an assembly line, and it just kept going. We were supposed to get two fifteen-minute breaks, and twenty minutes for lunch. If you wanted coffee or a sandwich, or needed to go to the restroom, you had to do it all in that fifteen minutes. We had to walk from the middle of the plant clear out on the dock, past all of the other restrooms, to go to one that they had for black womens. It took at least five or six minutes just to walk there. You'd spend your whole break just getting there and coming back. There was only that one restroom for all the black womens in the plant, and it was out on the dock! We didn't all take our breaks at the same time, but there was a lot of us.

I got sick a couple of times, and I had to be off. But, once you get used to it, you can work more. If you were just starting, it was harder. A lot of 'em quit, but I worked on 'til I got a better job. I worked at that job for about four years. When the mens started coming home from the war, they started giving the men their jobs back, 'cause it was a man's job. So, then I started sweeping in the same department and moved around some. A lot of the black womens they laid off. They didn't lay you off according to seniority, 'cause you didn't have no seniority over white womens. The white womens were there first, except for the maids.

The white womens were there ever since about '39. They didn't hire black womens then, other than the ones working as maids who cleaned the restrooms and things like that.

After the war, somebody had an agreement to lay off all of the black womens, until the union got over to it. We all was going to be laid off. The union put some kind of pressure on 'em.[15]

I think that most of the tension between blacks and whites, and the strikes, happened after the war. They had black jobs and white jobs. Really, there was more tension after they integrated, 'cause then if you had more seniority than a white woman, you could bump her. But if you did, the pressure would be on you so hard, until you would hardly be able to qualify on the job. They would make it so you couldn't do your work.

After they integrated, you could get on most jobs, but the thing was staying on them. They would treat you so bad, until you couldn't do the work. I'm sure I was the first black woman that went in the lab, that's where they test the rubber. They cook the rubber and test those big slabs of rubber, and cure it, and sample it before they make the tires. I was the first black woman in there.

15. See the interview with Lonnie Roland in chapter 4.

They gave me a rough time in that lab, even the supervisors. They'd tell you one thing and you'd do that, and then it was wrong. They'd tell you something else to do, you do that, and that was wrong. You just had to try to make it on your own, because they really wasn't particular about showing you what to do.

You'd get trouble from the supervisors and the white workers, too, 'cause they'd already told the white workers how to treat you and not to show you how to do the work, before you'd even get in there. They just wouldn't show you how to do the work. You might find one in the bunch who'd try to take the time and show you. And if they'd show you, they were gonna show you the hard way.

Now, the supervisor on the second shift, Joe Williams, was rough. He was rough! Duckworth, on the third shift, was very nice to work for. On the first shift, you'd work for the foremens, and Norton was the supervisor. They'd always send you to the second shift to qualify, because the toughest supervisor was there. Joe Williams's attitude was that a black woman never would qualify, as long as he was on the second shift. He was nasty. He was nasty! Yes he was.

But I managed to learn this job despite it all. Yeah, I sure did. I learned it. Most of it was just math, or something like that. When we did stock, all you had to do was go by your ticket number and count how many of those samples of rubber were there, and put that down. You just couldn't make a mistake, you just could not make a mistake. 'Cause if you did, it messed up the whole thing. You had to watch and be careful what you was doing, that was all. After you learned it, it wasn't anything. The thing was, you had to go through so much red tape to try to learn. It was an easy job, 'cause it had been a white women's job. They had all the easy jobs.

See, the lab was a job that nobody had worked on but white womens before. As a black woman, if you qualified with more seniority, that meant that you'd bump a white woman, and she would have to go work somewhere else. I qualified in there on vacation relief. One of those white womens would go on vacation, and then I would go in on her job and work the two weeks or whatever she taken off for vacation. I was laid off, and if I didn't have enough seniority to go to another job, I was laid off until they called me back. But they would always fix it so that you had about three good months work before you'd get laid off, 'cause they'd move you around on vacation relief.

Before they integrated, if you got laid off, you went out of the plant. After they integrated, if you had more seniority, you could go to a job in another department, any department. Before they integrated, your seniority was only good for that one department that you were in. You'd get laid off, 'cause you couldn't go anywhere else. Let's say you new in the tire room, and I had been five years in the tread room. I still couldn't come over there where you are, even though I had five years over you. I still couldn't bump you until after they integrated the jobs.

When I was in the bead room, you had a certain amount of beads to build. You could be building your beads, and they wouldn't be right. Or you could build a stack of so many beads, and when you checked out, they had taken half of your beads and given them to somebody else, and you wouldn't come up to what you were supposed to build.

The beads were made like a round ring, that's what you put on the end of the tires. They had a machine that you'd build 'em by. And then after you'd build 'em, you'd hang 'em up on a rack. A bead was just like a round piece of wire, and it was covered with so many pieces of rubber. That was the bead. It was a production job, [and] we were counting production. It had been all white womens building them. After they integrated the jobs, they put black womens over there.

I was checking beads together with a white lady. When we'd get ready to count the beads, she would go in the office to do hers, and I would have to stand out there in the plant and count mine. All night, we would tally the same beads, she had just what I had. But when she'd go to the office and come back, she would always run two or three hundred beads ahead of me. In the office, they were erasing some of mine and giving them to her.

So, the union president sent Lonnie Roland in at night to check us out.[16] He checked right along with me and her, and when he asked to see my sheet, some of my beads had been erased. They were supposed to disqualify me that night. Rip Clark [union president] came over there and told the supervisor, "If you disqualify her, it's going to be your job!" And the next night, I qualified. But the idea was, they didn't want me to bump a white woman.

The integration of jobs happened after the Supreme Court decision in

16. Roland was a black shop committeeman, responsible for dealing with problems in his area on the factory floor.

'54 [*Brown v. Board of Education*]. Before that, black womens couldn't be on the beads or nothing like that. Only thing a black woman could do in Firestone was sweep, work on the line doing heavy work like I was talking about, work up on the belt sweeping, where all that lampblack was, or clean the restrooms as a maid. They had a few black womens up in the cafeteria, on the black side. The white worked on the white side. That's all a black woman could do before they integrated the jobs.

But the idea was, the white women didn't want to sweep, she didn't want to clean up no restroom, so that was a black woman's job. It was just like you had black and white men's jobs. That's the way it was with the womens, too. Certain jobs blacks could do, and certain jobs whites could do. Actually, after they integrated the jobs, [the whites discovered] the sweeping job wasn't as hard. And after they found out that was easy, the white women would take those jobs.

Now, there was a lady, Juanita, we worked together. I would list the stock, put the stock out, and check the buttons. All she had to do was open the cans and pull the stock out. When they got on Joe Williams, that nasty supervisor, about it, he still didn't make her do anything but open the cans and test the buttons. But I had it all to do. When I had her job, I had it all to do, but she didn't. And that was after they integrated the job. It stayed like that until she retired. And after she retired, they fixed it so that every-body would have two jobs, which is what I had all along. It was aggravating to work alongside this woman every day, but if you had to work, it was a loss you took and swallowed it. If you had three children in school and wanted to send them to college, you take a loss!

It was in the '60s, when they integrated everything, and the plants, too. When all the civil rights were going on, like the sit-ins downtown. That's when the strikes were. We could go in the restrooms where they [whites] was. They'd strike. We drank from water fountains they drank out of. They'd strike. They even went on strike when they gave one of the men's lockers to the women.

It wasn't really integrated until the [black] sanitation workers was on that strike [in 1968]. It had been in the other cities, but it hadn't been here. When they passed the civil rights bill [in 1964], right then and there, it wasn't integrated.

So there were lots of changes, big changes, and people were excited about them. Imagine the idea that you worked all day and couldn't even sit down on the bus unless there was a seat in the back. [Ending that] was a great change. They'd [bus drivers] let the whites get on first, and then they'd fill the bus up, and we would have to stand. That was right out there by Firestone. Sometimes they'd fill up the whole bus. And you'd worked as hard as they had, or harder.

People talked about it, but what could we do about it? Times was not like it is now. We would take it, but nobody else [today] would take it. So it's just the change of time.

Or, if we could go on the other side of the cafeteria [where whites ate], they'd strike. They had a partition between the two walls in the cafeteria. The black on this side, and the white on the other side. A black cashier, and a white cashier. But after the integration, they tore that partition down and made just one big cafeteria. Folks could sit wherever they wanted. Sometimes people would still sit separate, but sometimes they'd sit together. It was just according to how you felt.

It take 'em [whites] a while to get used to it, I'd say about that! I think some of them opened up their minds and realized that it wasn't going to be like it used to be, and they just had to realize it. And some of 'em never did get used to it. When you were in the restroom, some of 'em would see you sitting there and act like they saw a snake or something jumping out. That's right. But you had a privilege to go anywhere that there was a rest-room in the plant. You could go and use it, whereas we didn't have but one before that. The civil rights movement really made it better for the blacks.

So, they eased up a lot, and at some point their attitudes changed. It sure did! It even changed with the supervisors. They'd see that you could do the work, then regardless of what color, if you could do the work, that was your job. I worked in the lab cleaning until the plant closed down. I'd say I worked in the lab about fifteen years.

I got to be friends with some of the white women, the very ones, some of them, that treated me like they did, became friends. Sure did. I mean, we would go in the lab, sit down, and talk. But beforehand, when I first went in there, uh-uh, we didn't do that.

If I remember, there were certain stores that blacks couldn't go in. They broke some of it down, but there were certain things that you could buy, but you couldn't try 'em on, like hats or dresses. You couldn't try those on, even if you had the money to buy them, at Gerbers, and Julius Lewis, and Landers [department stores]. Most of those stores went out of business, but it changed before '68.

Hillie Pride, pictured in front of his home in Memphis in 1989, was one of the first black workers hired at Firestone in the 1930s. Despite terrible working conditions, he took satisfaction in his work and felt that he and his union accomplished a great deal. Photo by Michael Honey.

Irene Branch in 1948. She had wanted to become a beautician some day, but, when industry finally started hiring black women during the war, she took a job at Firestone and worked there from 1944 until her retirement. Photo courtesy of Irene Branch.

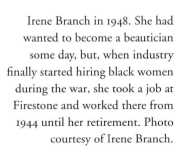

Clarence Coe, pictured outside his home in 1996, spent a lifetime fighting Jim Crow at the factory and struggling for civil rights in the community. Photo by Michael Honey.

Matthew Davis, a rural migrant to the city in the 1930s, did the heavy and hazardous labor that whites avoided. He became an elder statesman for the United Rubber Workers and a community leader in the New Chicago area of Memphis. Photo courtesy of Matthew Davis.

Edward Lindsey, pictured outside his home in 1989, was among the younger generation hired by Firestone in the early 1960s. Formerly a participant in the Nashville student sit-ins, he took direct action against factory segregation and was active in union politics. Photo by Michael Honey.

George Holloway, pictured at the first contract signing at International Harvester in Memphis, May 1948, was the only black member of the Local 988 UAW bargaining committee. He came from a union family and organized rubber workers, Pullman porters, and farm equipment and auto workers. He endured threats and racial insults throughout his organizing career. Photo courtesy of the Mississippi Valley Collection, University of Memphis.

Dr. Martin Luther King, Jr., and the young UAW leader George Holloway shake hands in the 1960s, symbolizing the meeting of civil rights and labor concerns. Black political leader George Lee looks on. Photo by Ernest Withers. Used by permission.

Rural blacks from the cotton economy migrated into urban food- and cotton-processing industries and made the Food, Tobacco, and Agricultural Workers' left-led Local 19 one of the fastest-growing locals in Memphis after World War II. The FTA was one of the most integrated of the CIO unions. White union organizers and black Local 19 members are pictured here around 1948. Photo courtesy of Ed McCrea.

Earl Fisher, pictured in a suit and tie with workers at a Local 19 shop in May 1968. Fisher, business agent and president for the local in the 1960s, survived the red scare of the 1950s and rebuilt the union based on direct action by workers at the point of production. Photo courtesy of Leroy Boyd.

Leroy Boyd (center) and other Local 19 members as participants in James Meredith's march against fear in Mississippi in 1966. Boyd and others had narrowly escaped lynching in Mississippi during their protest of the Willie McGee case in 1951. Photo courtesy of Leroy Boyd.

Leroy Clark, imprisoned for strike actions in New York and a veteran of the European theater in World War II, came to Memphis as a furniture union organizer. In the 1960s, by cultivating black rank-and-file leadership through strikes and a strong steward system, he rebuilt a local that white business agents had allowed to stagnate. Photo courtesy of Alzada Clark.

Alzada Clark, pictured on the left with American Tent Company strikers in Canton in December 1968, led strikes by black women against hostile white employers in Mississippi. The spirit of these women reflected the civil rights militance of the era, if not the strategy of nonviolence. Photo courtesy of Alzada Clark.

Joined in struggle and in marriage, organizers Alzada Clark and Leroy Clark (right) celebrate during a retirement tribute to Mr. Clark put on by the furniture workers union staff, January 19, 1980. Photo courtesy of Alzada Clark.

Taylor Rogers, pictured with his wife Bessie in front of their home in Memphis in 1996, became president of Local 1733 AFSCME after the 1968 strike in which Dr. King lost his life. Rogers felt the union transformed the lives of public workers such as himself and opened the way to black political power in Memphis. Photo by Michael Honey.

James Robinson, pictured outside his home in 1996, struggled to make a living as a sanitation worker. He survived the 1968 strike and the riots that followed to become president of the AFSCME Local 1733 sanitation unit. In spite of financial hardship, he felt his sacrifices benefitted the next generation. Photo by Michael Honey.

Ida Leachman (center) with workers at the A-Brant furniture plant in Texas in 1979. She came out of the shops in Memphis to become an organizer in the 1980s and 1990s, a period of attacks against gains made by the civil rights and labor movements. A woman-centered spirit and religion sustained her faith in organizing. Photo courtesy of Ida Leachman.

There was a lot of tension during the '60s. But if you had to work, you couldn't go to the union meetings. The union meetings would always be in the evening time, when I worked, so a lot of it I don't know anything about. I always cooperated with the union, though. There were no black womens in the offices in the union, you'd see black men, but no black womens.

The people at Firestone did better than most people. International Harvester opened up, but there weren't any womens working at Harvester, just mens. It [Harvester] was a good-paying job, but Firestone was the best in Memphis, and that was for a woman or a man. When I started working there, twenty-five dollars was a lot of money to me, 'cause I could do a lot with twenty-five dollars in 1944.[17]

When I started at Firestone, I was making fifty cent an hour. Fifty cent an hour, that's what we were making. And the whites were making more than the blacks, even though we were working side by side. That's right. They got rid of that when everything else changed, whites and blacks would get paid the same money then.

One of my sons, he got on out there. But, the younger people thought that things had always been better for us like they were when they started. They thought we were making big money all the time, and that we always had a easy job. It wasn't like that. The younger people came in and really didn't understand the struggle that the older people had gone through. No they did not. We went through with something!

The [black] mens were the ones that were [first] hired, in '37 and '38. To hear some of them tell you what they went through! They really went through with something. We thought we went through something, but we didn't near go through what they went through. When I first started, they had a jack, and the men was pulling all this heavy rubber. When the younger generation come in, all the new equipment was there for them, so they thought we had an easy time all of the time. But, we went through hell! Sure did.

When the younger folks came in, they could get a job anywhere. I always figure they thought, "Easy go, easy come." Well, when I started there, if you quit your job, you didn't get another factory job, most probably, not a black woman. You might could go to a little cafe, do housework, or

17. In fact, she made more than twice the wage her husband did at a locally owned lumber mill.

something like that, but factory jobs was hard for black womens to get. There were a couple of other companies that hired black womens: Bruce Lumber Company, Memphis Furniture, Nickey Brothers [lumber], and Humko. You could count them on one hand. I had been to those places trying to get on.

What we would take, the younger generation wouldn't have taken. The working conditions were better when a lot of them came in, and [even then] they didn't accept it. But, I want you to know, it was hard for some of the younger ones, too. Just like when the black tire builders come in, it was hard for them, too. They got it, too, they sure did. 'Cause tire building had always been a white man's job. Just like building beads was just a white woman's job. Really, the easy jobs were just for whites only. And blacks got what was left, whatever it was, until everything was integrated. They called it "our jobs," sweeping and cleaning the restrooms and like that. Later on, whites decided to accept it. If you had more seniority, they had to hit the street. And rather than hit the street, they'd take those jobs.

As I look back, in a way, I feel good about it, 'cause if I hadn't been able to get the job and work there, I wouldn't have accumulated what I did. So, I really don't have an attitude, 'cause I had to work, and I had to work somewhere. It was about as good as anywhere else, that's the way I feel about it. Now, maybe if I could have taken up nursing or something like that in other places, maybe I would have an attitude. But I feel that by working in Firestone, I have accumulated about as much as anybody with my education and my opportunity. If I were working at Firestone now, I feel like I would be making just as much as the teachers and nurses make.

That's the way I feel about it. I had two children go to college. My youngest son went to LeMoyne [in Memphis]. My oldest son went to the University of Chicago and became an engineer. I don't regret working at Firestone. I went through hard times, but I still can see something that I did with going through all that hard time.

Susie Wade Tells How She Built a Life around Work

I had work and I just stayed there, and I did what I was supposed to do.

Susie Wade, one of the first black women hired at Firestone, abandoned a cruel husband in Mississippi, moved her four children to the city, and created a new life for them and for herself though steady work and wages. She became close to the white managers in the main office of the Firestone plant but, at the same time, expected and demanded respect from them and from her fellow black workers, some of whom she had conflicts with. Her ability to lead a relatively independent life from an early age seemed apparent in her cordial but assertive manner. I talked to her by phone in 1989.

I was a farmer until '41 in Tunica, Mississippi. I came to Memphis August 25th, '41. I stayed with my parents. My parents came to Memphis, about '32 I think it was. My father was a minister. And my sisters and brothers, they came looking for jobs. Of course, they didn't find jobs, but when I came later I found jobs. I don't know what it is about me. It's very unusual. I can always find a job. So I got the job and that's that.

In Mississippi I went to school at Tunica County Normal High School. I taught school in Mississippi. Of course you didn't have to have a high school diploma or anything to teach in Mississippi in those days. I taught there. It was a grade school. In those days there wasn't too many high schools there for blacks. There wasn't too many high schools, period, in those days, you see. But at least we did have a high school.

Then I got married. I had four children. I left my husband down there in '41. I left him there. He was a very cruel man. His brother carried him to the woods to cut wood, and his sister carried me to the train station. So I came here with the baby. I left two, brought a baby, and had one in lay away [was pregnant]. Later I went back and got the other kids.

I came here and worked in a laundry for a while. I picked cotton in Arkansas, three or four hundred pounds, before my baby was born in February. He was eight months old when I went to Firestone. I started working at Firestone October 5th, [1942], one of the first black women to work there. I was there until October '78. I retired with thirty-five and a half years' seniority.

I had four kids. All of them went to school. My son is the baby, he was born in '42. I had a daughter born in '37, one born in '38, and one born in '40. All are self-sufficient. My son is in an attorney in San Francisco. My daughter in Los Angeles, she's an accountant. My daughter here is a nurse at Memphis Hospital. The one in Chicago, she's an assistant principal at a school in Chicago. So they are self-sufficient. I'm proud of that. That was my full intention of having them get an education. 'Cause in Mississippi you only went four months to school—three in the wintertime and one in the summer. And it wasn't compulsory.

I wanted to do something, and I did go to school. I was the type of person that would like to read, read, read, read. So that's how I got my education. After I left there I still read.

I'm seventy-six years old April 18th. By working at Firestone, I have a pretty good salary [pension], about $1,300 a month. And I own a few little pieces of property. [She explains that she accumulated four or five houses and other property at very low prices.] So I've been very, very, very lucky on those things. Very lucky. I don't know how I've come by all this, but I guess I am the kind of person who neglects themself for other people. So I guess that's how I'm getting my pay. I've also been a probation officer for about nineteen years, nineteen years in April. I want to quit, but they won't let me quit. They assign me three or four girls. I go see them once a week. And I call them once a week.

At Firestone Tire and Rubber Company, I was one of the first black ladies they hired. I worked house service and the first aid, in restrooms, house cleaning, and things like that. I had work and I just stayed there, and I did what I was supposed to do. I took orders. Well, I didn't get too many orders. But they had my job set out for me. But I'd do it, you see. Of course, if they'd say, Mr. Firestone will be here in five minutes, you've got three minutes to clean this conference room, I'd go in there and do it. That's how I got along with my supervisors. I know I made enemies with the rest of my peers, because I would do what I was supposed to do and I didn't argue. I did what they told me when they told me, then I could go on and sit down and make enemies with the rest of them.

I didn't work too hard. How could I work too hard and stay there thirty-five and a half years? No way. I just did what they told me they wanted done. And that was that. And they didn't order me to do it, they would ask me. I had one supervisor that told me once to do something. I knew I was going to do it, yet he didn't have to say it like that. He corrected himself. He said, "I'm sorry, will you do it?" When he said that, I did it.

Some of the blacks would say you were an Uncle Tom or something of that order. But I respected my supervisors. Because they also had supervisors. So I kept supervisors off him, so this way I got along with them.

The same identical place, I worked there for thirty-five and a half years, right there in the same place with the same job. In the main office. And I loved it. In '42, '43, you bet I was happy to have a job. The war was going on and I had four children. I didn't spoil my kids, because I wasn't around them too much, I was working all of the time. But they were nice kids, I didn't have any problem out of them.

It was all unionized. The pay was good, real good. [She acknowledges the pay differentials between white and black but emphasizes that these were eventually corrected.]

I noticed the other day I was out there where we would stand under the shed, where we would wait for the bus. The black place is there, and the white place is there. They had a section for the blacks and a section for the whites. I think that was the last thing they had that was exposed about segregation, under that shed where we would stand, one place for blacks to stand, the other was for the whites to stand, under the same shed. This year, I saw that someone had painted over it, they painted over the words, for black and white. I don't know who did that. I laughed about that. Anyway, it was a nice place to work, I'd have to say that. One of the best in Memphis.

I attended the union meetings, and of course, the union dues was deducted from our pay. So we still have our union office out there. We pay thirteen dollars a year now to keep the office going.

I know at one time you had to wear a dress, then you could start to wear pants. I didn't wear pants until, I don't know when it was. The ladies in the plant did wear pants, but [not] the ones in the office, around the office. I wore a white dress. When they could wear pants in the office, then I put on pants too. That was something of a big change while I was there. And everybody was using the same cafeteria—at first we wasn't. They had segregated cafeterias. Eventually they changed that. But they found that the blacks would still stay with the blacks and the whites would still stay with the whites. But it you wanted to, you could go over there. But I guess that's the way we are, birds of a feather, we just flock together. I don't think it really matters about we were wanting to eat with them, or they wanted to eat with us. It was just a matter of if we had wanted to, we would do it.

I had only had one problem there, with this gentlemen. I was going across the plant on this particular morning. Of course, I was probably a little late, and I was eating a sandwich. And I had this paper under my arm, and it fell on the floor. And this gentlemen was not even my supervisor, so he called me and he said, "Who are you?" And I stopped and I looked at him. And this is something I don't like, nobody asks me that. If you want to know who I am, you tell me who you are first. Then I spoke up, I said you want to know who I was, you're supposed to tell me who you are first. So he told me, "Where do you work?" So I wouldn't tell him. He followed me and saw who I was and reported me to my supervisor. He told me to go to the office, but before that time came he told me I didn't have to go. I guess they thought it over, see. That's the only time I had any problems. He wasn't even my supervisor.

Something that was very important to me was by being in first aid, I could do lots of things I shouldn't have done. [laughs] I did do some things. I won't say.[18]

I liked all my supervisors. I could sit and talk with them. I thought it was real nice. I didn't want to work any other place. Some of them call me, and we talk, talk, talk, talk, and we visit each other. I had better friendships with whites than I did with blacks. I did, really.

I just thought everybody was the same and I just treated them like they treated me. You'd be surprised how nice people can be. They wasn't abusive to me.[19] I guess, you know, if you wants a friend, you've got to show yourself friendly. That's the whole thing in a nutshell, show yourself. People ordinarily are good. That's my opinion about it. If you're nasty, they can get nasty too. I was all over the plant, washing water fountains, putting up salt tablets, whatnot. No one was nasty to me. I went there to work. So this is what I did, I worked. I tell people, my goodness, a person can't keep a job if you don't do what a supervisor says. But look what happened. Once the older people left, see what happened, the younger people just wouldn't do it. They would just drink, do dope, and all those times messed up. They just couldn't keep on producing bad tires and being sued. So they had to close the plant. That's the younger generation.

During the time I was there, I turned in I don't remember how many suggestions. They had a contest. It was a white man and myself that tied on those suggestions. So a couple of times I got awards. I had special parking space for a month. Those were some of the things that I did. These were safety suggestions.

18. She was supposed to have nurse's training to dispense medications.
19. Firestone management had exposure to or came from Akron, where racial prejudice was not as strong as in Memphis.

Something else. And you're not going to believe it when I finish saying this. It's the reason I made so many enemies with blacks. It's just an attitude blacks had. Some of the blacks was planning on cutting this white lady in the locker room. These are ladies. And I heard their conversation. They were jealous, you see. I went up there too, and I said [to myself], Well, I'm not going to let them cut this woman. I knew what they're going to do. So when they went up there and they saw me, they didn't bother this lady. They were jealous, just plain jealous, that's all. In those days, you might say that whites was hitting back, blacks was hitting back. This was after the riots, after '68.[20] But those ladies was not bothering those black girls. I know they wasn't bothering them. This was what they was doing, and I just wasn't going to go along with anything like that.

So another time, this supervisor of ours, his name was Mr. Armstrong, he was a very, very sensitive man. They'd upset him, do a lot of things that would upset him. I just didn't appreciate a person doing that. So when Mr. Armstrong came to the bathroom that day, and he knocked on the door, I was in there, and three more of the young ladies were in there. They went to the door and saw Mr. Armstrong and they said, "What are we going to do? We're going to tell a black supervisor that Mr. Armstrong came into this restroom." I couldn't hardly believe my own ears. And I really didn't think that they was going to do that. Mr. Armstrong [had] knocked on the door. They was in there lolling around. So they went to the door and Mr. Armstrong talked with them, then he left.

When they came back about half an hour later they were laughing about it. They had told this black supervisor that Mr. Armstrong had been in the restroom. The black man had called the white man in the office and he bawled that man out like nobody's business. I said [to myself], Oh my god, how can he do that? I just couldn't believe them people. Eventually they got around to calling me. Mr. Armstrong must have said, "Well, Susie was in there, you call her and you ask her." So when they called me in the office, I didn't lie. I said, "He didn't do it, they made up that they was going to say this. Mr. Armstrong did not come in there. He knocked on the door and they went to the door." So this is where I made a lot of enemies. But what was right was right, and what was wrong was wrong, and I wasn't

20. Racial polarization reached its height in Memphis following the murder of Dr. King in 1968.

going to stand there and let this happen to somebody else, just because I was black and they was black.

Then they had decided they was going to get me. This black lady told me that they had decided that, but she and her husband, I didn't know this, they followed me out. The husband had said they was going to get me outside the gates, so they followed me out. These were the things that happened. We bringed a lot of things on ourselves, I know that. I know about those cases. One time blacks claim a white man, a young white worker, was on top of the roof, peeking through a window at them in the bathroom. But I don't believe it.

But this is what they would do. I just didn't go along with it. It was wrong. I would go, "I'm not with you." This is why I made so many enemies. Maybe you'd better scratch that out. [laughs] Anyway, I had a lot of respect for the whites, and they had it for me. And I had a lot of respect for the blacks, if they wanted to be respected.

After I retired, these same girls called out to Mr. Armstrong's house and told him they were sorry. They sure did. I was so glad to hear that.

Rebecca McKinley Remembers the Strike at Memphis Furniture Company

I just didn't go back. I didn't want to give them
the pleasure of firin' me.

I searched high and low for survivors of the momentous 1949 Memphis Furniture strike, the failure of which destroyed the United Furniture Workers for some twenty years at one of the largest sites of black female factory employment in Memphis. I finally found Rebecca McKinley. She had written a poem used by strike supporters and gone on the radio as a spokesperson for the strikers. She was now blind and had lost much of her memory, but retained a sense of humor and consented to tell me what she could remember when I reached her by phone in 1983.

That was a long time ago. So many things . . . so many people I've forgotten. I'm an old woman now.

During World War II, I worked at Plough [a pharmaceutical company that turned to military production during the war]. I made 20 mm bullet boxes. They didn't have black women, I mean they had black women but they weren't *black* women. I mean they had lighter women, real light brown, had hair hangin' down below your shoulders or you didn't get on there at that time. They just hired light-skinned people, with real long pretty hair.

That's what I'm talkin' about. I take it you're white. I guess you know that blacks discriminate against each other. But that's the first place and only place that I've known that the bosses did that. I guess somebody around there just didn't like the look of real dark people. So they just didn't have anything to do with them. I've never heard of it anywhere else.

I think it was '44 when I started [at Memphis Furniture]. I was in the department that made chifforobe [a combination of wardrobe and chest of drawers] doors. Mr. Cecil Foster was the foreman. He's one of the nicest men I ever worked for. Lewis Thomas was the president of the local when I worked there. That was Local 282 [of the United Furniture Workers].

My brother-in-law got me the job and was working there when the CIO and the AF of L, both of them, wanted to come into the plant. He'd been around St. Louis and he didn't like the way the AF of L treated the blacks. Some of the locals, blacks couldn't join in St. Louis. He held that in his mind when he was working at the Memphis Furniture Factory. So he knew he wasn't going to join the AF of L. My brother-in-law didn't hesitate to tell me that the CIO was the one to join. My brother-in-law was the one that was workin' there when they organized it. I have forgotten what year it was. But the CIO was already established in the factory when I went there.[21] They bargained for what they could get in the contract, which wasn't very much. It was just two sheets of paper, most of it sayin' that they [the company] recognized the union.

All I had known about a union was readin' in the paper about [CIO President] John L. Lewis. We hurried to get the paper to see what John L. Lewis was doin' and that's all I ever knew.

[The 1949 strike was over] wages and workin' conditions. Wages were less than fifty cents [an hour], I think. We had long hours without a break. Restrooms were situated where you could look under the door at your feet, anybody could look, men or women.

21. The CIO won its first representation election there on April 28, 1942.

Some of the foremen rushed the people who were working, to the extent that they couldn't hardly make a thing. If they got fired there wasn't a lot that could be done, although the [union] president would do the best he could to get them back. But without proper contracts, you know, there wasn't a lot that he could do.

When we went on strike, I think they called them squads.[22] I had the early squad, something like six o'clock for two or three days. After that I was at the union hall because they wanted handwritten letters to thank the people, far and near, for the donations, because there weren't any funds in the treasury and they existed on donations from far and near. . . . A lot of people did wrap up [wear sacks on] their feet.

It was lost, because some of the people got other jobs, some went back [to work]. They took big old trucks, called eighteen-wheelers I guess, and would go to the people that weren't union members, and would go to certain locations and pick 'em up, and back that big truck up to the factory's ramp or dock. That's where they'd get the men so that the strikers couldn't harm them or yell at them. They just hauled them in. So, of course, we lost the strike.

A little group would get in one of the little rooms and decide what they goin' to do to the company truck, and what time. But, this man was in it, he would have some reason to stop on the way, to call somebody, he'd have some reason. He's the only one in the group that wasn't with them about every minute. And when they'd get to the place the police would be there. So they almost knew he was the one tellin' the company people.

The police carried people to jail, but I didn't ever see that. I'd go out there sometimes and stand on the sidewalk. I never did see the police harm anybody, but they arrested them. Somebody would say that they'd done something, threw a brick or a rock, or something like that. We had a young man that they kept him two or three days at the union hall and didn't let him go anywhere and still his name would come up. They'd tell the police that he had done something to them. But everybody knew that he wasn't doin' it because he was in the union hall. I mean, that's the way things went.

They had court hearings and some would come clear and some wouldn't. Somehow they managed to get out of jail.

22. Groups of union members who used to convince others to strike were known as "flying squadrons."

Other unions gave us support, especially Firestone. They had a commissary up to the union hall. People got food there, but I sort of supported myself. I already had some money. I could have gotten food, it was there for me. I just didn't take it. They [the United Furniture Workers] paid the rent for me. Some had a harder time. Some had other jobs. That's the way they existed.

[Memphis Furniture] had five times, maybe ten times more blacks than whites. Most of the white men were machine operators. The upholsters, I never did go in there—it was a separate building. They were white women. We didn't ever see them. They didn't join the union. They upholstered chairs and sofas. Now there was a few black women that worked in there but they serviced those white women.

The blacks did machine work, too. There were so many more blacks than whites. There were just a few whites. There wasn't a white person in my department, only the foreman, who was very nice. That's the only white person there. Across from me in another section, that's all there was, black women with a few black men. The real large section, on the third floor, was the same thing. There wasn't many white people that worked there.

I think there were seven hundred that went on strike. I think that's what they said. But the upholstery department kept on working as long as they could. When some departments stopped they had to stop too. But they kept on working a while.

I don't remember seeing any white people [on strike or] at the union hall, other than the union officials. And I was there all the time.

There is so much I've forgotten I can't tell you much about it. All I know is the picket line and the way they broke the strike was haulin' all the scabs in. There were some union members that went back to work too, but not a lot of them. But some did go back, even before they started to haul them in their trucks. The company trucks were red, white, and blue. That's the way they are still.

They [the strikers] just went about their business [after the strike]. Some got jobs. Some were related to members who used their influence to get them jobs at their plants. That's the way I got on at U.S. Bedding. This man was some officer in the union and so he got me on at U.S. Bedding because we had worked together in the union. He gave me a real nice job.

You know, it's very discouraging when you know you're not goin' to get back because they're haulin' people in big old trucks like that. And those

people had no idea about that and no conscience about our union. Some
still don't. So they didn't mind crossin' the picket line before they started
to haulin' them in.

But you know, they had to come out and people would do them in
sometimes. Some of the strikers would beat them up. So then the company
started haulin' them in.

They [the scabs] had come from the country but some of them was
born and reared right here in the city. It's just that the unions were new
here. [The] Firestone [union] hadn't been there a lot of years. Some people
never heard about them havin' a union. The people were not informed.
This is the reason they went in.

One woman would jump over the fence and get beat up and go right
back in the next day. She was determined. She wanted that job. That was
one of the scabs. They said that she jumped over a fence one day that a
man couldn't jump over, gettin' away from the people who was goin' to
beat her up. And they did beat her up a couple of times, but that didn't
stop her. She was desperate.

They would take chances. And then the company made it convenient
for them, that is, if you want to ride in the truck with no windows in it,
like cattle. Just like you see the cows goin' to slaughter, that's the way they
were. I looked at them back them big trucks up there and you could see
them jumpin' out of there and goin' into the plant. Some of them got
doors that fasten on the sides. They had them open and you could see
the people standin' in there. Some standin', some sittin'. They really
wanted jobs.

So it was people bein' uninformed is the reason that we lost the strike.
And the company helped them by makin' it convenient for them to get in,
if you call that convenient.

It was new then. See, I don't think that the people were really informed
about unions and the idea of paying union dues, because when I started
you didn't have a checkoff system. You go on a Monday morning, and
there's somebody collectin' for the union dues. Some would readily pay. It
was about one dollar and fifty cents at that time and I was on that committee for collectin' union dues [from various plants]. It's not easy. That's one
thing that made the union weak because for so long they didn't have a
checkoff system.

Every day, especially on pay days, they would send out a committee to
solicit at the plant gate. You would collect them anywhere you could run

into somebody, on your lunch period, because you didn't have a break period then. They didn't have a smokin' area, [so] if you smoked, you went to work at seven o'clock. And the people who smoked, they didn't get a chance to smoke any more until twelve o'clock. Memphis Furniture is the one where you had to go out in the cold, in the rain, and line up and go by the window and get your check. But after the union interceded they started to bringin' the checks around inside and I know that was much better. It was a small matter, but when you're standin' out there a-shiverin' it's not a small matter.

One man went on collection at one of the big plants, the gate collection you know, on payday. You know, they'd collect a lot of money. And he said, a grown man now, said that the wind blew the money away. He didn't get to the union hall with it because he said the wind blew it away. He had it in a shoe box or a cigar box and the wind blew it away. You know a grown man ain't going to let the wind blow it away. Anybody would know to lay a piece of brick or something in there to hold it down to keep the wind from blowing it while you put your hand in. I wouldn't go and tell somebody that, would you? A lot of funny things happened.

During the strike, Mr. Walter Carson[23] kept telling me about communism and asked me did they approach me. But I said I didn't feel I should have to tell him that. There were some people ahead of their time. We had a number of people, black and white, help out in the strike. All of these were not UFWA people, just union supporters. Like Ed McCrea, but also a black man from Louisiana and a preacher from Henderson, North Carolina. I knew Red Davis too. Charles Coeburn was also well informed and educated.[24] I think he was a Communist. He and I went to the Urban League building on Beale Street, and he refused to sit at the front but instead sat in the back with me. He wanted to walk right beside me, and I told him he couldn't do that. We sat at the back and he took my coat off. They [the whites] all looked very strangely at me. But he didn't go for any flirting, you couldn't tempt him.

They had a youth conference in New York and Ed McCrea and two

23. Carson was a UFWA district leader who favored purging the union's Communists. This issue nearly split the union. See chapter 5 for more details.

24. Coeburn worked for the UFWA. Ed McCrea worked as business agent for Local 19 of the FTA and had been a district organizer for the Communist Party, a post that Red Davis, a National Maritime Union member and port agent, took up after the war.

ladies from a union and a young man, we went to the conference to solicit money for the union. And when I came back somebody showed me the newspaper clipping, and my name was in it, that we went to a Communist meeting. We did go to a hall with a lot of people, and Paul Robeson sang there. I went to the meeting because I wanted to go to New York City.[25] Ed McCrea and Red Davis both approached me about being a Communist, but I couldn't understand why it was so good over in the Communist countries. If you're going to live in this country, you shouldn't undermine it. I'm not for communism, but I'm not for this system either. Why do people have to be so poor when we can go to the moon? So many things I see that I just can't understand.

I didn't go back to Memphis Furniture after the strike was over. I went on and wrote this poem [during the strike], it went all over. I just knew that the bosses over there had read that poem. There wasn't anything bad in there, but it said a lot of things. I can rhyme anything I know a lot about, so I did call some names. So I just didn't go back. I didn't want to give them the pleasure of firin' me. After that, I was working at a table factory. We also organized that plant. It was a small plant, but we did organize it.

The collective story that black workers tell is a deeply gendered one. Although black women appear throughout this volume, these life stories of some of the early pioneers in the industrial unions suggest that they were uniquely situated. The Firestone women clearly understood how the trajectory of their work lives was tied to the fate of their children, and their unionism and attention to community issues revolved around that fact. Because the wages of these women all supported their families and because both race and gender discrimination severely limited their opportunities, they of all workers had the most to gain by unionization. For Irene Branch, "freedom" meant unionization, first of all because the union saved her job when many other black women (including her sister) were being laid off at the end of World War II. Second, the union made Firestone "a good place to work" instead of the hell hole in which she began. It raised her wages, improved her working conditions, and, under pressure from black workers and civil rights forces, eventually opened up higher paying jobs to blacks. "By working in Firestone, I have accumu-

25. This was a meeting of the Communist-led Civil Rights Congress.

lated about as much as anybody with my education and opportunity," she concludes. Indeed, the wages of these women may have been better than most black women teachers, nurses, or others who found some alternative to domestic employment. As a result, they had an above average ability, in a mostly poor black community, to raise and educate their children.

The Firestone women understandably felt good about what they had achieved for themselves and their families through hard work and unionization. But the double duty of raising children and working prevented them from becoming union activists. Unions in heavy mass-production industries remained mostly the preserve of men, and mostly white men at that. Evelyn Bates had to work in the evenings, when the union met, while women who worked in the day undoubtedly remained at home in the evening with their children. The union, though interracial, remained male space, reflecting the considerable differences in opportunities available to black men and women. Child-rearing made it impossible for most black women workers to take a leadership role. Although they had the most to gain from unionization, they had the least time to devote to it.

Despite all that, black women proved as supportive as black men of unions and made an alliance with these men. Branch observes that black men "really went through with something," coming into industry during a reign of terror against unions and daily abuse in the factories. Their pioneering role helped make it possible for her and later generations to get jobs at the plant under relatively more favorable wartime conditions, when the federal government was pressuring mass-production employers into signing union contracts and hiring blacks. Yet the early generation of both black women and men still had to "take it" to keep their jobs. This was particularly the case for black women, who could count on one hand the other factories that would employ them.

These women of necessity tread a fine line between accommodation and resistance to racism. A later generation hired during the era of civil rights upheavals would disdain the ethic of "taking it" in favor of a more militant response to white racism, which, according to Susie Wade, sometimes went beyond the bounds of reason after Martin Luther King's death in 1968. This younger generation could easily misunderstand the older group, seeing their willingness to "take it" as passive acquiescence to racism. Some of the older people, on the other hand, felt the younger generation tended to be lazy, unreliable, and too materialistic. Branch and Wade both thought the irresponsible behavior of younger workers caused the Firestone plant to close—a belief that Clarence Coe convincingly discounts (see chapter 4). This generation gap resulted in part because the older group had so far to go and so much to gain, while blacks entering the workforce in the 1960s benefited from the radically changed circumstances wrought by three decades of unionism and from the emergence of a strong civil rights movement. Younger workers often took for granted what had been gained and did not feel the urgent need to stay in the industry in the same way the older group had.

Of course, the line between accommodation and resistance to racism and exploitation could sometimes be so fine that people could not discern it. Was working hard and "taking it" in order to feed one's family resistance or accommodation? Personal responsibility and hard work, forms of both resistance and accommodation, remained a constant part of the black working-class struggle for survival, even as union and civil rights initiatives began to redefine what "taking it" was all about.

While black workers all faced racial discrimination and repression, their opportunities and experiences differed a great deal by job, by gender, by generation, by region, and by industry. For the few black women working at Firestone who managed to make a career there, for example, "taking it" proved far more fruitful than it did in smaller and less profitable industries. Rebecca McKinley recalls the more active role that black women played in the strike at the Memphis Furniture plant but, at the same time, how little they got out of their endeavors. Subsequent generations of black labor organizers picked up this struggle where McKinley had left off, taking a union originally built by Communist and Socialist European immigrants in New York and turning it toward civil rights unionism (see chapters 5 and 6). Yet in the lowest-waged factories and in service and hospital work, they would continue to fight frustrating battles with stingy employers over low wages and bad conditions.

The stories in this chapter and throughout the book suggest how working-class black women used work and unions to further the next generation. While this necessitated some degree of accommodation to things as they were, unionists also pushed forward the struggle for a better life. As civil rights and union rights consciousness came to permeate black America during and after World War II, black workers redrew the line between "taking it" and openly fighting back. Their struggle for change would be increasingly at odds with the images many whites had of black women and men as contented servants.

INTERLUDE

NOT WHAT WE SEEM

Each day when you see us black folk upon the dusty land of the
farms or upon the hard pavement of the city streets, you usually take
us for granted and think you know us, but our history is far stranger
than you suspect, and we are not what we seem.

Richard Wright, *Twelve Million Black Voices*

Many white southerners maintained an elaborate pretense that
African Americans living under segregation were contented,
even happy. They could maintain this pretense only by keeping blacks silent, but the pretense wore thin from the 1940s onward as
blacks increasingly asserted their citizenship rights. During World War II,
blacks and whites alike flooded into crowded cities as industrial employment shot up to support a booming war economy. Gone were the days
of depression. In Memphis, twenty-eight thousand manufacturing workers, part of a larger group of forty thousand wage workers, now competed
for jobs, housing, and space on public conveyances in a rapidly growing
city of some three hundred thousand souls. By 1940, Memphis had also
reached a new high point of black migration into the city, now about
40 percent black.[1]

In this changing context, African Americans found new ways and more
opportunities to contest the rules of white supremacy. In particular, the
narratives in this book suggest, new workplace opportunities opened up
new struggles against Jim Crow. However, much of the black contestation

1. The Memphis population went from 253,153 in 1930 (37 percent black) to
292,942 in 1940 (41 percent black) to 396,000 in 1950 (37 percent black).

against racism, suggests historian Robin Kelley, "remained unorganized, clandestine, and evasive." Unions or civil rights organizations were not available to many African American workers, particularly in the South, nor could they encompass the many life situations that called forth black resistance. Daily acts of resistance, sometimes furtive or buffered by the presence of black onlookers, created a dissident black culture and discourse that provided part of the context for mass, organized protest. Much of this remained hidden from white eyes, and yet open resistance sometimes also erupted into a form of public theater, as Kelley calls it, in the "congested terrain" of cities during wartime.

Later generations will never know the full extent of the dissident black culture that existed under Jim Crow, but the narrators here highlight some of its dimensions. By their accounts, the war itself heightened black expectations and anger. Segregation clearly contradicted the antifascist rhetoric of freedom and equality the war generated. In the South, black soldiers were beaten in the streets by whites merely for wearing a U.S. military uniform, perhaps because such uniforms suggested that they were full citizens or that there might be a higher power than a local or state government. The contradiction between the rhetoric and practice of democracy could hardly have been more obvious.

George Holloway and other black Pullman porters focused on this contradiction when the segregation laws forced them to eat in the kitchen while German prisoners of war ate from good china and linens in the "whites only" dining area during a train stop in Arkansas. Such gross discrimination rankled the sense of fair play of many Americans; fifty years later civil rights leader Jesse Jackson still remembered an incident of discrimination suffered by his father as a worker on the trains during the war. In his own case, Holloway and his union successfully pressured the railroads to create better conditions for porters. Holloway felt that the wartime rhetoric of democracy would open up conditions for blacks in the larger society as well.

Clarence Coe's recollection of Corrine Smith's experience does not have such a happy ending. Smith was beaten, jailed, and fired by Firestone in 1944 for trying to enter a city bus before it had filled up with whites. A wildcat strike by black Firestone workers in response demonstrated that they would not tolerate such brutality. Their walkout exemplified a largely spontaneous but growing black resistance to the many degrading practices of Jim Crow, particularly the segregated seating arrangements on city buses.

Memphis segregation laws mandated that blacks fill conveyances from the back, whites from the front, with blacks always standing or sitting behind the whites. This movable reminder of supposed black inferiority provided many occasions for rebellion, especially during the war. In one case, an interracial group of sailors physically threatened a bus driver who tried to move them. "This is America," they told him, and they would sit where they wanted. In another instance, police arrested a black woman teacher who refused to give up her seat to a white boy, who struck her. Her minister and two thousand members of her congregation protested to the mayor. A black man in another case refused to give up his seat to a white, and when leaving the bus blurted out to the driver and the passengers, "This is that damned democracy you all been talking about."

Black workers, the great majority of those riding the buses, normally followed segregation's rules, but they demanded respect within those rules. They got tired of standing, and when whites would not move forward and make room for them their patience ended and their rebellion began. In these "public theaters" white bus drivers could sometimes only look on while black knife-toters or snickering teenagers at the back of the bus put some white man in his place. By the postwar era, intimations of black rebellion seemed to be everywhere. As Leroy Boyd and Alzada Clark tell us, African Americans utilized whatever theaters existed, in the voting booth as well as on the bus, to express their hostility to Jim Crow.

GEORGE HOLLOWAY

In 1941 when the war was starting, I became a Pullman porter. A. Philip Randolph met me in New York and asked me to be a junior organizer for the Pullman porters' union [Brotherhood of Sleeping Car Porters (BSCP)]. My job was to carry cards and wherever we stopped, I'd get people who didn't yet belong signed up, and then I'd turn in the cards to Randolph in New York. These were the young, extra porters who came in when they were transporting soldiers. The older porters were already pretty well organized when I came in.

I was located in the South: Atlanta, New Orleans, Birmingham, Montgomery, Richmond, mostly. Oakland, California, was another place I did a lot of signing up. Oakland was a center for the soldiers' cars to switch.

There were lots of boot camps in California. They weren't giving the young Pullman porters very good pay or benefits, so we needed to get in the union and be strong enough to get the things we wanted. The younger ones were the ones who changed the wage structure. Back in '41, they were only paying about twenty dollars a week for Pullman porters. We changed that. Another thing we changed with A. Philip Randolph was that we could borrow money against our paychecks.

During the war, I was on the train that carried President Roosevelt to Mexico. I wasn't drafted into the war, because we got exemptions for being porters. I was one of the six Pullman porters who picked up German soldiers in California and carried them to Mississippi. We stopped in Little Rock, Arkansas, that morning, and they fed the German prisoners in that beautiful, crystal dining room. They put the six Pullman porters in the kitchen. I was one of them. It came out in the newspapers all over, about the prisoners being served in the crystal dining room, and the black porters being served in the kitchen.

When I got home, my wife had an article from the paper that asked [Mississippi] Senator Bilbo if he had heard about this incident about the Pullman porters in the kitchen, and what did he think about it. He said, "The Germans are white, aren't they? Well, that's all right." My wife cut that out of the paper, because I had written to her about that day.

Anyway, after that incident in the kitchen, the black Pullman porters decided they weren't going to take that kind of treatment anymore. The union demanded that we would stay in hotels or in Pullman cars instead of YMCAs and places like that, and they paid the bills. The publicity in the paper helped, along with Webster and Randolph.[2] So we gained the right to stay in good accommodations.

CLARENCE COE

[At Firestone], the city buses would come and turn around right there in front of the plant gate. And the whites would load first. And if there was any vacancies on the back seat, you could pay your fee, and come in the back. You would pay up front, but then go in the back. They weren't

---

2. Milton Webster was first vice president and A. Philip Randolph was first president of the Brotherhood of Sleeping Car Porters.

going to let you in the front. They [white passengers] were going on first, and then you couldn't break into line, because you'd have to touch up against them.

[Coe relates how, one day in 1944, black worker Corrine Smith became angry with this procedure and tried to get on the bus without waiting for it to be filled with whites first. The security guard slugged her in the mouth, knocking out a tooth, and the Memphis police arrested her.] All of the blacks walked out [of the factory].[3] That resulted in a lawsuit that she won, and she got back to the plant. And she was picked on so much that she eventually left. Her and another woman. I mean, they [white workers] could keep that pressure on. She sued them for firing her unjustly. They had to bring her back and pay her. But they just stayed on her behind. And she wasn't super bright, and being a woman, too, you could very easily overtax her in job assignment, and so forth. They just made it so damn rough out there, she quit.

So I just kept some kind of old car, and come hell or high water, stayed off the buses to stay out of trouble. In certain places in the South they had curtains on the train. If you went to some towns back in those days, like Jackson, Mississippi, if your bus or train had a layover, you'd better not get off. But yet, when it came time to serve [in the military], you had to go in. Suffer and die, too, for freedom that you'd better not even act like you wanted when you got out! You'd just better not.

LEROY BOYD

After working on the job, I'm standing up. I used to ride, and go to catch the crosstown [bus] and transfer to 13 and go to the end of south Memphis. Shoot! On that line, it was bad. You couldn't sit down if a white was sitting in this seat and the [empty] seat was up there [in front of him]. You know, whites had the front of the bus. When we get on the bus, the bus would be full. And as it gets to them white neighborhoods, see, they'd [whites] be getting off. And [the white passenger], he's going to just sit back there after all those other got off the bus, and [he] wouldn't move up. And people standing up all in the aisle. He'd just sit there and look out the window.

---

3. Whites later walked out of the plant when the plant guard was disciplined, closing the whole factory.

I asked him real nice. I said, "Would you mind moving up to the front?" He just sat there. You ask him. You gave him a chance to move. He wouldn't move. Shoot, I just sat on down in front of him! I've did that many, many a time. He better not have said nothing to me. I'd be getting ready to mop that bus with him!

So I'll sit on down in front of you. There was quite a few of them [blacks] that would do that. They would respect it if that's the law, you know, by asking him to move up. And he wouldn't move, then sit on down in front of him. Just sit down. You don't start no ruckus with anybody. You just take your seat.

At that time, there was no Negro bus drivers. All the bus drivers was white. We had one on that 13, we used to call him Big John. He was a driver about six foot tall, weighed about two hundred something. And boy, he meant to be *tough*, you know. But he never did buck that. He just played it off. He'd act like he didn't see you. He knowed the guy was wrong. People want to sit down and he wouldn't move up. He'd act like he didn't see it. So Negroes then, they wasn't afraid.

Of course, the Negroes then—Negroes have always toted pocket knives. I guess any old policeman would tell you that. That's one thing black people will do here. They will cut you. So if one started arguing back, he run his hand in his pocket. So, you know, that would cease the argument. Yeah, if you had a knife in your pocket. Not a gun! You know. You started exchanging words, you put your hand in your pocket.

Yeah, Negroes was always toting those. That's way back in the forties. Switchblade knives. A little blade on it that long. Yep. That's all we had. That was our weapon. It wasn't all these guns and things on the street now.

ALZADA CLARK

We staged a protest on a bus on my way to work downtown at the five and ten cent store, long before I knew anything about unions or worked at a company that had one. There were plenty of empty seats up front, and the black seats were full all the way to the back. There was a long empty seat in the white section that no one was sitting on, so an old black lady sat down. A white man was sitting on the other end, and he told her to get up. She said, "Well, I'm tired."

We told her not to get up, and he reached over to hit her, and I kicked him. The white man told the bus driver to stop the bus and get after the niggers in the back. The men in the back stood up, and I heard one man's knife go "click," and he said, "Driver, drive on, everything is under control back here." He told the old lady to stay sitting, and told another one standing to sit next to her. He told the white man to get up, and then he told someone else to sit down. [laughs] All the way downtown, the white people stood up until that guy finally got off. When the bus stopped at the end of the line downtown, the police were there, but most of the original crew had gotten off somewhere along the line. That kind of incident was rare then, except for school kids once in a while. That was around 1950. All of the bus drivers were white at that time. We didn't get black bus drivers until after the civil rights movement in the 1960s.

The first strike I ever heard about was in June of 1952. It was a CTA [bus company] strike. The whole city was paralyzed. People were walking and carpooling, and I was hoping those bus drivers would get what they wanted. I didn't resent the white bus drivers. [But] blacks weren't really into that strike because there weren't black drivers. Most of the work the blacks were doing was washing buses and things like that.

LEROY BOYD

[The Crump machine] was the shackle that they [blacks] had to break. They say he used to do to Negroes, election eve, he'd go around, buy up a lot of watermelon, truckloads of watermelons. [laughs] Cut watermelons, let them eat them. Shoot! So what he said, it went. Policemen, he controlled everything here.

I was part of the vote to get Crump out. This was done through the union. Our union really was playing an active role in telling the people what they had to do if they wanted to change the conditions of the city. That you must prepare yourself and vote. You get out and vote. You can go up to the courthouse and register to vote. And I stood in line for four hours up there at the courthouse trying to get registered to vote. Shoot! I remember that line was a long line. You know, they can use psychology on you. They can register you real slow and make the people in line get tired of being in line and leave, see. It got late, late that evening, but I got registered. And a lot of people were wanting to go up and register, and they wanted to exercise their right to do it.

Black civil rights consciousness had always been present in the South, going back to Ida B. Wells-Barnett and earlier, but its open expression had been suppressed. By the time of the bus incidents described by Boyd and Clark that suppression was no longer working. By the 1950s, Richard Wright's warning that "we are not what we seem" must have hit home to many whites. Clearly, blacks did not look like the docile simpletons pictured in the racist cartoons of the Memphis *Commercial Appeal* or the Hollywood films of America's Jim Crow era. When the Supreme Court's *Brown v. Board of Education* decision finally ruled segregation in schools unconstitutional in 1954, it set off rolling waves of increasingly overt black resistance. In Montgomery, Alabama, a mass movement of predominantly poor and working-class African Americans went on to win completely unsegregated bus seating in 1955. Clearly, the time for breaking Jim Crow was at hand.

As blacks began to battle for equality in public accommodations, they also increasingly demanded the right to participate in a meaningful way in another public space: the voting booth. Never completely disfranchised in Tennessee, Memphis blacks had always voted, but only at the discretion of Boss Crump. As early as 1948, black and white workers in Leroy Boyd's Local 19 combined with other CIO unionists, most of them white, to defeat Crump's candidate for U.S. Senate. Crump's loss of Shelby County resulted in the statewide election of southern liberal Estes Kefauver, an upset that marked the beginning of the end of Crump's seemingly invincible rule. Unionized workers could afford to pay their own poll tax and no longer voted on Boss Crump's terms. Similar dynamics in some other parts of the postwar South resulted in the election of a significant number of relatively more progressive white politicians, and in Winston-Salem, North Carolina, unionized black voters spearheaded the election of the first black alderman since Reconstruction. As George Holloway recounts in the next chapter, his United Auto Workers also sued shortly thereafter to end the poll tax, and they succeeded in getting it annulled in Tennessee.

As the testimony here suggests, African Americans resisted white domination at many levels. In addition to struggling with white employers and white workers over the terms of work and of unionization, black workers also spent a lot of their lives building civic networks, the NAACP, churches, and self-help, neighborhood, and youth programs. This activity got stronger as their positions in the factories improved; as they unionized and made higher wages, their churches and neighborhoods prospered as well. Black workers also helped to mobilize voting rights activity and political action. And they participated in everyday, individualized, and spontaneous forms of resistance to Jim Crow. Within their families, churches, juke joints, beauty shops, and through the artistry of generations of black musicians for which Memphis is so famous, African Americans kept alive a struggle that went deeper and lasted longer than the momentous occasions for mass protest.

Throughout the rest of this volume, black union veterans testify to some of the ways that they participated in the quest for freedom. Industrial unions and the factory workplace provided them with a form of public theater not available to most workers. As black workers struggled for union protections, wage increases, vacation time, health benefits, and for a voice in union affairs, they also began to openly challenge the restrictions of Jim Crow at work.

In helping to create an economic backbone for black community life and the advancement of their children's generation, they carried out their own protracted guerilla war to end Jim Crow. For the workers who tell their stories here, that war lasted a lifetime.

4 FREEDOM STRUGGLES AT THE POINT OF PRODUCTION

> You had to fight for every inch. . . . Nobody gave you anything.
>
> Clarence Coe

Much as civil rights activists pursued the freedom struggle through practical attacks on specific aspects of segregation, black union activists tried to break the Jim Crow system down step by step at the point of production. They first sought the right to unionize, sometimes risking their lives merely to achieve that right. Secondarily, they sought to use unions to end workplace discrimination, including separate and color-coded hiring lists, rates of pay, and seniority lines for white and black that, among other practices, kept blacks in the worst paid, dirtiest, and most dangerous jobs. Beyond these workplace goals, black labor activists looked hopefully toward the ultimate eradication of Jim Crow.

The larger historical context in many ways dictated the pace of change and the degree of the activists' success. The opportunities for real change emerged with World War II. Antifascist rhetoric highlighted the obvious contradiction of fighting to save democracy while protecting Jim Crow, and A. Philip Randolph seized that contradiction to threaten a mass march on Washington to protest black exclusion from industry. In response, President Franklin Roosevelt set up the federal Fair Employment Practice Committee, which scrutinized racist hiring and promotion policies. The federal government also began to force industries with war contracts to abide by the Wagner National Labor Relations Act's guarantee of workers' right to organize unions. As floods of rural blacks came to urban industrial centers to gain a new economic foothold, the National Labor Relations Board, created by the act, enabled many of them to vote in union representation elections and to organize on the job, rights long denied to them in the larger society. Even before the first black serviceman returned from the war abroad, a new war for equal rights began in southern workplaces. In this war at home, black workers battled on two fronts, with white workers and with employers.

Black workers had understandable hopes that the postwar period would set off major social change, and to some extent it did. A disproportionate share of African American men had joined the military, serving honorably and well, while workers at home had gone along with wage freezes and seven-day workweeks to help the war effort. Like whites, black workers and returning soldiers expected to be rewarded for their service to the nation. Expectations for change rose further when workers across the United States engaged in a huge wave of strikes in 1946 to recoup earnings lost to wartime wage freezes and inflation. At the same time, the CIO began a campaign, called "Operation Dixie," to organize the nonunion shops of the South. In workplaces with large numbers of blacks, southern unions made some headway. Clarence Coe and other activists also began signing up factory workers for a rapidly expanding NAACP. In 1948, black and labor votes returned Harry Truman to the presidency, and the Democratic Party adopted a civil rights plank. And by 1954, the Supreme Court's *Brown v. Board of Education* decision opened the floodgates to equal rights initiatives. In the postwar era, the struggle for democracy was on the move, and black unionists knew it.

People like George Holloway thought this period would cause whites to at last shed their prejudices, and some did. Some white war veterans came home more interested in unions and liberal politics, and a variety of progressive organizations sprouted up in the South and elsewhere. Not just radicals but mainstream white unionists began to support interracial unionism. Richard Routon, for example, came to Memphis from rural west Tennessee with the racial prejudices typical of southern whites. Yet he helped establish the CIO's United Rubber Workers Local 186 during the war by convincing whites that the union had to represent white and black equally. Later on, after participating in an interracial delegation to a national union convention and integrated labor classes at Highlander Folk School, he began to see segregation as not only inconvenient but wrong. George "Rip" Clark, president of Local 186 in the mid-1950s, came to similar conclusions. Other mainstream union leaders in the Memphis CIO, such as its director, Red Copeland, were outright segregationists, yet even they understood the need to respond to the demands of black workers for organization. Furthermore, a small group of white Communists and leftists—Red Davis, Ed McCrea, Karl Korstad, Lawrence McGurty, and others—openly opposed segregation in the postwar years and did much to build an interracial CIO. Indeed, it would never have been built without the courage and commitment of a number of farseeing white liberals and radicals as well as that of black workers.

By the mid-1940s, blacks clearly had white allies in the CIO unions. Yet how far and how fast they could press for change at the workplace remained an open question. While blacks almost always joined the CIO when they had the chance, the biggest initial problem for CIO organizers, aside from Boss Crump and the police, was getting the majority of whites to understand that they could have no power until they joined with blacks in the same union. Given the pervasiveness of white supremacy, winning a large number of whites to this simple proposition proved no small feat. Under the pressure of wartime support for unionization by federal manpower and production policies, unprecedented numbers of workers—some thirty thousand of them in Memphis—did join CIO unions. But the commitment of most white workers to interracialism remained questionable at best.

Black workers understood the tenuous nature of their alliance with white workers, and at first did not quibble about the terms of their initial inclusion into industrial unions. But after the first phase of unionization and in the postwar climate of social ferment, blacks began to press for an end to the maze of discrimination they faced at work. Never content just to have a union, they also wanted equal rights. Yet as they pressed their demands, they found that most white unionists still expected to keep segregation. This hard reality undercut the CIO's Operation Dixie unionization campaign, as many whites refused to join the CIO or chose ineffective segregated units under the AFL. Even when white workers did join CIO unions, most expected blacks to remain subordinate to whites, sit in the back or on the side of the union hall, and stay in the worst jobs.

Other forces accentuated white resistance to interracial organizing and equal rights policies. The CIO's much heralded effort to organize the South hit a brick wall of police and company violence, firings of unionists, and virulent anti-union propaganda from chambers of commerce and evangelical Christian organizations. Republicans in 1946 regained control of Congress by attacking unions and "communism," and continued to level that charge at almost anyone who stood up for New Deal liberalism, unions, or civil rights. As Leroy Clark explains in chapter 5, Republican passage of the Taft-Hartley law in 1947 also encouraged state "right to work" laws outlawing the union shop and weakened the right to strike, while loyalty and security laws at the national level promoted a massive scare over the supposed influence of communism on American life. Southern "Dixiecrats," who controlled the key committees in Congress, began a movement to block civil rights initiatives within the Democratic Party. The *Brown* decision set off an even more rabid defense of segregation, led by the White Citizens Councils, southern politicians, and the Ku Klux Klan. Virulent opposition to black equality and unions, along with political inquisitions at home and military interventions abroad, became hallmarks of American political life in the 1950s.

In this poisoned climate, many white workers joined violent anti-desegregation movements. Even though racism had weakened unions in the South and led to wages far lower than in other parts of the country, many southern whites clung to its supposed privileges. During Operation Dixie, CIO leaders focused on signing up white recruits in the massive southern textile industry, to little avail, while often ignoring black workers, the strongest supporters of unions. Even when CIO organizing included blacks, many unions still negotiated contracts that ratified rather than challenged discrimination. In Memphis, as elsewhere, white workers organized "pro-Southerner" groups within CIO unions that were often tied to the White Citizens Councils. As many as three-fourths of the White Citizens Council members in the Birmingham, Alabama, area allegedly belonged to unions, and one source claims that 80 percent of the whites in George Holloway's United Auto Workers local at International Harvester belonged. As white supremacy groups tried to dominate or secede from CIO unions, the red scare began to fracture the CIO internally.

The narrators in this chapter do not refer to all these developments, but they certainly shaped the context in which the following stories took place. With few allies, and largely unheralded and unnoticed by the larger society, black union activists in the 1940s and 1950s undertook extremely tough battles to desegregate their workplaces and their unions. Clarence Coe, Lonnie Roland, and George Holloway suggest some of their methods. Of particular interest is the successful suit filed by blacks at Firestone Tire and Rubber Company, in the aftermath of the *Brown* decision, charging both the United Rubber Workers Local 186 and Firestone with violating their contract and the union's constitution, both of which prohibited discrimination. Most CIO unions and many CIO contracts with companies contained an equal rights clause, but it was usually ignored. Black workers now used the courts to enforce it. Likewise, Holloway and a group of black workers at his plant relied on the UAW's constitution and equal rights policy to stop a white supremacist group from taking over the Memphis UAW local, in a perilous fight that lasted more than ten years.

Black workers also fought racism by such workaday acts as deliberately bidding for "whites only" jobs, and both Holloway and Coe attest to the harsh personal consequences. Their daily battles against racism in the factory created palpable memories among black union veterans even while their actions remained largely hidden from the larger society. Black union pioneers opened their battle against Jim Crow at work even before the civil rights movement took the desegregation movement to the streets, and they continued their struggles long beyond the Supreme Court's decision to declare that "separate but equal" was no longer the law of the land.

Clarence Coe Fights for Equality

My God, man, when you'd given up thirty years of your life fighting
for something that should have been yours to begin with, it's a little
bit disheartening!

Clarence Coe had taken up the civil rights struggle as soon as he moved to the city in the late 1930s, working on the Scottsboro case, collecting memberships for the NAACP, and trying to organize a union (for which he was brutally attacked). He continued these activities while working at Firestone. For him, the struggle for equality became a life-and-death battle with whites at work, day in and day out.

I didn't go in the army. I could have, but I didn't. I can have asthma, so I had asthma. Every time a black soldier was pulled off of a bus and beaten in Texas or somewhere, we'd send a telegram to the Justice Department. To Roosevelt. And we'd get some response. Sometimes we'd send it to Mrs. Roosevelt. And then, on come the war, and I had to get off my job and go and register, sixteenth of October, 1940. There were two whites on the other side, comin' in and wanted to register, and the black line was about a mile long. And I said I want no damn part in this. It was just as segregated [as everything else]!

I can remember the first time I saw a white man shake hands with a black man, down in Crenshaw, Mississippi. World War II had started. A black man in a uniform crossed the railroad track, and he stuck out his hand to a white man. They knew each other. Twenty or thirty years ago you didn't shake hands with a white man. If you did, the white man would be called a nigger lover.

I worked at the post office a few weeks after Pearl Harbor was bombed, when I was laid off at Firestone.[1] But when Firestone called me back, I went, because there was no doors open at the post office. Every door was shut. You couldn't get the schooling, even those vocational classes would not admit you. I had a friend who went to school and worked at the post office in Michigan, but here in Memphis, this was the worst place on earth. It still is, it's just kind of camouflaged.

At Firestone I had to work seven days a week, and I did that. There was one whole year that I didn't see the sunset. I was working from three to eleven. I did my part then. And then some of the things that happened to some of the boys [in the military], I'm glad I didn't go, because I probably would have made somebody kill me.

I have known guys who had the hell beaten out of them in the street because they come back and maybe have on a service pin or something like that. "What theater you serve in, boy?" When he said, "European theater," [they would] knock him down. "You'd better not fuck around with them white women," just beat him up like hell.

What we did, NAACP would have a [fund-raising] contest every year, and we won first place every year for a number of years. There were some out there at the plant. There was Elma Bonner, Susie Wade, Sally Carter,

1. The U.S. Postal Service provided one of the few "clean-hands jobs" regularly open to black men in Memphis and most other southern cities during the segregation era, but the wages were not as good as working in a unionized, mass-production facility—if you could get in.

another one, too, that helped me to write the memberships inside of the plant. During the war years, at one time, we had seven thousand people in the plant. When I started, they were trying to get their first five hundred NAACP members, and we exceeded that at the plant. Mmm hmm.

They had a church that used to be downtown on Fourth and Beale. I remember one night I went down there to an NAACP meeting, and made a fervent appeal [for] membership for the NAACP and the CIO union. And I had people get up and leave, and said, "Hey you nigger, you're going to get your ass run out of Memphis talkin' like that." I said, but if we band together, there's nothing Mr. Crump can do about it. They can't run us all away from here. But at that time, you just didn't even talk about the CIO.

They [whites] were ready for them [black soldiers] when they came back. You had about thirty days to get back to Firestone when you got out of the army. I remember one of the first guys who got discharged, William Trice, came back to the plant just on a visit, he wasn't ready to come back to work. And he came down on the job where I was, and I was glad to see him, but I didn't neglect my work, I kept working. This old [white] guy, George Cruz, came down and for some little old bitter reason, there was some scrap rubber on the ground, and you'd either sweep it up or cut down your machine and crank it out. But he came down to call me every kind of son-of-a-bitch in the world, to let Trice know it hadn't changed a goddamn bit since he'd been gone. Of course he'd been in the European theater, [but] don't come back expecting any damn thing. This boy had been gone about five years, because he was single. First to go.

Some of the black soldiers had a little trouble adjusting, depending on what theater they were in, when they came back. Mayo Williams, that boy was an army employee. He stayed out of the United States for sixty months. He went to England, Europe, Italy, and on to Japan. And one morning he was coming from the locker room to his job. And there was a white guy drinking out of a fountain, and the damn thing's stem broke. There was one source down here at the bottom, but there was one black bowl and one white. If a white person was drinking, you weren't allowed to drink out of the other one even though that was your fountain. You had to wait 'til they were finished. So, having been gone that long, he just came on up and was drinking the thing, and the white guy had a goddamn fit. And we had an old foreman at the time, old man E. W. Woody, he jumped sky-high. He jumped on Williams saying, telling me, "Did you see that?" And then I jumped on Woody.

We kind of got it squared away, but in the next five minutes, I was called to the office. "What are you trying to do out there, start a damn race riot?" I said, "No, that fellow has been out of the country for five years and he still has a little more freedom." I said, "It's going to take him some time to adjust." Mr. Williams didn't have nothing to do with it, [but] now Williams and that white man will go out there in the yard and kick each other in the ass until their noses bleed, I'm not going to say a word. Don't nobody else say nothing. They read me the riot act on that one.

I promised at that plant, [Willie] Harrel and some of the guys out there can tell you, that we would get some Negroes in supervision, and on up as high as they could go, that we would get a black nurse, and that was a fight. I brought a girl out there who had finished nursing at the University of Tennessee, at the top of her class, but they said she's got to have four years of experience. Where the hell are you going to get four years of experience if you can't get a job? I got that broken down. I wanted black guards on the gate, they said, "No nigger's going to tell us [what to do]." When I left [in 1981], the captain of the guards was black.

Lord, I was working in a lot of areas. I wrote to the credit union, for black tellers, I have the original letter. I hand-delivered it one day, but it still took three [more] years to get the first black teller. When I left the plant, they had black managers.

I don't have a farm to speak of, I don't have a big fine house like Harrell and some of those guys. I spent all of my time fooling with this kind of stuff. Everything that I saw at that plant, I did something about it. But it took all of my time! And it's just not fair for an individual to have to waste a life. If I had gone into business and put in as much time as I have doing civil rights, I'd probably be [very well off].

Matthew Davis [in the 1960s and 1970s] had three kids in college, but he would always go with me to the office about discriminatory practices. He just had enough faith to do it. But the average guy wouldn't risk butting their head against the wall, their family suffering. Most people wouldn't go with me. A lot of people would walk around you. We had some educators too who wouldn't sign a petition, afraid they'd lose their job. [Only] a preacher wouldn't lose his job.

That grinning and scratching goin' on, I just couldn't handle it. They just didn't like a Negro if he was sincere. You always had to be playing and grinning and dancing, and [then] you could get away with murder. I had to work like hell every day, dot every *i* and cross every *t*, because I wouldn't play that game. They found out I was a little bit intelligent, and they didn't like it. I'm seventy-five years old and I still don't have to write down telephone numbers. I'll remember it. I never carried numbers around with me.

You had to fight for every inch of it. Nobody gave you anything. Nothing.

I tell you when both of us get in a ditch together and stay long enough we'll find the means to get out together, and CIO was that. But once they got it set up and got that thing working, the white leadership just wasn't going to support you in job equality or equal pay. We had the dirtiest, the cheapest job—there was a certain job the white man didn't do, he just didn't do it.

[This was true] even in 1952, when they started hiring a new batch of young people. You see, for twenty-five years they hired a person now and then, but once they got it settled with all the young people it lasted for a long time before everybody was retiring. Now the way the white got elevated was some of the white moved up or went back to Akron or went somewhere else, and some of the local whites could move up into higher positions [they had vacated]. But we were set. Couldn't move nowhere. . . .

And the union wouldn't give you no support on it. None whatsoever. They passed a buck with you. But I was just one of those hardheaded guys with nobody but that little woman you see back there, no children in school that they [whites] knew about. I had a brother pass, left seven kids and we took them, but they didn't know it. I didn't have none [children] at the plant. And in certain areas I just stuck my head in and whatever I had to do I just did it. And some of them respect you for it but they wouldn't help you. I had a brother out there worked on final inspection and you had three or four [black] guys out there, they had what they called a "white man's job." The whites wouldn't necessarily bother you, but they wouldn't help you either. They couldn't help you. If they did they would be called a nigger lover.

Even after we got the CIO we had to fight like hell for individual help. Just certain areas they wouldn't support you in. They weren't going to support me if we had a falling out or got in a fight or whatever. I wouldn't get no support from the union. I mean they was going to say enough or do enough to avoid a lawsuit or something like that, but they weren't going to give you any real support. We had to get it through the courts. Everything we got.

[The CIO would not have gotten the plant organized without the blacks.] But we had this element that thought, "I want the progress, but I don't want to see you do it," if you was black. When we first started getting raises for instance, they would give us percentage raises. So if you're makin' eighty-seven cents an hour, and I'm makin' forty-five cents, hell, you get a percentage rate, you see how you're starting to move away from me? Whoever had the higher wage would always do better. And whites just moved plumb out of sight of where we were. When I was makin' twelve dollars an hour at the plant, they were making twenty dollars on account of those percentage raises over ten or twenty years.

And then the next thing I set out to do, steadily got my neck out, and decided to integrate the job. I felt that was the only solution. Because they had us on one seniority board, the whites were on another. I'm tellin' the truth! So finally we had to raise money, hire a lawyer, fight it, take the threatening phone calls and all of the other abuses that came along with it. We hired a lawyer named [Anthony] Sabella . . . had to give him $2,500 to initiate a suit.[2] And we had to go around and collect $1.50 at a time over a period of two years.

And once we got that thing in progress everybody that was involved in it they caught hell. But, as I said, a few of us who didn't have large families just stayed with it. Oh, man, we got a lot of threats! A lot of nights I went to bed and didn't expect to wake up. Really, when you're pushed into a corner, you reach a point where you don't care. The only thing that really bothered me is that my wife didn't deserve to be blown up.[3] And you can't come home telling your wife what has transpired that day. There's nothing she can do, why worry her? But, you go through these things. In the '50s and '60s, all the way through.

I remember one incident we had, a white lady said she saw a black guy urinating in a coffee cup one night, and maybe he was, 'cause the cycle was so tight, you know, you had a certain amount to do in so much time. Maybe he did and she could have looked away. But she made a big fuss out of it and they sent the guy home and she had him arrested, and went uptown and the police and the jury dismissed it, and then the whites shut the plant down. I went around and took a dollar here and a dollar there—

2. Interestingly, Sabella also served as Martin Luther King's lawyer when he fought injunctions against the right to march in April 1968.
3. Throughout the South, blacks who fought for civil rights had their homes bombed by whites, and Coe expected the worst.

he was making about thirty dollars a day at that time. We kept him away from the plant for three days. Mr. McCune wouldn't touch it, Mr. Guthrie wouldn't touch it, not one of those company officials would touch it.[4]

They wouldn't touch it. They left it to me. I kept him away from the plant for three days, took up money, and paid him to keep him away from the plant. When they did get him back, that night I was getting off at 11:00 and I went over there and there was about ten or fifteen white guys ganged around his machine. So he was sweating and trembling and called me and said, "Coe, I can't work with all these guys standing around me like this. Can't you do something?" So I took the telephone and called Prentis Lewis. He was union president at the time. I said, "Mr. Lewis, tire builders and mold men and everybody else is ganged around Glenn." I said, "He can't work like that, and I'm afraid they're going to do something to him, and he is too."

He said, "Go and get McIntyre"—he was the chief steward at night. "Tell [union representative] McIntyre to get off of his job and go and stay with him the rest of the night and tell him to get a hold of Mr. Pruitt, the night superintendent, and tell him that those guys are in there, and they must have jobs [to do]." I go out there and talked to McIntyre, but he says, "I can't get away now." And I lost my cool. I said, "Look, let me tell you one damn thing." I said, "Mac, goddamn it, if you weren't having this trouble you'd be over there in the feed room with that woman where you be every night at this hour." I said, "Why you can't get off?"

We kept the guy off, paid him, kept the blacks from rebel-rousing to try to keep the peace. But damn if I didn't lose thirty pounds. Because any fight, any disturbance, racial trouble that come up, that was my job. I left here and went to California. And I can show you some pictures before I went and while I was out there and I looked as old as I do now. Man, oh man.

4. White workers walked out of the plant numerous times over racial incidents, as did blacks. Such wildcat strikes violated the union contract, but union leaders and company officials tried to get the workers back into the plant without disciplining them, which they feared would stir antagonisms even more. Union leaders used the well-known "strikitis" at Firestone over a period of years to get what the union wanted from management, while they joined with management to avoid a race war. According to Billie Willis, a Firestone worker who became director of the Memphis Labor Council, the workers at Firestone went on strike fifty-nine times in one year. Personal interview, February 3, 1983, Memphis.

You knew that [racist] element was there and you knew you didn't have any support. Whatever the white man said, that's what it is. I remember one day I was driving a forklift at that particular time. I had a guy, when I'm at full speed he shoved a four-wheel truck out in front of me. One of the mechanics. If I'd hit that truck that would have been my job!

You are both union members, but then how would the company treat you when they knew you had this relationship with your white brothers? They know they didn't have to treat you too well.

Back during the war years, we thought that the mill room was [designated] predominantly black. The company hired some white boys once and brought 'em over there once, and I admit, we shut the thing down until they moved 'em. We thought we were gaining some strength, for the fact that we had enough strength to do that. But once they got us segregated, they put the foot on our neck. I mean it's easy to get a bunch isolated, you know. Next thing I knew, base rates, classified average earnings, had changed. Once they got us separated, whites just moved away from us [in terms of wage increases].

Then the only alternative we had was to try to integrate the jobs and filter out into some of these other departments. And they tried every trick in the world to disqualify you. And only a few people had enough education maybe to take the risk of qualifying in some of those departments. I took the risk.

You know collecting money and doing this and that—I guess for twenty-five or thirty-five of my forty years at this plant I had to dot every *i* and cross every *t*, 'cause they were watching. They knew I was the troublemaker. Yeah, when I first went out there.

And a chemical I was working in got me down to about 145 pounds. I went in weighing 155. Doctor sent them a note to get me out of that stuff and then they started the process to get rid of me, see. So I had a talk with Mr. William Norton, head of the lab. I had a high school diploma and had done some major in chemistry and I would like to work over in the lab, because I was going to have to transfer from the department I was in. And he said, "Well, bring your diploma in tomorrow morning and we'll get you over there." So I brought it and went on down in front and waited there til 9:00.

The person that I was to deal with, Mr. Edwards, didn't come in that morning but he sent another guy over there, and when I got there they had my money ready. I haven't taken a speed reading course in school, but I can look at a paragraph. And I shoved it back in the office. I said, "I didn't ask for my money, I asked for a transfer." They said, "We ain't going to fool with you no more."

And I do believe that God intervenes in things. I had been talking to the union president, [at that time] Ray Allen. He was building tires. He knew the whole thing and it looked like something touched him on the shoulder and he looked back. The guard had told me I couldn't go back into the plant, and I said [to Allen], "He's supposed to transfer me, but they're firing me!" He rushed right into [plant manager] Cliff Reynolds's office, and as the Lord would have it, Reynolds was not busy. He just walked straight in and stated the case. Reynolds said, "Well, put him back on his regular job for the day and we'll get into it later on."

Man, I was on the hot seat and I never did get the transfer. He [Allen] dropped it, even though he was president of the union!

When I got back inside and went to the superintendent to get my pass, my department manager wouldn't give me a pass out of the plant. So a guy named George Cruz said something vulgar about me and I heard Richard Routon [first president of the union] say plainly, "Mr. Cruz, there's some Negroes just don't take that shit. He attended school, and that shit, it just doesn't work with him. You got guys you can kick in the butt, but don't kick him. You know, some of them are just different, and I don't know where he came from, but I don't think it was up North." Richard Routon was a liberal, he stood up.

[And] they trained some of us over there to handle our own union business. You've got to handle your own business and you've got to handle it right. So I became so proficient in it until I never even carried a contract in my pocket. I could walk into your office and say, "Mr. Honey, you've done such and such a thing on this job, and article so and so says it's done this way, and that's the union position." No contract in hand, and that really had an impact on them. They knew you really knew what you were talking about. I didn't lose many cases over there.

We had a contract and I knew it. But not where it came to separate departments or racial discrimination. You couldn't get support from the union on that. You just couldn't. They just wouldn't deal with it.

You have always had some white people, [even] in Biloxi, Mississippi, or wherever, who would be fair. If you were decent and intelligent, the initial group [of white supervisors], they were fair. They would hear your side and they would hear the white man's side. But after this, they began to go back to Akron [Firestone headquarters]. And management began to shift over to local whites, and [then] you didn't have a chance. You didn't have no voice, no say, no anything. And your union, the CIO, just didn't support you in some areas. What are you going to do about it? They just wouldn't go to bat for you.

They were afraid they would lose office and they could get bombed or anything. We had a lot of Ku Klux Klan. I've had guys that called here right at this house and identify themselves as Grand something. But I never was afraid of them.

I remember one New Year's night about twenty minutes to twelve, you know, when you go out and shoot your gun. I got this call, and I knew who he was even though he had been drinking. I could distinguish his voice. And he said, "We're going to get you nigger, starting right on this New Year," and so on. And I said, "Well I'm just in here waiting 'til 12:00 to load up some ammunition. Now you said if you knew where I stayed you would come over and do such and such a thing to me. You don't have to come over here," I said, "the supermarket, they're closed tonight. At 12:00 the lot's going to be vacant—nobody out there but you and me. Meet me over there." So he hung up the telephone.

But it's pathetic when a young man has to live ready to die all the time. All the time. Wouldn't make no difference now. But a young man, thirty-five years old, got to live daily ready to give it up. No progress, no nothing. It was just tough.

I got out of that department and out of some of that situation after I had twenty-five years' seniority. I finally transferred out of the mill room to the calender room in '65. So I had worked at Firestone for twenty-five years before I made fifty dollars for one single day's work. I stayed on the broom for six months [waiting for an opening doing skilled work], but I knew I could make it. And I knew I could set the pattern and open the way for some of the lesser qualified people.

They kept me on the broom six months. They had vacancies [in white departments] that they kept in their pocket, but they wouldn't tell you about it. They would call people in around the clock, working overtime on a job that I could do, but they wouldn't call me. And one day I was over in the tire room sticking up some liners, and the treasurer, who was a young one at that time, [union official R. L.] Tracy, I don't know what provoked him to ask me the question, but he asked, "Coe, how are you getting along in the calender room?" I said fine. He said, "Coe, how are you getting along in the calender room?" I said fine. "Coe, how are you getting along in the calender room?" And I said, "Not worth a damn, Tracy, and you know it." And the next day my job was on the board.

I don't know what provoked him, [but I guess it was] because he had been seeing my situation. I was picking up liners, something that we used in my department that he was using in the tire building, and he saw me all day everyday and he knew I had twenty-five years' seniority and could do something better. I went to the third shift.

When I transferred over there we had a guy named Vic Bourgenni, an Italian that had been a calender operator, and he had been vice president of the union and I had worked with him and supported him. So when I was transferred over there, I had to work with Vic and I asked him, I said, "Do you have any suggestions," and he said, "No. Just go on and do your work." And he stood there a while, and on the second thought he's saying, "Have as little to say to them [the whites] as you can." And [in this new job] I just followed that, I didn't complain. After I transferred to the calender room, I didn't say anything about anything.

From that day on I had to watch, watch, watch because they try to hurt you. They would do anything in the world to get you off of the job. Anything.

Let me give you an example. On the tandem calender was a great big machine, as big as from here across the street. You couldn't see everybody in the group. The operator had signals for what area the problem was, and the others knew where you were, you know. He could give you the wrong signal and get you. I remember one day a guy gave me a reversed signal to back out the cold rubber and put in a new strip of warm rubber, and it took off forward as fast as the damn calender would go. I'd have been flat as this table. But I didn't say anything. I just got down and stepped out in the aisle and stood there and looked at him about five minutes.

Another incident of trying to hurt me: you had what you called a hot house. The fabric inside a tire was dipped in a solution two or three times, and that is what they called a hot house. And when it came out it would be dry and you could take the next processing step. Behind each four hundred- or five hundred-yard roll you would have to sew them together. And you had what we called a compensator. You didn't have to stop the calender. You get your compensator all the way up to the top, and when you stopped the roll the compensator would start down slowly. And if you did your work on time you had plenty of time to get it sewn together and let that roll go, and then the compensator would pick back up. But every now and then that fabric would pull loose somewhere in that series of drums and rollers and [you had to go fix it]. I suspect it was five hundred degrees in there.

So they called us one night to shut down our machine to come down to help find the broken splice, and they sent me in there to find it. I had a trouble light. Something told me to take off my glasses, I was using plastic glasses. Go up the steps, go on in, got maybe thirty feet to where I was going and I realized something was wrong, you know. And I was becoming confused 'til I just lay down on the floor, and I remembered what direction I came from and started crawling on back.

I'm in the aisle, but the heat, the heat, man! If I had had on my glasses it would have melted them. But I just happened to pull them off. So I just lay down, turned around and started crawling back. And when I got back to the end of the step I could get some air. Some of them was down there grinning. They didn't let it cool down enough, or tell me what precautions to take or masks to use or anything. They going to get you, see. [They let me go up there knowing] I wasn't going to get back.

And I lost my cool that time. [Cursed] everybody. I didn't feel right for three months. But they seemed to have more respect for me after they found out I could stand up for myself. It seemed to make it better all across the plant. You see, I was just playing one of those Jackie Robinson roles.[5] The union told me to take it easy, because I was the first black that bumped a white man in that plant. In the whole plant. They just couldn't handle that.

I could watch on most of the jobs [to learn how to do them]. One guy on one side of the belt and one on the other, they didn't tell you nothing. The first job I told you about that the guy tried to hurt me on, they had

5. In 1947, Jackie Robinson became the first African American to break into major league baseball, which had been segregated. He endured much harassment and threats of violence by white players and fans. His grit, determination, and success inspired many African Americans, like these factory workers, trying to break open previously all-white occupations.

opened a new calender, what they called a four-roll calender. And I had
to bump into another job, and that's when I bumped the first white man.
Went in that Sunday night. They "didn't have time" to show me anything.

That Monday night I went in this guy was gone on vacation and I had
to do the job. Nobody showed me anything but I had been observant, see.
And I could watch this guy over here and I could think fast enough, I was
forty-eight years old and I could think fast enough and move fast enough
to see him begin something and have mine done when he would get to his.
And I just made it, but after about three years or so it eased it up, and I
was treated like any other person.

[After a while] it blew over. [But three years is a long time.] A long time.
It's a waste of life. That's where the union let me down. Even when you
brought in the federal government and made them bring in people to try
out on the job, the people there brought in the worst welding machine
they could find. The man trying out just about did it, but they turned him
down. They said he could try again, but he got in at Caterpillar [tractor
factory]. He had been a welder, there was no doubt about it. But those
guys at Firestone wasn't gonna have no black welder. And you had to live
with it.

[In] the '60s, one night we was setting here [at home]. The TV sat
right there. We had a little old white German pit dog who was laying
down in front of the TV, and he growled. I wonder what's wrong with him.
So he growled again. And I get up and look and there are two white guys
out in front of the house. No white people in this neighborhood. They
have no business, no nothing out here. I got those German shepherd dogs,
I put a fence around the house, I got guns all around the damn place in
every room. You have to. And keep one in the car.

[These white guys] just look and leave. Until today I don't know who
they were, but I know there was two of them and they had no business—
there isn't a white person's neighborhood within five miles of here.

The last time I had to go downtown to a hearing [on discrimination
in the plant], the company lawyer had gone and told the jury that certain
things had been done [to end segregation], and then when I came in the
jury started questioning me. And I said, no, the plant's still the same, I said
the lockers are still segregated, the showers and the fountains. And he [the
judge] said, "You mean to tell me? . . ." I said, "No, I'm not meaning to tell
you anything. Would you recess the court, and go out to the damn plant?"

And he said, "That's all." And I left. I don't know what transpired after that. But the next morning at 7:30 the air hammers was running, tearing out walls. The lockers and everything was completely integrated. So that really straightened the plant out.

That was as late as '74. Some areas and some things were segregated that late. I mean you just weren't comfortable.

But I couldn't even win the delegation [run for office] after that. I was a marked man. But even leading up to that, when I was still in the all-black unit, I had finally reached a point where I couldn't run for no more offices or anything like that because I was getting only a certain percentage of white votes, see. The plant was set up 65–35 [white to black ratio]. So even if you got all of the black votes you couldn't win.

We had had a plant manager at that time, J. W. McCune, he was just as fair as could be. But even so, there were certain things wrong. I remember we had some trouble out there. One of the [black] tire builders called a white guy "Red" and the white guy called him a "nigger." And that's when Mr. McCune told us. He said to all the white [and black] people, "There's no 'Mr.' in here. If a white man is named 'John' call him 'John.' You don't have to call him 'Mr. John.' But if he has a pet name that some of the others call him affectionately, 'Red' or 'Slim' or 'Whitey' or something you call him 'John.' Tell him 'yes' and 'no.' No 'Sir' to it."

But, man, it took, hell, thirty-five years of my work out there to reach that point. I have seen the time when a young white boy came in and maybe I had been working at the plant longer than he had been living, but if he was white I had to tell him "yes sir" or "no sir." That was degrading as hell. I had to live with it.

I stayed there '41 'til '81, and today we are in good shape. Good living coming in, good retirement, wife never worked. When I retired they gave her half of my social security and I have my pension. It all totals about $1,800 a month—about $400 a week. But I earned it. I've had many a sleepless night and had to work like a dog because somebody is watching every move you make, trying to find any little bitty thing that you might have done.

It's not fair for a person to have to live like that. And you know what? I know you're white, but you know what? The only difference is a white guy could do anything he wanted to do to you [if you were black].

The last fifteen years I worked, I worked in different departments. And then they started trying to move me into management, supervision, and so forth. But I never accepted it. I would have had a better retirement plan, but I just wanted to stay on with the union and try and get everything I could for them, and we did. We did. Before they left here, we were virtually equal. If you qualified for something, you could just about get it.

But my God, man, when you'd given up thirty years of your life fighting for something that should have been yours to begin with, it's a little bit disheartening!

And then the very people that got the big promotions were ones that were never reprimanded, never were called to the office, never put on the spot. You know, they went out and found the good boys. [chuckles] We had some leadership at that time, even though they were black, they were tricky. I don't know how they managed to get sucked into it, but some of them had been there since '37, '38. And we have some Firestone people who are living like kings and never lost any skin off their butts for any of it. Looked like most of it came off of my butt.

But all of that's life, that's life. And I'm happy. My wife and I, the Lord has allowed us to grow old together. When a man's worked forty-eight and a half years, no aches, no pains, no arthritis, no nothing, that's a blessing.

Lonnie Roland and other Black Workers
Implement the *Brown* Decision on the Factory Floor

We finally got justice, and it worked pretty good all the way around.

Following the 1954 *Brown v. Board of Education* decision by the U.S. Supreme Court, which invalidated segregation in schools, black hopes for desegregation soared. Lonnie Roland, Clarence Coe, and others covertly collected money and in 1956 sued both Firestone and the United Rubber Workers for discrimination. Their civil suit in the chancery court of Shelby County documented the cases of blacks who had been laid off from work even though they had more seniority than a number of whites who kept their jobs. The company even hired inexperienced whites off the street while laying off blacks with years of experience. The suit charged both the union and the company with conspiring to follow "practices, customs, and arrangements . . . to deprive them of their rights, job assignments, and employment, which their seniority would entitle them to[,]

solely because of race and color." These practices, they charged, violated
federal and state constitutions and laws, and the union's own constitution
and the union and company's joint contract. The court ruled in favor of
the black workers, and Lonnie Roland suggests that the court case desegregated the entire plant. But what it really did was force the union and
the company to invalidate the practice of following a color-coded departmental seniority system. According to Clarence Coe, complete desegregation of plant facilities required many more battles, but the suit did open
the doors to change. I interviewed Lonnie Roland, a quiet and composed
man, in 1984 at his home.

When Firestone came here, they said blacks could only have certain jobs,
certain jobs for whites and certain jobs mainly for blacks. And the salary
would stop at a certain point. We went along like that for a while. But
[George] Clark suggested, he was [Local 186] president then, that I get
an attorney and recommended the attorney that I go to. I went to the
attorney and we filed suit against the company, the local union, and
the international union, and the main company in Akron.

At that time, the black women that were working there, when they got
laid off, they weren't called back. And they were laying off black people
with fifteen or twenty years of seniority and keeping white people on the
job with ten and twelve months' seniority.

Vice President Richard Nixon, who Eisenhower had working in fair
practice and policy, sent a man down here. We met, had two, three meetings with the company and the union and finally went to court. The case
was on the docket, but our lawyer presented his case, they asked for a recess, and when I went back that evening, they had decided to settle out
of court. And they ended up paying all the lawyers' fees and whatnot. And
they had to hire back all the black women and black men that they had laid
off, and they began integrating the jobs. They were equal for everybody.

That was in '57. Before that time, there were no black foremen, no black
supervisors, and black people only got to a certain status and stopped there.
There was an unwritten law that black people couldn't work high-skilled
jobs, couldn't have no top jobs operating no machine. Blacks worked
mainly in the preparation department.

That was processing the rubber when it first come in. When it was
building the tires, the tubes, the molds and all that, and the finishing pro-

cess, it was operated by white people [with much less seniority than black workers]. Your seniority was confined to your department. When the blacks was brought up to the status quo with the whites, it was a matter of the man with the most seniority stayed on the job, if he could qualify. It wasn't easy to get black men qualified as tire builders because a white had to say if he was qualified or not. But we found a way and went ahead. [Eventually], some of our best tire builders were black.

You had a brown fountain to drink out of[6] and a black restroom to go to, and a black section in the cafeteria. Black women had one restroom over on the Moorhead [Street] side. Them that was working on the other side of the plant had to walk over there for any reason they needed to go to the restroom. White women had restrooms all over the plant. The black men, they did have more restrooms, but you didn't go in the restrooms where the whites were. You didn't bathe where they were, you didn't use the restrooms they used, you didn't drink out of the fountains they drank out of it. You didn't punch the clock that they punched.

[While the lawsuit was being fought] there was a lot of intimidation, threats, and all that kind of stuff. I was called just about everything. I got threatening telephone calls and all like that. I didn't have a family at that time, so it didn't make too much difference. I didn't have too much to lose. I wasn't a young man, but I was in my forties, and I was able to roll with the tide.

[Blacks in the plant took up a collection to pay for the court suit.] That was to pay for the lost time, in negotiations and things, 'cause the union wasn't going to pay for that, and you know the company wasn't going to pay for that. They were very generous. A lot of them gave who didn't want their name disclosed, but they gave. Some people were afraid for their jobs. They hadn't ever went through nothing like that, and they didn't see how I could win suing a company like Firestone, most of them felt like that's the way it was. We had to educate them to the point where they could apply for these jobs and get 'em.

Personally, I didn't see how I could win either, but I had a notion that if it was possible, to go ahead and try. And like I said, being a single

---

6. A number of interviewees commented that blacks got the dirty, literally "brown," fountain to drink from.

man with no family, I didn't have too much to lose. I didn't feel like I would lose my job. [But] if that's the way I had to go, well, you can't go but once.

Our suit was to integrate the plant. It started in January of '56, and it was July of '57 when the case was settled. We finally got justice, and it worked pretty good all the way around. We didn't get any cash settlement, but all the attorney fees were paid. [After we won the suit], they integrated the locker rooms and the bathrooms and the lunchrooms, and the showers was integrated and the black fountains was removed, anybody could drink out of them. It was a big change.

[Whites] found out that this was a bigger help to them, because whites who probably would have been laid off out of their classification, they were able to lower their classification and take other jobs when their job would be eliminated through lack of work or something like that. They'd take jobs in housecleaning and various other things. It worked out smoothly. When I left there in '74 it was a pretty harmonious place to work.

There was a few diehards still in there. Their biggest problem was they didn't want black men working with white women. They found out that we were human and we didn't want their women any more than we wanted nobody else. They found out we were human. If a man said something to a woman, she didn't have but one thing to say, and that was yes or no. We didn't have any racial problems at that stage. But that was the point they would throw up all the time: "We don't want them working with our women." They had quite a few white women working there. There wasn't more than about forty black women working there then. There's about twenty-five or thirty black women now drawing pensions that wouldn't have been drawing anything if this hadn't taken place, because they was laying them off without recall as a job was eliminated.

The people I used [in the suit] was a black women and two black men as ones who was laid off out of turn. They all got their jobs back. I couldn't go through with it now at the age I am, but it was a lot of fun.

The three men [local presidents] who went through with this was Tom Taylor, Rip Clark, and Prentice Lewis. And H. B. Griffin, later on. Griffin was an officer in the union, but when he got to be president, it had all been worked out. [Our attorney] Anthony Sabella is a criminal court judge now.

I worked there since December 1938. It was different, like night and day.

I started there at thirty-two cents an hour and left there at five dollars and fifty cents an hour, so that was a big boost in salary. And I was able to get any job that I could qualify for when I left.

When I first went, there was just certain jobs that I was designated to. The AFL didn't mean nothin' to us. The AFL was the craftsmen's union. Black people really didn't have no place in that union unless they was a bricklayer or something, but we didn't have nobody like that out there. When George Bass and the different Akron representatives came in here and set the CIO union up, we did pretty good under them. They turned his car over, they did everything they could to hurt him, but he survived. A few of the white workers accepted him, Griffin and Clark, guys like that. But the general workers, they didn't accept him, because he was making the union available for all races. The blacks accepted [CIO] wholehearted. We had to meet in a different place every Sunday in case the police was after us. But we finally met until we could get organized. I retired in 1974.

George Holloway's Struggle against White Worker Racism

I was a target all of the time.

In chapter 2, George Holloway told how segregation had poisoned the atmosphere for African Americans growing up in Memphis in the 1920s and 1930s. Despite his several years of college education, work at the Firestone factory had been the best employment he could find. When violence and race-baiting defeated his efforts to organize the plant, he moved on before the company could fire him and, like his father, became a Pullman porter and a leading recruiter for the Brotherhood of Sleeping Car Porters. Of all those hired at the new International Harvester plant after the war, Holloway had perhaps the most union experience and education. He became a key strategist in organizing the factory and perhaps was the most active shop leader in the plant, representing black and white alike. He spent his life seeking to advance the cause of all workers, all the while under attack by many of the white workers he so ably represented.

When the war was in the thick of it, after Pearl Harbor, I got a sense that everyone was going to live as one and love each other. They were always talking about the Japanese destroying the ships and the rest of America. So that was the main concern that people united against. So, whites set aside some of their other prejudices perhaps, towards the goal of defeating the Japanese.

Well, to some degree there was some change. Towards the end of the war, [Tennessee] Governor [Frank] Clement opposed Crump. He was a Democrat, and he gathered the blacks together. This changed the atmosphere and image of things. I think some of this came to be because of Tennessee State College [a black college]. Many people there worked with Clement, [and] our own teachers began to educate us about justice. Coming out of college, [they] began to educate us much better than we were in the second-rate black schools earlier. We began to realize that we had to elect school board members and others to change the system. The NAACP began to move, and young people began to be dedicated to change.

That was when the United Auto Workers union [UAW] was coming in, too. After World War II, General Electric, Globe (who made street globes), and [James B.] Carey's [United] Electrical Workers union came in [to Memphis].[7] With Walter [Reuther]'s help, Carey organized GE. In 1946 I got into the UAW. You couldn't find any local lawyers who would support the UAW. They would support the AFL, but not the UAW. Crump had said that the UAW wasn't coming into Memphis, that was a threat he made. It was in all of the newspapers.

Some whites started fighting Crump by paying the poll tax for blacks to vote freely. [Then] between 1946 and 1948, the UAW had a young lawyer by the name of Schlossberger working for them. The UAW had four plants here at the time. Schlossberger came down to Memphis and took the lawsuit against the state for the poll tax. I went with Schlossberger to the courthouse, but the legislature changed it for the entire state before it got to court.

Things changed completely when Senator Kefauver beat the Crump machine in 1948. The Crump machine started to crumble. Following Crump, it was like a new Memphis. People began to see that they could

7. James B. Carey, allied with Reuther, later became president of the International Union of Electrical, Radio, and Machine Workers, a CIO union that sought to displace the more left-wing United Electrical, Radio and Machine Workers (which was forced out of the CIO in 1949).

protest what was happening, and they weren't afraid. The UAW later spent a lot of money on registration and education drives to help people understand why they should vote.

At that time, too, we began to have more black letter carriers. Senator [Kenneth] McKellar controlled the post office, and there were only black mail handlers. Blacks couldn't do any job accept letter carrier, because they wouldn't let us handle money. I quit the post office because I had a high test score, and they would only let me be a mail carrier. I remember one day when I got out to the post office, and they didn't furnish raincoats in those days. I'll never forget how hard it was raining, and a piece of junk mail got wet. I got back downtown to the Front Street Post Office and the supervisor chewed me out. I left after three months. I decided there was better work for me to do.

But the overall [white] attitudes were going back in the same rut. The whites wanted unions to a certain degree, but they didn't want to change the structure of jobs. They didn't want justice in jobs, they still wanted the blacks to be janitors, and they didn't want blacks to advance. That was a big struggle there. A lot of blacks thought it was time to get some justice, especially some of the youngsters around my age. Some of them refused to accept the old prejudiced ways.

A lot of veterans were hired into Harvester. At that time, Harvester was one of the big plants that had moved into our area. I was hired at Harvester in December of 1946. I was about the three hundredth person hired. Jobs for whites at Harvester included the punch press, bulldozers, crane drivers, truck drivers, drill machines, assembly line, warehouse loaders, tool room jobs, and many others. Blacks weren't allowed to have these jobs. At that time, blacks were only janitors, lift drivers, and warehousemen, those were the only three job classifications for blacks.

The farm equipment workers, a Communist union, came in and tried to get me to help them organize, thinking they could get the blacks to join them. The farm equipment workers were a strong group, and went from East Moline, Chicago, to Kentucky.[8] Grant Oaks was the president, and

8. The Farm Equipment and Metal Workers (FE) followed a strong equal rights policy and was attacked by segregationists as "un-American" for doing so in its Louisville, Kentucky, local and elsewhere. It competed with the UAW for membership, and UAW leaders helped to expel it from the CIO in 1949 for having Communist leadership.

was stationed in Chicago. They may have had some of the John Deere plants, too. But in Memphis, they just had about three organizers. They handed out leaflets that said Walter Reuther was a racist. They wanted to get the blacks mad, but my daddy told me that Walter Reuther was the greatest labor leader in the country, and to follow him. I went from that and I convinced the others in the group to follow the UAW.

Ford and General Motors of the South agreed with Reuther: if you get the cards signed that the workers wanted a union, they would automatically recognize it. "Acclamation" meant that people wanted a union in the plant from the beginning. No election is necessary. The union representative gets all of the union cards signed to prove that the people want the union. Then they make a contract which might take them two or three months to work out. You can pick up seniority from the day you come in that way. The Ford plant in Memphis came in that way, and other auto plants in the South came in with acclamation, too.

The union wanted to be recognized. We went to National Labor Relations Board in Memphis, and they told us to come back in a month. This went on until February of 1948, before they recognized our cause. By that time, they had 837 people in the plant. We had an election on April 8, 1948. The union should have been in [recognized by acclamation] by 1946. [But International Harvester] stalled because they thought if they had more employees, the union would be less likely. But they were wrong. We won the election by 833–4. Those against it became foremen, so that was their reason.

At that time, Harvester and Boss Crump were determined that the UAW would not be in Memphis, or even have an election. Crump made a newspaper statement saying there would be no UAW, and he opposed Walter Reuther. They tried to interfere by writing in the paper that Harvester was a good company that would treat everyone right without a union, so there was no need for a union and not to worry. It was a big story in the press saying Reuther was a socialist. Crump didn't like Walter Reuther, period.

To prove their point, they brought Crump out to our plant to visit. He came through, and shook hands with all of the whites. None of the blacks would shake hands with him. Crump didn't have any influence on the white workers either, because Harvester was giving us hell. That's why we won the election so unanimously. For example, if you walked up to the clock to punch out at night, and the supervisor told you to work overtime, you had to work several more hours without any choice. The same thing would happen if he told you to go outside with a bucket of nuts and bolts, you didn't have any say about what he could do, and you couldn't get any help or anything. There was no job description or anything.

I started off at Harvester at forty-five cents an hour, some of them made a little less than that. The minimum wage was around thirty-five cents at that time. You had to buy your own work gloves and anything else you needed at work, and they wouldn't let you go to the toilet when you needed to. Guys would have to urinate in back of the machines sometimes when they weren't allowed to go to the toilet. You didn't want to be smelling that stuff, but you couldn't get them to change it. Locker rooms were separate for blacks and whites, and they usually didn't keep toilet paper in the toilets, or soap or towels or anything else. These were the kinds of things that made people really want the union.

The first union contract in 1948 only got recognition of the union, and saying the people had seniority according to when they were hired. That's all that we were after at that point. International Harvester had already given us a forty-five cent an hour raise to keep us out of the union, so we didn't ask for a wage increase.

After the UAW won the election in April 1948, the first negotiations were held at Peabody Hotel. The company and the union met at the entrance door of the hotel on Union Avenue. Mr. Condo, the manager of International Harvester Memphis Works, and two others, and seven union members, met there at 2 P.M. The manager of the hotel met us and told them [that] all of the white members of the bargaining committee could come in, "but not that black one out there." Mr. Condo asked him why couldn't he come in, and the manager told him that this hotel would not allow a black man disputing a white man's word. Mr. Condo almost cried.

Then they called the Chisca Hotel and talked to the owner, Mr. Snowden. He accepted us to negotiate a contract in the Gold Room, but he told Mr. Condo that a black man could not come through any doors of that hotel, front or back—although both hotels had black bellhops. We accepted the room after much discussion, and the bellhop met me and took me up the alley to the freight elevator, where all the garbage and filth was. Every morning he would meet me and ride to the third floor. This elevator had all of the garbage, trash, waste water, and foul odor. The elevator would jump to each floor and splatter water all over my pants and shoes.

I wasn't allowed to eat lunch or supper in the dining room, therefore Mr. Condo would order our lunch or supper to the Gold Room, and the company would pay for it. I also had to leave the hotel by the freight elevator. I knew the bell captain at the Chisca, and he did his best to stop the kitchen from putting the garbage on the elevator, but he couldn't stop it all. The company felt very bad about this, as they could smell the foul odor on me. The company tried to get other hotels, but wouldn't any of them accept us.

I also want you to know that when I came on the staff of the UAW Region 8 in 1962, only one staff member would eat with me and his name was Carl Moore. I was the fourteenth member of the Region 8 UAW staff. They used to tell me we will meet you to eat and give me the time, [but] many, many times they would not show, or they would fill the tables and I wouldn't have any place to sit but by myself. I never ate a meal with the director or the assistant director at any conference or meeting, other than in a group banquet. This hurt me very, very much, but I took it.

I want you to know that after we negotiated the contract in Memphis, for one year Mr. Bryson, the superintendent of International Harvester Memphis Works, would use the word "nigger" at every grievance meeting. Such as "niggers are slow, they are not doing their work, we are going to get rid of them." I used to lay my head on the table and cry within, because the other six union committee men were white and wouldn't defend me. I was the secretary of the bargaining committee,[9] therefore I keep the minutes of each grievance, and I didn't have time to speak up. Many times, I asked the bargaining committee to stop this, but they wouldn't.

I want you to know that after one year of Mr. Bryson using the word "nigger" at every meeting, they called me up to the front office and told me, "George, you can take it, and we are proud of you. The word 'nigger' will never be used at the bargaining table again." I was on the bargaining committee for twenty years, and the word "nigger" was never again said in my presence. I want you to know I was overjoyed.[10]

I was on the Local 988 UAW Executive Board for twenty years. I was

9. Due to his several years of college education, Holloway undoubtedly made a better secretary than most factory workers.

10. International Harvester ended the use of racial slurs and opened skilled jobs to blacks earlier than other companies (it was reported by the media to be more liberal in its race relations than other Memphis companies), but Bryson's commendation to Holloway for being able to "take it" must have been cold comfort.

the only black, the rest was white. Our executive board originally used to meet at Firestone Hall, before we bought our own. I'd have to leave the plant an hour early to get to the board meeting. [At that time] I had no car, and there were no streetcars out there. Sometimes a trucker would pick me up and give me a lift. Other board members would pass me, and wouldn't pick me up. When I got a car, people tried to sugar the tank one day. There was sugar all over the hood of the car, but it had a locked hood. The company let me park inside the gate after that.

If I made a motion, even just to discuss something, no one would second it during those first two years. They wouldn't eat with me, or talk with me, either. As you know, without a second you can't discuss anything. I told Walter Reuther and Emil Mazey, the secretary-treasurer, UAW, about this. They told me they couldn't do anything about that, but keep making motions, which I did. They also told me that if any of the candidates run for office that I supported and they won the election, and they didn't second my motion, to tell them I would not support them again. And [then] they started seconding my motion. I knew I wasn't going to win, but at least it was discussed.

When they hired me at International Harvester, I was the only black in a training class. I learned the various machines, but they put me in the warehouse anyway. I guess they had the idea that they might move me, but they didn't do that until Larry Carlston, the UAW international representative, told the company that [until something was done] they wouldn't negotiate a damn thing. I thought they would pick someone else, but when they came to me, I didn't have any other choice than to take it. I didn't want it, because I didn't want to deal with "you've got less seniority"—because I was a union official—"than I." I didn't want that. I wanted someone black with more seniority than me to go. I thought we should have a seniority system.

But we didn't have any choice or bidding rights or anything, they could still do with us as they wanted to do. I was put on a machine somewhere around December 1948 or early 1949. I was the first black to ever operate a machine [at International Harvester].

After we got organized at the plant, I met with Reuther in Detroit. I found out that the workers at all of the other plants were making twenty-five to thirty-five cents more an hour than we were, and that was when I decided to fight to really change the situation. We were operating the same machines and doing the same work, [but] we were making about a third less than at the other plants in the North, which was typical all over the South.

When we made our first contract, each plant had to negotiate its own individual contract. Today, there's a master contract. So, Reuther got us to form a council from all of the farm equipment plants, and we got a chance to meet each other and find out what was going on elsewhere.

In the second year, we got the grievance procedure, which was the greatest thing that you can have. Then, you have a chance to have things checked out if there is a problem. If you are discharged or suspended, you have a right to be defended. It's worth money to you.

In that second contract, the company had actually agreed to give us a quarter [per hour] raise, but what we wanted was medical insurance for our family. We struck Harvester for thirty days in the second year for a company-sponsored insurance that we could pay for ourselves, so all workers would be eligible. [He explains that they only won partial health coverage but got full family coverage in the third year of the contract.] As you know, unions have strikes to obtain justice for all, and I have been involved in many, many strikes. The union gives assistance to strikers, but I want you to know that I have received assistance for strikers, but I have never used any of it [personally]. As a committeeman and as a service representative, I gave my own strike assistance to black or white members of the local, because many of them had large families. I also gave them money out of my pocket. We could do that because my wife's father was a lover of unions, and he had a small business. And he helped me and my family during the strikes. We never wanted for anything when we was on strikes.

The union was active then, we set up our leadership, and I was elected as a trustee and a committeeman. The trustees check your books every week, to make sure money is paid out correctly. We had a plant-wide election for union president, vice president, secretary-treasurer, three trustees, a sergeant-at-arms.

The union proposed the zones, and a committeeman was over all of the stewards in a zone area. I was in number seven. I had all of the punch presses, warehouse, truck drivers, janitors, and foundries. I had maybe a hundred different stewards under me, from about a hundred departments. There had to be at least one steward for each department, no matter how few worked in it, working under a committeeman (myself). Foundry workers had twenty stewards. My zone covered all of this.

While I was there, I was the only black elected as a committeeman.

These [other] zones never had a black elected official. I was [also] elected to chair all the union committees (we had ten) in the local except the bargaining committee. I was vice chairman of the bargaining committee. That committee decides which grievances to pursue and meets once or twice a week. I was also chair of the trustees for ten years. The steward's job was to handle grievances, and if he couldn't handle them, he'd turn them over to me. I negotiated the contract with the other six committeemen (seven total) and the international representative. I am the one that wrote the grievance procedure for Local 988 UAW, and the layoff and recall procedures which are in effect in all of International Harvester [now called Norstar] contracts today.

This was a brand new plant, right on the Wolf River. There were nasty foremen riding people constantly. The reason we organized in the first place was that we as workers felt we were entitled to certain rights, such as job bidding [employment open to all], [and] the right to return from job layoff with seniority. All of these things are with the company today, at Norstar, which used to be Harvester. Job-bidding procedure and how you progress is a section that I wrote, which stops the foremens from giving jobs to an employee that they liked. Today, the company can't just walk up and fire you because you didn't make so many pieces. As long as you make progress, you're protected. Other Norstar contracts picked that up from ours. We [eventually] obtained a pay scale that was the same as the northern employees, [and] we obtained a pension plan, group insurance, improved vacations, more holidays, break time.

After a couple of years of union recognition, we purchased a union hall [in Memphis] for $175,000 [on November 19, 1951]. We paid for it within a year, and we stayed there for a while. Every time we had a board meeting, the whites would go out and meet, about three different times during the meeting, so I knew something was up. It turned out, the whites didn't want to use the same toilet with the blacks. They sold the old hall for $170,000 and built a new hall across from the plant, but I knew something was amiss. Sure enough, they put in segregated toilets.

I called Walter Reuther and told him what had happened. Pat Greathouse[11] came down and changed it back to ladies and men. Two weeks later, at about 4 A.M., all thirteen windows in my house were broken with bricks at the same time. I called the police, but they didn't show up. The

11. UAW vice president in charge of farm equipment plants.

UAW didn't find any handprints, the brick throwers must have used gloves. I don't think it was done by anybody I knew. I think they hired people to do this. My son was nine years old, and he said, "Daddy, how come they're doing this to you?" Glass was everywhere.

After that, I got on the phone to Walter Reuther, and he said not to go to the police or newspapers. He said they were trying to destroy the UAW and I was the greatest influence in it. Walter said he would get the members to help. So I told the members what had happened, and three of the whites collected money and replaced and put in all of the windows. We never did go to the newspaper or the police. They wanted publicity, but we didn't give it to them. We had an idea of who it was. I saw three or four cars of people when it happened, and they [the people] were all white. I couldn't get the licenses. They were most likely hired by the Crump machine who was trying to get rid of the UAW. We were quite sure that none of this was caused by white union members.

About one week later at a stewards' meeting, the segregated signs were back up in the union hall. I called Walter again, and I got hold of Mazey. They said Doug Fraser would be in.[12] Pat Greathouse, Doug Fraser, and Bob Johnson, the Chicago director, came to town and called an executive board meeting of the local union. They said if they didn't correct the problem, they would go into receivership with an administrator over them. Some of the members kept putting [the segregation sign] back up. So I called Walter again, and we ended up with an administrator over the executive committee for two years. The only other person who could function was me. I could use the union, but the others could only come in with permission of the administrators. Mike Marshall and Red Collins were the international representatives who administrated for two years, and they carried guns. They changed all of the locks. We didn't even have union meetings for two solid years. We had a two-year contract, and then they made the move to correct discrimination in the contract.

At that point, we began to break down the segregation of toilets and watercoolers in the plant. Walter was talking to International Harvester people in Detroit. They took all of the "white" and "colored" signs down, even in the locker rooms and on the coolers.

The whites in International Harvester pressured the company to change

12. Fraser, following Leonard Woodcock, later succeeded Reuther as president of the UAW.

the cooler to one with cups. At that point, we discovered that five people owned the first union hall, instead of the local. The international union didn't know it, but they had signed it [the property deed] as Local 988 Executive Board under their names, and my name was nowhere on it. There were nine of us on the executive board, but those five guys got away with it and got the money.

For the next two years, when I left the hall every evening, I got ticketed. [About] every other day. I had a red Buick, and some guys said I should change the color of my car. I called Walter, and he said not to change the color. He said just to stay with it. I had to pay all of those tickets, even when I went to court and pointed out that I couldn't have been speeding when there were cars right in front and behind me. The judge asked me if I was saying that the policeman was a liar. He said that I called the police a liar, so he fined me ten dollars instead of five. All of this was against the UAW, of course.

From then on, I continued to get those tickets. I kept paying the tickets, but I stopped going to the courthouse to fight it. The union members helped me to pay the tickets.

Then we corrected the ownership to the Local 988. Doug Fraser came to tell people about the settlement, that the international executive board had ruled, and how the local union would have to be run. We had close to four thousand members by that time. [During one meeting over these controversies], I knew there was something going on and that something was going to happen to Pat Greathouse and Doug Fraser. While Doug was speaking, I got up and I got about twenty-five black members to line their cars up in the alleyway, and park mine by the door. So we had two cars in front and twenty some behind, and no one couldn't get out until we got out. I was thinking, "Lord God, give me the wisdom to figure this out!" Sure enough, I wrote a note up to Doug that when he was done speaking, he should follow me out of the union hall. At that point he and Pat got up, and I came across the room. (We were still sitting with whites on one side and blacks on the other.) I guess they thought that they could catch me before I could get Doug and Pat to the airport.

Doug got in my car, and I had two cars in front of me and twenty-some behind. The rest couldn't get out of there until all of us had come through. I carried Doug and Pat the short route to the airport. Those who stayed in the hall told me afterwards that people pulled out weapons and were planning to kill Doug. People had knives, sticks, and bricks and all in the union hall. After we left so quickly, they knew Doug was with me, but they didn't know where we had gone.

The next day, Art Shy from the UAW Education Department came in to speak in the union hall, sent by Walter Reuther. A guy named George Ellis, a mechanic, had a big chain in his coat and he came up front and swung it at Art Shy. I jumped in front of him, and the chain hit me. I was George Ellis's committeeman. Some of the whites said there would be a race riot now. Art jumped out of the way, but Red Collins and Marshall came out of the office with the big gun they had in there and made Ellis leave. This was in 1958 or 1959. This guy was going to knock the hell out of him, and I just happened to catch the blow.

So the executive board had to accept the conditions set up by the international union or lose the contract. Carl Moore was the service representative during much of this period, since 1953 or 1954. He didn't live very far away, and they shot into his house with shotguns.[13] [Three of the] executive board members [Holloway was the fourth] lived out in Frayser[14] and were also supporters of Reuther. After hearing about Carl Moore's house, they were afraid they would be harmed too.

After people found out about the dues money being used to buy the house [union hall], all but four of the officers got defeated. The "Holloway law" at the 1959 convention said no one could buy anything without the signatures of the international leaders and the local president. The same five guys who stole the UAW hall sued the International UAW and International Harvester. I was the UAW's only witness. I had to sit in the back balcony of the court until I was called, and I testified for an hour and a half. The judge dismissed the suit against the UAW. They [former union officers] were suing Harvester because Harvester wasn't sending the check to the local treasurer of the union.

So, at that point, only the plant fountains and bathrooms were desegregated. We had obtained plant-wide seniority, but the company wasn't administrating it right. This is where I came in and wrote the section on seniority in the contract, and we worked all of this stuff out with the com-

13. Moore carried a shotgun in his trunk for a number of years because of the threats against him. Phone interview, Carl Moore, February 7, 1983, Memphis.
14. Frayser was a mostly working-class white suburb north of Memphis.

pany after the union hall incidents. No more departmental seniority, and you had a right to be laid off instead of fired, and they would have to hire you back again. Finally, International Harvester began to cooperate with me at that point. Until then, they hadn't cooperated, because they didn't take the union seriously.

I heard that Crump went to Mississippi to investigate a boycott of [mechanical] cottonpickers. They were encouraging people to boy-cott Harvester products because they had integrated the plant. It was much later when we really achieved integration. The Memphis Urban League was praising Harvester, and Crump was against it. He didn't want integration.[15]

We had a White Citizens Council working in the plant at one time. Once we won the election and got the plant up to around two thousand workers, white rural workers from Mississippi and Tennessee came in, and they didn't like what was about to be changed by integration.

So they started to disrupt the union meetings. They wouldn't let you have a union meeting without trying to filibuster whatever was going on. We had six hundred to nine hundred members at every union meeting! We had day meetings and evening meetings. I could get six hundred black people to come to a meeting, but the supportive whites wouldn't come, be-cause they didn't want to be associated with this white citizens group. You had to have three-fourths of the vote to pass anything, according to the by-laws. So if I had five hundred blacks out of nine hundred members present, they [the whites] could never pass anything. That's what I did, for four or five years. I kept the membership going and got large numbers of blacks at every meeting.

In one election at Local 988, maybe the fourth election, a white guy ran for me, to represent us. We had a black caucus, and we supported this white guy. He was about to win, when White Citizens Council and KKK types broke in the door as the election committee was counting. These guys threw in a bunch of new ballots. As a result, our candidate lost. Whites stole the election from the blacks. The next time, we used [voting] machines and won, with the same candidate.

15. The Urban League saw International Harvester as a model company, but Carl Moore recalled that some of Harvester's management supported segregation, and that its cooperation with the union in Memphis resulted only from actions taken by company leaders outside of Memphis. Phone interview, Carl Moore, February 7, 1983, Memphis.

I let the company know what was happening. I got in with Mr. Hallet of the industrial relations and with the managers, and the company began cooperating. Mr. Condo, then Mr. Mayhall, were the first plant managers who cooperated with us. They'd trade ideas with me. I had the largest territory of any committeeman, [and] they feared disruption of the plant. People could start running bad stock if they wanted, so managers cooperated.

Then I bid on running the biggest machine in the plant, and I got it. We had staggered fifteen-minute lunches in three shifts (we called it a "continuous trick") so they wouldn't have to shut down the plant. I'd go and set up my punch press machine, then I'd cut it off when I had lunch. I'd check it out to know if it was set up properly when I came back. I'd always know I had it right when I left, but one time when I came back, something told me to inch the machine down. And as I inched it down, all of the punches fell out. I could have been killed if I had just turned it right back on.

So I went straight to Mr. Condo's office, and he came to see what had happened. I don't know where the foreman was. Condo stopped the entire department, questioned everyone, but no one had seen a thing (or so they said). The entire department was white except for me. Condo and Mayhall both read them the riot act. They told them not to ever mess with any machines again. They said, "George Holloway is here to stay, and there are soon going to be many more like him. You can't suspend him or run him out." Eventually, they did bring in lots more blacks with seniority, but they'd been janitors and lift operators before. All of this was in the contract procedures.

I was the committeeman for the man in the department who tried to kill me. That's how relations were with whites at the time. Soon, blacks moved into Departments 10 and 11.

Around the same time, I won an arbitration case for a union member by the name of Ham, a white guy, for one thousand dollars back pay. When we broke for lunch, after the case was won, I went out into the shop and told Ham I had won the case. He thanked me, then I left and went to the coffee machine and was telling another black employee that I had won the case for Ham. And just about that time Ham called [out to] another white employee and told him that he had won his case. The other white employee asked him how did he know, and this is what he said: "That nigger committeeman told me so." Another black guy heard this. This really hurt me because Ham and I was hired together and he knew my name. Ham and I came to the plant at the same time, and I always treated him nice. This went all over Department 10, the department I worked in also.

We almost had a race riot. That's how relations were between us and the whites at that time. I want you to know that some of the black employees boycotted talking or eating with Ham for two years. The company came out and told them they didn't want to hear that or any other slur against anyone, again. I didn't say anything to Ham, but he knew that I knew.

My department was the first to really stop the use of the term "nigger" and other derogatory terms. Moore said that if we heard it from anyone we should fine them, and the company wouldn't do anything to support them. This had to be in 1959 or 1960.

I was a target all of the time. Many times, I didn't come home. I'd be in the street with my car, but I wouldn't come home for fear they would get me. For a solid three months during one summer, Lint Coe, Clarence's older brother, stayed at Mr. Hamilton's house across the street with his shotgun, to see who was going to come by the house. I'd go to my mother-in-law's house.

For two years after I organized Local 988, our phone rang at 6 A.M. every day, seven days a week, at 2 A.M., and other hours, too. For two years, the FBI came to my house every other day to check on me, after our second or third contract. I believe someone told them I was a Communist. Walter told me not to worry about it. They used to come to the door around 5 P.M.

I borrowed money to send my son to college. He went to the University of Michigan his first year, and he graduated from Lincoln University. When my son went to the University of Michigan, the FBI followed him. They ask[ed] my son what schools and meetings he went to, what courses did he take, did he know certain people. Two or three days later they came by again. They ask[ed] him where his parents worked, when was his daddy in the union, and all those kinds of questions. My son said the university called to tell him that the FBI came to investigate him, and he was only eighteen years old. They only bothered him personally two times or so.

The FBI seemed to be trying to find out my background. They'd send different people to question me. I knew Earl Fisher, we were good friends. He looked very militant and he'd speak up, so that's probably why the FBI went after him.[16] The FBI knew I was dealing with Walter and Mazey, so maybe that's why I was followed. I was in the civil rights movement at that time, too. I used to sell four hundred to five hundred memberships to the NAACP every year. My wife got so sick of people calling for their cards.

I was appointed to the Memphis [AFL-CIO] Labor Council. We had three or four thousand people [in our plant], but each little craft local had an equal number of votes [on the council]. Any time that you raised black problems, they wouldn't support any UAW proposals. There were scattered numbers of blacks as delegates, but they were under white control. In the whole time I was in the council, I never did get elected to a committee position. Through the grapevine, or by phone, we would discuss things among the blacks at the other plants. Henry White was effective among the Red Caps [train terminal porters, whom White had organized into the CIO]. I had met him when I was a Pullman porter. He wasn't very dynamic, but he was a smart fellow. He'd speak up, but not forcefully, we [black labor leaders] used to talk about that. He raised with me the problem of Red Copeland, [and] he didn't think too much of Copeland's handling of contracts.[17]

I knew Leroy Clark, too. Leroy Clark and his wife [Alzada] got things well organized.[18] They were good friends of mine. If they would have had more autonomy, they would have been more effective. But Red Copeland and other [whites] restricted their actions. We used to talk about that a lot, too. Clarence Coe and I were friends, I encouraged him to run for union office. We got married around the same time, though he was younger than me. I also worked with Earl Fisher in voter registration drives.

I was on the staff [of UAW] for eighteen years, the first black to be put

16. Earl Fisher was president of the left-led Local 19 of the Distributive, Processing, and Office Workers and a prime FBI target. See chapter 5 and "Interlude: Arts of Resistance."

17. Red Copeland was CIO director in Memphis. Numerous CIO activists complained that Copeland did not stand up for black workers in contract negotiations, opposed strikes, and was more concerned with maintaining control over blacks and Communists than organizing the unorganized. By all accounts, he expected blacks in the unions to treat whites with deference.

18. Leroy Clark was a black organizer for the United Furniture Workers of America and later president of its Local 282 in Memphis. Alzada Clark began as a member of the union, married Leroy, and became an organizer herself. See their interviews in chapters 5, 6, and "Interlude: Not What We Seem."

on the UAW staff in the South, starting in 1962, and the first black to negotiate a contract.[19] I was a service representative in Region 8 in the South,
from Miami to Delaware to Tennessee. I negotiated their contracts, got
them a pension plan, insurance, and everything.

During the servicing, I went to Local 34 in Atlanta and Local 10 to set
up a fair practice group.[20] At first the Local 34 guys wouldn't let me in. And
Local 10 wouldn't let me set up the fair practice meeting. The region director, Tom Starling, was so bad that I didn't bother with him. When George
Wallace was running for president, I went to the Ford plant in Georgia, Local 882, for a fair practice meeting. The company had bought ten or twenty
thousand Wallace bumper stickers. Placards and signs and everything that
they had in the union hall, for George Wallace. But the UAW wasn't supporting Wallace![21]

We didn't have a fair practice meeting because no one showed up. Staff
member John Young and I took all of the Wallace bumper stickers and
everything and we put them in the trunk of my rented car. I carried them
to the city dump, and a black man that was operating the scoop shovel covered up the material and it would never be found. I gave him ten dollars.
No one knew who took all of that Wallace stuff. I was scared, but they
didn't have enough money to buy more. If they would have caught me,
I would have been hurt.

The CIO really contributed to the civil rights movement, I think. The
CIO brought better wages, so parents got interested in schooling and began to send kids to college. The UAW came in fighting for education and
better schools for all. [But] many people in Memphis at that time came
from Mississippi and was afraid to join the union. The Tennessee right-

---

19. Holloway said he negotiated a contract even before black UAW leaders from
Detroit Nelson Jack Edwards or Mark Stepp. Region 8 Director E. T. Michael ap-
pointed Holloway as staff representative on August 3, 1963. *Fifty Years of Progress,
UAW Region 8, Past and Present* (Detroit: United Auto Workers, c. 1985), 91.

20. Holloway handled Equal Employment Opportunity Commission complaints
and for a time served as political coordinator for some parts of Region 8. *Fifty Years
of Progress*, 91.

21. Alabama Governor George Wallace gained fame as one of the most violent political opponents of segregation. He claimed to be a populist and appealed strongly
to white workers on economic as well as racial grounds, and ran in presidential primaries in 1964, 1968, and 1972. The election Holloway refers to probably was in 1964,
but it may have been 1968.

to-work law made it possible to fire people for organizing.[22] People got fired [and] there were no leaders left to carry on. Most shops have a small leadership and a small shop, so they don't have the financial base to defend people in court. All newspapers in Memphis was against the unions. Many white and black had a lack of education. That is the reason why it was so hard to organize them. They didn't understand the great help and benefits that a union could do for them.

Black workers used industrial unions to expand black freedoms, but they did so within severe constraints imposed by the labor movement itself. First they battled the segregation and conservation of the older AFL craft unions. And then, where the industrial unionism of the CIO took root, long battles ensued for union representation, grievance procedures, better wages and working conditions, and health insurance and other benefits that unionized workers came to think of as entitlements. White and black workers could agree on obtaining such goals. But the war, urbanization and industrialization, the *Brown* decision, and the stirrings of a broader civil rights movement also opened up new opportunities to dismantle segregation on the factory floor and in the union hall. Unionized black workers acted on these opportunities but paid a high price for doing so, since it put them on a collision course with white workers. Whites feared the loss of their privileges at the workplace and in society at large, especially in the South. Here, defenders of segregation whipped up massive propaganda and instigated violent acts of intimidation to stop desegregation. For taking jobs previously closed to blacks and trying to end segregation in factory and union facilities, people like Coe and Holloway faced threats and actual attempts to maim or kill them, which served as warnings of what would happen to other blacks who tried to end Jim Crow at work.

Under such pressures, sympathetic white union leaders usually supported desegregation covertly. Hence, when it came to ending the racial

22. The Taft-Hartley Act of 1947 allowed states to pass "right to work" laws that outlawed the closed shop, in which all members of a workforce covered by union contract had to join the union as a condition of employment, and that contained other provisions which undercut union organizing. Tennessee and other southern and western states where unions were weak passed such laws, making it difficult for many unions to maintain their memberships.

seniority system at Firestone, the white president of the United Rubber Workers Local 186, George Clark, secretly advised blacks that they needed to get the courts behind their demands. Their 1956 court action, suing the union and the company for discrimination, brought documented proof that the company was hiring whites off the street while laying off blacks with years of seniority, and getting away with it largely because seniority in the plant accrued by department instead of plant-wide. This meant that when the company laid off blacks on the banbury machine or in other "black" jobs, their seniority did not move with them into "white" jobs such as tire building, allowing whites with less seniority to be promoted or hired ahead of them. Everyone knew that departmental seniority was discriminatory and in violation of the union's constitution, but nothing had been done about it.

The threat of court intervention finally gave Clark the impetus and outside support to take a public stand. At a Local 186 meeting, he argued that, as the union's leader, he had no choice but to follow the higher law of the union's constitution, the courts, and the international's master contract, all of which outlawed discrimination. He had tried to get the international president to do this, to no avail. Now under the pressure of a court settlement, Clark told his audience that nondiscriminatory contract language would be enforced. When "pro-Southerners" tried to stop this change, Clark used parliamentary procedures to outflank and split the group. Clark told the workers that eventually they would be glad for an end to departmental segregation: when they got too old for stressful production jobs, they could bid for some of the less demanding traditionally "black" jobs such as janitors and sweepers, and thereby extend their own work lives. If other white union leaders across the South had taken such a forthright leadership position in support of desegregation, he felt, much of the turmoil among white workers could have been defused. Perhaps he was right.

Clark's unusually open support for plant-wide seniority and open bidding on all jobs to whoever could qualify to do the work and had the most seniority, regardless of race, led the union in a new direction. Yet Clarence Coe and other blacks still had to implement this decision. To do so required absorbing years of harassment and abuse when blacks obtained tire building and other formerly "white" jobs. In this respect, probably no one had it worse than George Holloway. When he became the first black welder in the International Harvester plant, he faced the wrath of whites who hailed from rural areas, admired the KKK, and belonged to the White Citizens Council or the John Birch Society in the plant's local environs of Frayser, a mostly white suburb of Memphis. As he tried to integrate the workplace, Holloway's efforts to end segregation in his union hall took on epic proportions.

In 1951, when his local purchased a new building, Holloway himself removed the "white" signs from the toilet and had a black janitor burn them. Segregating the restrooms was against both CIO and UAW policies, but in 1956 the segregationist "pro-Southern slate" took control of the local's executive board and put the old union hall up for sale. They put the new hall's ownership in their name, claimed they had the right as private owners to segregate it, and tried to raise the price of union dues to pay the mortgage. By 1958, Holloway found himself as the only black member on an executive board of racists, fighting his own local tooth and nail for violating their international constitution and oaths of office. Although blacks made up one-third of the UAW local's members, UAW regional representative Carl Moore could remember only one white sheet metal worker who voted with blacks in their continuing battle with white supremacists. Moore himself, supporting the blacks, carried a shotgun in his trunk for protection.

Holloway's struggle almost created a civil war within his union. He won only because of the support of black workers in Memphis and of the International UAW Executive Board, which put the local into an administrative receivership in February 1960, dispossessing the "pro-Southerners." This group continued to spearhead resistance to desegregation, supported the Republican Party against the increasingly liberal national Democrats, attacked Walter Reuther for "running a socialistic dictatorship," and led pro-segregation marches to the state capital. As late as June of 1961, Holloway reported to the national UAW that this group's segregation signs were still up in his union hall. The creation of a "moderate" slate, which took over the local executive board and ended the trusteeship, occurred only after ten years of struggle on Holloway's part, during which whites sabotaged his punch press, put sugar in his car's gas tank, punctured its tires, broke the windows in his home, and constantly threatened him with death. He won his battle largely because black unionists came out in the hundreds to support his position at confrontational meetings with white supremacists and guarded Holloway to and from work and at his home. Remarkably, he eventually won the trust of many white UAW members, and he served UAW Local 988 for sixteen years as committeeman and one year as vice chairman of the bargaining committee. He later became the UAW's first African American regional representative, servicing Region 8 in the Southeast.

Holloway, like black workers at Firestone, did get some support from white union leaders, but again tempered by timidity. Holloway constantly called on Walter Reuther, Emil Mazey, and others at the top of the UAW leadership in Detroit, and he gained local support from Carl Moore. The UAW's action in putting the local in receivership smashed white suprem-acist control. Yet it took UAW leaders nearly ten years to act decisively, leaving Holloway under incredible attack. Yes, blacks at Firestone had a warm place in their hearts for George Clark, and Holloway revered Reuther. But black union activists in this period gained most of their strength and insights from informal meetings and discussions among themselves and from varying degrees of support among the black rank and file. The red scare had eliminated the most militant white desegre-gationists and blacks remained in a distinct minority in CIO leadership bodies, even though they were probably the overall majority of CIO members in a place like Memphis. As Leroy Clark comments in the next chapter, such dynamics left black leaders and activists in a frustrating po-sition within the CIO.

Breaking down workplace and union segregation required tremendous courage by a few individuals willing to hold back their emotions, to take whatever whites dished out, and yet persist in the struggle for change. People like Holloway and Coe, and others who tell their stories in this book, were exceptional leaders, putting considerable skill and intellect into factory organizing. Their survival encouraged others to emulate their actions. As black Harvester worker Ralph Thompson later told Paul Or-tiz, Holloway was the "driving force" in Local 988 and "some of that rubbed off on some of us." Said Thompson, "When he moved up to the staff, then we started running and we tried to do the Jackie Robinson role, you know. Everybody wanted to be George Holloway." Not only at the plant but also in local politics, Thompson recalled, "George was that pi-oneer and he was that lightning rod in Memphis as far as the black side was concerned." A few individuals took the risk, Clarence Coe emphasized, so that others could move even further ahead. This was the essence of "playing the Jackie Robinson role."

However, those who took the risk lived in a pressure cooker. Like Jackie Robinson himself, those playing this role put a tremendous strain on themselves and their families. The price they paid for ending Jim Crow at work came clear to me several years after I interviewed Holloway. I found a poignant note in his handwriting, sandwiched in with many other union documents in a folder marked "Personal, 1965–1969," in Holloway's files at the Walter Reuther Archives of Labor and Urban Affairs at Wayne State University in Detroit. Written after the 1968 deaths of Martin Luther King, Jr. and Bobby Kennedy, both heroes and acquaintances of Holloway's, his note describes the deep pain that racism caused him on a personal level.

"Dear Lord," he began, "if there is a God, what have I done wrong to cause me to have such a hard time?" Why, he asked did whites hate him so? "This is a hard country on black people. Why?" Holloway knew enough history to have the answer to that question, but he remained amazed at the refusal of whites to accept school desegregation, equal job rights, or any other measures breaking down the barriers of discrimination. "My life is so unhappy," he exclaimed, calculating that 90 percent "of all white people" still practiced discrimination, "for they feel that this is a white people's country." In his moment of doubt and defeat, Holloway wished to God that he had never been born or even raised a family, for he felt his children would have it even worse than he did—which was pretty bad, since "I have caught hell all my life." Holloway addressed his frustration and anguish to his God, while also asking, are you out there?

Even an optimist such as Mr. Holloway could feel utterly devastated by his daily struggles with whites, and the burden of his work weighed even more heavily on his wife Hattie. Some months after Mr. Holloway's death from a massive coronary in 1990, she recalled how unprepared she had been for the consequences of her husband's union activism. She had been raised in Memphis sheltered from whites—her father had been a successful businessman, a dry cleaner and tailor—and she was shocked and unnerved by the threatening phone calls that went on for two years, every morning at six o'clock, seven days a week. News reporters also called constantly, even though she refused to talk to them, and "made my life very miserable and unhappy," she said. When her husband left for work and gave her an embrace, he often said they might never see each other again. "It was rough on me and my son," she told me in an understatement. "I am still affected by it, I'm very nervous, the result of all that stress, nobody home but me and the boy. Once you get your nerves up, it's hard to get them back down."

Black workers fighting for equal rights have not usually been identified as part of the broader civil rights movement, but they clearly are. Black factory workers did not usually take the lead in civil rights battles in the streets, although their ability to send their children to college did provide one of the important platforms for the new generation of civil rights activists. If they did not lead the civil rights movement, the pioneers in this book did work for change in their workplace, built up the NAACP and other community groups, and remained acutely aware of the civil rights movement going on around them. They were as much a part of the freedom struggle as the Montgomery bus boycotters or the freedom riders in the 1960s. The union struggle itself was a part of the human rights revolution that swept the world in the twentieth century. For black workers, it was about more than the right to a job, decent wages, and working conditions. For those who began their union initiatives in the segregation era, this was a lifelong battle to be accepted and respected as human beings and as workers. Generations of African Americans in factories and other workplaces participated in the black freedom struggle at the point of production, persevering, as we shall see, even during the height of the red scare.

5 ORGANIZING AND SURVIVING IN THE COLD WAR

We told them [the company] we wanted to be treated like other decent Americans.

Leroy Boyd

Afrrican Americans in the Jim Crow era contested the meaning of citizenship at all levels. Black workers like Leroy Boyd first of all believed citizenship should not be the sole preserve of whites but should be bestowed equally. Moreover, he believed that its benefits should include economic as well as civil and political rights. Why should people fight wars for democracy when they do not have democracy themselves? Why are many of the economic benefits of industrialization denied to those who produce the goods? In the wake of a war against fascism, colonized, darker-skinned peoples as well as labor organizers throughout the world raised such questions, as did black people raised in the Mississippi Delta. From Vietnam to Memphis, those who wanted to maintain the old order often identified such questioners as "reds."

In the South, political leaders and journalists applied the Communist label to anyone who sought to break the color barrier, especially those involved in interracial union organizing. Communist Party members and other like-minded leftists did often provide the most forthright support for black equality. Communist-led campaigns to free the nine Scottsboro youths, and other African Americans victimized by white violence in the 1930s helped to draw back the veil that hid racial terrorism from public view. Communists and assorted leftists also braved gun thugs and police repression during early union organizing and helped to generate a climate favorable to interracialism within the Congress of Industrial Organizations (CIO). Black workers made allies wherever they could find them and joined numerous unions described by their enemies as "Communist dominated," in food and cotton processing, meatpacking, mining, and auto, steel, furniture, garment, longshore, and other industries. The exemplary equal rights policies of most leftist unions and their organizers made it difficult to convince black workers that anyone with socialist sympathies was an enemy of progress.

In places like Memphis, the authorities not only did everything possible to eradicate Communists but also accused virtually anyone who supported black rights of being one. Police and prosecutors rationalized their persecution of Thomas Watkins, for example, by claiming he might have been a Communist. Despite much repression, workers joined the Communist Party (CP) even in the deep South. In the Birmingham steel district, black workers made up the majority of CP members in the Depression era. In Memphis, only a few CP members existed, but they played an important role in the early organizing on the waterfront and among low-wage workers, creating a space for civil rights unionism in the CIO that otherwise would not have been there.

While most black workers probably had little contact with the Communist Party, many black workers concluded, reasonably enough, that if segregationists hated leftist unions and their organizers they must be good for blacks. Daniel Powell, a long-time white CIO leader in the South, believed that charges of communism attracted rather than repelled blacks. "Among Negroes, they didn't pay any attention" to Communist-baiting, Leroy Boyd relates, because blacks knew that any white who spoke up for blacks would be called a Communist. Black workers were not blind to the real differences between unions: George Holloway, for example, chose the more powerful anti-Communist UAW over the Communist-led Farm Equipment and Metal Workers union. And many CIO activists believed in militant unionism, interracialism, even socialism, but did not belong to the Communist Party or accept its discipline. At a time when many whites used the slur "nigger lover" and "Communist" interchangeably, however, most black union activists rejected red-baiting as simply another means of driving equal rights advocates out of the unions and scaring away white workers.

Until the late 1940s, many CP members and non-members worked together in the CIO. The Food, Tobacco, and Agricultural Workers Union (FTA) played a particularly exceptional role as a weapon of the weak against the strong in the South.[1] Organizing in agriculturally related industries, the union reached out to some of the poorest workers, took a clear stand for racial equality, and provided a vehicle for outstanding black union leaders such as Moranda Smith in North Carolina, the first black woman to become a regional union organizer in the South (or probably in the country). The union also employed a cadre of white labor organizers who took bold steps toward racial equality. These black and white organizers built the union's base among ethnic minorities, poor whites, and women, and their equal rights commitments became even stronger in the postwar years, when labor leftists sought an all-out assault on the barriers of Jim Crow. In North Carolina, the union registered black voters and created a freedom movement not seen in that state since Reconstruction. In Memphis, it not only organized the working poor but helped to mobilize them to vote against the Crump machine.

Leroy Boyd illustrates how FTA Local 19 provided blacks in Memphis with a more powerful means of self-assertion than did most CIO unions. African Americans made up a majority, around 60 percent, of Local 19's membership of some 2,500 to 3,000 workers scattered throughout a number of cotton compressing, cottonseed oil, and food processing plants. The union's leftism translated into a degree of white support for black equality that existed nowhere else in Memphis. From the local's inception, a succession of white organizers helped to convince white workers that they needed black support and leadership to succeed. These leftist organizers followed interracial practices all down the line, in defiance of Jim Crow conventions, while opening increasing space for black leadership of the local. Karl Korstad organized interracial picket lines during a strike at Buckeye Cellulose company in 1946, followed by Ed McCrea, an energetic and astute man whose trademark of militance combined with sound tactics and negotiating skills helped build Local 19 into one of the strongest union locals in Memphis. He and other leftists worked closely

1. The FTA began in the 1930s as the United Cannery, Agricultural, Packinghouse, and Allied Workers of America, or UCAPAWA, and was among the first unions in the CIO.

with Red Davis, a National Maritime Union member and, like McCrea, both a Communist and a decorated war veteran. This cadre in the CIO organized white worker support for black strikes in numerous industries after the war; for example, at the Nickey Brothers lumber company in 1948 they stopped other whites from scabbing against black strikers, saving the strike from defeat.

Local 19's success hinged not just on its militant white organizers and supporters but also on its strong black leadership. Henderson Davis, a black CP member, played a critical role in the union's formation in the late 1930s. John Mack Dyson, the local's black president, participated as a contract negotiator during and after the war, a time when most white employers refused to negotiate with blacks directly and when most white unionists would not think of encouraging such a practice. Dyson was the CIO's only African American union president in the city in the 1940s and was a popular leader among black workers, as they demonstrated by turning out in the thousands for his funeral in 1951. Soft-spoken Lee Lashley followed him as president, but Earl Fisher increasingly became one of the local's strongest black leaders.

In Leroy Boyd's description, Local 19's cadre of white and black organizers worked together on a day-to-day basis to challenge both employers and the white supremacist practices of some workers. Such shop floor actions emerged naturally in a union that successfully promoted black leaders and followed exemplary racial practices when compared to most CIO unions. It held integrated parties and picket lines, employed a black woman at the front desk in its office, attacked occupational discrimination within the factories, and enforced a clause in its contracts banning employment discrimination (other CIO unions had the clause, but few implemented it).

More important than formal declarations or informal practices, the union actually began to achieve its goal of ending segregation in the factories. As early as 1946, black worker George Isabell at Buckeye Cellulose took the lead in breaking down the unwritten rules prohibiting blacks from working as mechanics and skilled workers. As mechanization eliminated unskilled laborer positions, efforts to integrate departments saved blacks' jobs, allowing workers with seniority to shift to other jobs on a plant-wide basis, rather than losing work as they would have under departmental seniority. Buckeye also removed segregation signs over water fountains, pay windows, and time clocks (causing some whites for a time to bring their own water in canisters rather than drink out of the same fountain as blacks). Such early resolution of workplace segregation saved blacks at Buckeye from the lengthy guerilla warfare that Clarence Coe, George Holloway, and others endured in other shops. The Buckeye company's northern-based management (Proctor and Gamble owned it) certainly proved more ready to make such moves than southern-owned plants, but the initiatives for these changes came from the FTA workers themselves. Few other unions in Memphis could, or would want to, boast of such a record of effective organizing combined with a clear policy of racial equality as could Local 19 of FTA.

Indeed, Local 19's practices conflicted with the rest of the CIO in Memphis. A black majority at the workplace did not ensure egalitarianism, especially during the cold war. The CIO's International Woodworkers of America in Memphis had an even larger percentage of black members than Local 19, probably 90 percent or more. But like most CIO unions in Memphis, it steered clear of taking stands on racial issues and always relied on a white business agent to make decisions. And, like many other unions, at the national level it purged leftist radicals who might have had a different approach.

By 1949, any union with antiracist policies was at risk within the southern CIO. Both Local 19 and the United Furniture Workers (UFWA) Local 282, also with majority black membership, came under fire. At the local level, the Memphis CIO began to attack Local 282's leftists after the failed Memphis Furniture strike in 1949 (described in chapter 3 by Rebecca McKinley), while UFWA national leaders purged those staff members considered Communist in order to stay in the good graces of national CIO leaders. This purge, Leroy Clark explains, removed many racially progressive whites and some of the most militant blacks, sometimes replacing them with union functionaries who drew their paychecks and drank coffee while staying away from the tough job of organizing. The removal of white leftists robbed the Memphis CIO of interracial strike support, and strikes indeed began to fail. The loss of militant organizers translated into stagnation in many CIO unions across the country.

In the South, the CIO's older leaders opposed "communism" and antiracism as if they were interchangeable evils. When Ed McCrea and Red Davis demanded desegregation of the CIO union hall at a meeting of the

Memphis CIO's Industrial Union Council in 1947, the council expelled them both for "Communist" agitation. Although the national CIO later ordered the Memphis CIO and other labor councils to desegregate, many southern whites resisted. As George Holloway's story documents (see chapter 4), the failure of CIO leaders to desegregate union halls left the painful and difficult task of implementation largely to black workers at the local level. And whites continued to resist such desegregation efforts, often justifying their actions as "fighting communism."

Anti-communism as a tool to destroy integration and unions was nothing new, of course. It had long been used against the labor movement, and after World War II it became the operating method of Republican politicians such as Richard Nixon to remove New Deal Democrats from power. The Republican-dominated Congress's Taft-Hartley Act of 1947 held that unions with Communist leaders could not participate in National Labor Relations Board (NLRB) elections, while a massive government and media crusade against "communism" in the U.S. intensified with the division of Europe into East and West, the Chinese Revolution, and later, the Korean War. But now the CIO itself participated in the red scare, purging its own Communists and presumed Communists and even kicking out of the federation, in 1949 and 1950, eleven unions with nearly a million members for supposed "Communist domination." Attacks on union leftists led by the House Un-American Activities Committee (HUAC) and the Senate Internal Security Subcommittee (SISS) set off many local purges and blacklistings. CIO participation in inquisitions against leftists and in raids to take over the memberships of left-led unions only accelerated its internal stagnation. When the CIO merged with the more conservative, craft-oriented (and mostly segregated) American Federation of Labor (AFL) in 1955-56, its organizing days seemed to be over.

The red scare combined with the segregationist upsurge to put every black trade union activist at risk. At a time when many blacks admired and sometimes joined Communists in union and civil rights struggles, anti-communism put intense pressure on them to reject allies they desperately needed. In Memphis, the SISS held hearings on communism in 1951, targeting Local 19. This and regular FBI questioning of black unionists further complicated the racial tightrope walking required of blacks in the unions. The price of staying in the union movement increasingly required bending to the dictates of anti-communism, which also usually meant giving in on equal rights principles in order not to be suspected of being a "red."

Leroy Clark and Leroy Boyd tell us in plain language how they coped with such pressures in quite different ways. They each found themselves in agreement with many of the policies and people associated with the left, but they also both had to survive within the CIO. For Clark, a relatively well-educated New Yorker with little tolerance for racism, this meant going against some of his basic principles in order to stay active in his furniture union. For Leroy Boyd, raised in poor circumstances and with little education in Mississippi, it meant sticking with a "Communist-dominated" union while trying to stay out of the way of the sledge-hammer blows directed at alleged Communists. Their narratives remind us of why such people became involved in the union movement in the first place and how they sought to bring about change. In the era of the red scare, they occupied increasingly difficult, and sometimes contradictory, positions in the labor movement.

Leroy Clark Follows the Pragmatic Road to Survival in the Jim Crow South

He wasn't a Communist, he was just a black man who was way ahead of his time.

Leroy Clark began his organizing career in the rough days of the 1930s as one of the original members of the CIO's UFWA in New York state. He became one of the few black organizers within a white- and male-dominated union hierarchy of Jewish and eastern European immigrants. A soft-spoken man of sharp intellect, he guided his actions pragmatically: he sought to do whatever seemed necessary to make the union survive. In the 1960s he became one of only a few black union presidents in Memphis, and led the Memphis NAACP after King's assassination there in 1968. But he came to these positions only after years of perseverance and many distasteful compromises, particularly during the era of America's red scare.

I was asked by the International president to come here to Memphis because of my activities in our local union in New York, which is Local 76, the upholsterers union.

I came from New York. I was raised in Harlem. I became active in the labor movement around 1938. The factory I was working in was being organized by the furniture workers union and we got engaged in a tremendous strike. We made the springs for the furniture trade in a Long Island factory, which employed predominately black and Puerto Ricans. In 1937, John L. Lewis [first president of the CIO] called a conference of all furniture workers in order to set up a furniture workers union. There was a carpenters and joiners [union] and there was an upholstery union already established. He brought them together to see if he could set up one union out of all of them. The result of that was the United Furniture Workers of America, CIO, but the upholsterers and carpenters stayed with the AFL.

The AFL policy was they didn't even want blacks in the union. In fact my father was a carpenter and he could not get a job as a carpenter in New York, and he had to finally wind up gettin' a job as a porter in the subway station.[2] He had worked on the Panama Canal, and he could build anything, he could build this house, he could build a little birdhouse, anything! But he couldn't work at his trade in New York. He couldn't practice his trade because he couldn't belong to a white carpenter's union, [and] the hiring was all done through unions.

So that's one of the reasons why when the union first came to where I was working, I didn't want no part of it. I knew the history of the unions and their treatment of blacks. I knew! I knew how A. Philip Randolph used to get in the conventions and get booed down and shouted down at the AFL conventions. So I didn't want no part of the union movement when it came and knocked on our door. 'Cause I didn't think it had anything to offer blacks.

It was only through our own experience with the boss that we turned to the union. We found that we weren't getting nowhere with him, so we had to turn to the union. We found out that we couldn't get no fifteen cent a week raise, there was no way to deal with the boss and get anything—we just had to go and form a union.

The [United] Furniture Workers had sent their [white] organizers to our plant, you know, and of course we didn't so much go for the organizers. [But our] committee decided that we needed a union and we went on

2. Clark's father had a master's degree in divinity and came from either Jamaica or Trinidad, and Leroy's mother was born in Cuba, according to Alzada Clark. Leroy attended City College in New York for two years.

down to the CIO office. Alan Haywood was the organizer at the time.[3] We took the membership cards and our little committee got together and worked out a plan, and in forty-eight hours we had the entire plant signed up. We had a system that would keep somebody in the bathroom and somebody would send people in there gradually, one at a time, and sign them up. And in forty-eight hours we took the cards back down to the CIO. They didn't believe that we could do it like that, you know, they really didn't believe it. But we had the cards signed.

Anyway, as a result of the efforts we formed a Local 91 spring makers union. We couldn't get nothing [from the boss] and we had to strike, so we were out on strike for almost a year. The employer had a tactic that he was going to pick off all the leaders and have them arrested and jail them, mostly on charges of assault. Most of the leaders were arrested and served some time because of the employer's influence with the district attorney and the courts. I mean it was just a routine thing. I probably got the second highest time and one other guy, he got a couple of years. And the rest of them got thirty and sixty days, ninety days. [So I spent] fifteen months [in prison] in Riker's Island.

[After Clark got out of jail Local 91 elected him as an organizer, but he was drafted into World War II and served as an officer in Germany, France, and England. Clark preferred to say nothing about his experiences in the war, which his wife, Alzada, felt upset him profoundly. When he returned, his local had become predominantly Jewish and Italian, but as the result of his volunteer activities they elected him as the local's first black officer. As he became more active, Clark became aware of the struggles of blacks in the South.]

They had a strike in Thomasville in North Carolina. This was around 1946 or '47, when the CIO had a campaign that they called "Operation Dixie." This is when they had started organizing furniture and textile and concentrating on those industries, and as a result a number of local unions were established in the South. Operation Dixie was a time when the CIO was doing a tremendous job of organizing. It established a foothold for labor in the South. If it hadn't been for that, we wouldn't have had as much as we did [in the South].[4]

3. Haywood became national organizational director for the CIO (in October 1939), one of the top spots in the organization.
4. Operation Dixie was a dismal failure among white textile workers, but did have some success among black and poor white workers in other industries.

We were in a fight during that time from '48 to '50-something with the Upholsterers International Union because during that time we were in noncompliance [with] the Taft-Hartley law. The Taft-Hartley's whole purpose was to undermine the labor movement.[5] It didn't destroy it as it was intended to, but it did weaken it. It had the unions feeding on themselves, raiding each other instead of organizing the unorganized. They would petition for an election and we would have to tell the people, "No, you don't want no election," because we couldn't get on the ballot, 'cause we were a noncompliant union. [But] it wasn't the Taft-Hartley so much as the raiding business [that would] take away the members.[6]

I was one of those that fought for us not to sign the affidavits, up until the Supreme Court's decision, five to four, to uphold it. Then I said we had to go along because it became the law of the land. To me it was just an instrument to help try to destroy the union. But you couldn't take the same opposition in face of the Supreme Court's decision.

No question that I was opposed to it, and I know why it was designed. You see John L. Lewis, when he was setting up the CIO, he knew some of the hardest workers and the best people were Communists, and he sent for them to help organize and develop the CIO. So wherever you found good unions you find they were Communists, you know. He was concerned about building the CIO, so he went and did what he had to do to build it. He didn't question whether they were Communists or not as long as they did the job in building the steelworkers, furniture workers, or any other union. [But Taft-Hartley took the CIO's] most effective workers out. In fact our union, the [United] Furniture Workers, was one of those that was supposed to be expelled, but our president, he went to Walter Reuther and

5. According to Taft-Hartley, union officers had to sign an affidavit that they were not Communists. Those unions that did not comply with this provision could not participate in National Labor Relations Board elections, making it almost impossible for such unions to gain bargaining rights in unorganized shops or even hold onto the shops they had. Those unions that complied began to take away, or raid, the membership of noncompliant unions, adding to a destructive cycle of internal war within the CIO. Taft-Hartley also limited union political contributions and imposed government "cooling off" periods to interrupt strikes, and included other measures that have undermined unions ever since.

6. The United Furniture Workers vigorously opposed Taft-Hartley but went into compliance to stop raiding of its membership by compliant unions, which took away over 10 percent of the furniture union membership.

he worked with Reuther and so we weren't expelled.[7] We got rid of some leadership that were [Communist] Party guys, and this saved us from being expelled. Whatever staff guys that were on the left [in the furniture union], they got rid of them. You know, the union just goes on. They looked around for new staff guys where they could get 'em.

[In the United Furniture Workers], quite a few people active in that 1938 New York strike [had become] leaders, and when [union leader Morris] Pizer wanted to send somebody down to Memphis he called me. That was in 1951. My first experience when I come into Memphis and hittin' south, I landed up in north Memphis somewhere when I hit town, and I was in a black neighborhood. I saw a barber shop so I went over there to find out how to get to the address I had of 136½ South Second Street. That's where the CIO was. They gave me directions, and when I come out the police car was sittin' behind my car. When I went to the car he called me over and asked me was that my car, and I told him yeah. He said, what was I doin' there? You know, I had New York license plates, and a brand new car! [laughs] In that day, blacks weren't supposed to have no new cars. In fact, I bought the car in order to make the trip.

They questioned me what I was doin', and I told them I came here to do some work and I had a letter of introduction, and I showed them the letter and told them I just went in there to get directions. They give me back the letter and as I walked away they called me back. "Look, nigger, you're in the South here and when speakin' to white men you say SIR!" So I looked at him and said, "OK" and turned and walked away. "Come back here, nigger!" [laughs] It's funny now but it wasn't funny then.

I come back and he looked at me for about five minutes and then he said, "What are you, a wise guy?" I'm all innocent and I know what is botherin' him, I say "No." "Well I just got finished tellin' you to say SIR when you speakin' to a white man." And I'm figurin' what I'm gonna do. Give him his "SIR," and if I don't give it to him they may kill my mission, you know what I mean? I say [to myself], OK, I say, "Yes sir," and then I went on to my car. That was the police in '51. I don't think that would hap-

7. Walter Reuther was president of the United Auto Workers, and also became president of the CIO in 1952, until its merger with the AFL in 1955. He supported the purges of Communist-led unions from the CIO but helped the furniture and the packinghouse unions to stay in the federation on condition that they eliminated or muted the presence of Communists within their ranks.

pen now, but that's only because we've had to fight the police all through the years in order to try to change their attitudes.

And of course I wasn't too welcome here anyway by the labor leaders, because they didn't like my attitude. I was the guy who came from New York, and I didn't have the attitude they were accustomed to getting from black people, you know. In my local union in New York you didn't have that, you were just another person that's all, it didn't make no difference of your color. You just another person. 'Course you couldn't be an apprentice! You couldn't get the better jobs if you were black! [laughs]

The reason the union sent me to Memphis was they had a problem with the president of the local union here, a fellow named Rudolph Johnson. He was having a close relationship with Local 19, and the labor people in Memphis here branded him a Communist. He got elected president and they didn't want to accept a black Communist as head of the local union here, so they put the pressure on Pizer to do something about it. Oh yeah, he was in the papers a lot. See, the local people in the labor union was hot on him 'cause they were hot on Local 19 too. They were with the Food and Tobacco Workers union and that was one of the unions expelled from the CIO because of their Communist leanings, you know.

So I was sent down here [to Memphis] really to get rid of this Communist that had been elected president. Well, after I came in here I talk with the people supportin' him. They told me, "No, he's not a Communist" and they were going to support him no matter what happened. And so I went and talked with him and I found out that it wasn't a question of him being a Communist, it was just a black young fellow who was a way ahead of his time in fightin' racism—he was just way ahead of his time. And what the local union leaders were hot about was the fact that he wrote Philip Murray a letter complaining about the segregated facilities in the union hall, and behind that Philip Murray issued a letter that all segregated facilities in all CIO halls had to be done away with.[8] So they was after him for that. You know, they had separate drinking fountains in the union hall, separate bathrooms, that was in '51. He explained his position to me and came to me very clear just what he was doing, and people who believed in him, you couldn't shake their belief at all—he was their leader.

8. This letter, under direction of CIO legal counsel Arthur Goldberg, went to all CIO industrial union councils. While councils in the South sometimes complied formally by passing resolutions for desegregation, many of them continued to segregate.

Then I figured out what I had to do. It was get more people to the election that had not voted, period. And that's what I did—I got more people who hadn't voted at all and who weren't committed to him one way or the other and argued that it's not good for the local to have a guy at the head of it who was labeled a Communist, whether he was or not. But the power that be didn't even take a chance on him losing the election because they had him drafted, they had him drafted. They had that much influence.[9]

There was an election and he was defeated and another fellow named Brown was elected president. He [Johnson] was defeated but Johnson got the same amount of votes he got in the election before [laughs]—he didn't lose a vote! It's just that I organized more people to come to an election to vote. [The local], I would say it was maybe 95 percent black. In shops we had under contract most of the whites wouldn't join the union. There was some that did but the majority wouldn't join.

Well, I was sent there for movin' Johnson out, and after that election I stayed for a few months or more tryin' to build up the morale of the membership. And at the same time, there was an international representative assigned to the local union, Doyle Dorsey was his name. And I found that he wasn't no good. He was a guy that just was given a job. I don't know how he got the job, but he was a very dishonest guy and semi-alcoholic. He had two signers to the checks, the president and financial secretary, and he used to have them sign a bunch of blank checks and then he would fill them out for whatever he wanted. The secretary-treasurer was a much older guy and he just couldn't say no to a white person. [I told the officers what Dorsey was doing and they stopped signing checks, and] Dorsey put pressure on Pizer to get me out of there, move me out of Memphis.

In Memphis, there was no black leadership in the labor movement, except for Henry White, he was a CIO organizer. You couldn't tell whether Henry White was white or black, you didn't know it, see. And let me show you a picture of Henry White so you can see what I mean. He knew his place and he stayed in it, you know. He's a very intelligent guy, but he knew what he was supposed to do. He was the first one told me I wasn't going to be in Memphis long. He addressed them all [white CIO members] as "Mr.," and he was older than me, and I never did. They called

9. It is difficult to know whether the CIO leaders, the FBI, or the Crump machine, or all three combined, had Johnson drafted, but there is no doubt that such a thing could occur in Memphis.

me "Leroy," and I called them "James" or "John" or what have you, and I found out they didn't like that and they resented it. I didn't go to them for no lot of advice or anything. Anyway, I found that they were unhappy. The main guy who was unhappy was [CIO director] Red Copeland.

While there were a few local unions and they had black presidents, you know, they generally had a [white] international representative who really was over the local union. It was strictly the case with the woodworkers. They had a regional guy, he was [white]. They didn't have local presidents in different shops, they'd have what we call an "amalgamated local." The real leadership was given by Forest Dickenson, and the way he run it, it wasn't about to develop no black leadership. Steelworkers have that same setup and they got a lot of locals here and they didn't have no black leadership either. Most of their locals were majority black, and they had this as a district, [with] fifteen or sixteen local unions, and they'd have a district director and a staff representative, and the two of them took care of the servicing of the local unions.

Earl Crowder [the steelworkers union's director] was a typical southerner's approach to the black folks in general. I remember him the first time I met him. I was introduced to him when I first came in, and he said, "Well, ain't no question he's black." [laughs] I wondered why he said it. The reason for it was Henry White.

Henry White really was sort of semi-retired. He attended meetings and maybe make a little speech, but he didn't do nothin'. In fact a lot of the CIO staff just before the [1955 AFL-CIO] merger were in semi-retirement, those that were kept on didn't do too much. That basically was due to the philosophy of [AFL-CIO President] George Meany. He felt that it wasn't the job of the AFL-CIO to organize, it was the job of the international unions to do their own organizing. So they didn't get rid of the staff but they just let it die away, you know. Naturally, guys working under those circumstances didn't work too hard, and then if a guy passed away or somethin' they didn't replace them.

When I came here, I think they [the Memphis CIO] had taken the [segregation] signs down, but the custom still remained where they still had the separate bathroom but they didn't have no signs. [The opposition to that] they mostly attacked on the basis of communism. But this was what their attacks were about. Red Copeland pretty well had me investigated by the FBI while I was here, too, in fact I'm pretty sure about it. Later on down the road I had a company attorney to make a statement about me being a Communist, and that was based on government records, this is what he said. I challenged him, and he said well he knows, that this is what he was told.

I didn't have that much dealing with Copeland because I saw the kind of person he was—he's what I call a "redneck"—and I avoided him as much as I possibly could. Yeah, I only had any deals with him when I just had to. They [most of the local black union leaders] were more like Henry White. They just accepted it. They just accepted it. Rudolph Johnson, [on the other hand], what he told me is he did a lot of reading, and he just felt that his people were being wrongfully treated. And as long as he got a mouth, he was gonna open it. This is what he told me.

That senator, what's his name, [Eastland] from Mississippi, he was always callin' [Lee Lashley, president of Local 19,] in and questionin' him and things.[10] And of course they knew that Lee wasn't a Communist but they just felt that he was going along with 'em. But they was really after [Local 19 business agent] Ed McCrea. The position that that local took on the Emmett Till lynching—that was one of the things that really upset them you know. The CIO council, they made a big deal out of it [too], but Local 19 was correct in its position as far as I can see.[11]

But you see, before I came I watched the development of the CIO in New York, and it went out of its way to recruit and get black leadership for the local unions and train them. It went out of its way, which was entirely different from the AFL-CIO policy.[12]

[Clark explains that after employing him to remove Rudolph Johnson, the furniture union moved him out of Memphis to Martinsville, Virginia,

10. See "Interlude: Arts of Resistance" for more information on, and a transcript from, the Memphis SISS hearings.

11. Two white men murdered fourteen-year-old Emmett Till for allegedly making a "fresh" comment to one of the men's wives. The incident took place in Mississippi in 1955. Clark is referring to Local 19 members' protests against the 1951 execution by the state of Mississippi of Willie McGee on charges of rape. See Leroy Boyd's comments on the McGee case later in this chapter.

12. The CIO in 1935 began as a group of industrial unions that later broke away from the AFL. Clark gave examples of black workers speaking out and having some power on issues that concerned them in the CIO, and compared it to what he saw as a lack of black leadership in the AFL. He and many other African Americans felt the AFL and CIO merger in 1955 undermined CIO equal rights policies.

where he and white organizer Gene Day, labeled a "red" by many, organized workers, black and white, and successfully won an election at the
American Furniture plant. Clark then went back to work in a shop in
New York, until the union's leaders asked him to go back to Memphis
again in 1958.]

They had gotten a lot of letters of complaints from the members in
Memphis that the representative here wasn't doin' his job. [Furniture
union leader] Morris Pizer sent two of us in here, he sent a southern vice
president in and he sent me. Nobody knew I was here, but in the meantime I took all the letters that was wrote to the international, and I visited
all the people that wrote the letters. I visited other people in all the shops,
and I got a good picture of what was going on from them.

This guy Walter Carson, he only ran the union on a part-time basis
'cause he had another business—he was lending money on second mort-
gages and he was in close contact with Senator Eastland from Mississippi.
After our report, then the international president decided to go get rid of
him, but we found out that he had written a contract with the local for his
services for five years. We were of the opinion that the contract wouldn't
hold, due to the circumstances in which it was made, you know he just
got a couple of officers to sign it. But I think we propose[d] to give him
five thousand dollars to terminate his services. Then in the meantime we
had sent to the telephone company a request for all the phone bills and
[laughs] Fred Fulford [organizational director] found out that he had had
all his phone calls to, what's his name, to the senator in Mississippi. Then
Fulford says, "Fuck it, I ain't goin' to give him a damn thing!" [laughs]

I guess we were still a sort of a "red-tinged union," see. So he [Carson]
was keepin' them informed about us, I guess. [But the workers told us]
they could never get hold of him, he was never in the office, and when
he handled their grievances he always favored the boss. I talked with him
about it and he didn't deny it, he says you can't get these people to do
nothin' for theirselves. So only thing you can do is beg the bosses for a
favor. And that's all! And his position was, you know, go along with the
bosses an' they'll let 'em live. He wasn't servicin' the workers, he wasn't
lookin' out for their grievances. No faith at all in the workers.

I don't remember where he came from, but I got the impression that
this was the first union he worked for. I know [Doyle] Dorsey, he had
never worked for no union before. See Pizer was concerned that he have

the face of the union be reflected in the white southern person who had all the morals of the southerners. And that's the way he looked at it and that's what he would try to find in a staff person. They weren't people who were caught up in the movement.

[The union's leadership then returned Clark to organizing in North Carolina, where he led a six-month strike in High Point. His wife, Alzada, had remained in New York and gave up a well-paying job to go with Clark when the union moved him to Chicago in 1960. He ran into opposition when he tried to bring blacks into leadership of the local in Chicago, and the union returned him and Alzada, who resented the union's treating them as moveable furniture, to Memphis in 1961.]

There was a guy who came to Memphis, and he asked the international to give him help. He was a former typographical worker but he was a good organizer, and the union was growing. But he couldn't get to organize no new shops 'cause he didn't have the time. What was happening [at the union when I arrived], the kind of people [there] weren't too interested in really building a union or organizing, but holding a job was about all they were interested in. This guy Steve, of course local [labor] leaders were a bit after him. He was a Socialist, I think he belonged to the Socialist Party. I know there'd been questions raised, he was one of the persons involved in the literacy organization, concerned about teaching adults to read and write.[13]

And they started attackin' him for his political beliefs and tried to get him to say if he was or wasn't a Communist! [laughs] He was a very capable guy and we worked together for one year, and then he just disappeared in thin air, he just disappeared! Years later I found he was in the home for typo workers, a retirement home for typographical workers. I think he purposely left so that I would handle the local union. And so I just took over and took care of the local union and built it up, as the international representative, from a local of 400 or 500 to about 1,700, from about half a dozen plants to about eighteen plants. So I was sent down here to Memphis and I've been here ever since.

13. Highlander Folk School organized a citizenship and literacy program led by Septima Clark that proved instrumental in black voter registration drives during the early civil rights movement, and was taken over in 1961 by Martin Luther King, Jr.'s Southern Christian Leadership Conference. It seems likely that the activity Clark describes was related to those efforts.

Leroy Boyd Battles White Supremacy in the Era of the Red Scare

What the union stood for was being called un-American.

Leroy Boyd grew up in a rural neighborhood near the Mississippi Delta town of Greenwood, where his family of ten children (he was the sixth) and two adults lived in a drafty two-room wood house without plumbing. He recalled that "we were the last one to go to school, the first one to quit." To get an education, he walked five miles, past the white school to which whites were bused, during the few months out of the year he wasn't in the fields. He spent his early years working for his father, raising cotton and corn on shares, and raising animals and food crops. When I met Leroy Boyd, I was impressed by his humble yet self-assured manner and his shrewd and realistic understanding of power relations on the shop floor and in society. Unassuming yet direct and sincere in his demeanor, he reflected the knowledge of a man with little formal education but with years of schooling in the union movement. Although he had no knowledge of unions in his home state of Mississippi, the heartland of segregation, Boyd's roots there in many ways guided his actions in the labor and civil rights movements. I interviewed Mr. Boyd in 1983, and spoke with him numerous times after that. I have also drawn on Paul Ortiz's interviews with Mr. Boyd in 1995 for the Behind the Veil Oral History Project at Duke University.

I'm from Black Hawk, near Greenwood, Mississippi. I stayed there twenty-one years, and then came to Memphis in 1945. It make your blood boil when people tell you about a lot of things that happened. Because my mother used to tell us [about] maybe certain girls that some of the white men was going with. "You better not fool with that girl. She going with a white. You can get killed." So I say to myself, I can't court their race, and I got to pick who I got to court. I didn't feel like that was right. If a girl want to court me, that's her business. And if she didn't, that still was her business. That's the way I felt.

[So] I got me a gun. Now I'm a young boy here. My daddy didn't know I had it, see. I always kept protection. [Whites], they'd get on the road and shoot you down. And that would just be all to it. I got big enough, I searched around until I got me a pistol, a pistol and bullets. Yeah, in fact I had a knife. I done had the tools to fight with. I had the tools. The pistol, I always kept the pistol for last results. Some people would think of it as first. That was just a backup, just in case. For more power, then you've got to use your gun. But thank God, didn't nothing happen to me.[14]

Well, 1944, I helped my daddy out. I was about twenty years old then. . . . Well, it was during the war. And we was talking about what the defense job was paying. I said, "Shoot, my last year of farming." I didn't go in the service. So in 1945 I left. I was going to go to Detroit. But after the war was over they said they was closing up all the defense plants. So I had a sister and a young brother in Memphis, and I said, Well, I think I'll go to Memphis. I came here the last day in '45. And I've been here ever since. My family still has a farm in Mississippi.

I began working at Federal Compress on January 4, 1946. I was twenty-one years old, and I was engaged at the time. They sent me out [there] from the employment office. It wasn't what I wanted. I was just going to go down there until I could do better, and got stuck while I was courting my wife. Then we got married in '47 and started raising a family. That's the way you just start getting tied down, see, start buying furniture. So family just kept increasing. My oldest son was born in '48 and in 1950 my oldest girl was born. And I believe that was during that Korean War. They was trying to get me to go to the army, but I got deferred on account of I was married and had three dependents, you know, two children.

Oh, man! When I first came there [to Federal Compress], boy it was rough. When I first started working, I was trucking. Pushing a pair of two-wheelers with a bale of cotton on it, back to the scale and weigh it, take it to the warehouse to be stored up, or take it to the press to be reprocessed. Of course, everything was then [done] by hand. Before machinery come in effect, shoot, you had to put one bale up on the other one, prop it up on the next one. Just keep on until you got it up five high, six, seven high. Down at the south Memphis plant, it was maybe 175 [worked there]. But as machines come on, one machine would cut out eight truckers.

Well, at Compress it was just like on some of these plantations. We had

14. At age eighteen, Boyd did use his knife to cut an older black man who attacked him.

those people right off the plantation. I've heard a lot of them [blacks] talking about how those guys used to do them on the plantation, that the guys used to be down there with a bull whip and be cursing you and be telling the Lord, "Teach me something to call these black so-and-sos." Man, it was rough. They didn't believe in treating the employees decent—long hours, cheap wages, and no ice water. And them warehouses hot. You know, you working in a hot place where you ain't getting any breeze, it's rough, handling them bales of cotton. We were storing maybe 150 or 200 bales an hour up in the warehouse. You was working, man.

So that's the way it was. And they just wanted to get all they could get out of you. We had a union, but the union people weren't too active. During '46 the wages was low. I started making fifty cent an hour, and after ninety days, I was raised to fifty-five cent an hour. That was it.

Down at the Compress, it was no white workers pushing no bale of cotton. They didn't hire any for that, they hired them all as supervisors. The bosses had a terribly nasty attitude. Being in the [military] service didn't affect the company people for the better. Well, not William Woods. He was a scoundrel boss fellow when he came out [of the army], just like when he went in. Well, you get those bosses right off those plantations. [At Federal Compress] they didn't have no bull whip, [but] you couldn't act like he was another man, you had to act like he was your boss. If you disagreed with him, you couldn't tell him he was lying, even if he was lying. The bosses would hire and fire you. They were rushing you and cursing at you.

When I came in I didn't even know what a union was. You know how it is when you come out of the country, you don't know what things are all about. In July '46, Earl Fisher taught me. He was working in the same shop, and talked me into joining the union, and in the latter part of that year I started going to the union meetings. I was there about eight months, and [Local 19 leaders] Earl Fisher and Ed McCrea and John Mac Dyson they started having meetings with us. Well, see, at that time the contract was expired in December. We have a number of people that wasn't union. Number one, if you want to be a threat to a company, like an army, you got to get your people together. If your people ain't together, the company going to say, "Well, you don't even represent the majority of the people. There's no threat to us." Which is true. You come down to a fight, so what you got? So you have to consolidate.

I was there about eight months and I was elected steward. You know, they started having meetings electing crew leaders, so I was one of the crew leaders. You know, each supervisor had a gang of mens. And you elect a steward in each gang so if a problem arise a person wouldn't have to be going all over the plant trying to find the chief steward, see. You have someone right in your department, you know, to take the case up.

In '47, Earl Fisher was elected chief steward. The struggle began when Earl took up the first grievance. Earl was a outspoken person, and this is when we began to feel the effects of the union. He began to get the people together down at the union hall. With the help of Ed McCrea, he taught us how to handle grievance, how to conduct ourselves, and how to protect ourselves against the boss. They taught us how to do.

From then on, he [Fisher] attempted to take up the grievance, and we had to let the company know that we had a union, so we had a number of work stoppages during the life of the contract [wildcat strikes]. We were just lucky that no one got terminated from the work stoppage at that time. But we had a number of them afterwards. Finally, Earl was picked out along with two or three others, and was fired from Federal Compress on account of the work stoppage. They accused him of leading the people out.

It was about working overtime. That's what the work stoppage was about. After working eight hours, then Fisher thought the company should pay a man to work extra hours, but not by force. But the arbitration board upheld the company. Most of the time, we lost more cases than we won, and arbitration usually sided with the company. At that time, looked like the company had the upper hand, knew the people picked for arbitration. Usually the mediator would pick five company people, so they had the advantage over us. During negotiations for the next year, the company would sometimes offer a nickel or two-cent raise. They might say, "Well, we had a bad year." Most times we got two and a half cent each year for a three-year contract. That's seven or eight cent over a three-year period.

They told us during negotiations that Federal Compress was owned by 3,500 stockholders. But, it was being run by just a few people from Mississippi and Arkansas.[15] The shiproom guys were from plantations in Mississippi and Arkansas, and some of them had been guards out at the work

15. Federal Compress, which used high-density compressing machines and stored cotton in warehouses, had scores of plants throughout seven southern states, with approximately 3,100 employees in 1966. The company had tangible assets of over

house. Some were ex-policemen. The company's attitude at that time was like the bosses, and the bosses were people right off of the plantations in Mississippi. They believed in working you just like the people worked you down there on the plantations. They didn't pay you anything decent. That was the sentiment of the company from top to bottom.

This was before my time and I didn't witness it, but a supervisor pulled a gun on one of the workers. So all of the workers got together and said they wasn't gonna work until the company discharged the guy. But the company didn't discharge him. At that time, the supervisor had a time book, instead of a time clock. The company just took his time book away, so he couldn't be a boss over the workers. The only thing he could be was just a shipping clerk, and that's the only punishment he got.

Years ago, they said, the superintendent or general foreman would curse you, calling you a black son-of-a-bitch. The workers, they'd ask the good Lord to teach him to stop. That's just how things was. They were fighting us, and we were fighting them. We was cutting out on their profit, because they weren't able to get their merchandise out for the customers. We would have work stoppages that lasted two days. Not too often, but maybe once a year for that long. But it often happened and lasted a day. It happened when Earl was fired [see chapter 6].

We'd be out there at the gate, and they'd say we were fired the next time we came back. So we got together and put out leaflets, and everyone stuck together and didn't go back. The next morning the union officials came down and talked to the company, and then they came to get us to go back to work. That's the way it was done, we all went out together, and we all came back together. We never would drift back. We knew that if we drifted back in one at a time, we'd have been beaten, we'd have been whupped.

Workers was afraid. At that time in our contract, we had to take them in before the superintendent. They had to witness their signature, because they had a checkoff in the plant. That was a stick. The average worker wouldn't want to come up and sign one of those things before the boss. That kept us from signing up a lot of workers before we got that changed.

During that time, we didn't have a clause in the contract to protect the

---

thirty-two million dollars, with 3,600 shareholders. It was a big business, but its executives came from cotton-related commercial activities in Tennessee, Arkansas, and Mississippi.

worker from getting out of the union during the year. The bosses was loaning money at the office, and if a person came to him and wanted to borrow money, he said they'd have to get out of the union first. "Either you're on my side, or the union's." When a man was standing on the fence, well a lot of them said they were going to get out. One superintendent then was Cliff "Fat" Thomas, and he was a tough one. He was the one who would loan out money. See, we had a problem. We'd sign people up—shoot, you think the guy's with you—and then we hear later he's done got out of the union under pressure. But now that's changed. If you sign up, you have to give written notice a certain number of days prior to the expiration day of the contract. This curbed all of that.

The supervisors resented the union at first, like when we first got rest breaks. Why did we need to take them? they thought. Of course, we had to have work stoppages to get breaks. We waited until the company got real busy, and one day at noon, we just didn't go back to work at one o'clock. We all went to the office, and they want to know what was the matter. The stewards went in and talked to the managers about it. So this is how we got breaks. We told them we wanted to be treated like other decent Americans. We wanted to have a fifteen-minute break, but we did get them to give us ten minutes twice a day. Our lunch hour was from thirty minutes to one hour. It all depended if the company was getting behind or not.

When we had work stoppages, to keep the steward from getting fired we had the stewards continue working. The other members would quit work. You'd have to be together. The boss'd come and tell us that X number of people have quit work. Stewards'd go down there and try to get them back to work, as the contract said, although we'd be knowing what it was all about. When we'd tell them to go back to work, they'd tell us to go to hell! They'd say they weren't going back until they got certain conditions, whatever the work stoppage was about. We [stewards] were just the go-between people, between the union and the company. We'd go back to the company and tell them the workers said they not going back to work and ask what we should do?

So we'd assist and make every effort to go from the bottom to the top! The next step was to call the union representatives on the phone and get them to come down. Then they'd come down to talk with the workers, but they'd take their time coming down! [laughs] So, it might be three or four hours later, and they'd talk for a couple hours with the workers. Then the union would tell the company that they were still refusing to go back to work. [The company], they'd get mad at us and say, "Well, you've all been off this long, take the rest of the day off!" The day's almost gone by then, and they'd all go to the union hall for a meeting.

So this is the way we done. We know we've violated the contract,[16] but the reason the company don't fire us is there's too much work to be done, and there are too many people involved. If they fire all the members, they'd had to hire new people, and they'd be defeating their purpose doing that. Over a period of years, this is how we were able to change conditions in the shop.

See, in your grievance procedures, it says that all grievances should be taken up with the supervisor, with the assistance of the steward. We knew that. But, see, what happened, if someone did that he got fired, and so did the steward! Even if there were five people, for any reason. They'd get fired at the drop of the hat. If your supervisor said you couldn't work, or lied and said you took too long a restroom break, they wanted to fire you. The way we dealt with that, the rest of us would time the person, and be showing them on our watches that it wasn't true, we'd time each other to prove it when a supervisor lied. That's how we kept them from doin' that.

At that time, they had two restrooms in the plant, and it would take you from five to seven minutes just to walk to one. We had to walk from here to maybe two blocks to the restroom. I had grievances about that many times. The breaks weren't long enough to get there and back! Finally they gave us fifteen minutes. They wanted you to ask before you went, and that was something we felt we didn't have to do. When you did ask a supervisor, he'd tell you to wait until so-and-so comes back or say you'd already been once. We felt that was our own business.

Supervisors might say something to one of the workers, curse at him. [The worker], he'd use the same word back to him. Then he fire him. As long as you tuck your head, he going to continue to pull it on you. This is why together, you got to be knowing what's happening. Your workers have to keep your eyes on to *know* what's going on. You have to stand up for yourself, because the supervisors got together, too. We had to fight, man. I've been in a lot of battles.

They made me a steward. Took me a while to be trained. And, boy, me

16. Most union agreements prohibited strikes during the duration of the contract.

and the boss had some good hassles. They tried to make it hard for me. [chuckles] See, my job was just like a lawyer for workers' rights, and I'd defend them. But he tried to make it hard for me by putting me in hard places. They going to bend me. I know I had to be at work on time to be able to protect myself. So I just kept myself covered. If I had to go to the restroom, I let someone know. I know [the supervisor] he's watching me. Once you well organized, you can bring him down because you get everybody working together.

The [work] gang leader have to train his people. Our businessman [union agent], he taught us all that. Then the trouble black women had with the supervisors was that they would pat them all of the time. If they let them [do it], they were all right. If a woman stood up for herself, she didn't stay in good with them, and she wouldn't be around long. She would have to find some other work. At that time, the only thing black women did was clean up and tie on tags when a bale of cotton came in. Some that had some education did clerk work like whites, but they didn't get paid a clerk's wages.

In the shop, all the whites were considered bosses, regardless of what they did. In fact, they belonged to the union but they didn't attend any of our meetings. But working in the shop, if a white person took too much time with a Negro, they'd always call him a nigger lover. That's what you'd be branded, a nigger lover. So they [the whites] wouldn't associate with us too much. And that's a mistake with the whites, not to associate with the Negro. The union representatives were branded with another name, they were called nigger lovers, and also Communists. White men in the shop would use these names. I never heard a white lady call names, it was always a white man. There were white women in the office, but not in the shop. They would hire Negro women in the shop, but not white women. The only Negro working in the office would be a janitor.

I can remember back when I first came here, we had a number of raids [on Local 19 membership by other CIO unions]. What led up to those raids: we were a part of the CIO at that time. In the Memphis CIO council, we had segregated sides in the union hall. All the white mens sit in groups by themselves, you know. And they had segregated restrooms. This was white men, white women, that was colored men, colored women. Four different restrooms for the people.

We were still part of the FTA, the Food, Tobacco, and Agricultural

Workers union. We thought there should just be men's and women's [bath-rooms], like they do now. We always felt like Local 19 always treated a person as a human being. And we didn't have segregated restroom. We had just men's and women's. At that time, we was expelled from the CIO, we was kicked out.

After we were expelled from the CIO, the CIO began to raid our plants where we had a union in them. During that time, of course, a lot of our people were branded Communists. In fact, during that time, they investigated our local. I don't know if it had anything to do with McCrea resigning from his job here, or not. They gave him a job in New York in the shop. They felt like he would be a hinder to the union.[17] He was very popular. In fact, it hurt me when he left, because he really would speak up for you. He was just as good as an attorney. He was good. He had people behind him, too.

But any time a white man spoke up for the rights of the Negro, he was called a Communist. As time went on, you don't get that name. Since the civil rights movement began, you don't hear about being called a Communist.

Among Negroes, they didn't pay any attention, because they knew how white men felt about another white man speaking up for the Negro. He was just branded as a Communist. I don't think it made any difference if he *was* a Communist. But they used that sometimes when they were raiding some of the shops. They used that to discourage the whites in the shop. The white people in the Local 19 shops were poor whites, mostly.

I imagine it worked for a few whites. You see we have white workers in there, well, they want to get a union to themselves. The companies got in with a lot of the white labor unions to get them to raid our plant. They [CIO] were passing out leaflets, and they'd get so many people to say they don't want Local 19, and they'd petition for election. Then they'd get a majority of the votes. That's how they were able to take the shop away from the union. Where a lot of white worker was, they were succeeding in winning some of them over.

17. The FTA removed McCrea from Memphis after banner headlines in the Memphis papers, reporting on the Senate Internal Security Subcommittee hearings on communism in the southern labor movement in 1951, called him a "bigtime red." The union didn't believe McCrea could work effectively after such negative publicity.

In the 1930s many African Americans in the South remained tied to the failing rural cotton economy. Between 4 and 6 A.M. Memphis laborers were hired by drivers to work on Mississippi and Arkansas plantations for 50 cents to a dollar a day. Photo by Marion Post Wolcott, October 1939. Farm Security Administration (Library of Congress).

White men who ran the Memphis cotton exchange, along with the banks, real estate, and trade connected to the cotton economy, formed the ruling elite. Manufacturers came to the economy late but also used segregation to their advantage. Photo by Marion Post Wolcott, November 1939. Farm Security Administration (Library of Congress).

Black men on the riverfront (this group was in New Orleans) moved cotton and other goods up and down the Mississippi River to national and international markets. Stevedores, among them Thomas Watkins in Memphis, were among the first blacks to unionize. Photo by Russell Lee, September 1938. Farm Security Administration (Library of Congress).

Because whites paid black men such poor wages, black women had to work to keep their families together. Domestic workers sacrificed time with their own children to take care of white families for even poorer pay than black men received. Photo by Marion Post Wolcott, Atlanta, May 1939. Farm Security Administration (Library of Congress).

Segregation and low wages translated into poor housing and schools. This unpaved street full of "shotgun" shacks might appear to be a rural area, yet it was among many such black neighborhoods in Memphis during the 1930s. Photo by John Vachon. Farm Security Administration (Library of Congress).

African Americans were not passive victims even in the worst of times. Creative outlets for the expression of their humanity included dressing well, playing music, going to church, or jitterbugging in a juke joint, as in this scene in Memphis. Photo by Marion Post Wolcott, November 1939. Farm Security Administration (Library of Congress).

Whiteness, upheld by law and racial violence, remained a badge of superiority for some and a symbol of degradation for others. African Americans increasingly protested segregation during and after World War II. This photo of a Memphis bus station in September 1943 is by Esther Bubley. U.S. Office of War Information (Library of Congress).

Unions provided one of the few vehicles available for blacks and whites to join in common cause. Workers at Memphis Firestone became famous for their many strikes, which led to generous health care and pension benefits for retirees. By 1976, when this photo was taken, virtually all barriers to black advancement at the factory had been eliminated. *Press-Scimitar* photo. Courtesy of the Mississippi Valley Collection, University of Memphis.

Black workers in the public sector had the worst jobs at the lowest pay. Hauling garbage was nasty work and paid so little that many of the workers qualified for welfare. Photo by Roy Lewis, 1973. Courtesy of the Mississippi Valley Collection, University of Memphis.

In 1968, accumulated grievances and the crushing of two men in a garbage truck set off a spontaneous strike in the dead of winter. Sanitation workers marched and held mass meetings for sixty-four days until the city of Memphis recognized their right to union representation. *Commercial Appeal* photo. Courtesy of the Mississippi Valley Collection, University of Memphis.

On April 8 sanitation workers and an estimated twenty to forty thousand others held a silent march of solidarity and grief after the slaying of Martin Luther King. These members of AFSCME Local 1733 carried two simple signs: one read "Dignity," the other said "I Am a Man." A Del Ankers photo. Courtesy of the Mississippi Valley Collection, University of Memphis.

In the 1970s a younger group of black labor leaders emerged from the civil rights and black power movements. Willie Rudd, successor to Leroy Clark as president of Local 282, is shown here speaking to strikers in Indiana in 1982. Photo courtesy of Ida Leachman.

Black workers, most of them women, struck the Memphis Furniture Company in 1980 when it refused to bargain for a contract. The company sought to break their union, as it had in 1949, by bringing in strikebreakers by the busload. The strikers won, but the company soon closed its operations. *Press-Scimitar* photo by Larry Coyne. Courtesy of the Mississippi Valley Collection, University of Memphis.

Black women have taken an increasing role in factories, as employers have sought cheaper labor in the U.S. and around the world. These furniture workers in Memphis in 1980 came under increasing duress as employers sought to bust unions. Photo by Earl Dotter. Used by permission.

Industries closed across the U.S. in the 1980s and 1990s, gutting employment in urban areas. The closing of Memphis Firestone, shown empty and deteriorating in 1996, dragged a once relatively prosperous black neighborhood down with it. Photo by Michael Honey.

Every year, black workers in Memphis hold a memorial
march to remember Dr. King's death on April 4, 1968.
Backed by members of the United Furniture Workers Local
282, this marcher in 1982 speaks to the job crisis facing
inner-city black youth. *Press-Scimitar* photo. Courtesy of
the Mississippi Valley Collection, University of Memphis.

During that time we lost two plants. The Cudahy oil plant, the CIO raided and the AFL also. Malone-Hyde grocery warehouse was lost. We lost, I guess, four or five different shops. This Buckeye plant out here, we never did lose it. There were quite a few white workers out there, but [they] finally got a good white steward out there. And he would stand up, just tell [it] like it is. And they finally stopped trying to raid the plant.[18]

What the union stood for was being called un-American. Of course, there were some people at the shop who didn't agree with the policy of the FTA, and they wanted out of that union. I remember Red Copeland [of the CIO], he was really *deep* down on people. Those were some of the reasons that we lost [members].

Back in '50 or '51, I was arrested over Willie McGee in Jackson. That's the only time I've ever been arrested. I was picked up down there. That McGee case, shoot . . . they would come out of there with a special newspaper, accusing him. He was in World War II, and he was a driver for some truck company. He didn't return one evening with the truck company's money. He was an out-of-town driver, and he pulled out. He was actually going with this white lady, and her mother-in-law called, and she cried rape. She never did identify him. I think they just thought he was a Negro in the state of Mississippi, and they executed him. Boy, that's rough.

Seventeen of us went from Memphis, almost all from Federal Compress. We got down there early in the morning. The highway wasn't like it is now. We left at 9:00 the night before, and got there around 6:00 or 7:00 A.M. There wasn't a highway patrol anywhere. We were supposed to have a prayer meeting in the capital at 9:00 A.M. So, we went to some of our friends' houses in Jackson and came downtown together. About 8:00 A.M., things began to pick up. I'm sure they was working on a strategy for catching a bunch of us. It didn't work, so they had to pick us up one by one.

I was up on Capital Street that goes around the capitol. About 8:30,

18. Leaders of the CIO unions in Memphis combined with the Memphis Urban League in urging workers to vote out the "red front group" at the Buckeye Cellulose plant, a Local 19 stronghold and its biggest subdivision in Memphis. Two concerted raiding efforts by CIO unions after the SISS hearings could not budge black workers from their support for Local 19. White workers petitioned to secede from the local at some plants, but where blacks were the majority, as at Buckeye, Local 19 held firm. Over time, however, it lost many members during the red scare, as employers increasingly resisted bargaining with the union.

some of the boys were sitting on the lawn, and they arrested them. I saw them just sitting there talking, and the police formed a circle around them to keep them from getting away. I saw the police were picking up people, so I came right up to them. I figured I couldn't get away, as there was nowhere for me to go. They had formed a circle all around us, too.

We started across the street, when one of those detectives said, "SSSSST." The cops were on motorcycles, and they nodded their heads at us. We walked over to the motorcycle. They wanted to know why we were up there. He said, "Where do you live?" I said, "In Memphis." He said, "What are you doing here?" I said, "Visiting my cousin." By that time, a squad car had squealed up, running a siren, right to the curb, and told me to put up my hands. I put my hands up, and they searched me. He said, "OK, get in the car. We have some fellows that we think know y'all," which was our buddies, the guys who had already been arrested.

He said, "Where do you work?" I said, "Federal Compress." He said, "Federal Compress had to close down today, didn't it?" He'd picked up so many people from Federal Compress. He took us on up to the jail. They were picking up people, anybody who was walking the streets close by got arrested. I think there was about forty-two of us including some whites, but most of us was Negroes.[19]

That's when, Lord, things began to shake. It was Saturday morning, and they said they was going to keep us in jail until the next Monday. We had attorneys there from the NAACP, a white woman, and there was a white man lawyer, too. They kept us in jail until 2:00 or 3:00 A.M. the next day. The lawyers was working on them to get us out of jail. We hadn't done anything, they'd just picked us up on the street. The state wanted to have the Negroes' trial last, and the whites' first. The lawyers told them they'd have one trial or no trial, since they had us all charged with the same thing.

So they agreed, and all of us got up. We didn't know what was going on. They had us all get out on the lawn. Then they took us downstairs in the old jail, they had us all around, and said all of our names. I saw more state troopers and more cops all lined around the walls than I'd ever seen before. They marched us over to the courthouse, and some of them said, "We're

19. Red Davis, Memphis National Maritime Union and Communist Party activist, was among those arrested, as was Anne Braden, a white journalist from Louisville, Kentucky. According to the Jackson newspaper accounts, state police arrested forty-one people for "conspiring to obstruct justice."

going to march these so-and-sos right on down to the river!" What they often did at that time was march you down to the river and kill you. That's what they were saying.

But they marched us over to the court, and they had a trial. The lawyer got the judge to drop charges if we would all leave the city at their earliest convenience. So we did. The lawyer asked for a private room to talk with us, and he asked us how we felt about leaving and going back to Memphis. I said I didn't think it was too safe to go back on the highway. A lot of the police had made cracks that they'd get us when we was going back on the highway.

So they suggested that we bring our cars over to the police station and turn our keys over to one of the white men. A white woman couldn't get close to a Negro man, but white men could come up to us and talk to us and transfer the keys. The white women then got the keys from them, and the white women drove the cars back. At that time, they wouldn't bother a white woman. They were going to get us if we had all come back by car. The men all came back on the train, we had Pullman service. We was instructed not to cause any disturbance, because they'd be looking for something to arrest us on again.

So we set out for the train station quietly. They walked all along with us. At the train station, they was looking in at us just like cats through a glass at mice. Those peckerwoods wanted to get us, man! These were just switchmen and white guys hanging around the station. I was prepared to die. We had all been schooled to watch them, because they might try to hook something on us. We was supposed to watch for other women at the station to get on the train and do the same. So that's what we did.

You see, they had on the [ticker] tape when to go out there, but they told us something different. They were trying to fool us. They told us to go out early, but we didn't. So we got on the train without trouble. There was detectives on the train with us. If I got beat up, it would just have to be the best man, because I wasn't going to sit there and take no whuppin'! I had said I wasn't goin' to get a whuppin'. I went around to each room on the train to make sure everyone was safe before I went back to mine.

But some of the boys was so scared they could hardly walk. I had a brother like that. He was so scared, he could hardly walk. That was how bad it was, what we went through that evening, with some of the cracks the police and others were making.

In the Memphis black community, everyone was afraid. At the airport, they beat up a [white] guy coming in [as a reporter] for the *Daily Worker* [Communist Party newspaper], and nothing was done about it. The police department wanted to see what would happen, said they didn't know who beat him up. So after we got back here and got off of the train, we made the headlines of the paper all over the U.S. Seventeen from Memphis got arrested, but there was lots more there from Memphis who got away. I've been lucky since that time. I think of James Cheney who got killed,[20] and certain people who have been beaten. I was raised in Greenwood, right around where a lot of that was happening. I've been lucky. Lots of people have gotten killed down at that river that no one even knows about.

We had a contract with the Federal Compress. They didn't like it, the supervisors showed us that they didn't like it. But what we did in the street was our business. As long as we were back at work on Monday morning, they didn't have any control over what we did outside. They didn't have anything on us.

When we got back to Memphis, the FBI wanted to know who got us to go down there to the capital. They were after Earl, also. They made trips to his house from then until about 1960. They would either come to his house or send him a Christmas card! One day in the Huguenot Grocery, he met an old FBI man. The FBI kept steady track of him for about ten years, they would call him and want him to go out with them, but he wouldn't.[21]

The FBI told him that someone accused him of being a Communist. He wouldn't tell them any names, since he figured they were trying to frame somebody on something. They made five or six visits and many phone calls, and any time he moved they would know where he was. He asked them why they didn't do something about crime with their time instead!

The FBI were trying to get as much information as they could. That's why they were pumping me. They were trying to get as much out of me as they could, preparing themselves for the Eastland hearing. The detective

20. James Cheney, an African American, and whites Andrew Goodman and Mickey Scwherner were murdered for their civil rights activities by police and white vigilantes in Philadelphia, Mississippi, and buried in an earthen dam during the summer of 1964.

21. A copy of the FBI's file on Fisher is in the author's personal archives, obtained under a Freedom of Information Act request.

told me, he said, "Leroy, you're not fooling us. You're not as dumb as you pretend to be." I just let him talk.

Actually, if I don't share my information with you, you don't know what I know. Regardless of what someone else tells you, you don't know how much truth there is. That's no proof unless I tell you. The more I share with you, you can go to somebody else. Much as I was reading then, I wasn't about to convict no one. I know as long as you don't say anything, they don't know what's in the back of your head. They told me, "We can prove that we saw you X number of places with so-and-so, and so forth," and I said, "Well, prove it!"

I knew they was trying to scare me, but I decided not to scare. If they have enough to pull a string on you, they goin' do it. They'll try to bluff this and that out of you, and get a little piece here and there, and try to put something together. I've seen them work. They was fishin' around. And if they've got the goods on you, partner, they aren't going to be fishing around.

Some of the FBI's wives caught Fisher's wife coming home from work once, and picked her up. They made her get in the car, and took her out and kept her until real late at night. They slapped her around, trying to make her tell.[22] Earl told me, about the pressure they was putting on them. He was getting pressure from his wife over his associations and activities. A lot of what affected Earl was what they were doing to his wife. He came by my house a couple of times to try to get me to stop selling NAACP memberships because of the pressure. He thought things were too hot.

I was doing NAACP the same as I would getting people signed up in the shop. I wasn't getting anything out of it, but just trying to get people signed up. Being a worker, I'd do things for what it was worth, trying to do a good job. Fisher told me not to be a hero, but I kept selling anyway. It was legal.

They used to come by and ask me about a lot of the guys. A guy from Atlanta named Hosea Hudson, the FBI asked me about. He had a lot of different identifications to use spur-of-the-moment. He'd slip in and out. He had certain places he would go. I think they were watching Earl's house. They had him staked out, they figured he [Hudson] would go there.

22. Hosea Hudson remembered this incident, and thought it was wives of white steelworkers union members who attacked Mrs. Fisher. Personal interview, May 28, 1985, Takoma Park, Maryland.

After they checked on him, you knew he really got to run, because they're going to come back for him.[23]

Well, I wasn't scared, in fact I was young, and I think we got a kick out of it. I had a young family, though, so I really couldn't get off into it. I was trying to raise a family, and my wife worked until ten or eleven at night, so I would babysit. I had two then, a girl and a boy. I had two more later, but they're all grown now. That's how it was.

Actually, Local 19 was the onliest one [active in civil rights]. Even the NAACP was afraid to speak up. Guys like Red Davis, a bunch of them would attend [Memphis CIO] council meetings, raising different issues about things. The FTA was the only local to keep up like that. That's really the reason they put Eastland on it. I never forgot that. After that period I got more active in the union.

Fisher and McCrea taught me most of what I know. Ed McCrea told me how to conduct myself on the job. Those people at Federal Compress were out to get any stewards they could. We were involved in a lot of civil rights struggles, too. We had people from the local who participated in the [civil rights] marches, some who were involved in demonstrations.

When I started in '46, it was just whuppin' and cursing by the supervisors at some of the workers. You go down there now and [it's quiet] like being in a church house! [laughs] So things have changed that much, from the fights that we put up, due to the older heads dying out and being replaced, and everybody having new ideals. [And] Negroes is a little bit different now as when I was growing up. I guess as times went on that we wasn't as afraid.

Now, it's mostly younger people. You start talking about the past and they don't see how most of the past could have happened. When you talk about what you had to do years ago to survive, they think that's unbelievable.

The stories of Leroy Clark and Leroy Boyd provide glimpses of how the red scare ravaged portions of the labor movement and undercut inter-

23. Hudson, a Communist Party trade union and African American leader in the South, told me that after the indictments of national CP leaders under the Smith Act (passed in 1940), which in effect outlawed the party, he left Birmingham and went underground. The FBI constantly looked for him, and he stopped in Memphis trying to evade them. Authorities nearly picked him up at Fisher's house, which they ransacked after Hudson had left.

racial organizing. People like Clark, trying to stay within a CIO union, felt increasingly compromised. Clark was a World War II veteran, but he was also a veteran of some of the earliest and toughest CIO organizing, attested to by his fifteen months in prison for strike activity. He had strong equal rights principles, and felt the left, which was very strong in his own union, had moved the CIO forward on racial issues. Clark spent most of his life working to create strong black union leaders, yet in removing Rudolph Johnson from the leadership of Local 282 he destroyed exactly such a leader. This contradiction reflected his pragmatic approach to unionism: he did what he felt had to be done, or would be done anyway, for his union's survival. He also sought to remain acceptable to a frequently factionalized union hierarchy at the national level, while looking for new opportunities to organize workers wherever he was. In the end, he rebuilt the predominantly black Local 282 after incompetent, corrupt, and do-nothing white union leaders had left it in ruins. Throughout the 1960s he played a dynamic leadership role in both the unions and the civil rights movement in Memphis, but he would be forced repeatedly to compromise his ideal of black leadership in order to maintain the support of white union leaders.

Leroy Boyd faced a different kind of problem: survival at the workplace, within the bowels of white supremacy. Like thousands of others who streamed out of Mississippi's mechanizing cotton fields, he came to the city with no knowledge of unions, hoping to move on to Detroit. Instead, he spent the next forty years in one place, battling for his rights as a worker in the low-wage cotton compress and seed oil industry. In this struggle, he drew on new information imparted by Local 19 and on traditions from his past. His father had a degree of autonomy on his sharecrop land; he somehow remained out of debt, he rarely dealt with whites, and, unlike many sharecroppers or tenants on big plantations, his family never went hungry. Speaking to interviewer Paul Ortiz, however, Boyd also remembered a white man who hit his uncle in the head with an axe handle and beat him, and an incident in which whites dragged a black man behind their car with chains. He knew that whites could be vicious but followed his father's example of speaking up to them. Early on he learned to protect himself, with knife, gun, or fist. He saw unions as another means of self-defense, but when he turned to Local 19 for help, white folks called him and his associates "Communists."

Unlike Leroy Clark, Boyd never sought leadership positions, and the necessity of deferring to white union leaders never entered into the equation. Always a rank-and-file activist, Boyd fought it out with bigoted foremen, supervisors, and company owners for most of his life. He followed a straightforward logic. As he told Ortiz, "The union is the people. You got to have your people with you. If everybody fighting for one cause, you got a strong union." Boyd, like Earl Fisher and other FTA stalwarts, continued to support their union while hoping not to be destroyed by the hurricane of the red scare. The difficulties of being a black unionist remained, but at least Boyd had no ambivalence about his union, "the onliest one" active in grassroots civil rights struggle in Memphis during a dark period of repression.

Indeed, Boyd and other black workers, in the absence of support from established civil rights organizations, took on one of the hoariest of white supremacy's myths. As Boyd explained it, he had always been angered by the idea that women and men had to choose their partners on the basis of color. Like Ida B. Wells-Barnett, the Memphis anti-lynching crusader of the 1890s, he knew how rape frame-ups could be used against black men, particularly when someone caught a white woman and a black man in a sexual liaison. The left wing of the labor movement and the Communist-led Civil Rights Congress believed that exactly such a frame-up was being used against Mississippi truck driver Willie McGee. A mob nearly took him out and lynched him during his first trial in 1945, and an all-white jury, after two minutes of deliberation, convicted him of raping a white woman. Ousted left-wing unions or CIO unions with large black memberships, through the Civil Rights Congress, provided McGee with some of his strongest support, but they could not save him. The Congress's lawyers got McGee's first and second murder convictions overturned, but after his third conviction (again by an all-white jury) he was executed in May of 1951, while five hundred whites celebrated in the streets.

When Boyd and the group of nineteen workers from Federal Compress went to Jackson, Mississippi, to protest McGee's pending execution in May of 1951, they took a daring step, one that most people would find hard to imagine. In that dark period of the cold war and of lynch mobs, they placed themselves under jurisdiction of the Mississippi state police, with none of the national media exposure or influence from friends in high places that occasionally supported 1960s protesters. Boyd knew full well about the many blacks murdered and thrown into the Mississippi River in his home state. A courteous, responsible family man, Boyd nonetheless knew about fighting back, and when arrested, he resolved to die fighting. Fortunately, Boyd survived, only to watch a few years later the equally dreadful case of Emmett Till, a fourteen-year-old from Chicago who was mutilated and killed for allegedly being "fresh" to a white woman in a store in Money, Mississippi. An all-white jury acquitted his murderers. Both cases demonstrated that lynching remained sanctioned by the law in Mississippi. After his protests in the McGee case, Boyd steadfastly refused to reveal what he·knew about union activists to the FBI, ducked his head to avoid other blows, and continued recruiting NAACP memberships and fighting shop battles. The impulse to resist white control had been with him since childhood, and he continued, quietly, to resist.

Some years later, Local 19 organizer Ed McCrea explained the significance of the protest by Boyd and other black workers in the McGee case. "That's what scares the powers, when they see rank-and-file workers doing things like that. I'm not talking about middle-class blacks. I'm talking about workers right out of the plant. That shook the whole town [Memphis] up. That scares hell out of them. 'Cause that's getting down to the roots." Local 19's brand of unionism provided the vehicle that enabled them to take such a stand, and its meaning for someone like Boyd can hardly be underestimated. Boyd had first hoped to use Memphis as a way-station to escape the low wages of the South, but marriage and children instead caused him to settle for a life of hard and oppressive work that he had never wanted. Boyd made meaning out of his life at the workplace and in the community through the union. The union gave him training, allies, and a legal framework to make work tolerable instead of a curse. It also provided a vehicle to imagine and fight for full citizenship rights.

Daring civil rights protests, usually associated with the 1960s, were not limited to college students and ministers. Factory workers during the heyday of Jim Crow had taken similar risks. As novelist Richard Wright observed, "We are not what we seem": the reserved demeanor of the humblest-looking black man or woman could conceal the soul of a fighter. Necessarily, both resistance and some degree of accommodation marked the lives of black trade unionists, who looked for opportunities and watched for danger signs. These were increasingly marked "red" during the cold war. Many in the Memphis black community regarded Boyd and his fellow workers as heroes for the stand they took in the McGee case. Yet their protest also set off a major inquisition led by Mississippi Senator James O. Eastland against "communism" in the labor movement, one intended to destroy civil rights unionism.

INTERLUDE

ARTS OF RESISTANCE

I don't see where I've been in anything political.
                                                    Earl Fisher

Leroy Boyd and other Local 19 union members faced heavy repercussions for their protest of the Willie McGee execution. Mississippi's
Senator James Eastland, owner of a massive plantation in Sunflower
County, a leader in the White Citizens Councils, and one of the most
powerful segregationists in the country, saw the protests as a sign of subversion. How could black people possibly take such a stand in his home
state? His opening investigation into "communism" in the southern labor
movement, held in Memphis on October 25 and 26, 1951, provided the
answer: black organizing resulted from the efforts of conniving white outsiders who sought to use southern blacks in their efforts to overthrow the
U.S. government on behalf of the Soviet Union. As during Reconstruction, ignorant Negroes had been led astray.

During the course of these highly publicized hearings, Eastland and his
Senate Internal Security Subcommittee (SISS) ignored the U.S. Constitution's First Amendment, publicly exposing and vilifying people for their
speech and organizational associations. Marshals seized the records of Local 19 and made its members' names and addresses public, jeopardizing
their jobs and sending fear into their communities. Huge headlines ac-
companied the compulsory testimony of Local 19's business agent Ed Mc-
Crea, labeling him a "bigtime red," while a paid informer, Paul Crouch,

as well as Memphis CIO leader William Copeland, gave names and dates linking McCrea and other unionists to Eastland's Communist conspiracy. The atmosphere in the hearing room resembled that of a modern inquisition, in which people were forced to testify, without benefit of counsel and upon pain of imprisonment, against themselves and others. When New Yorker Victor Rabinowitz tried to fulfill his role as attorney to accused union members, Eastland exploded in what appeared to be an anti-Semitic rage, shouting "Get that damn scum out of here." Marshals slapped the lawyer and expelled him from the room. Such were the conditions of free speech during the 1950s red scare.

The ejection of Rabinowitz forced Local 19 Vice President Earl Fisher to be a reluctant witness with no one to advise him on a perplexing matter: which questions did he legally have to answer and which ones could he refuse to answer? Witnesses could cite the Fifth Amendment right against self-incrimination and refuse to answer all questions, but according to the news media and the inquisitorial committees, this meant one had something to hide. To be a "Fifth Amendment Communist" was to destroy one's public standing and career. Alternatively, civil libertarians asserted that under the First Amendment no one should have to testify about their own or other people's political beliefs and associations, an area in which the First Amendment prohibited the government from legislating. Congressional investigators did not accept First Amendment privilege, however, and integrationists Carl Braden and Frank Wilkinson went to prison when the Supreme Court, too, denied this right in 1961.

The last alternative was to cooperate but take the Fifth Amendment whenever specific testimony might be deemed self-incriminating. Eastland and others believed this immunity did not apply to questions asked about other people. Yet such questions led exactly to the sort of "fishing expedition," aimed at getting people to name names and tell about others, that Leroy Boyd had refused to participate in on behalf of the FBI. He understood that efforts to exonerate oneself could get other people, and oneself as well, into trouble. Earl Fisher understood it too. By forcing Fisher to be a witness, the hearings put him in the position of possibly betraying friends like McCrea to enemies like Eastland, or going to jail if he refused to cooperate at all.

Without legal support and before a battery of reporters and government and law enforcement officers, Fisher faced Eastland and subcommittee counsel Richard Arens, two men highly skilled in entrapping witnesses in their own words and getting them sentenced to prison for perjury or contempt of Congress, or in browbeating them into incriminating others. Eastland had built up to a grand moment after two days of hearings, with Fisher as the final witness in what was to be a triumphal exposure of communism. Fisher now confronted, in a sense, the same dilemma faced by Leroy Clark: what price was he willing to pay, how far was he willing to bend, to persist in his role as a black union leader? The following exchange spotlights how segregationists used anti-Communist hysteria to attack labor and civil rights organizations. It also suggests how African Americans in the Jim Crow era sometimes used dissembling as a form of resistance when the weak faced the strong. I have edited out repetitive portions of the testimony, marked by ellipses. In the original text, interruptions are marked by pairs of dashes (———).

TESTIMONY OF EARL FISHER, VICE PRESIDENT, LOCAL 19, DISTRIBUTIVE, PROCESSING, AND OFFICE WORKERS OF AMERICA, MEMPHIS, TENN.

MR. ARENS: Please state your name, and your occupation.

MR. FISHER: Earl Fisher.

MR. ARENS: Would you speak a little louder? We can hardly hear you.

MR. FISHER: Earl Fisher; work with Federal Compress & Warehouse Co., South Memphis.

MR. ARENS: Are you also connected with local 19, DPOWA? [1]

MR. FISHER: Yes, sir.

MR. ARENS: And what is your connection?

MR. FISHER: I have been a member up until, just a member—shop steward in the plant until about last May or June, something like that; I don't remember the date. At that time I was elected vice president of the local . . .

MR. ARENS: Where were you born?

MR. FISHER: Dublin, Miss.; between Dublin and Clarksdale, Miss.

1. Distributive, Processing, and Office Workers of America, an independent union based in New York City, was created from the merger of several unions purged from the CIO in 1949-50. Formerly, Local 19 was part of the Food, Tobacco, and Agricultural Workers, and before that the United Cannery, Agricultural, Packinghouse, and Allied Workers of America (UCAPAWA).

MR. ARENS: And how long did you live in Mississippi?

MR. FISHER: I be in Mississippi other than the time that I spent in school until 1939, I believe it was . . .

MR. ARENS: In 1949, August, did they have a regional meeting here in Memphis of FTA?

MR. FISHER: A regional meeting? In the union hall?

MR. ARENS: Yes.

MR. FISHER: I really don't remember. I can't recall. It might have, it might have been such, but at that time I wasn't so active in the union.

MR. ARENS: Do you remember making a speech at the union hall here during the regional meeting in 1949 about the trial that was going on up in New York City at that time?

MR. FISHER: I don't recall that.

MR. ARENS: Now, I put it to you, Fisher, as a fact, that in August 1949, during the meeting of the FTA here in Memphis, you delivered a speech in which you were condemning the trial of the 11 Communists in New York City. Do you remember that?[2]

MR. FISHER Sorry, I'm not saying I did not, saying I didn't, but I just don't recall it. I'm afraid of saying something that I might get in trouble.

MR. ARENS: Is that why you don't remember, you think you might get in trouble?

MR. FISHER: I don't want to say something under oath that is not true.

SENATOR EASTLAND: Do you remember making a speech back there?

MR. FISHER: I really don't recall. I'm not saying that I didn't, not saying that I did, but I don't remember.

SENATOR EASTLAND: You did condemn the trial of the 11 Communists whether it was in a speech or not, did you not—the 11 Communist leaders in New York?

MR. FISHER: To be true and fair, I'm afraid to say it.

MR. ARENS: I can't hear you.

2. Communist Party leaders went to prison in this period under the Smith Act, a law passed during wartime emergency that made it illegal to "conspire" to teach or advocate the overthrow of the government. The Supreme Court in 1956 declared much of the law an unconstitutional invasion of the right to free speech.

MR. FISHER: I don't recall doing that.

MR. ARENS: Remember last year circulating a petition around here in Memphis?

MR. FISHER: Yes, I remember that.

MR. ARENS: Did you help circulate the petition?

MR. FISHER: Did I help circulate? You mean going around to people's homes, circulating?

MR. ARENS: Yes.

MR. FISHER: I don't recall that either.

MR. ARENS: What petition is it that you remember?

MR. FISHER: I remember they had a petition out called "peace petition" down here, and at that time I heard a lot of talk about it, but so far as me participating in some activities, I don't recall that.[3]

MR. ARENS: What did you do about the peace petition? Did you sign it?

MR. FISHER: I don't recall signing the petition.

SENATOR EASTLAND: You say you do not recall signing it?

MR. FISHER: No, sir.

MR. ARENS: Did Larry Larsen circulate the peace petition?[4]

MR. FISHER: I don't know; don't remember that either.

SENATOR EASTLAND: Who circulated the petition?

MR. FISHER: You mean from the union hall?

SENATOR EASTLAND: Yes. You said you remember it was circulated. Who did it?

MR. FISHER: I don't remember whether it was circulated from the union hall, but I remember in the city here there was a petition. I saw in the paper about the petition being circulated.

SENATOR EASTLAND: Is that all you know, what you read in the newspapers?

3. The Stockholm peace petition, circulated during the Korean War by W. E. B. DuBois and other peace advocates, called for an end to the development of nuclear weapons and for de-escalation of the cold war. The police in Memphis arrested Carmen Davis, wife of National Maritime Union organizer Red Davis, and took custody of her baby in a stroller and her other small child as well, when she tried to circulate the petition in the streets of Memphis.

4. Larry Larsen was a regional director for the FTA, based in Memphis.

MR. FISHER: I saw a petition in the union hall at one time. Yes.

SENATOR EASTLAND: That was the Stockholm peace petition, was it not?

MR. FISHER: Just what was on it I don't recall.

SENATOR EASTLAND: Who had that petition there?

MR. FISHER: You have a table out there with literature on it and it was just out on the table with the rest of the literature.

SENATOR EASTLAND: Who put it there, do you know?

MR. FISHER: No.

SENATOR EASTLAND: You knew that was a Communist plan to try to undermine the United States position in Korea, did you not?

MR. FISHER: I say I knew there was a———

SENATOR EASTLAND: Yes. Did you know that?

MR. FISHER: I'm telling you I don't know. I don't want to get any trouble here by answering a question that I don't know about, that I am not acquainted with, but I refuse to answer that.

SENATOR EASTLAND: You refuse to answer that?

MR. FISHER: It might incriminate me some way.[5] I don't want to get into something I am not well acquainted with and I don't know so much about. I'm not a politician.

SENATOR EASTLAND: You just don't know. That is the truth, is it not?

MR.FISHER: Yes, sir; I don't know.

MR. ARENS: Did they have some meetings of the local in which they discussed this petition and urged everybody to sign it? Do you remember that?

MR.FISHER: You mean general membership meeting?

MR. ARENS: Yes.

MR. FISHER: I might remember some discussion on it. I don't recall. I never kept up to date with all those things. I never kept no memorandum or nothing like that on it . . .

MR. ARENS: You are a pretty good speaker at the union meetings, are you not?

5. As Fisher seemed to be well aware, it remained very unclear which comments before inquisitorial committees would be protected by the Fifth Amendment and which ones would not. Hence the sparring throughout his testimony about which questions he should answer.

MR. FISHER: When it comes to something I know about, union activities or grievance or what not, I can, but when it comes to political questions, I'm not so well off.

MR. ARENS: Did you get up in the meetings pretty frequently and make speeches?

MR. FISHER: When I'm in town and when around. I drive truck and sometimes I'm out at nights.

MR. ARENS: When you are here at meetings, do you get up and make speeches?

MR. FISHER: Sometimes I do; sometimes I don't.

MR. ARENS: Did you make a little speech about this peace petition?

MR. FISHER: I refuse to answer that.

SENATOR EASTLAND: You have to answer that question. You will have to answer that question. It is not a privileged question.

MR. FISHER: If I answer it I wouldn't be sure.

SENATOR EASTLAND: I want your best judgment.

MR. FISHER: I really don't recall it.

SENATOR EASTLAND: You do not recall?

MR. FISHER: No, sir.

SENATOR EASTLAND: And that is your best judgment, you just do not recall?

MR. FISHER: That's right.

MR. ARENS: Did you take a copy of this peace petition that was there on this table in the union hall?

MR. FISHER: I refuse to answer that, too. I don't remember that far back. I refuse to answer because it might incriminate me in some way.

MR. ARENS: That was just last year, was it not, during 1950?

MR. FISHER: I don't even remember what year it was.

MR. ARENS: Didn't you take that peace petition around and get other people to sign that peace petition?

MR. FISHER: I refuse to answer that.

MR. ARENS: Why is that?

MR. FISHER: Because of the fact that I might be incriminated in some way with something that I don't remember clearly, and don't want to be tied up with something——

SENATOR EASTLAND: Wait a minute. You are about to incriminate yourself. You better think now.

MR. FISHER: I don't know.

SENATOR EASTLAND: I know you don't want to. You are about to incriminate yourself. You just said you do not know anything about
it. You do remember about it, do you not?

MR. FISHER: (Shakes head negatively.)

MR. ARENS: You are bound to. You first said you did not remember anything about the petition. Then you said you saw it on the
table in union hall. You do not want to incriminate yourself,
do you?

MR.FISHER: No, sir, sure don't.

SENATOR EASTLAND: You answer his questions.

MR. ARENS: Fisher, you went around with that petition and got some
signatures, did you not?

MR.FISHER: I refuse to answer.

SENATOR EASTLAND: You are going to have to answer the question.

MR. FISHER: If I don't know———

SENATOR EASTLAND: If you don't know you can say you don't know.

MR. FISHER: Well, I don't recall.

MR. ARENS: Did Mr. McCrea ever tell you what to do on these peace
petitions?

MR. FISHER: I don't recall that either.

MR. ARENS: Do you know Red Davis?

MR. FISHER: Yes, sir.

MR. ARENS: Who is Carmen Davis?

MR. FISHER: Must be his wife.

MR. ARENS: You know him pretty well, don't you?

MR. FISHER: I met him when I came in the union. We all was in the same
hall together on the city [labor] council.

MR. ARENS: Is Red Davis a Communist?

MR. FISHER: I refuse to answer that because———

SENATOR EASTLAND: Now, wait a minute; you are going to have to answer
that question. That will not incriminate you to tell what you
know about Red Davis.

MR. FISHER: I don't know. I refuse to answer, that is all, because it might
incriminate me.

SENATOR EASTLAND: No; that could not incriminate you.

MR. FISHER: I don't know nothing about these people. In fact, I heard more this week than I heard about the whole situation.

SENATOR EASTLAND: Did they ever talk communism around you?

MR. FISHER: I refuse to answer that, too.

SENATOR EASTLAND: Did they ever tell you they were Communists?

MR. FISHER: I refuse to answer.

SENATOR EASTLAND: We have not asked you if you were a Communist. Have they ever told you they were Communists?

MR. FISHER: I refuse to answer that question.

SENATOR EASTLAND: That would not incriminate you and you are going to have to answer.

MR. FISHER: If I can recall all that, then that——

SENATOR EASTLAND: Do you want to be cited for contempt? I thought you wanted to stay out of jail.

MR. FISHER: I want to answer the questions that I know.

SENATOR EASTLAND: All right, answer it now. Did they ever tell you they were Communists?

MR. FISHER: I refuse to answer that.

SENATOR EASTLAND: I want you to answer the question. Did they ever tell you they were Communists? You can answer that "Yes" or "No." That would not incriminate you.

MR. FISHER: I don't have anything to do with these political questions because I'm not so clear and I can't tell.

SENATOR EASTLAND: It is not a political question and I just want to know what they said about it.

MR. FISHER: I refuse to answer because I can't recall all the incidents——

MR. ARENS: Can you recall whether they told you they were Communists or not?

MR. FISHER: I can't recall that.

SENATOR EASTLAND: You don't remember?

MR. FISHER: No, sir; I don't remember.

SENATOR EASTLAND: You would not say they did and you would not say they didn't?

MR. FISHER: No, sir.

MR. ARENS: Fisher, I want to make a little statement before I ask you the next question. I am not in the next question going to ask you whether or not you are now or ever have been a member of the Communist Party. I am going to ask you this question, however: Who asked you to join the Communist Party?

MR. FISHER: I refuse to answer because—I refuse to answer that because it might be tied up in something—what do you mean who asked me to join the Communist Party?

SENATOR EASTLAND: Yes; just who asked you to join it?

MR. FISHER: I can't recall anybody asking me to join no Communist Party. If I am clear on the question—get me right——

MR. ARENS: Nobody asked you to join?

MR. FISHER: I can't recall anybody ever asking me.

MR. ARENS: Did you ever pay dues to the Communist Party?

MR. FISHER: I haven't paid any dues. What do you mean "dues to the Communist Party," me knowing that I have paid dues? I never have. I can't recall that incident. I don't know, because I don't know——

SENATOR EASTLAND: Did you ever have a membership card in the Communist Party?

MR. FISHER: I never have.

SENATOR EASTLAND: You never had one?

MR. FISHER: No, sir.

MR. ARENS: In 1949 and 1950—that is last year and the year before last—did you subscribe to the Communist Daily Worker?

MR. FISHER: No, sir; I did not. You mean did I do that myself?

MR. ARENS: Yes.

MR. FISHER: Let me clear this question before I answer it. I never subscribed to the *Daily Worker*. If somebody sent my name in, I don't know who it was, and the paper is coming to my address now, but I did not subscribe for the *Daily Worker*, and I haven't had any communications in my own handwriting to the publishing house.

SENATOR EASTLAND: Do you know who subscribed for you?

MR. FISHER: All I know the paper started coming in.

SENATOR EASTLAND: What is your best judgment now about who subscribed for you?

MR. FISHER: I really don't know. I'm sorry, I don't remember.

SENATOR EASTLAND: Don't you think the business agent of the local did that?

MR. FISHER: I'd rather not answer that.

SENATOR EASTLAND: Yes, you have to answer that. I just asked you what you thought. What you think is not going to incriminate you. It is not a crime to think. Now, your best judgment is that the business agent sent you——[6]

MR. FISHER: No.

SENATOR EASTLAND: That is what you think, though, is it not? You cannot refuse now. You are going to have to answer that.

MR. FISHER: I don't have no thoughts about it because the paper came in there. I got a letter today some place—I don't know how they got my address—from some reserve life-insurance company. Why they got my address, I don't know.

SENATOR EASTLAND: If you are getting a newspaper other folks in your union get it, too, don't they?

MR. FISHER: I guess they do. I don't know.

SENATOR EASTLAND: You know they do. Now, does the union buy those papers? . . .

MR. FISHER: I don't have no opinion; just don't know.

SENATOR EASTLAND: You get a paper and you never did even think who might have sent you that paper?

MR. FISHER: I don't recall.

SENATOR EASTLAND: And the other officers in the union get the paper and none of you have ever thought who paid for it or how you got it, have you?

MR. FISHER: I haven't thought anything about it . . .

SENATOR EASTLAND: The Communists were trying to save Willie McGee down at Jackson, Miss. You know about the delegation that went to Jackson from your union?

MR. FISHER: I know about the one from my plant.

SENATOR EASTLAND: Who was on that delegation?

MR. FISHER: About 19 of them, I think.

SENATOR EASTLAND: About 19 of them? Who sent them down there?

MR. FISHER: The way this happened, some person came by there one day at noon and was talking to fellows on top of the hill.

SENATOR EASTLAND: What person?

6. Eastland was trying to establish that business agent Ed McCrea was behind all of the political activities at Local 19.

MR. FISHER: Don't know; supposed to be from California. Never saw him before and haven't seen him since.

SENATOR EASTLAND: He was just a stranger, and he talked to the fellows on the top of the hill. Now, go ahead.

MR. FISHER: Came in and talked to those men at the plant gate where they eat lunch; asked about participating in some kind of prayer meeting—that was before he discussed Willie McGee—and asked them to come down and pray in the prayer meeting.

SENATOR EASTLAND: Was the prayer meeting in Memphis?

MR. FISHER: No, sir; Jackson.

SENATOR EASTLAND: Jackson, Miss.?

MR. FISHER: Yes, sir.

SENATOR EASTLAND: It was a Communist demonstration in Jackson, Miss., and 19 went from your plant; is that right?[7]

MR. FISHER: That's right.

SENATOR EASTLAND: Just a stranger came there—you don't know who he was—and talked to you, and 19 of them pulled out to Jackson?

MR. FISHER: They had a meeting among themselves and they took up the donation there among the plant, workers in the plant.

SENATOR EASTLAND: Did the union approve that trip?

MR. FISHER: I don't think the union knew anything about it.

SENATOR EASTLAND: There has been testimony here that the union sent them.

MR. FISHER: Sent those men down here?

SENATOR EASTLAND: You better watch what you say.

MR. FISHER: I know this fact to be a fact: that those donations up there were among themselves, regardless of who said what.

SENATOR EASTLAND: Why is it that when there is a Communist cause to be promoted this local here always cooperates to promote that Communist cause? What is the reason for that?

MR. FISHER: I don't know whether I'm able to detect, to answer that question, but yet I mean I don't—if you make it a little more clearly what I understand "Communist cause"——

7. The "prayer meeting" was a protest organized by the Civil Rights Congress. It was not a Communist Party demonstration.

SENATOR EASTLAND: Well, to "save Willie McGee"; Civil Rights Congress, Stockholm peace petition; everything the Communists have advocated your local has advocated. Why do you do that?

MR. FISHER: I don't know whether my local advocates all those things or not.

SENATOR EASTLAND: Well, now, actually the business agent runs the local; does he not?

MR. FISHER: Well, to clear that up, from my understanding that we try to make our union as democratic as we possibly can.

SENATOR EASTLAND: I know that.

MR. FISHER: And, in the electing in these resolutions or any program that is to be adopted, then we urge every rank and file person to come from the plant and participate in this affair.

SENATOR EASTLAND: But the business agent is the smartest man there and he actually runs the union; does he not?

MR. FISHER: I wouldn't say that.

SENATOR EASTLAND: Be frank with me.

MR. FISHER: I wouldn't say that . . .

SENATOR EASTLAND: What political organizations do you belong to?

MR. FISHER: Political organizations? I am not so up on political organizations. I just participate in politically nothing. I don't see where I've been in anything political. The only thing I have devoted most of my time to is union activities and problems in the plant.

SENATOR EASTLAND: Well, were you interested in Henry Wallace's campaign for President?

MR. FISHER: I wouldn't say that I was. I wouldn't say that I wasn't . . .

SENATOR EASTLAND: As a matter of fact, you know that your union did support Henry Wallace; don't you? . . . Is it not strange, now, that if your union was not run by the Communists they would support along with the other Communist unions the Communist candidate for President in 1948?[8]

8. Henry Wallace, former Secretary of Agriculture and vice president under Franklin Roosevelt, ran for president on the Progressive Party ticket in 1948. While supported by Communists, he was not a "Communist candidate," as Eastland asserted, but sought an end to the cold war developing with the Soviet Union and China.

MR. FISHER: I don't follow you. How do you have that?

SENATOR EASTLAND: I say, isn't it strange that if your union is not controlled by the Communists that they would line up with
other Communist unions and support Henry Wallace
in 1948?

MR. FISHER: I refuse to answer it.

SENATOR EASTLAND: You are going to have to answer.

MR. FISHER: I try to answer the best I can. I want to cooperate, but I don't
want to get myself in trouble here. When it comes to this
political questions, I'm not so up.

SENATOR EASTLAND: You are liable to get in trouble if you do not answer
the questions.

MR. FISHER: If I don't know them?

SENATOR EASTLAND: If you don't know them, say you don't know them,
but I am not going to let you refuse. Did you ever join the
Communist Party?

MR. FISHER: I refuse to answer that question. It might incriminate me,
Senator.

SENATOR EASTLAND: Might incriminate you some way?

MR. FISHER: Yes . . .

[Eastland asks a series of questions suggesting that Fisher
joined the Communist Party in 1939, but Fisher refuses to
confirm or deny.]

SENATOR EASTLAND: What have you got to hide?

MR. FISHER: When it comes to these political questions I don't know.

SENATOR EASTLAND: You do not know?

MR. FISHER: What I mean, I don't want to get tied up in something I
don't know about and I have no understanding about it.

SENATOR EASTLAND: If you did not belong to it, the way not to get tied is
to say you did not belong, if you didn't.

MR. FISHER: Like you say now, about the local send a delegation to Jackson; my understanding is that they didn't send a delegation to
Jackson. You said somebody might come up here and say in
1939 and say Earl was this or Earl was that and I don't know
what these people say and therefore I am not going to tie myself up to it.

SENATOR EASTLAND: In 1939, now, if you did not belong to the Communist Party say so and declare yourself. Then nobody can get
you in trouble.

MR. FISHER: I refuse to answer.

SENATOR EASTLAND: Have you ever been a member of the Communist
Party?

MR. FISHER: I refuse to answer that, too, because it might incriminate
me . . .

SENATOR EASTLAND: It has been testified here that Mr. McCrea was the
Tennessee organizer for the Communist Party and the head
man in the Tennessee district. Have you been on any trips
with him over the State where he saw people? . . .

MR. FISHER: I refuse to answer that, too.

SENATOR EASTLAND: As to this stuff that it might incriminate you, where
did you hear about that?

MR. FISHER: In other words, what I'm trying to say is I don't know whatever been said. I'm trying to stay clear of all this stuff so I
won't get myself in trouble.

SENATOR EASTLAND: All right. Who was it that told you to say that?

MR. FISHER: Who was it told me? I had some legal advice, but he didn't
tell me what to say or what not to say.

SENATOR EASTLAND: Who was your legal adviser?

MR. FISHER: Lawyer for the union, but he didn't tell me what to say.

SENATOR EASTLAND: What is his name?

MR. FISHER: Rabinowich or something like that.

SENATOR EASTLAND: Mr. Rabinowitz of New York?

MR. FISHER: I guess.

SENATOR EASTLAND: You began to sing a little song and before I even
asked you, you were going to say that he did not tell you
what to say.

MR. FISHER: I mean he didn't put words in my mouth.

SENATOR EASTLAND: All right, he told you to say that he had not told
you what to say, did he not? He told you to tell me that
out here — that he had not told you what to testify.

MR. FISHER: May I put it the way I understand it?

SENATOR EASTLAND: I want you to answer my question "yes" or "no."

MR. FISHER: He didn't tell me what to say because he didn't know what I mean. He just told me what my rights were . . .

SENATOR EASTLAND: Yesterday, did you talk to the employees of the Compress, the Federal Compress, about this hearing?

MR. FISHER: Yesterday?

SENATOR EASTLAND: Yes. I want you to think because I want to warn you now that I have a statement from somebody who was there . . .

MR. FISHER: I don't know nothing about what I told the workers. I didn't get in town till 4 o'clock the other morning from New York and I didn't get up until around 10:30 and I was at the union hall at 11.

SENATOR EASTLAND: Where were you between 7:30 and 8 o'clock yesterday morning?

MR. FISHER: That was—that's Thursday morning?

SENATOR EASTLAND: Yes.

MR. FISHER: I was in the bed, I thought, unless I was walking around in my sleep . . . Last time I went down to the plant was yesterday at noon and I only saw one or two people.

SENATOR EASTLAND: Did you have a meeting yesterday morning and tell them not to pay any attention to these hearings and tell them not to testify, that we were only trying to prevent the workers from getting an increase in wages? . . .

MR. FISHER: I haven't saw the workers yesterday, only one or two people that come down to the plant. I was up on top of hill at lunch and only saw one or two people down there. We didn't have a meeting down there yesterday. If there is, somebody else held a meeting; I didn't.

SENATOR EASTLAND: Your name is Fisher, F-i-s-h-e-r?

MR. FISHER: F-i-s-h-e-r . . .

SENATOR EASTLAND: You would not want to belong to a Communist union, would you?

MR. FISHER: Well, if it's against the law I wouldn't want to belong to nothing, if it's against the law.

SENATOR EASTLAND: You know the Communists are against the United States and trying to destroy the United States, do you not?

MR. FISHER: Yes; that's my understanding about it.

SENATOR EASTLAND: They are controlled by Russia.

MR. FISHER: Don't ask the question too deep for me because I never gave it too much study.

SENATOR EASTLAND: But you hear that.

MR. FISHER: Yes; I hear that.

SENATOR EASTLAND: You would not want to be affiliated with an outfit like that.

MR. FISHER: I don't want to be affiliated with nothing trying to overthrow the Government.

SENATOR EASTLAND: You are. Those people are using you. Why don't you tell me just what Mr. McCrea, the business agent, has told you about Communists? He's a Communist.

MR. FISHER: I refuse to answer because it might incriminate me.

SENATOR EASTLAND: It might incriminate you?

MR. FISHER: Yes, sir.

SENATOR EASTLAND: You do not remember whether he has even told you anything or not? Which is it? Which is true?

MR. FISHER: I don't remember, so I don't know what.

SENATOR EASTLAND: Well, you do not remember, then.

MR. FISHER: I don't remember. I just want to get saying something here——

SENATOR EASTLAND: Are you afraid of him?

MR. FISHER: No, sir; I'm not. I don't think I am.

SENATOR EASTLAND: Has he ever threatened you in any way?

MR. FISHER: No, sir.

SENATOR EASTLAND: If he has made some statement to you, why don't you testify about it? Are you afraid of him?

MR. FISHER: No, sir; I'm not. He never said anything or made no threats to me. If he did, I didn't hear.

SENATOR EASTLAND: Are you afraid of him?

MR. FISHER: No, sir; I'm not afraid of him . . .

SENATOR EASTLAND: Did your lawyer tell you that if you were asked if Mr. McCrea or Mr. Red Davis or other members were Communists, or if officers in New York were Communists, to refuse to answer on the ground that it might incriminate you?

MR. FISHER: Just told me what my rights were. He didn't call names to me. He didn't say anything.

SENATOR EASTLAND: How did you know when to refuse to answer on
                     the ground that it might incriminate you when the ques-
                     tions were asked about somebody else that did not con-
                     cern you?
MR. FISHER: I am answering that because of the simple fact I don't know
               and I don't remember occasions and therefore I'd rather not
               commit myself to something that I'm not clear on . . .
SENATOR EASTLAND: That will be all. You are excused.
               Gentlemen, I am going to close the hearings in Memphis. I
               am going to order the investigators at a future date to see if
               the testimony of the activities of these people in Mississippi,
               Alabama, Arkansas, and Kentucky would furnish the neces-
               sity for further hearings at those places.
                  I think the record is absolutely clear that this is a Com-
               munist organization and that it is directed and controlled
               by men who are able and who are ruthlessly carrying out the
               policies of the Communist Party. I think instead of being a
               labor organization that it is, in reality, a Communist organi-
               zation and that the Negroes who belong to it are dupes and
               are being used and bent to the will of people who desire the
               mid-South to set up a Communist organization.
                  I think that is the issue and I do not think there is any
               doubt that its purpose is to set up in this community and in
               other communities a Communist organization, an organiza-
               tion designed to overthrow the Government of the United
               States and designed to aid and promote the objects of the
               Soviet Union. How such an agency as this could be certified
               as a bargaining agent by the National Labor Relations Board
               is beyond me, but it has been, and I think as a result of these
               hearings there will be legislation to deny organizations of this
               kind bargaining rights.
                  I think that the Negro officials who testified here are
               dumb. I do not think they know what has happened. I think
               that they have simply been used by designing people.
                  I desire to thank in particular the United States marshal
               and his deputies for the very fine cooperation and assistance
               they have given us.

I also desire to thank the Federal judges and the United States attorney and his assistants for their help and for their assistance.

Every one here has been very nice to me. In fact, I have never been better treated in my life.

We have the membership records which were seized and I am going to order those records to be made a part of the permanent record and thrown open to the public. I think that the public interest requires that the names of people who belong to organizations such as this be made public and the public can get the full information about them.

I also desire to thank the press corps for their courtesies and for the fair way in which they have covered these matters. I have had to be discourteous to some of the people at times, because I have had to be firm to prevent people from taking over the hearings and running away with them, as they desire to do and as they have done in other places. I was not going to permit this hearing to be a sounding board for Communist propaganda, and yesterday when I saw certain people here I was certain that that was the object—to use this as a sounding board to promote the interests of world communism.

That will be all, gentlemen, and I thank you.

(Whereupon, at 4:30 Friday, October 26, 1951, the hearing was recessed, subject to the call of the Chair.)

Before the Eastland hearings, the Memphis CIO, including its one black staff member, Henry White, had campaigned to destroy Local 19, joined by middle-class civil rights leaders. While the CIO petitioned the National Labor Relations Board for elections to decertify Local 19 from representing workers, the local NAACP banned identifiable leftists from its ranks, and James A. McDaniel, director of the Memphis Urban League (a SISS-friendly witness), led black ministers to the homes of Local 19 workers, urging them to leave their union. Nonetheless, black workers defeated two decertification efforts at the Buckeye plant. If the unions themselves could not destroy the local, perhaps Senator Eastland and the attendant publicity might. Indeed, after the hearings, employers began to refuse to bargain with Local 19. A union that had been the largest local representing cotton industry workers in the area, with three thousand or more members, became a shell of four or five hundred in the mid-1950s and never regained the larger base it once had.

The federal government contributed to the fearful atmosphere of conformity through investigative committees and through the FBI, which continued a campaign of intimidation against people in and out of unions whom it suspected of being Communists.[9] Intercepting mail, tapping phones, following workers, talking to their employers and landlords to get them fired or evicted, and arresting individuals suspected of subversion all became standard procedure. As Leroy Boyd related in chapter 5, Earl Fisher, who didn't go to Jackson for the McGee demonstration, suffered much worse FBI harassment than anyone else after the hearings, and that harassment continued for many years. A physical assault on Fisher's wife by white women, an incident in which the FBI tore apart his home while looking for southern black Communist leader Hosea Hudson, and the 1952 arrest by federal agents in Memphis of Junius Scales, the last victim of the anti-Communist Smith Act, increased fanfare in the press about the charges of subversion and put more pressure on people like Fisher.

It was not a good time to be a black union leader. As unions eliminated the few whites speaking openly for civil rights, black union stalwarts were left with almost no reliable white allies. Under these circumstances, Leroy Boyd remembered, Fisher became leery of openly standing up for the NAACP or any other cause. In many ways, he turned hard-shelled and reclusive and dispensed with anything that interfered with building the union. In the South, well into the 1960s, anyone associating with unionism and civil rights came under suspicion. This included, rather absurdly, Leroy Clark, who had participated in the anti-Communist purges himself, Alzada Clark, who had nothing to do with leftist groups, George Holloway of the anti-communist-led UAW, and even Holloway's college student son, all of whom came under FBI surveillance.

Yet, through exceedingly hard work and obsessive determination, Fisher and his colleagues rebuilt Local 19 into a respectable union that

9. FBI records on Fisher, W. E. Davis, and other individuals and unions in Memphis, obtained under the Freedom of Information Act, are in author's possession.

had significant contracts with a number of employers by the 1970s. It had lost most of its white members, with blacks making up probably all but two hundred of the union's 1,400 to 1,700 members in Memphis. Bereft of Ed McCrea and other leftist whites, Local 19 eventually gained grudging acceptance by the local labor establishment.[10] The union survived not because of mainstream acceptance, however, but because of the loyalty of its black members and Earl Fisher's single-minded efforts to rebuild it. Black leadership, emphasized even more by the removal of white leftist organizers, remained the hallmark of Local 19, which continued to provide an important vehicle for civil rights unionism, as Leroy Boyd documents in the next chapter.

Fisher's survival, and that of his union, must be seen as significant accomplishments. Few victims of the inquisitorial committees survived as public leaders of unions anywhere in the United States. Fisher survived in part because he managed to get through the SISS hearings without being vilified as a radical in the white community or destroyed as a credible leader among blacks. How did he do it? Fisher's testimony reminds the reader in some ways of the B'rer Rabbit stories, in which the weak and defenseless used cunning and deception to divert or entrap a more powerful and vicious foe. Fisher used "weapons of the weak" and "arts of resistance" crafted by a people long oppressed by a dominant group. These included subterfuge, dissembling, and speaking with ironic double meanings. Fisher used racist assumptions as a shield, hiding his proficiency as an organizer. By all appearances, he could not have been an upstart black labor leader, as his friends knew him to be (a "hothead," Boyd later explains). Rather, in the hearings, Fisher became an apolitical, inarticulate, stammering Negro from Mississippi.

Unlike actor and singer Paul Robeson, who thunderously denounced the southern chairman and the House Un-American Activities Committee as racist, Fisher survived the SISS hearing by taking advantage of Eastland's preconceptions about how African Americans thought and acted in his home state of Mississippi. Here, under the incredible pressures of white supremacy, blacks had developed highly stylized arts of deception

10. The remnants of the Distributive, Processing, and Office Workers at the national level became a part of District 65 of the UAW and was allowed back into the AFL-CIO. Local 19 remained the affiliate in Memphis under all these titles.

in dealing with whites. Fisher knew these arts well, and Eastland's stereotype of the "dumb Negro" or "Communist dupe" offered him a defense from a jail sentence for refusing to cooperate fully with a congressional committee. His testimony provides an interesting and ironic picture of black survival skills at work. Without a lawyer, Fisher outflanked Eastland's and Richard Arens's questions. He never denounced or implicated those who put in *Daily Worker* subscriptions for the workers or organized peace activities, nor did he accuse McCrea or anyone else of being a Communist, as was almost obligatory before an inquisitorial committee. Nor did Fisher implicate himself. He admitted nothing, conceded nothing, got entrapped in no indictable contradictions, and to some degree gained Eastland's confidence. Using phrases such as "I have no opinion," "just don't know," "haven't thought anything about it," "I don't follow you," Fisher's vague, confusing, contradictory, and inarticulate responses to substantive questions caused Eastland at one point to admonish him that "It is not a crime to think." Clearly Fisher understood that it was, and acted accordingly.

Fisher thought well enough to avoid a citation for contempt or to reveal any information about others. One can hardly read his testimony without thinking that he did not know what he was doing, did not care about politics, or perhaps was not very principled or smart. But all of these conclusions would be wrong, for his fellow unionists knew Fisher as an astute and thoughtful leader. Behind Eastland's stereotype of a mumbling Negro was a shrewd and quick mind at work.

While playing dumb, Fisher at the same time defended his integrity and that of his union as best he could. In taking the position that workers in his union made their own decisions, and that the union was democratically run, he stated his core belief forthrightly. And in a number of ways, if one were to read between the lines of his testimony, Fisher refuted Eastland's assumptions that blacks could not think for themselves. When the Senator said that former Secretary of Agriculture Henry Wallace was a Communist candidate, Fisher responded "I don't follow you. How do you have that?" a question many opponents of the red scare had been asking as well. Fisher served as one of Wallace's electors in Tennessee,[11] and

---

11. According to Tennessee law, independent candidates for president had to be sponsored by a group of electors in order to be placed on the ballot.

he must have known full well that Wallace, unlike any other candidate, had barnstormed the South for racial equality during 1948; indeed, a rally for Wallace had produced the largest interracial meeting in Memphis during the 1940s. What did Eastland really mean by associating Wallace with a "Communist cause"? Fisher innocently asked. Was it "Communist" for the former vice president of the United States to speak for equal rights? This was a question many others around the country were asking.

In a real way, Fisher did refuse to cooperate. Repeatedly, when Eastland told Fisher to answer questions, Fisher did not. "I am not going to let you refuse," Eastland said at one point, and yet Fisher did refuse, and without being cited for contempt. When Eastland insisted that Fisher had been indoctrinated by union lawyer Rabinowitz, Fisher asserted that he spoke for himself, and he similarly refused to acknowledge that the white business agent McCrea might have made decisions for the workers. When Eastland asserted that McCrea "is the smartest man there and he actually runs the union," Fisher dryly replied, "I wouldn't say that." Fisher neither condemned communism nor its supposed mastermind, McCrea. Nor did he accede to Eastland's suppositions. He let him draw his own conclusions and never directly challenged him, but indirectly he questioned some of Eastland's basic assumptions. The contradictory nature of Fisher's testimony frustrated Eastland, but attempts to explore contradictions led nowhere. As Leroy Boyd puts it in chapter 5, "If I don't share my information with you, you don't know what I know." Although Eastland gave the news media his a priori conclusions that white outsiders had misled blacks to go against their best friend, the southern white man, his grilling of Fisher produced no revelations for the red scare's propaganda mills.

One can see in Fisher's testimony the main position that Fisher held to throughout the rest of his life: the union came first. His testimony may not have made him feel good about himself, for he could not speak from the heart. Yet he lived to fight another day. Years later, some of the union's old-timers remembered the perilous time of the red scare so strongly that they feared to speak about it. Earl Fisher has died, and we don't know what he might have told about what happened. We only have one clue, an interview with Anne Braden in which Fisher forthrightly told her how employers and politicians used racism to divide poor whites and blacks. He suggested that the main objective of the organizer was to help the workers see that they had power if they would only unite. Far from being timid or inarticulate, he struck Braden as a courageous and principled fighter for workers' rights.

Fisher, like Boyd and other black workers, had carried experiences and ideas formed in the depths of the Jim Crow era into the 1960s and beyond, when the civil rights movement helped them to sweep aside many racial barriers. They understood the union as a transformative agent, a weapon of the weak against the formidable forces arrayed against them. They lost many battles, but they never completely lost the war. Black unionists during the red scare had few options, but they exercised the ones they had to the fullest and so created a base for the more formidable assault on white supremacy yet to come.

6 CIVIL RIGHTS UNIONISM

Negroes is a little bit different now as when I was growing up.
I guess as times went on that we wasn't as afraid.

Leroy Boyd

When they started integratin' jobs . . . now you're talkin' about a
hurtin' thing for the white man.

Matthew Davis

The labor movement and the civil rights movement went hand in
hand, absolutely.

Alzada Clark

The life stories in this book implicitly contain a vision of what we might call civil rights unionism, a unionism engaged simultaneously with striving for decent jobs and equal political and legal rights. Labor and civil rights objectives were not always the same, and unions often provided ambiguous partners for black workers. One side of the labor movement resisted civil rights and minority demands, while another side sought an expansive agenda for social change. But the workers and organizers interviewed here had no doubt which side of the divide they were on. Allied with the broader civil rights movement, they sought to move unions beyond rabid fears of communism and integration toward a vigorous challenge to Jim Crow at work and in the society.

This proved difficult, for the cold war's demands for conformity in the 1950s to some degree had split the labor movement away from the emerging black freedom struggle. By the time craft and industrial unions joined together in the 1955 AFL-CIO merger, the unions had lost the drive to organize the unorganized. In the South especially, hopes for a sweeping unionization of industry waned, beaten down by repression, anti-union propaganda, racism, red-baiting, and restrictive labor laws. Most workers in textiles, furniture, tobacco and other low-wage, labor-intensive industries went without unions. Nor did unions spread into the expanding service sectors or clerical work, where minorities and women might have provided a strong base for organizing. And although the AFL-CIO officially took stands for school integration and civil rights legislation, its constituent members, even powerful industrial unions like the United Auto Workers, had a difficult time getting white workers in local unions to accept even the smallest steps toward integration. And AFL-CIO craft unions in places like Memphis proved to be among the forces most hostile to any kind of civil rights demands. Although labor unions were larger and stronger than ever before, or since, the labor base for civil rights demands remained weak.[1] At the same time, mainstream unions and the AFL-CIO became more heavily invested in anti-communism through their involvement in American foreign policy.

This weak union base for social change bedeviled the civil rights struggle. Industrial union supporters, including Martin Luther King, Jr., hoped that white workers, once organized, and black workers, once they had the right to vote, together would vote out reactionary political leaders, particularly southerners who had a stranglehold over U.S. congressional committees. Instead, in the 1960s many white workers shifted from the Democratic to the Republican Party or supported segregationist George Wallace, who won numerous presidential primaries in northern as well as southern states. In Memphis, Barry Goldwater's appeals to segregationists attracted a solid block of whites into the Republican Party, leading ultimately to the 1966 election of Dan Kuykendall, a congressman who "hated liberalism, civil rights, and Communism." Instead of a progressive, labor-based coalition for civil rights and economic justice, a greater chasm emerged at all levels between white workers and the poorer and minority segments of the working class.

1. The NAACP labor secretary Herbert Hill in 1961 thoroughly documented the prevalence of union racism since the AFL-CIO merger, and A. Philip Randolph repeatedly attempted to get the AFL-CIO leadership to confront the problem of racism in its member unions, to no avail. By the early 1960s, civil rights advocates in and out of the unions had become increasingly disturbed by the failure of the AFL-CIO to attack hiring and workplace discrimination. In Memphis, white craft union leaders adamantly refused to desegregate their unions throughout the 1960s, and those unions remain mostly a white preserve even to the present.

Momentum for change had shifted from the labor movement, which had shaken up the society in the 1930s and 1940s, to civil rights and community mobilization, beginning with the Montgomery Bus Boycott in 1955 and followed by a multitude of community-based actions against segregation throughout the South. Across the nation, the civil rights struggle heightened the consciousness of African American workers, whose initiatives often reflected the timing, strategies, and tactics of the broader movement for change. Just as the *Brown* decision precipitated black challenges to segregation in various factories and unions, the passage of the 1964 Civil Rights Act (with major support from the AFL-CIO, the UAW, and numerous other unions) provided another. The act's Title VII in particular created a new means to pursue equal rights at work. It established a federal Equal Employment Opportunity Commission (EEOC), which prohibited both unions and employers of more than one hundred from discriminating in union apprenticeship and membership or employment and promotion because of "race, color, religion, sex, or national origin." The Voting Rights Act of 1965 and the desegregation of public facilities through local mass movements also liberated black workers from many of the constraints that had kept them powerless as citizens.

The civil rights movement's legislative and organizing gains opened new citizenship rights for black workers, but conversely, black workers also provided important support in the battle for civil rights. As Matthew Davis emphasizes in this chapter, black workers did not usually lead broad social movements for equality and sometimes feared even to participate because they might lose their jobs. Yet they did play a role in desegregation battles. In Memphis, Clarence Coe and George Holloway recruited workers at their plants to join the NAACP during the organization's toughest years before the 1960s, and Coe helped the NAACP screen and recruit test cases for black youth to desegregate Memphis State University. Coe, Holloway, Alzada and Leroy Clark, Leroy Boyd, and others in this book remained involved in civil rights, community, and church organizations most of their lives. Working-class blacks served as foot soldiers for the freedom movement during the Montgomery Bus Boycott and other actions, while leading black unionists such as Pullman porter E. D. Nixon, A. Philip Randolph, Coleman Young, and Cleveland Robinson played important organizational roles.

Unionized black workers, through their wages and their unions, provided strategic financial support to the civil rights struggle[2] and helped to keep churches and community organizations alive. At a more general level, in attaining a standard of living that allowed them to send their children to college, such workers helped create a new generation of educated young people with heightened expectations for change, some of whom became civil rights activists. George Isabell, the first black to qualify as an electrician at the Buckeye Cellulose factory in Memphis, raised a daughter who became one of the first black college students arrested for trying to "integrate" the public library in the early 1960s Memphis sit-ins. Leroy Boyd's children joined many of the civil rights battles in Memphis, as did the children of other workers interviewed here. The children of black factory workers who went to college also broke down many racial barriers in the professions. Leroy D. Clark, the son of Leroy and Alzada Clark, for example, became general counsel for the EEOC in the 1970s, a professor of law at Catholic University, and author of a textbook on employment discrimination. Susie Wade's son Booker also became a lawyer, and George Isabell's daughter became a heart specialist. Numerous other children of unionized factory workers undertook distinguished professional careers.

Within the labor movement itself, black workers in the industrial unions provided the most progressive element in the South and in the nation. They were usually the first to join and the last to leave union organizing drives. As Edward Lindsey and Leroy Clark recall, black workers also began to form caucuses and produce slates of candidates to put black leaders and issues at the forefront of union concerns. And with the spread of black voting rights, organized black workers began to build a progressive political base outside the unions. Where African Americans could vote, unionized black workers, especially when mobilized by AFL-CIO political action campaigns, were among the most active. In Memphis, the death of Boss Crump in 1952 made it possible for African Americans to elect numerous Democratic moderates in the 1950s and 1960s. In 1972,

2. Martin Luther King and the various movements he is associated with, for example, often went to the United Packinghouse Workers of America, the Brotherhood of Sleeping Car Porters, the UAW, Hospital Workers Local 1199, District 65, and a number of other unions for financial and moral support.

with the help of Alzada Clark and other black unionists, they removed from Congress the conservative and anti-labor Republican Kuykendall, replacing him with Harold Ford, the first black congressman in the deep South since Reconstruction. White voters in Memphis established a dreadful record of backlash against civil rights, while blacks, with unionists playing an important organizing role, went on to elect a number of relatively enlightened officials, most notably black mayor Willie Herrenton in 1991.

In the minds of the industrial workers testifying in this chapter, civil rights and union movements followed parallel and mutually supportive paths. They felt that they, just as surely as the new generation of college students and ministers, were a part of the freedom struggle. Black working-class and poor people, tied down by jobs and families to provide for, could only rarely take the lead. They continued to suffer the stings of racism and the frustrating resistance of white workers and employers. But where they could, they joined the movement for racial equality and used unions as a battering ram to break open doors to opportunity previously closed by racism and economic exploitation.

Leroy Boyd Tells How Black Workers Used the Movement for Civil Rights to Revive Local 19

I always felt it, the only difference in white, black is just the color of the skin.

External attacks such as those launched by Senator James Eastland's hearings on "communism" in the labor movement combined with the succession of raids by other unions to decimate the ranks of Local 19 in the 1950s. But in the 1960s the local, affiliating now with District 65 of the United Auto Workers, regained acceptance within organized labor as Earl Fisher, Leroy Boyd, William Lynn, and a handful of others rebuilt it through battles waged in local shops in tandem with the burgeoning of the civil rights movement. For Mr. Boyd and many other black workers, labor and civil rights struggles had never been separate, a fact emphasized for them by the events of the 1960s. I include here a segment from Paul Ortiz's interview with Mr. Boyd as well as my own.

Well, things fireballed back up after Earl became president, because he got out and organized new shops. He was more of a leader, a different kind of person than the previous president, Lee Lashley, was. See, after Earl Fisher was fired at Federal Compress and lost his case in arbitration, then William Lynn [union vice president] got him in out at Buckeye [Cellulose]. See, before that, when a company would find out who it was, he just couldn't keep a job. At Buckeye, they made him shop steward before they knew who he was. Out there, shop stewards have super-seniority. So they couldn't touch him. That's how they [the union] protected him. First he got a job, then they [management] read about it. Otherwise, he'd have been there for two or three days and gone. That was around '56.

This was why Local 19 began to get back on its feets. We were still paying rent down on Vance Street. We got enough money to pay down on this building on Fontaine Road, and we started our own union hall. So things just began to look up. Lashley had been an easygoing guy, unlike Earl Fisher. Earl was more hot-headed, he didn't take a back seat. Lee Lashley was mild-mannered and treated the whites like bosses. Lee was older, too, but he was more cool and didn't have the temper that Earl had.

You had to watch Earl a bit, because he'd get mad and have a tendency to go overboard to fight for things he couldn't win. I know working in the shop, if they made him mad, he'd be out to get 'em! You'd have to say, "Earl, you just don't do it like that, man. Look at how many people are going to suffer from it, and you can't win." If he heard it from a friend without getting critical, he'd listen. When you have a group of people, you can't be making mistakes. You've got to keep your people behind you, and then you don't have to worry about the boss messing with you, because they know there are too many people to mess with. But in negotiations, he was real sharp, real sharp.

[At Federal Compress], they used to work in them concrete buildings down there, it'd be over hundred degrees and they don't want to put a fan in there. But they look for you to produce. How can you produce when you just scuffling trying to stay alive in a hot place? You working in a hot place drinking warm water. Oh, boy, we had a fight about that. Just about that! Shoot! [But] if you go to having trouble at the peak season, see you got them by the nose. So we tell them, we just want to be treated like humans. We had work stoppage, and that's the only thing we would demand. We was human beings, and we demand to be treated like human beings.

Well, the company brought [up] some of the young dudes. They got rid of the old ones. They was giving us too much of a break, you know. They brought some new young fellas, new managers, in from Mississippi. They going to run the plant. That's what they told us. "I'm going to run the plant just like I run it in Mississippi." Yeah.

So that's why we had a lot of work stoppage. We tell them we want a fan. As a steward, I ask for a meeting with them. They promised it, but never would do anything about it. So what we all decided one morning, instead of going to work, we going to go to the office and talk with the manager about the working conditions. So that's how things got started. And it's just like you roll a wet ball on the ground, you know, if it rolls, it's going to pick up dirt.

So at first he didn't want to come out and talk to us. So we just held the line, said, well, he promised he was going to have the restroom cleaned every day. That was another thing they wouldn't do. Filthy places. Well, down there [in Mississippi] they used to have them places just be over a hole and you got out there and do your business.

But we stuck together as a team. So he wasn't able to pick nobody off. He tried to call it a work stoppage. We said it wasn't no work stoppage because we had started to work. That's one thing we pledged in the contract, not to call any strike or work stoppage, slow down of work during the life of the contract, see. And when that happened, they'd get right on the phone and call for the union to come down there. They want to know what's the matter, you know. Well, they be knowing.

So when we leave from meeting with the workers, go back in the office and meet with the company, [the workers say], "We not going to work under those conditions. We not going back in there unless he do something about it." And this is how we got things accomplished. So we got, shoot, five-gallon cans or ten-gallon cans of ice water. We got one of them big fans for people working in the area, you know, where you can get some fresh air.

They hired them [whites] to tell us what to do. And they didn't know what to do, they didn't know what to tell us! And as time went on, they hired the white boy for supervisor or hire them for clerks, then go get some of the blacks to train them. For clerks! Now, we wasn't "qualified" to be a clerk, but we qualified to train them!

And we started applying for the clerk's job. They say we didn't have the qualifications, even if one of the bosses brought one of his sons down here and put him with one of the Negro clerks to train for so many days. He's good enough to do it to train him! We could do the same job [as whites], but they wouldn't pay us for that job. If they were short and had to put a Negro up for a clerk, he'd just get his usual rate of pay. And so that went on for a few years, [until we struck]. Yeah, oh man, that strike back in '64 was rough. We didn't lose the strike, but we fell to the draw. We stayed out for two weeks. The local couldn't back up the people on the picket lines, they didn't have a strike benefit, so we had to finally go back to work.

[But] we accomplished a lot there. We got a lot of things corrected. A lot of times we had to file to the Equal Employment Opportunity Commission, and to the labor board [NLRB].[3] They could get the company to agree. We filed discrimination charges. They tried to say that we didn't have enough education to do it, perform the [clerk's] job. And that's when we pointed out that's all they [black workers] did every day. And they was doing it when I started to work there, checking the cotton leaving one part of the plant, you know, going into the press room.

So this is how we got through those charges we filed against the company, through the Equal Employment Opportunities Commission. [And] we finally got the [black] mechanics making up to the rate of the whites, through the results of the EEOC.

During that time, all white mens was considered bosses, even though they was just shed clerks. At that time, a hundred fifty to three hundred people worked in those sheds. There would be maybe twenty-five or thirty clerks. They wanted to keep them all white, so they didn't want the whites to be part of the bargaining unit. They always considered them the Negroes' bosses. If you had any trouble with one of them and he recommended you be fired, then the supervisor fired you. It was a way of keeping the Negroes and whites divided.

Earl Fisher confronted them with the fact that they were not bosses but were covered by our contract. They said they wasn't, so we went to the labor board and filed charges against the company. This went on for about two or three years, bringing up a big investigation. The board here

3. Boyd was one of a group at Federal Compress complaining to the EEOC after their 1964 strike. Earl H. Fisher to Frank Parker, April 1, 1965, and Alvin Heaps to Fisher, September 10, 1964, in the "Federal Compress" files of Local 19, in Memphis.

[in Memphis] ruled that the shed clerks was under our contract as workers, they wasn't bosses and didn't have the right to hire and fire. They had to take those people off of straight time and put them on our hourly wage. And this opened up the way for Negroes . . .

The company appealed over those twenty-five or thirty white clerk positions, and filed a petition to the board in Washington, [D.C.], and the board in Washington upheld the ruling. The next step the company did was to file to the U.S. Sixth Circuit Court in Cincinnati. That went on for two or three years, and finally after the court heard the case, they upheld the ruling.

The company would give the whites a little bonus in the middle of the year, and wage increases to keep them on their side. But since we've been getting pretty sizable wage increases, all of that's been cut out. Now there's no difference in wages. There are still white supervisors, but there are Negro supervisors also. They've offered me a job to be a supervisor, I've had the opportunity. I was afraid to take it, because I was the one who signed those [EEOC] papers along with the guy from Washington. There were about six of us who signed those papers.

I always felt it, the only difference in white, black is just the color of the skin. And I felt like if I was able to master a certain job, I shouldn't have been deprived of it because of who I was. And if I could do it, then I should get the pay that the other person get. All the best jobs was white, and that's one of the things that I don't think there was no other company as bad about that as the Federal Compress was. And I survived there forty-four years.

Negroes is a little bit different now as when I was growing up. I guess as times went on that we wasn't as afraid. It was mostly my mother, she used to be scared something was going to happen to us and [told us] don't be saying no "yeah" and all to whites. Well, down there [in Mississippi] then, I didn't say, "Yeah" and "No"; I was just accustomed of saying, "Yes, sir." But in later years, after the Supreme Court ruled that, you know, the white kids and Negro kids go to the same school, well, they ain't no more than we. We just said, "Yeah" and "No." We had a little problem on the job with that. They [white workers] expected you to say, "Yes, sir."

[When they] said you're supposed to say, "Yes, sir," [I say], "Hey, man, I'm as old as you is." Really, I was taught to honor my elders. You know, if he was an older person, yeah, I'd honor [him]. But just because your skin is white, I don't have to honor you. And I'm old as you is. You're supposed to say the same thing to me. So, I remember one dude. He broke to the office and told the supervisor I wouldn't say, ["Yes, sir"]. [They say], "Well, he's right. Ain't no law for him to say, 'Yes, sir' to you." So that was the end of it. Never was no legal action taken, you know, about this. We had a union there. If we hadn't had the union, [I'd] a been gone.

When Earl died, we lost a good man. He died of a heart attack. He left his wife behind, and she died about a year later. After Earl died, Francis Owens came on the scene, and Scotty [Robert Scott, a Local 19 organizer]. They had new negotiations, and we was able to get much more money and a better contract.[4]

We got a union, this begin to change things. After we got a union and got the people active in the union, [they] weren't afraid to stand up for their rights. That's a way of surviving, of getting something decent from companies.

I think the civil rights movement had a big effect on that. The civil rights movement woke some people up, and they lost some of their fear. Those people in Mississippi have really woken up. Since the civil rights movement we were able to organize the shop in Mississippi. I used to go all through those towns, and it used to be that if you were from Mississippi, they'd hire you here in an instant, because the people down there was working by the day and thought the minimum wage here was big money. You couldn't tell them nothing. Shops started moving South, so the union organized shops down there, and now people [factory workers] are living there like they are here.

[During the civil rights movement] they marched from Memphis to Jackson. I participated in the march when it was marching here, I didn't go all the way to Jackson. One Sunday, we marched sixteen miles, there were about two or three carloads of us. We left here and went to Greenwood, got with the march just the other side of Greenwood there. We marched from there to Belzoni, down 49 Highway, we had police escort.[5]

4. Francis Owens had worked in the Local 19 office, and took over the local after Fisher's death. Fisher and his wife had no children and apparently left no family behind, according to Francis Owens, personal interview, February 2, 1983, Memphis.
5. This appears to have been part of the "march against fear," initiated by James Meredith in June 1966, from Memphis to Jackson. Meredith was shot and other civil rights activists took up the march in the nonviolent style. Stokely Carmichael and Willie Ricks used the march to popularize the "Black Power" slogan.

I point out to [my children], you know, how things was. And some of my kids was brought up in it. They was in on a lot of these demonstrations and sit-ins and marches. You know, you go to training them, and after they went off to school, you know, the kids use their training to improve conditions where they was going to school at.

I learned about unions and all that after I came to Memphis here, after '45. I didn't know anything about nothing like that then. That wasn't even thought of back at that time. In fact, a lot of people here, you talk about organizations, they didn't think very much of you. After the struggle, they learned you need an organization.

Factory Worker Matthew Davis Becomes a Community Leader

It's the way you carry yourself.

In chapter 2, Matthew Davis recalled how he had hauled and cleaned huge blocks of rubber in freezing conditions at Firestone, doing brute labor whites consigned to blacks. Over the years, through hard work and persistence, Davis earned respect on the shop floor and became a grassroots community leader. Clarence Coe remarked that Davis had always been willing to fight for equal rights in the factory, even as he devoted time to building his church and supporting civic organizations and civil rights activism. He provided a strong backbone for the less fortunate in his community.

The three years and seven months I was in the army, when I come back to Firestone was added to the two years and somethin' I already had.[6] I was right at the top of the list in seniority. So many guys come back to Memphis, they leave, and I think, I'm going to Detroit, Michigan. So I thought about that. I said well, seniority means something, you can't beat that. I made a lot of guys kind of angry because according to my seniority I could move up in my department. Then I got married, Palm Sunday, '46. I have a wife and three children.

It didn't go as bad with me, I guess, as some blacks. I was one of them kinds to speak out, whether I got fired or not, you know, if I felt too much

6. Factory workers who went to war accrued seniority all the while they were in the military.

pressure comin' down. Most of the time the supervisor or foreman would believe what I said. You had a few friendly whites, regardless of the circumstances. They knew it [segregation] wasn't right. They would come talk to me. Some like Rip Clark, you might meet them down the aisle on the way to the lunchroom.[7] You had time to chat with each other. I didn't have any problems. I think it's the way how you carry yourself on any job. They walk up behind you wantin' to goose you or whatever. I didn't take that.

That has something to do with any job. It's the way you work. I didn't jump when they said jump, but my work would go on. I'd be on the job, I'd be there at 7:00. I'd be on the job maybe ten or fifteen minutes before seven. You was supposed to stay there until 3:00. I either stayed until 3:00 or [later]. There wouldn't be no complaints. You can't come up and just demand you work, just because you was the boss man. Like I say, I got along real good even back in the tough days. Well, if they [foremen] wasn't good, I'd make 'em good! [laughs]

I know once we went off on strike, one man, he was one time top man but he got busted down. He had a way of hootin' and hollerin' at you. He hollered at me one day. I said somethin' that wasn't in the Sunday school book back at him, and so he said, "Let's go to the office," and I said, "OK, let's go to the office." I got to the office and he said, "Davis, you ain't got no witness and I don't have none either so we better just drop this thing." We dropped it right there. See, he figured unless he has a witness, just because his face was white and he was a supervisor, that wasn't going to be enough. I say, it's the way you carry yourself, you can get along. I got along real good.

[Firestone workers] was somewhat looked up to. It was just known that Firestone was one of the best paying jobs in the city of Memphis. That was a good payin' job, compared with the other factories. When they got the [union], we was going strike, strike, strike. Families would suffer sometimes when you go on strike. But I can see the value of sometimes those strikes we went on now because of the benefits we have today, the comfort of benefits that you can live on. But we had to fight for those things. We had to fight for those things.

Of course, strikin' back there, I think, it got out of hand at one or two

7. George ("Rip") Clark, one of Local 186's most popular presidents, was elected several times in the 1950s and 1960s. Clarence Coe felt he was one of the shrewdest leaders the local had.

points because it seems like, the whites, a lot of guys had farms down in Mississippi and at a certain time of year they would want to go on strike. I think the factory caught on to that stuff, the fact that they wanted to go on strike to go down there and plant their crops or somethin'. But as a whole, most of those strikes, they paid off in our benefits today.

On the race question, most times they'd go around it. They started puttin' those signs up, that everybody was equal. They started gradually breakin' [segregation] down. But then we had to get that stuff out of our system. We'd go to the lunchroom and we'd just automatically sit where the next black man sits, you know. And right here in the union hall, at the meetin's. Whites just tried to gather together, and blacks tried to gather together. [By that time] there wasn't no law said you couldn't sit together but that stuff just happened.

Now, when they started integratin' [jobs] out there a little bit, now you're talkin' about a hurtin' thing for the white man. It didn't bother the black because the black'd been used to all this hard-workin' stuff. But see, they had some white guys out there being supervisors that couldn't write, couldn't read, they had to lose them jobs and go back to work. There was one fella out there, they named him Duckheal, 'cause he come from Duckheal, Mississippi. He was one of those that had to go back to work because he couldn't read or write or nothin'. But yet and still, he could stand up and holler and tell you what to do. The foreman had to come out there and fill his papers out. Like, I'm already workin' there, say maybe a year before you get there. And they put you with me, I got to train you. We had several of them like that. But their face was white and they had the job.

Oh, yeah, [the white man] he'd get the best job. All you had to do was come in there and your face was white, brother, and you'd move up. And that thing went on for years and years, up till the plant closed almost, 'cause they'd pull in [white] guys out of the street just because they had been to school. They brought them in there to be a supervisor. That's part of the reason that the plant commenced to losin'. 'Cause brother, they messed up many, many batches of rubber 'cause they didn't know one thing from the other. Schoolin' is good, but working with that rubber is something different.

I had worked in that compound so long, like on inventory, man if anybody's gonna work on inventory I'd be the one to work. 'Cause see, if the ticket got knocked off the rubber, off them bales, got so much dust on them you couldn't make out what it was. I could smell that stuff and tell them what it was. And they just had to take my word 'cause they didn't know. I knew that pigment. You see, I worked with, let's see, forty or fifty different pigments out there you're workin' with. And I could just smell it. "Whatever Davis say, that's it!"

[But these young white guys out of school], they sent them to a training place and then they come out there and they gonna be a supervisor, they gonna be your boss then, you know. And some of them [black] guys, they would do what they ask them to do, but it was wrong. My point is, the fellas what were workin' there, they knew better, but, see, the [white] supervisor be tellin' them to do it wrong. They go on and do it because the supervisor said to do it this way, but it just messed up a lot of stuff.

I say, you got to have some experience. I don't care how long you go to school, when you're working with something like that you got to know what you're doin'. Your schoolin' won't get it. [The guys who worked on the job for a long time], they was the best. That's what saved the company all the years. Them old guys, supervisors, they just wanted to stand around and boss you. They could go in the office and sit down 'cause they had fellas out there that knowed what they was doing. And they was goin' do the job right. Until that young generation come in there, back in the late '60s. That's when so many of our fellas commenced to gettin' old enough to retire, and man, they commenced puttin' young boys in there.

This young generation, black and white, when they put their foot in Firestone and work for a day they felt like the world owed them something. And man, them guys wouldn't work. Women worked themselves to death, black and white. But them lazy white boys and young black boys! Man, I'm tellin' you, you felt like you was out a place workin' with them. You know, you be trying [to help], and they wouldn't do it! Them young generation just didn't work the same way.

But, I don't know, I've been involved with a lot of activity. When I moved out there to that community where I am now, I just saw a bunch of boys one day and I just decided that I was going to start working with boys, and I guess the Lord was working with another lady, so she called me that morning and said, "We got to get these boys in an organization." We called them together and organized a Be Better Boys Club out there in New Chicago [in north Memphis]. We started teaching them parliamentary procedures and things like that and, of course, from that it was Boy Scouting. I've been working with Boy Scouting now for I guess thirty-three years. I served as scout master, representative, committeeman, and just about everything you could name.

I was blessed to receive the highest award when I got this Silver Beaver award for working with the Boy Scouts. Also, I got the George Meany award, that's through the AFL-CIO. That's the kind of award they present for working with the Boy Scouts. He [Meany] used to be president of the AFL. He was a great old man, a great old man. He's been dead about three or four years now. He used to be on television all the time. [I got to meet Meany], hell yes.[8]

See, that's what I liked about my union, my union sent me on so many trips for community service. H. B. Griffin, when he was president [of the local] I have to give him credit, that man's a politician. I would go to work, I started carrying me a necktie and a suit of clothes. By the time I would get to work he was liable to call over there and tell my supervisor to let me off and to go downtown to a luncheon and represent the union. And I really liked to go. [laughs] The first trip I got, somebody else was supposed to be going, but I guess his wife wouldn't let him go, so I got ready overnight and went the next morning on the trip. We've had all kinds of conventions in New York, California, Chicago, Philadelphia, and Atlanta, just about every major city you can name. I've been in those cities for some kind of a union meeting or something. So, I really enjoy working with the union.

Like this election time coming up, I would get out two months before the election and be campaigning. I would come in and work with the headquarters and we would be putting up signs or calling folks and asking them to vote for the union ticket or something like that. I really enjoyed that and getting away from that plant for a while.

I moved up to be chairman of the community service for the AFL-CIO Labor Council here in Shelby County. I served in that capacity. That's where all union, all AFL meet together once a month. I served in that capacity for about ten years, 'til 1982, when I retired. I retired and they didn't want me to give the job up. I stayed with them for about a year after I retired and then I gave it up. Last year they come back and appointed me the chairman again, so I'm still serving as chairman of the Community Service

8. George Meany, a New York plumber, came from the AFL craft unions, which had a history of racial discrimination, to become president of the AFL-CIO when the AFL and CIO merged. A. Philip Randolph and other equal rights advocates clashed with him repeatedly and did not see him in such a positive light.

Committee. [laughs] That committee consists of helping people, like if your union goes on a strike, we be the committee, if you owe bills, to go downtown and tell those people you're on strike and get them to extend your bill, and maybe they'll give you another month or something like that. Or if a family need food or clothing we'll get out and hustle some way of getting them food and clothing. That's why we're called the Community Service Committee. And I served on the executive board of the A. Philip Randolph chapter here.[9]

People give Martin Luther King a lot of credit, but A. Philip Randolph was way ahead of Martin Luther King. The Pullman service, he was the president over that thing. He could write. So he goes way back. He served as vice president of the national AFL-CIO one time. Everybody is supposed to have equal opportunity and that's what they push for at A. Philip Randolph [Institute]. You're supposed to have a better job and higher pay and equal opportunity.

And I've had so many positions in my church. I'm a member of what you call a Christian Methodist Episcopal church and now I'm servin' as chairman of the steward board. That position in your church is really next to the preacher. If the preacher happen to be out of there, it's your task to kind of conduct the worship service that Sunday. You're in charge of all the finances that come through your church as steward. On the district level, I have served as the president of the district board. On the annual conference level, I served as the lay leader of the west Tennessee annual conference up until this year. And I also served as the vice president of the annual conference. And I've been a delegate to the general conference. That's where we elect bishops and general officers.

Now, I went through somethin' sure enough when the NAACP started this integration program. A couple of times we've had walkouts, strikes [over that]. I always like to be in those marches. I've been downtown with [NAACP leaders] Jesse Turner and Vasco and Maxine Smith and all the lawyers walking pickets, 'cause I wanted to see a better America.[10] They

9. A trade union equal rights organization affiliated to the AFL-CIO.

10. Jesse Turner, president of Tri-State Bank, Vasco Smith, a dentist, and Maxine Smith, director of the Memphis NAACP, were a part of the college-educated generation that revived the Memphis NAACP and initiated a variety of civil rights struggles in the 1960s.

give a write-up in the newspaper once, *Commercial Appeal* come out and interviewed me, and I had my picture in the paper one Sunday morning.

The thing that really disturbed me when my children were growing up, especially my oldest son, I'd be driving by the fairground or the zoo. And you had [only] certain days you could take them. You see, they didn't understand, you know. They'd say, "Daddy let's stop and go to the fairground." Well, if it wasn't Thursday you couldn't go. If it wasn't Tuesday you couldn't go to the zoo. And yet and still, you pass on by those places when I'd be goin' on down to see some of my relatives.

All three of my kids have gone to college. My oldest son seemed like he was the smartest one of the kids. He went three years up at Lane College up in Jackson, Tennessee. He works for a railroad company in Cincinnati. He's learned everything concerning a railroad job. My youngest son has just about got his Ph.D. He teaches English at Woodstock Junior High now, it was a high school, not far from our union hall. I just have one daughter and she's finished her master's degree. Both of them got their master's down at the University of Atlanta. She has a good job down at the Universal Life Insurance Company.[11]

I said, I'm goin' to get on out here and whatever it takes to make this a better world to live in, I'm willing to sacrifice my life for it. Now, we didn't have nobody at Firestone to do that but one or two of us, to go downtown and picket, because you'd be all over television and they'd be afraid that their foreman or their supervisor would see your picture down there you know, walking the picket line. You didn't find too many [Firestone workers] was community leaders. They figured they'd lose their job. If you wasn't brave, it was best for you not to do it, 'cause I've had a couple of them [whites in the factory] say, "I saw you downtown." I say, "Yeah, how you like it?" They walk on away and I talk like I'm half crazy to them. It took some guts to do those things.

When that sanitation strike was here in Memphis, the day that hell broke loose I wasn't but about two or three rows from the head of the line, when Martin Luther King was leading the line. The police started shooting tear gas. What started it, there are always some wild dudes. We was walking down Beale Street, almost to Main Street, and had some fellas on the side-

---

11. A black-owned insurance company in Memphis.

line just started breaking out all of the windows out of the showcases, and they just broke up the march. They started shooting that tear gas. I had my little daughter with me. She wasn't but about seven or eight years old, and me and my wife was back there havin' a fit.

[During civil rights conflicts], most the time the union would send a representative, maybe one or two [to demonstrations or meetings]. 'Cause somebody might call the union and ask them could they send somebody to a meetin' or somethin' like that. They sent a black representative, maybe Josh Tools, or somebody like that. In later years, I started going. But as a mass, you couldn't hardly get no volunteers to go to nothin' like that no way. You couldn't hardly get volunteers to go downtown to picket. Guys, really, they really was afraid. They was afraid of their job. They was afraid the police was goin' to beat you up. You had a whole lot to be kinda fearful of.

Now, like if they're goin' to join in a march, if they knew you from the local union, they might put that one representative at the front of the picket line. They tried to get all the leaders together, Maxine Smith of the NAACP and some of the top ministers. We had quite a few white ministers join in, especially Jews and Catholics. They tried to put those right up in the front line. But you just didn't have a lot of volunteers from the union folks, even when they had the opportunity, when we was out on strike, or something like that. They just didn't bother to go too much.

I think what hurt me, I'd be downtown, and we'd ask people not to go in Goldsmith's to shop. You see some of your own folks cross the picket lines and go in there and come out. You ask them, "If you owe a bill, mail it in," or something like that. But they go in there and pay a bill, then they come out of there with a shopping bag.

I'd have to give [credit to] some of these local unions, especially these all-black unions, like the [United] Furniture Workers, like Leroy Clark, and AFSCME, Reverend James Smith.[12] Naturally, they'd be right up front. Like our union, where you got a white president, and you didn't have too many black presidents in those days, they might send a representative down there, but there wouldn't be no mass of people. Those black unions, like the furniture workers [and] the Local 1733, they have a mass of people

12. James Smith was an organizer for the American Federation of State, County, and Municipal Employees Local 1733, the union to which Memphis sanitation workers belonged.

here at any kind of activity we had going, if it was somethin' they thought would improve conditions. But the leadership was ministers.

Edward Lindsey Recalls Black Union Politics

It was a civil rights struggle and it was a labor struggle also.

A new generation of black workers came into the Firestone plant and the union during Firestone's hiring expansion in 1963. It was the same year as the March on Washington, with the civil rights movement in full swing, and black workers sought "freedom now." But black union politics were not as simple as the freedom now slogan of the student sit-ins, complicated as they were by black intergenerational differences and conflicting political loyalties. One of the few African Americans elected to the United Rubber Workers Executive Board on a plant-wide basis, Edward Lindsey easily remembered those divisions but also the points of black unity. I spoke with him at his home in Memphis in 1989.

[Before I came to Firestone] I had a good attitude about unions, but I didn't have any experience. I spent two years at Tennessee State. So I had little jobs like waiting tables, and stuff like that, where you didn't have any unions, but a lot of my friends' fathers had been railroad men. [My father worked at] the Illinois Central. He worked in the service department, in a shop. He was in the union. He wasn't an officer, he was just a dues-paying member. He was always concerned about what issues took place. So I had a pretty good working idea what the unions are all about.

I had planned to be a doctor. I got involved in sit-ins by my freshman year, around 1960, at Tennessee State in Nashville. At that time it was Tennessee Agricultural and Industrial, a predominantly black school. I knew James Lawson because at that time he was in graduate school in Vanderbilt.[13] We were trying to integrate the lunch counters at that time. I participated at a sit-down at Havarty's. Luckily, there was no violence. Havarty's

13. A prominent leader in the Vanderbilt student movement and the Student Nonviolent Coordinating Committee, Lawson later became the leading minister organizing support for the Memphis sanitation workers. It was upon his request that Martin Luther King came to Memphis.

[was] a big department store like Goldsmith's here. They had eating counters at that time. I didn't get arrested, [we] just shut it down.

[But I got married], naturally. Had to worry about taking care of the family at that point. I kept saying I was going to go back to school. I'm sorry that I didn't.

[I went] to work at Firestone April 26, 1963. Race relations were bad at the time that I got in there. We stood at the brown and white fountains, had separate locker rooms, eating places. As a young group, a bunch of us just hired, we began to rebel. We'd go and drink out of the white fountains, periodically show up in the white locker room and white cafeteria. They had a partition where black employees had to eat. You had this big other side—there was a hole in it, you could just walk through—for the whites. Of course the same employee had to service and to clean up both sides, so they always had a partition where she could walk through. And we began to go on the other side, go into the locker room, drink at the water fountains.

Eventually, they broke it down, in order to avoid some trouble. Firestone had a guy come in named Paul Borda. He worked with the union, to help them remove those kinds of things, like partitions, so all people would have the same locker room. He was brought in specifically to save the plant, period. That was prior to us getting there, too. They couldn't get any production out. Of course, when production is down, there are numerous problems. That was one of the problems, race relation problems. And he came in to save the plant. He was real aggressive. He would do anything, whatever it took to get production up, he would go ahead. He had the guts to go ahead and do it, whatever it was.

I remember one incident—that was right after we got in there—a black employee was accused of just pissing on the floor behind a machine. Supposedly he exposed himself to some white women.[14] And of course the next day the women and some white men refused to come to work. Paul just stood up there and looked at them and he walked out. He told the guard, "If anybody don't want to come to work, just ask them to put their badge in the garbage can." That's the kind of guy he was.

14. This incident is also described by Clarence Coe in chapter 4. Josh Tools said that whites concocted this incident to get him off a machine job that he was trying to qualify for.

He just challenged them. The shift was changing, about 2:30 in the afternoon. It was time for the second shift, and that's when the problem occurred, on the second shift. These people were standing out in front of the gate and refused to go to work unless something would have been done with this black employee. Paul wouldn't have anything to do with that. If you didn't want to work, just go ahead, go off. They went to work.

I got to know people. You got some flack from white workers. But as a whole, most of them thought [desegregation] was right, they couldn't just come out and say it.[15] Some of them have told me in privacy that we were right, we should stick to our guns. There's always that small percentage that shows up [in opposition] and you get the wrong impression. But most of them wanted us to stick to our guns. Some people even received telephone calls, saying you need to stick to your guns and even suggesting some things that you ought to do.

When we started to eat our lunches in the cafeteria, there were people that threatened to do something to us. We always stayed together, two or three of us. We wouldn't be caught alone for fear of that. Thankfully, nobody ever attempted to do anything. But I was young and crazy enough I would have tried to do as much to them as they did to me. Yeah. Wouldn't hesitate. I was just that headstrong about it. I am thankful that nobody ever did.

The removal of [segregated] water fountains and locker rooms and things, it was a gradual process. People just began to accept it. I would guess people's jobs were critical at that point, too. Firestone being one of the better jobs, I imagine both side weren't going to take a chance of losing their jobs. There wasn't a lot of physical abuse, like fighting, but verbal abuse, yes.

Prior to us [the new generation] going in there in '63, they had what you'd call black and white jobs. There were some jobs that blacks just were supposedly not able to do. They did still have separate restrooms, eating facilities, the colored fountains, brown and white fountains, that was obvious. And naturally there was no policy-making people—black, that is—in the union.

They [blacks] weren't on the executive board. The executive board were

15. Lindsey's comments suggest a significant change in attitudes among at least some white workers since the 1950s.

[plant-wide] elected people. I think it was seven executive board members. The president, vice president, secretary, treasurer [also]—all were members of the executive board by virtue of their [elective] office, for eleven total. They set the policy, as to how things would go. At the peak we had probably about one thousand black employees, against two thousand white employees. With those numbers it was just virtually impossible for them [blacks] to get elected [to plant-wide office].

We had some very good black labor leaders that were capable, they just never had an opportunity. Lawrence Garrison was one, Clarence Coe was another, Josh Tools was another. When I went in, they were there. I remember those guys, they helped us a lot. Hillie Pride and those guys paved the way for us, in order to be able to have a chance to work at Firestone.

But the people elected the stewards by department. [And] the division chairmen were appointed by the administration. A division chairman is a person that represents all three shifts [in a given area of the plant]. Everybody has to be subject to the division chairman. Major decisions had to be made by him. He was the right hand of the [union] president. I think we had something like sixty-five division chairmen. You had black shop stewards, you had black division chairmen. You had Clarence Coe at one time, you had Josh Tools at one time. Lawrence Garrison, he was division chairman. Lawrence was in the compound room and the mill room, some of the jobs that were restricted to black people at that particular time. Of course, you had others.

You had almost in the plant like political parties, you had two or three political parties. It was just like the Republican and Democratic Parties, that's the way it worked. Many of them were able to get blacks elected on an executive board. [Then] you had some black executive board members. That wasn't a big problem [because they would be part of a ticket].

There was a guy, when I went in there, by the name of George Clark who was the president. Lawrence Garrison was a part of his administration. A young guy got elected by the name of Chester Turner, he was [also] part of Clark's administration. He was the first young [black] guy I knew that got elected overall by the plant as an executive board member. He was the only one at that time. Chester was a real aggressive, assertive person. Very able person. And you know what happens with that. In time, he would run into trouble with the administration. Chester only lasted one term, three years.

Chester was sensitive to black needs. He came into the plant at the same time I did. He just didn't see enough black movement as far as the union was concerned. If things went down at an executive board meeting he disliked, many times he got on the floor and spoke against 'em. It was political suicide. But it really didn't bother him because he was really concerned and sensitive to the needs of the people. If that happened to him, so be it. He didn't care.

[Among the black workers] here were some people who were loyal to a particular administration. Some of them thought Chester was wrong. Of course there was a division there. They thought Chester went about his grievance wrong and they were loyal. Then there were those that understood it and went along with Chester. So it was just a divide and conquer type of thing, where you divide the blacks. There was a real division there. Yeah, it always happened like that. I would guess many times it was by design, to do it that way.

Once all blacks got together beating the same drum, then they would get things changed. It happened one time, during the time when I was elected overwhelmingly as treasurer. But that happened only because the blacks got together and combined with the white voters. For a number of years it was just the opposite, where some issue would divide blacks. Maybe you had two or three factions. And you can see what happens, you never get the job done.

To be in the labor movement, you really have to love, be obsessive about people in general, I don't care if they're black or white. If they're workers, if they're dues-paying members, you have to be concerned about those people and try and take care of their needs. It really doesn't become a black and white issue because the problems out there, those problems don't care whether you're black or white. I guess what I'm saying is, if you don't learn to be together, stick together, you'll never get anything accomplished. And I think that that's a lesson that all of us at Firestone had to learn in the final analysis.

I would hate to think the company would like it the other way around, where you got everybody divided. I think some of the issues people just brought into the plant as a result of what was happening in the communities. The communities were divided. They just simply brought those divisions to the workplace.

I think the only significant issue [where blacks united] would be like when blacks were restricted to a particular job, where he couldn't bid on certain jobs. Like I said, they had taken care of that prior to us getting in there, prior to '63.[16] But I can remember, like in the tire room, they had very few black tire builders. You had a certain time you had to qualify. It was ninety days you had to qualify as a tire builder. What they would do many times, was they would change you from different types of machines. By the time you learn how this machine operates, they would move you. It makes it awfully difficult. There was certain blacks that went in there that had, what you'd call a "don't give up" attitude, he could stay around and qualify.

Most of them [blacks] that went into tire building went on to become excellent tire builders. It's like athletic skills, some guys are just better athletes. Some guys were just better tire builders. And they were just efficient, made good use of their time, they could just build them in less time. A guy that was efficient, making good use of time, he could make good money. At that time, you're talking about '65, '66, a guy could make close to forty-five, fifty dollars a day, about two hundred fifty to three hundred dollars a week. You got paid by the number of tires you built. Of course, if you didn't do anything, you didn't make any money.

I worked at that position for a while. I was hired in as a tire builder. I think the advantage that I had, I was hired into the department as a service man, therefore I learned a lot, just watching. What happened was, I was laid off. I asked for a transfer to come back there as a tire builder. I came in as a trainee. I didn't have any problems qualifying.

The two times that [Martin Luther] King came, we were there in support of the sanitation workers, we collected money out there, also participated in the walks. And we were prepared to go to the rally that night, prior to his assassination. In other words, we were in contact with other unions with similar problems. We also worked a great deal with the Memphis AFL-CIO. We took an active part in city elections.

It was a civil rights struggle and it was a labor struggle also. Being that the predominant number of those [sanitation] workers were black, that in itself made it a civil rights struggle. But it was just as much a labor struggle

16. Clarence Coe maintains that desegregation of some facilities took until 1973, but open bidding on jobs had been accomplished earlier.

as anything else. When you go through it, the labor struggle and the civil rights struggle is parallel, you can't hardly get away from it.

Memphis itself has always been anti-labor for some reason. Even though you've had strong labor movements within the city, it has always been anti-labor. And I guess it goes back, I guess it's where Hillie Pride and Clarence Coe would remember. The older guys can really give you a better view of it than I can.

It seems like a thing we just inherited for some reason, but it goes back far. You have to somewhat understand the way politics goes in this city. Like certain families control, and have always controlled ever since I can remember. It's just a small sector in control. Maybe that's true in all cities, I don't know. But it's always been that way. From the Crump machine on back. I've heard my father talk about that. Memphis is a city that has been [one of] divide and conquer. That same mentality still holds true.

Alzada and Leroy Clark Fight for Unionism and Civil Rights

It was just a series of battles that we won.

While some women married to male factory workers or union organizers remained isolated from union activities, Alzada Clark joined the labor movement when she married. She grew up in Memphis and went to work in a factory because she could not afford college. She met Leroy when he came to Memphis from New York to organize the furniture industry, including her shop. They created an organizing partnership, which provided glue for their marriage. I spoke with her in her living room on March 24, 1988; Mr. Clark had died from cancer only a short while before, on December 22, 1987. I had interviewed him in 1983, and unfortunately never got to talk to him again. I have combined both of their voices in this section in hopes of telling a more complete story.

ALZADA CLARK

People here began to learn about unions when Firestone moved in here, [in 1937] I think. Firestone was located just down the street from the black high school. Quite a few guys got jobs and worked at Firestone, and if you had a job there, you had a good salary. People started taking note of this sort of revolution in the organized labor movement in Memphis. Finally people made more money and had a little better working conditions. It was more humane.

My parents were working on low-income, low-paying jobs. My mother worked for Sam Forest Furniture Company, she was what they called a decorator. She would place the furniture in the windows and dust it off. My stepfather worked at Pillsbury Flour Company as an errand person, he would do the mail, clean up the offices, and things like that. My mother was the only black at the furniture store. I don't know what kind of pay they both earned.

My mother had hopes of me going to school to take advantage of a scholarship that I had won. I went to Manassas High School, that was the only black high school in the north side at the time. I won a sorority scholarship to go to LeMoyne College, but it wasn't a complete scholarship, and the extra cost was too much for my family to afford, even though I was an only child.

I was working in a shop, the Memphis Dinette as a supervisor/inspector. Conditions at the Memphis Dinette were bad. We didn't have adequate restrooms or places to eat. You couldn't go to the washroom without having to ask. Those were the kind of conditions that I resented, so I felt that no human being should be exposed to that. It was very difficult. The whites in the shop were either in a supervisory capacity or they had the better jobs. They marked the furniture or worked on the loading docks or [as] inspectors. I was one of the few blacks that had an inspecting job. Memphis Dinette made dining room furniture, and I inspected seats. Sometimes I stopped the line and checked it. At lunch time, we would have to eat outside or sit out in our cars and eat, and we would all hover together and talk. There was no inside area where we were allowed to eat. There was an area for the whites to eat, but not for us.

There were about one hundred workers, less than 1 percent were white. Blacks made the seats, pulled the plastic on them, put them together, make the padding, transport them and box them, put them on the shipping dock, things like that. We went to work from 7:30 A.M. to 5 P.M. or so, about a nine-hour day. There weren't enough facilities there for the blacks, [and] they [only] kept them halfway clean. The supervisor didn't want you to talk or go to the bathroom, and we never had breaks. It was pretty hard on the women, because the plastic be cold. It was under a big light, and you had to let it warm and pull it around fast. The machines were made square, and you had to stretch it and get it stapled.

I met Leroy in 1950, he came to Memphis on assignment. I was interested in the union, [and] a fellow who was a steward asked me to come work with him in the union. So I did. I had an opportunity to move around among the people, and ask different people to come to the [union] meeting. I didn't have any fear about the union when it started. My mother had more fear than I, but she soon decided it wasn't necessary to be afraid. Leroy would come to the shop in the evenings and load up his car with as many people as we could, and we'd go to meetings at the [CIO] union hall at 136½ S. Second Street. We would discuss conditions in the shop and organizing the union.

Leroy came along, and he kind of enlightened people about things that we could do about it, like forming a union. I became interested. I'd heard about unions before, but this was the first time I had participated in one. I had no other family members involved in the union, only my mother. I was about twenty-five or twenty-six at the time. I grew up in Memphis. We got off to a good start, but before we could get really organized, Leroy was transferred to Chicago. I continued with the union, and I worked in the factory for about a year. Super said, "You married a union man, I bet." I had nerve enough to take a week's vacation then. Most people were afraid to even ask for a day or two. Leroy came back, and we got married. I quit in November of 1952.

Leroy's father was a carpenter and had a master's degree in divinity. His father was from Trinidad or Jamaica, and his mother was from Cuba. Leroy was born in Panama City, Panama, and he came to New York at the age of two or three. Leroy seemed to have gained much of his political and social attitudes from his father, who may have had some [bad] union experiences, which might have been why he went to Panama to work on the canal. His mother always insisted that Leroy stay in school, and she would go and get him off of the picket line to get him back to school. She got him to City College for two years, and then he was in World War II as an officer in the army in Germany, France, and England.

At one point the army sent him to Camp Shelby in Mississippi, and they told him he was no longer in the U.S. He never set foot off base until he was shipped off to Europe! Leroy saw too much suffering and pain in the war and didn't want to talk much about it. He mentioned discrimination some, but not in any detail. I saw his pictures of Paris and France, though, and he told me a lot about the two Germanys. After the service, he worked his way up in the union and became recording secretary of his local union in New York.

We moved to High Point, North Carolina, right after we married. He was working on [organizing] several places there. Then we went to New York, and Leroy supported Jack Hochstad [for union president], who lost. Leroy went to work in the shop for a while then, because [furniture union president] Pizer fired him. Then Pizer asked him to go back to North Carolina in 1953. Then I was in the hospital, so he came back to New York and worked in the shop again.

[Finally], I was working in the New York garment district in a good job that paid $110 [a week] in 1958. That was good money then. Leroy went back on staff with Pizer a third time then to go to High Point, since they said he was the only one who could settle the strike there. Pizer moved us out to Chicago in 1960. I went to work for Sam Sloane, director for the Chicago UFWA [United Furniture Workers of America]. We had a strike in that plant that Leroy had so well organized. We were winning that strike, until the company called me at home one night and said [someone] was paying $500 to kill Leroy. I told them if they'd pay me $1,000, I'd do the job! I was of the opinion that Sloane had something to do with this. After Leroy told him of his hopes of building up the union, Sloane felt threatened that he might be replaced. Leroy was talking about getting other blacks involved in leadership. When Leroy had an opportunity to take a year's leave at the University of Michigan, Pizer told him not to go as he had too much education already. They transferred him to Memphis. So I had to quit my job again, and we moved to Memphis.

LEROY CLARK

The local [AFL-CIO] Memphis Labor Council, they didn't want no blacks on their executive board at all. I think Henry White got on the executive board because he was of the establishment.[17] And as I got more active in the union I got more involved in the council, raisin' my voice and tryin' to induce members to come to the council meetings so they could have some

---

17. On the situation in the Memphis AFL-CIO, see Clark's account in chapter 5.

influence. Eventually I got elected to the council executive board. I did my best I could to make some changes in the setup. The black workers generally became more militant and speak out more for their rights.

[But] they didn't get to the point that we were in the early 1940s in New York when the CIO was really workin', you know. You had black leadership on all levels within the unions in the CIO, and of course a lot of them were bein' attacked for bein' left wing, like the office and professional workers [Office and Professional Employees International Union]. But they went out of their way to train black leadership, they had all kinds of trainin', while this is not done here in the South, you know.

A guy had to fight his way through a whole lot to become a leader in the South. And generally it's only to become a head of a black local. And there was a definite change from the CIO policy of involvin' blacks, back to the old AFL policy to toleratin' 'em, you know. Really they didn't want blacks in the unions.

[In Memphis], the steelworkers had a large black membership, the woodworkers, furniture workers, the brewery workers, the ones that worked on the soft drink trucks. They had a [white] business agent, used to be a former policeman, and he ran the local union, and they had local union officers all black, because most of the union was black. But the top official was the business agent and he ran the local union, until they got rid of him. Also, you had the laborers union, which was predominately black but all of their officers was white. And then they got rid of all but the man that took care of the money, he was white. [laughs]

I was a lone voice hollerin' about black leadership for these unions around here. I was always complainin' that the internationals were not sendin' in and not developin' no black leadership for their local unions here, and I complained bitterly about it in council meetings and my views are well known. They [the council] took the position it wasn't their business, it was each international supposed to do their thing.

Only one union I think responded, that was the steelworkers, they sent a guy in here he's now vice president of the steelworkers, Leon Lynch. Me and him worked together, 'til he became the vice president of the labor council, and the vice president was the chairman of the [council's] board. Of course, the steelworkers were havin' problems with the blacks in their international, they formed a black caucus. In fact that's what I did in my international and did in the state [AFL-CIO] council, was to form a black caucus to put pressure to get some things done as far as leadership is concerned. They weren't trainin' them and givin' them opportunities, you know, and puttin' blacks where they were needed. I knew that it could be done 'cause I seen it done! You know, I seen it done in the early formation of the CIO.[18]

[As the international representative here], I established a "steward system," everything had to go through the stewards, you know. Took me time, but I eventually worked it out that stewards had to be responsible to take care of their shops, and that really strengthened the union more than anything else. But prior to that the only way the grievances or the problems were handled were you just got in touch with the guy that was the head of the local union, and then he would see what he could talk the boss into, and that was it.

The problem I found difficult was to get the people to go on strike. Their position was he go up there and get an increase but don't be talkin' about no strike.

The Memphis Furniture strike was a lost cause when they got finished with it, and it was a [negative] example for all workers. I was in New York at that time [1949], and I fought like hell that our local union vote a weekly amount to the strike. The problem with Memphis Furniture, they had a contract, but they didn't have no checkoff of dues. The company fired a union activist and then they went out on strike and that was the tough time for them. [At] the same time they were red-baitin' the union leadership, during the time of the [Taft-Hartley] noncompliance.

The company used to go down to Mississippi and Arkansas and load up their trailers with scabs, and then they drive a trailer-load full of scabs up to the loading docks and back in. And you had a whole lot of police around the entrance, so there was no way you could stop the scabs from goin' in. And the company used to manufacture the clubs for the police. Yeah, special clubs was made by the company for the police—extra long—the ones the police regularly had wasn't long enough and heavy enough! [laughs]

The steelworkers had their American Snuff strike [the next year], you

18. Clark described how a group of black trade unionists defended the National Maritime Union's Ferdinand Smith, the first black vice president and secretary-treasurer of an international union, before CIO President Philip Murray in 1949. The U.S. government deported Smith under the McCarran-Walter Act as an alien and Communist Party member during the red scare.

know, but we were just a little small international, we didn't have the resources that the steelworkers had.[19] So it was a job to remove that fear [of strikes] from the workers' minds.

It was a question of education, [to show them] that they had to force a strike issue or they were only beggin'. I conducted one strike and it only lasted about a week and the company give a few pennies more and I accepted it and went back. That's when the workers got their strength, when they knew that they could go on strike and they didn't lose their jobs! Because prior to that, winnin' strikes just wasn't done. Strikes was just a lost cause and workers knew it, you know they knew it! And therefore they didn't want to be involved in losin' their jobs.

So I figured out let's have some strikes of short duration and if we get some concessions and settle, that encouraged the workers that they could strike and not lose their jobs. When they got that, then there was no problem of callin' a strike. And the employer know and he negotiate with me and we either reach agreement or we had a strike. He knew that. But it took years to get into that position. Then I suspect we had a strike with every employer under contract—sooner or later we had a strike. Our biggest job was tryin' to stop strikes! [laughs] When they weren't necessary, you know. You got some guys get up there and they shoot out those things that sound good to the workers, "a dollar an hour increase," you know. [laughs] And you say, "Let's be real," they say, "Oh, you talkin' for the boss." [laughs]

I know one strike we had, in the [Ivers and Pond] piano company, and the vote was very narrow—there was maybe five hundred people in the hall, and I think the vote was about ten votes different between not strikin' and goin' on strike. And of course [some] swore that there was a miscount and I had screwed them some way. I said, "I didn't do any countin'." I just added up what the tellers said. But at the end of that contract there was no stoppin' the strike—they were determined to go on strike! The end of that [three-year] contract they did go on strike.

But that was a whole lot different than when I first came here. And of

19. A long strike by mostly white women at the American Snuff factory in Memphis in 1950 led to fighting and other forms of violence, at a company whose leaders later became prominent in the anti-union John Birch Society. Although the strike was heavily funded by the steelworkers union and supported by other CIO unionists, the workers eventually lost.

course the attitude of the police changed also in the course of the years, you know. Before the police were tough on your picket lines. But over the years they changed, and they were friendly and took the position if they didn't see nothin' they wouldn't arrest you. Before, they didn't have to see anything, they'd arrest you. They'd arrest and whatever the employer told them to do.

In my young union it was just a series of small strikes, gradually you know, it was just a series of battles that we won. Of course you had people going to jail and all like that. But I had one philosophy where I tried to avoid anybody spending a night [in jail]. I always got 'em out, I always got 'em out. There's nothing better than seein' a guy you'd lock up today, he's back on the picket line the next day. You see that helps the morale quite a bit, quite a bit.

[He describes the work situation in upholstery factories, where black women, most of them pro-union, did the heavy lifting and white women, most of them reluctant to join, did the sewing.] They were hard to get to join the union. They were in the vanguard of those women who were workin' for a livin', and generally were single parents. They were the main breadwinners for the family, and they were afraid of losing their jobs. If they didn't work, they didn't have nobody to take care of 'em.

Where there was a better chance to make higher wages, you'd find that's where the whites were. They had those jobs. That was the same way in the piano company [Ivers and Pond], which had the largest group of white workers. The company had tried to keep the easier and better-paying jobs exclusively for whites, even if the rest of the whole plant is black. It had to do with changing company policy. I had to make the company change that, you know. It was quite a job. I told the company if there ain't gonna be a change, there ain't gonna be no contract and we're gonna strike. So we worked out where the workers could bid into the jobs. Before then they were always locked into the jobs. If a white worker quit, they'd hire another white worker to take a good job. The black workers couldn't get it!

So we finally got a bidding right so any worker could bid for a job, and once there was a vacancy they had to give that worker a shot at it. You put your name up [on a board for jobs]. When a job becomes available, you give 'em the first opportunity to try out for it. You had a better chance than a new person coming in, because you been seein' the job and a worker wants a job, they make it their business to learn it, through lunch hour, going around and learning it. The whites didn't like the idea, but they accustomed to it. Even then, you have to encourage the [black] workers to bid on the jobs, because workers have the tendency to stay with what they know. What the company wanted to do, was if you bid and you didn't make it, then you lost your job. That was where we hung up for quite some time. You can't call workers out on strike for just that, because they can't understand that. But this is the key to advance, 'cause if you let the company keep that position, ain't nobody gonna bid! And then the bidding process is just a farce. So, you don't make your agreement on the money [with the company] until we reach agreement on that.

All companies tried to do that, to lock you in so you can't move about, especially when it's a question of blacks movin' into jobs that whites had. It took time, but we eventually broke it down.

ALZADA CLARK

Leroy was the president of the NAACP during the dreadful times here in Memphis in 1968–71. Things were really in confusion then. The white community, especially the Jewish community, sent so many letters and calls [of support]. Leroy was the cohesion and adhesion that kept the city together at that time, according to them. Without his level-headedness and his attitude about things, the city could really have been torn apart, they said. Since the time in '68, when Dr. King was killed, into the latter part of that summer, that was really true, he kind of kept the lid on things.

The NAACP was the focal point of the civil rights movement in this city, we didn't have CORE or SNCC[20] or anything else, because we had sophisticated leadership with college degrees in Memphis. You had to have degrees to have any power here. The president of the Tri-State Bank [Jesse Turner] preceded Leroy's leadership in the union. Maxine Smith, Leroy Clark, two female local school teachers, a man teacher from the state tech, a minister from the CME [Christian Methodist Episcopal] church were all leaders here. This made Memphis different than some cities that had branches of NAACP. Jesse was independent from whites in his job, and so was Maxine. Jesse was the national treasurer of the NAACP.

20. The Congress of Racial Equality and the Student Nonviolent Coordinating Committee were civil rights groups that specialized in civil disobedience and direct action.

After Dr. King's death, everything was ready to explode. Blacks couldn't be out in the street, not here so much as further east in the city in white areas. Police would stop blacks in white areas at night. [Down south of the city], it used to be called White Haven, now we call it "Black Haven" because if only one black person moved in the block, the whites started moving out. Now it's all black.

Back at that time, we received threats constantly. We never changed our phone number, because I always had an answer. We weren't afraid. One time Leroy went to Brazil to study the labor movement for a month, and I got lots of calls and threats then. Leroy went to AFSCME late in '68–'69. He was the first director after Martin Luther King's death.

LEROY CLARK

I don't know when the Memphis NAACP got started. They've been in existence, but they were like a lot of the branches in the South—they were very quiet and people hid their memberships. They didn't do too much, and people who were members didn't let it be known. And that's the way it's been in the South in a lot of the branches. It's only recently that people would acknowledge that there was an NAACP in Memphis. I was always in the NAACP wherever I went, even as a youngster. Here I did the same thing and became active and was on the board. My wife became active too.

In the early '60s we had demonstrations every week for about a year and a half and we had sit-ins at the banks and downtown area, and they finally sat down with the leaders of the black community, asked, "What do you want?" And they reached an agreement on no segregation in any of the public places. A long list of demands, all of them weren't met, but the majority were, so that we ceased the demonstrations downtown, but it took about a year and a half of constant work, every week, every week. Sometimes there would only be a small group of us would go down there and picket and demonstrate, but kept it up until they finally gave in. Then we had to test it. We sent out teams to test every restaurant, every theater, and then would see what would happen. I was very much involved in marches and so on.

Then, of course, [after the sanitation strike here in 1968] there was what they called the Black Mondays, when they had the children to come out of school, and they [AFSCME] was striking St. Joseph's Hospital also. The agreement between the union and the NAACP was that either side could settle without the other if they found a way to settle. They [the NAACP] reached a desegregation agreement with the school authorities, but the union didn't want us to stop the demonstrations on Black Monday, they wanted to maintain the pressure on St. Joseph's. Well, the NAACP board didn't agree with it, but the president of the NAACP, he was in the pocket of the union and he went along with the union. He was forced to resign, and I became the president after that. They [AFSCME] lost. [St. Joseph's is] not organized now. None of the private hospitals are. The city hospital is, but private hospitals are not.[21]

The labor movement on a whole didn't participate much in the struggle that was going on in the black community here. Very few of the labor leaders participated. Tommy Powell [president of the Memphis Labor Council], he took the right position, you know, 'cause he was president of a predominantly black local [the Amalgamated Meat Cutters and Butcher Workmen]. But when the sanitation strike came, they [the AFL-CIO] did support the union in the strike. They gave it support.

Alzada Clark Organizes Black Women Workers in Mississippi

The chief of police always said that they couldn't control the "niggers" in town after I arrived.

When Leroy Clark started organizing plants in Mississippi, the companies hired women in hopes of defeating his efforts. The union counterattacked by hiring Alzada Clark in 1967 to organize these women. She became one of the most effective organizers the United Furniture Workers had in the deep South. Her determination and passion for civil rights and unionism and her buoyancy and verve as a community leader, well known

21. The NAACP organized Black Monday protests in the fall of 1969 to put pressure on the all-white Memphis school board, elected by at-large elections, to open up to black participation. Eventually the electoral system was changed, and NAACP leader Maxine Smith and others were elected to the board. AFSCME had some one thousand people signed up at John Gaston, the city's public hospital, but after the failure at St. Joseph's, organization did not spread into private hospitals.

in Memphis, soon spread to parts of Mississippi. Here labor organizing capitalized on the energy unleashed among blacks, black women in particular, by the civil rights movement.

Between 1961 and 1965, the *Commercial Appeal* labeled Leroy and myself as Communists. Red Copeland said we would bear watching, but he never said anything of substance as to what we had done. The only thing we belonged to was the NAACP, the union, and my church! We had had a little strike at a broom or mop factory over on Third Street, and a lawyer for the company said we had Communist traits and branded us. The FBI started going through our files and tapping my phone, and all of those kind of nonsensical things. We had a nice headline in the press, and everyone called us to joke that we had made the paper again!

Later, when Leroy became president of the NAACP and I was working for the Tennessee State Labor Council, I found the letter from Red Copeland to [state labor council leader] Matt Lynch. The letter said we were "two smart cookies" and they should keep their eyes on us, because we were working for the communists. I found the letter in the waste basket in the office. I got laid off at the Tennessee State Labor Council because the whites complained so much about my being black. They just abolished my job, saying they didn't have enough money. So I went on staff with the furniture workers.

I came on board with the United Furniture Workers on February 27, 1967. There was a campaign on in Canton and Leland, Mississippi. They had lost the election prior to 1967 in Canton, north of Jackson. The union's district director, Auggie Barr, asked me to come down there because they had a lot of women to organize. He said, "Don't let those white folks scare you when you get down here!" When I got there, we talked about how to organize. Auggie said that the white guys were scared to breathe, their organizing wasn't very effective. I said I could win that election.

Leroy came down to help now and then. I had two security guards to go everywhere with me at night, because the Ku Klux Klan had made some threats. One black policeman told me that I was the top of the conversation every Monday morning, [and] they were afraid for me. Many police, even the police chief, were involved in the Klan, and sometimes they would follow me around in an unmarked car to intimidate me.

The Cullmer Company said they beat every union election in the state

but one, until "that black woman came around." They had a lot of respect
for me there in the union. They said they couldn't have organized the
women without me.

Carl Scarborough[22] and I and three others were organizing the Gilbert
Manufacturing Company, called the DeSoto Company, which made furniture parts and employed over three hundred workers. We came in one
morning to talk with the employer, Mr. Gill, and negotiate the contract.
He said, "Good morning, Alzada!" His lawyers were filing in behind him.
I said, "I beg your pardon! I didn't know that you and I were good enough
friends to be talking on a first name basis. I reserve that right for my
friends, and I don't think you and I are friends!" He said, "Well, how is
Leroy—I mean, Mr. Clark?" I said, "Does that really concern you?" and
I walked around the table and sat down. He turned red as a beet. I told
the blacks later that I considered us of equal status, and that he should
treat us with respect.

I had the right written into the contract to allow me to go through the
plant, and I did this so the workers knew they had power and representation. I wouldn't interrupt their work, but I'd talk to each of them, or whoever I needed to see. We got the contract, but Mr. Gill sold his interest out
of DeSoto, and he bought another plant over across the field.

I had also organized No-Sag, a division of a spring [mattress] company
out of New York. It had a plant in Canton and paid better than anybody in
the area. But I managed to get three of their workers interested in starting a
union while we were sharing a beer at a local tavern. (Leroy always taught
me to go where the people are!)[23]

So the people I met at the tavern got some other workers together,
and we met using our car lights out by an old nightclub every week for a
month. We didn't have any other place to meet. Leroy always taught me
that eye contact was important, so I always sat in the center. They told me
their problems, and I would write them down, and then I'd go visit each
person who spoke later and get to know them so they'd trust me. We'd try
to get people to sign cards for the union, and then we'd talk about better
working conditions, facilities, and pay.

22. Carl Scarborough, a white worker at Ivers and Pond for a time became president of Local 282 and later president of the UFWA international.
23. Leroy Clark mentioned that some of his most effective organizing in North
Carolina in the 1950s had been "over a bottle" with furniture workers.

Then we'd work to get people to sign membership cards, but we had to talk with each person outside of company property. Some of them were afraid, but most of them came around. When they had 75 percent of the workers signed up, they petitioned for an election.

The thing that turned the election around for me at Gilbert was a black guy who had been working at the owner's house as a gardener, and he couldn't read or write. He said he didn't need a union. I spoke to him outside a window on the main street of Canton, [and] a superintendent was drinking up in the window, and he [the superintendent] said, "Those people don't know when they need help." The next Monday that black gardener came to me and apologized, and he signed up more people in that plant than I did!

Four white folks and a black man told me after we won that they were making more money than they'd ever made in their lives. One man said that his wife went to buy all of their children shoes, with leather soles, and now they could all go to school. We talked about how they could save a little money aside each week, maybe ten dollars or so, and find decent housing to rent, and take things slowly.

A third plant I organized, the Jackson shop, Milsap, was mostly men. They had a black guy who didn't like me. One night at a restaurant he took a lit cigarette right across my face, just missing my eyes. Another guy with me pulled out a razor, and I yelled at him to stop. He said to the guy with the cigarette, "I'll cut your throat if you don't stay away from her and leave her alone, or this town will eat you alive." I told him to put his razor in his pocket and leave it there!

In the meantime, I was also working on organizing a fourth company, the American Tent Company. They made cabinet parts, and had four hundred people. I started on the union, and they laid off two hundred workers. We won that election, but negotiated for almost a year to get a lousy nickel. The owner of that plant was Bob Yandell, I was told he was a member of the Klan by both whites and blacks. We went into negotiations at American Tent with six women, but we lost two hundred workers. Finally, we called a strike. International supported me, and we settled that contract.

Then Milsap went out on strike. I was out on the picket line with them one day, when a big truck pulled in, knocked me over deliberately into the ditch, and I landed on a pile of red ants. I was bitten and burned by those ants, and my dress was torn. The constable was called, and he came and said I was interfering. I said I wasn't interfering with anything. He twisted my arm right out of the socket and carried me to jail. When we got there, I called the president of the union to call Leroy and tell him to come for me at the jailhouse. Then the jailer reached up to hit me, and I almost scratched him, but thought these two white men all alone with me would kill me, so I ducked instead.

The jailer handcuffed me and put me in the car, and I rolled down the window when we were coming through a little town. I yelled out, "Hey, they're taking me to the county jail! Call Memphis and call Leroy." He swore at me and rolled up the window, and pretty soon I rolled it down again and did the same thing. Then we got out of town, and I let it alone then, because there was no one around.

Just as we got to the county jail, Howard, the local president of the union, pulled up behind us and saved my hide. He said, "Miss Clark, we come to see about you." They locked me up, and Howard asked how much my bail was. They wouldn't tell him what the bail was. So he called Leroy in Memphis. When Leroy called, they said, "That nigger from Memphis called, and he sounds like he's white!" Leroy asked what the bail was, and they told him five hundred dollars. He said he was sending out a man with the money.

I slept on that iron for about five hours, and they hadn't done anything with my arms yet. When I got out, they took me to the doctor in Jackson, and when I told the doctor what had happened, he just jumped and said, "Well, I can't do anything about it, the police have to take you to the hospital." So I put it in a sling and slipped up to Memphis that night without anyone knowing, and the doctor there looked at it and gave me some pain medication. I saw Leroy there, he wanted to make sure I was all right. I slipped back by morning, and no one had missed me.

When they set my trial, the judge was the desk sergeant from the night I was arrested. We had everyone who looked like me [blacks] in town at the trial. They all took the day off from work, and they had Peace Street, the two side streets, and the street behind full of people, all pushing into the courthouse. There wasn't enough room in the courtroom, and they postponed my trial until January. When I came out in the courtyard, the crowd wanted to have a rally in the square. I got up on the steps and made a speech. Leroy said, "You turned Canton out today!" I was charged on five counts, including resisting arrest for saying ouch when he twisted my arm!

Leroy told the lawyer to get me off. I wanted to plead guilty and go to jail. Leroy was afraid I'd get sick staying in jail, he thought I was crazy.

Meanwhile, American Tent factory was still on strike. I kept them out on their strike, the international sent me fifty thousand dollars. Each week we got about eight or nine thousand dollars to pay rent, house notes [mortgage payments], food, and necessities for the workers on strike. Six women sat that strike out with me whose husbands had other jobs. They never did get a nickel. The strike lasted a year, two months, and two days.

Then Gilbert sold out DeSoto to set up Gilbert and Rine, and I organized that. There was a woman who helped me in there. We boycotted a number of businesses as part of our strike strategies. Mr. Aikens, the white man who ran the motel, protected me more than once from angry people looking for me. One time I was being followed and I jumped out of the car and left it running, Mr. Aikens brought me the keys and checked on me all night long. The FBI came down once, and they followed me and asked questions about me. One night I passed by the FBI car, they got out, and I went around the corner and they missed me.

Al May [an international union organizer] and Leroy weren't served in a restaurant once, so they went to a black restaurant. I went to the restaurant where they were refused and asked to be served. After they served me, they splashed coffee all over me, and I walked out.

Whenever we went to [the union's] District 9 meetings, Canton always had the best reports. Leroy would straighten out the grammar, and May would type it. I sent pictures of the strikers to the international. When I closed that strike down, we had a union of about one thousand people in Canton. We had about fifteen thousand to sixteen thousand dollars in the local treasury.

The only shop still there is No-Sag, the rest of them went out of business. DeSoto, Gilbert and Rine, and American Tent went out of business. When President Reagan came in[to office in 1981], a lot of businesses went out.

We closed American Tent down ourselves. Everybody in Canton carried a pistol. One night they got tired of the white superintendent splashing water on them with his car. Four women got in the car with their husbands and took along a great big container of baking soda. They went to the white superintendent's plant where all of these beautiful Black Angus cows were. They dumped soda all over the grass for the cows to eat. When the cows ate that and drank some water, they fell over just like flies. It poisoned the cows. It wasn't until two years afterwards that I knew who did that. The black supervisor who kept working when the rest were on strike had his house riddled with bullets by some of the women workers. They never got caught. I didn't know that until a year later, either.

That plant soon sold out at a complete loss to some place in Virginia. We closed them down. When they pulled the last piece out, I called the strike off. This was the really long strike of over a year, at American Tent Company. Bob Yandell, who was the head of the [local] KKK, and someone else were the owners. They were making tents for Vietnam. After we closed it down, we got complimentary and thank you letters from many people who were against the war. The six women who went on strike with me at American Tent Company found out that every Wednesday, Bob Yandell's secretary Patsy would go to Jackson. They trailed her to the Jacksonian motel every week, and they found out that Bob Yandell was meeting her there. They spread the news all over Canton! I said, "Lord, y'all are too much for me!"

The chief of police was killed in Louisiana, and the police who arrested me were later imprisoned as thieves. They were sneaking into peoples' houses and stealing. These were our police! [Yet] the chief of police always said that they couldn't control the "niggers" in town after I arrived from Memphis! The attitudes of people started changing after we organized. Dr. King came in there once, but only briefly.

I stayed there from 1967 to 1976. I worked in Mississippi and in Little Rock and Pine Bluff, Arkansas, during those years, I was the business agent and the international representative, and everything else. I organized Brown Company in Pine Bluff, and helped to get the black women involved in the union. I worked on Little Rock Furniture Company in Little Rock, too, and then Dillingham Manufacturing in Leland, and Guthrie Furniture Company in Guthrie, Oklahoma. We had all of them organized, but we couldn't do anything with the Memphis Furniture Company.

In Natchez, Mississippi, they had a bombing, and they killed a union organizer down there. People phoned me at the hotel, thinking it was me when they heard the news. But it was a man from the automobile workers who was killed.

The workers at that company showed me how to check to make sure my car was not rigged with a bomb, because they were worried about me. If you put a match under the hood and one under the trunk, if that match has moved when you come back, don't touch the car.

Then they told me how to tell if someone was following me in my car. I'd put the brakes on in the middle of the street block, and if they stopped too, they were following me. I was followed lots of times! Once Mr. Dan Thomas, chief of police, and Mr. Aikens, both of the KKK, were following me at night. But I made it back to the hotel anyway. That was after I exposed Bob Yandell. He went out of business, and they gave me some terrible times.

Yes, they assassinated my character over and over again down there. One time a friend told me that the white cafes had placed a fifty dollar bet to poison me. So I went to a particular cafe where the owner was my friend, and I just ate there. I left Canton [for good] on February 27, 1976.

Leroy worked in Mississippi and anywhere else that he was needed. Leroy always said the union was his religion. Leroy felt that he was able to make a difference in labor, so it was very important to him to be working for the union. He wanted to live to see the difference that his work made, and he did. He eventually became the international vice president of the furniture workers union, which was unheard of for a black person. He wanted to come to Memphis to see what he could do to build the union up. He wanted to bring both whites and blacks together in order to build the union, and help eradicate racism.

He saw the labor movement and the union as a way to do that, the civil rights and labor movements were interwoven. The police would try to control the blacks and the labor people, black, white, Jewish, whatever. [But] he wasn't worried about coming to the South or going anywhere. The labor movement and the civil rights movement went hand in hand absolutely, they've always been partners. Both had the same goals.

Leroy died of cancer in the end. He was in remission after 1979, so we knew it was coming for a long time ahead. You were here in '83, he was doing well then. He started going downhill in 1987, he got cancer in his leg, and there was nothing they could do for him. He just took his pain medication and did the best he could.

He slipped away from me on a Tuesday night. He began to lose his voice, his vocal chords became paralyzed. I told them to do everything they could for him, to help him and make him comfortable, but to ask him about any big decisions. He told them to give him no life support, only pain medication to the end. We never discussed it, but we respected his decision.

That night he died, when I came in he said in what little voice he had left, "Hi baby, how are you doing?" He told me to go home and get some rest. I asked him how he was doing, and he said, "I'm still here!" Later as I went home to get some rest, I held his hand and told him I was leaving for a bit. I kissed him and said, "Don't you be running any races all over the floor here, stay here until I get back." He said, "I'll try." Those were the last words he said to me.

The next day, December 22, a few days before Christmas Eve, he died about 11 A.M. They said he just quit breathing when they were bathing him, he never made a sound.

The state passed legislation to leave a memorial to Leroy Clark on February 2, 1989. I have it here. I have letters and telegrams from the governor and people all around.

He said quite clearly a couple days before he died that he felt he had lived a good life. He said he did what he wanted to do, helping people to help themselves, and helping some people in spite of themselves. He said he was so proud of me and loved me so much for coming into the union and working with him all of those years, and for understanding what it was all about. He said we made a contribution and a difference in how people could live. He said that people were his religion.

After he died, people said I didn't seem as sad as they thought I would, and I said that Leroy had told me not to let anyone see me cry. There were lots of nights in this house alone that I cried my heart out because I miss him so much, but no one else saw me crying. I done my best.

As black workers confronted the challenges of the 1960s, struggles for civil rights and labor rights intertwined in many ways. One of the fruits of the civil rights movement, the Equal Employment Opportunities Commission, aided black labor organizing very directly. The courts had largely failed to implement the *Brown* decision to desegregate the public schools, but use of the EEOC combined with strikes allowed many African Americans to implement desegregation at work. In Memphis, schools had long denied blacks equal education, and as a result employers could claim they lacked qualifications for skilled jobs, such as inventorying cotton at Federal Compress. This double-bind system, denying workers an equal education and then denying them good jobs because of it, had long been used to keep blacks stuck in positions as low-paid laborers. In reality, Federal Compress denied checking jobs to blacks not because they couldn't count or write legibly but because they were black. Managers already had blacks training whites as checkers, while denying them access to those same jobs, a practice Matthew Davis also described at Firestone.

Through the job actions and cases Leroy Boyd and others filed before the EEOC, blacks in Local 19 overturned such absurdities, demonstrating how unions and civil rights laws operating together could cause years of white privilege to come crashing down. Many whites had opposed industrial unions from the very start for fear that they would place them on an equal level with blacks. Now their fears were realized as the EEOC removed them from their perceived status as bosses. Such a loss of privileges was "a hurtin' thing for the white man," observed Matthew Davis. It stigmatized racist behavior and an artificially elevated status that whites for generations had accepted as a right.

Davis and many others among the early generation of black industrial workers, after many years of "taking it," could only feel vindicated as such barriers to black occupational advancement began to fall. As jobs and union positions increasingly opened up to blacks at Firestone, white employers and white workers alike increasingly had to treat Davis as a citizen with equal rights. This turn of events authenticated a sense of equality Davis had always had, and it also created significant new resources for his community. From the time he came back from the war, Davis turned down overtime work in order to put his family and community first. As blacks gained greater standing at work, the union sent him to city hall to represent black and labor interests to the larger community. As a black unionist, he increasingly found himself serving as advocate for his north side community, where he continued to build church, community, and youth organizations for many years after retirement.[24] Davis looked

24. In his later years, Davis volunteered within his community, helping people pay their bills, working with kids, and attending to family and neighborhood difficulties through the New Chicago Civic Club, his church, and the union retiree's organization.

back with pride to the work he had done to elevate the human condition through his union, and he was not the only one.

Edward Lindsey, from the generation coming into the workplace in the early 1960s, had similar motivation but a different perspective and method. Lindsey's generation had higher aspirations financially and chafed at the compromises inherent in a labor movement still dominated by whites. Lindsey recognized that "Hillie Pride and those guys paved the way for us." But unlike the first generation of Firestone employees, he had hoped to be a doctor, not a factory worker. As a college student he had also participated in one of the startling and powerful moments of awakening in the freedom struggle, the Nashville sit-in movement. By the time he came to Firestone in 1963, the culture of black factory workers to some degree had changed. While older workers criticized the younger people for refusing to "take it" or work as hard as they had, this generation defined itself by direct action. If, indeed, some refused to work hard, others like Lindsey simply refused to go along with the segregated facilities in the factory, sitting anywhere they wanted and using whatever drinking fountain they chose. He believed that the time for accommodation to white prejudice was over.

Much as George Holloway did, Lindsey used his unfinished college education to put his youthful energies and militancy into union politics. Here, however, he found compromise unavoidable. To get elected to the rubber workers union's executive board, blacks had to adhere to one white union leader or another; outnumbered by whites in the factory two to one, blacks running for office joined "tickets" that put their interests at varying levels of priority. Conflicting choices and schisms led to black disunity in the largest union local in Memphis. Lindsey eventually concluded that some degree of compromise was in the nature of interracial unionism. So he chose to work within the system and make some compromises with whites in the interests of getting blacks elected and having an effective union. Such necessary compromises and black disunity, as well as the fear that they might lose the best-paying factory jobs in the city, kept many blacks at Firestone from taking a stronger direct action role in the civil rights movement.

Like Edward Lindsey, Leroy Clark made compromises and pragmatic choices, based on long experience in organized labor going back to the 1930s. Merely to be part of the labor movement, for Clark, had been a form of compromise. He would have seen George Meany not as the "grand old man" of Davis's imagination, but as a representative of the white craft unionists of the AFL who held back people like his father from remunerative employment. Clark well knew that while CIO unions had a policy of interracialism and equal rights, the AFL unions had pioneered in using initiation rituals, constitutions, apprenticeship programs, and occasionally brute force to exclude blacks from the crafts. Within the AFL-CIO, the AFL's cherished principle of "local autonomy" canceled out sanctions against union discrimination, in marked contrast to the centralized control over affiliates both the AFL and the CIO had exercised to eliminate "reds" and their disfavored unions. The new AFL-CIO federation created a political climate hostile to black leadership initiatives, in the context of a stagnating labor movement that concentrated on servicing the workers who belonged to unions, or on building union halls, rather than on organizing the unorganized. This climate often allowed white business agents to represent blacks with little or no participation from the rank and file.

Clark realized the AFL-CIO merger had constrained what he as a black union organizer could do. He remained as conscious of the labor movement's flaws as he was of its potential for good and carried forward his own brand of civil rights unionism within these constraints. Inaction, corruption, and declining membership created a leadership vacuum in the unions, and he attempted to fill it. He pragmatically sought to organize workers and build a black union leadership whenever and wherever he could. In Local 282, he created a strong steward and grievance system, and rather than relying on labor boards, he educated workers to the idea that they had to be ready to strike if they wanted any improvements. Step by step, he rebuilt furniture locals in Memphis that had been allowed to stagnate by uncreative white leaders. Clark sought to break black women out of the lowest paying jobs in the furniture industry by making it an axiom not to settle other contract issues until first reaching agreement on the right of blacks to bid for every job in the plant. Strikes became his primary weapon to achieve this goal. In reviving Local 282 by such methods,

Clark followed lessons he learned in the CIO era, making demands on employers to activate workers and building black caucuses to put a fire under white-dominated unions.

Such leaders paid a price. Clark's independent decision making and reserved demeanor, intentionally perhaps, put distance between him and white leaders in the Memphis AFL-CIO; Alzada Clark felt that officials in his union were not yet ready to see a black man call the shots. At the same time, Clark's modesty and his pragmatism left him open to charges from other black workers that he was not militant enough. Clark made a career of combining militancy with compromise in attempting to balance the interests of individuals against what he perceived as a larger good. At various times this meant participating in expulsions, stepping aside for white leaders, or even laying off his wife Alzada from the organizing staff to avoid the appearance of nepotism. Similarly, during his tenure as president of the Memphis NAACP in the wake of Dr. King's death, Clark avoided provocative militancy, even on behalf of a union local in the hospitals, in favor of a more measured effort to win concrete gains for the good of the greater community.

This sort of civil rights unionism, balancing militancy and the search for results, brought both successes and frustrations. Clark fought throughout his life to promote blacks into local, state, and international union leadership, and he himself provided one of the few exceptions to the rule of white male leadership. Although honored by many colleagues upon his retirement, however, Clark had a sad feeling that some of those he helped to organize and to bring to union office had turned against him. In a painful intragenerational conflict, Clark lost office as president of Local 282 in 1975 to Willie Rudd, a younger black worker who sought to make the union-community mobilization of the 1968 sanitation strike the operating method for what he saw as a more militant form of civil rights unionism—a promise he carried out during a strike against Memphis Furniture Company (see Ida Leachman's interview in chapter 8). Of course, after he lost the local presidency Clark also lost his union job. To his credit, Clark retained an analytical sense of distance and sense of humor, and he remained true to his belief in organizing to the end of his days. "You've got to do what you do because it is right," he told me, not because of the personal rewards it might or might not bring.

Civil rights unionism could be a compromise of sorts, but it often required much the same sort of direct action and willingness to die as the civil rights movement. This can be readily seen in the career of Alzada Clark, who for nine years became a full-time union organizer, reaching out particularly to black women, who were among the lowest paid and most exploited workers in the furniture industry. As her husband had already demonstrated, one had to go beyond business as usual to represent such workers. To do so in Mississippi meant taking on some of the most hard-bitten employers in the great cold heart of segregation.

In that extremely unpromising setting, Alzada Clark took on the persona and many of the methods of a civil rights worker, which also were union methods: meeting people privately, speaking to them directly and hearing their grievances, building up a cadre of people who would take leadership and define their own struggles. Most important, she, like Leroy, carried through her commitments regardless of personal consequences. Even with her arm dislocated from its socket, followed by the police and the FBI, she refused to abandon the fight in Mississippi. In a state where civil rights workers had been brutally tortured and killed, the class and race war with company owners and police, who sometimes belonged to the Ku Klux Klan, required bold, obstreperous, and some workers believed, violent actions to achieve victory. In the end, organizing in Mississippi yielded closed up plants and only a few transitory economic gains for the workers. Yet, like many a civil rights worker who lost the battle only to feel they had won the moral war, Clark took pride in the fact that she helped oppressed people to stand up for themselves in one of the darkest corners of the South.

Black labor organizing in the late 1960s and early 1970s held some promise of stimulating the next wave of the black freedom struggle. Civil rights unionists reinvigorated the African American church, family, and community while helping to break down Jim Crow at work. Their agenda, which included voter registration and political campaigns, lead, for example, to the election of the first African American to Congress from the deep South since Reconstruction (Harold Ford, in 1972). However, black labor organizers operated at a time when the limitations of the labor unions had become dreadfully apparent, as the older generation of white union leaders held on to power and often stifled the initiatives of others. In this climate, unions desperately needed the link to the moral agenda of the larger civil rights movement, which people like Alzada Clark and others who tell their stories here represented.

Yet the limits of the civil rights movement also had become increasingly apparent. As the wave of civil rights protests from Montgomery, Birmingham, Selma, Mississippi, and many other places crested between 1955 and 1965, leaving new laws and new rights behind, manifold issues still confronted African Americans. It became increasingly obvious that attaining citizenship rights to vote, march, use public facilities, go to school, sit on juries, and hold public office could not substitute for establishing the right to a decent job at decent wages. Neither the labor movement nor the civil rights movement had yet fully addressed the crisis affecting a large portion of the black working class, which was increasingly marginalized and impoverished. Nowhere did that crisis hit with more ferocious impact than in Memphis during the 1968 sanitation strike, which fused labor and black freedom struggles in a new way.

7 "I AM A MAN"

UNIONISM AND THE BLACK WORKING POOR

You are reminding the nation that it is a crime for people to live in
this rich country and receive starvation wages. . . . This is our plight
as a people all over America.

Martin Luther King, Jr.

We just got together, and we decided to stand up and be men, and
that's what we did.

Taylor Rogers

The history of endurance, struggle, and achievement by black workers remained largely invisible to others. H. Ralph Jackson, a minister who became a key supporter of Memphis sanitation strikers
in 1968, remembered that prior to their strike he was highly aware of
racism, but a full appreciation of class issues and his own class privilege
had eluded him.[1] The working poor suddenly became visible in 1968.
In Memphis, the sanitation workers' fight for union recognition, better
wages and conditions, and dignified treatment upended the "good race
relations" that paternalistic white leaders (who refused to bargain with the
workers) thought they had achieved. The strike exposed the poverty and
abuse suffered by many black working people, and when police maced
Rev. Jackson and other ministers during a demonstration supporting the
strikers, he and others suddenly understood how powerless they felt. This
identification of black ministers and indeed the entire black community
with the plight of the strikers opened up a new chapter in the civil rights

---

1. Jackson said that "I and others had become unaware of conditions in trying to
make it under the system," which "were unfolded to us" in the course of the strike.
Jackson directed the minimum salary division of the African Methodist Episcopal
Church, a program designed to subsidize the salaries of the poorest AME ministers,
with his headquarters in Memphis.

and labor movements. The strike lasted nearly three months and ultimately brought Martin Luther King, Jr., to Memphis to place national attention on the plight of the working poor.

"I Am a Man," the slogan of the all-male group of some 1,300 striking sanitation workers, signified that this was not just a labor dispute. The call to assert black "manhood" struck a strong chord among people like Clarence Coe and Leroy Boyd, who had always detested being called "boy" by whites. "I Am a Man" meant black sanitation workers would no longer accept white supervisors and city leaders treating them like children. Rev. James Lawson explained that Mayor Henry Loeb "treats the workers as though they are not men, [and] that's a racist point of view. . . . For at the heart of racism is the idea that a man is not a man, that a person is not a person." [2] As Dr. King put it, "We are saying that we are determined to be men. We are determined to be people." Put more colloquially by James Robinson in this chapter, "I Am a Man [meant] that they weren't gonna take that shit no more." The slogan demanded both a living wage and personal respect for people who had received neither during generations of Jim Crow.

It also highlighted the fact that black poverty resulted from both racial and gendered forms of oppression. "We are tired of our men being emasculated so that our wives and daughters have to go out and work in the white lady's kitchen," King told strike supporters, "leaving us unable to be with our children and give them the time and attention they need." Low wages had forced both black women and men to work, sometimes two or more jobs each, in order to provide even minimal standards for their families. Hence, "I Am a Man" resonated with black men and women alike. Ortha B. Strong Jones, speaking to interviewer Laurie Green years later, related the slogan to her own struggle to organize a nurses union in the wake of the sanitation strike. "We felt like we could say we am a woman, . . . we felt like we wanted justice." For her and other nurses, having the union meant that "we feel like we had a man that had backbone. We feel like that we had somebody that we could lean on and we felt like that we had somebody who would protect us if we needed help." The call

2. Lawson pastored Centenary Methodist Church in Memphis. A long-time veteran of the nonviolent movement, he organized much of the strike support among ministers and in the community.

for "manhood" in this sense meant not reinforcing male domination but overturning inequalities that for generations had placed huge burdens on black men and women.

The slogan and the strike emanated not just from conditions in Memphis or the South but also from a growing crisis of the black working class, one which took distinctly gendered forms. Black workers had made great advances through factory employment and industrial unions during World War II and its aftermath.[3] But by the 1960s industrial employment had passed its peak. While white males still monopolized most of the best jobs in unionized mass production industries, both white men and white women increasingly moved into rapidly growing professional, technical, and clerical fields, work still largely closed to blacks. White workers seemed to have joined the "affluent society," yet for black male workers in particular, the economic trajectory arced downward. Historically, employers had discouraged black men from obtaining skills or a higher education, which they felt would make them unsuitable for, or unwilling to accept, hard, physical labor. Low educational levels continued to force many black men into unskilled labor, but in the factories and on the farms such jobs were being mechanized out of existence. The percentage of cotton harvested by machines in the Mississippi Delta jumped from 5 percent in 1950 to 50 percent by 1960 and 95 percent by 1970. As more and more rural workers fled the shrinking cotton economy, they found fewer opportunities for unskilled labor in cities. Black male unemployment rates shot up two to three times higher than those of whites, and black male incomes compared to white male incomes dropped. Income gaps widened, and unions largely failed to address the problems of workers at the bottom.[4]

Mechanization of factory jobs and a shift toward white-collar employment in the 1960s thus turned the American economy into a real nightmare for many black workers. As men lost jobs, families disintegrated and

3. In Memphis, black men went from 20 percent of factory workers in 1940 to 32.3 percent in 1980, while black women went from 8.6 percent to 16.4. Prior to the 1940s, many such jobs had been closed to African Americans.

4. The average income of black male workers in the U.S. had been 37 percent of that of white males in 1939, but this figure had gone up to 62 percent by 1951. By 1962 it had dropped back to 55 percent of white male income, about where it had been in 1945. In 1964, the overall black unemployment rate was 10 percent, compared to 5 percent for whites. Unemployment rates were easily twice that high among young men in the inner cities.

black women took on more work in an economy that still made little room for them. In 1960, some 40 percent of white working women in the U.S., compared to 5 percent of black women, had clerical or sales jobs, and black women still did the vast majority of domestic service. Many black women raised families on wages that averaged less than half the wages of white women, who made a little more than half the wages of white men. However, black women often stayed in school longer than black men, and found work in larger numbers as teachers. As a result of the 1960s civil rights movement, black women with higher levels of education made increasing inroads into the lower levels of "pink collar" clerical and sales work, and into professions such as teaching. The gap between black and white women's income would begin to narrow, as larger numbers of black women moved away from domestic, laundry, and cleaning jobs and gained some share of employment in the expanding areas of the job market.[5]

The cry "I Am a Man" protested not only racism and low wages but also the shrinking position of black men in the job market and as family breadwinners. It gained support because the declining position of many black men and their families translated into black community impoverishment, leaving 57 percent of the black population in Memphis during the 1960s living below the poverty line, as compared to 14 percent of whites.[6] A growing sense of racial-economic oppression, combined with rampant police brutality, made the black ghettoes of America the proverbial "powder keg" of the 1960s. With massive factory closings in the 1980s, job opportunities for black men with low educational levels would only worsen, continuing to wreak havoc on black communities across America (see chapter 8).

5. Memphis census statistics show a greater occupational advance for black women than black men from 1950 to 1990. In the metropolitan area only 2.1 percent of employed black men in 1950 worked in professional (including administrative and teaching) jobs, compared to 5.05 percent by 1990, whereas the percentage of employed black women in such jobs went from 4.4 percent to 11.6 percent; black men moved from 3.2 to 9.8 percent of clerical and kindred workers, while black women in these jobs increased from 2.3 percent to 22.2 percent; black male sales workers went from 1.4 percent to 5.7 percent, while black females climbed from 1.3 percent to 11.5 percent.

6. Some 70 percent of Memphis African Americans had lived below the poverty level in 1959. One might say the situation had improved in the 1960s, but it certainly did not appear that way to black men without jobs or decent incomes, or to over half the black families still living in poverty.

James Robinson and Taylor Rogers illustrate how most black workers were left out of the nation's rapid expansion of wealth. Mechanization of the cotton economy forced sharecroppers like Robinson's family to leave their homes and head for the cities. With few job skills that transferred to urban employment, and with almost no formal education, such workers could not make it into higher-wage employment. Mechanizing factories at the same time began replacing male with female workers, cutting back employment, or even shutting down. The scarcity of unskilled industrial jobs forced country people like Robinson, but also men raised in the city with few educational advantages like Rogers, to take dead-end service jobs. Given that white males in Memphis generally obtained nearly four more years of schooling than black men and that an eighth-grade education in black schools was considered to be the equivalent of a sixth-grade education in white schools, few employers would hire black men for white-collar jobs. And while the expansion of government in the 1960s provided new jobs for black men, many states and cities kept wages low by banning public employee unionism. The City of Memphis in just this way kept workers like Robinson and Rogers impoverished.

In many ways, the plight of the black men who worked in sanitation epitomized that of the urban black poor. Many sanitation workers and their families lived below the poverty level even as they worked two or more jobs. A large percentage of the sanitation workers qualified for welfare, and as a group they had virtually no benefits, vacations, or health and safety protections. Many came from rural Fayette County, Tennessee, where black unemployment reached nearly 70 percent, and for them, as one worker put it, "there is no worst job. I would take anything." Whites treated these men carrying garbage tubs over their heads as servants, giving them cast-off clothing and holding their wages to little more than a dollar an hour. Few white leaders in Memphis seemed to notice or care about this impoverishment. When black sanitation workers walked off the job in Memphis on February 12, 1968, few suspected the situation would escalate into one of the climactic struggles of the 1960s.

Their strike, called spontaneously and without support from their international, the American Federation of State, County, and Municipal Employees (AFSCME), happened when it did because, as Taylor Rogers explains, the workers "just got tired." On that day, supervisors sent blacks home without pay during a rainstorm, while keeping whites on at full pay. A recent incident in which a malfunctioning garbage compactor had crushed two black men to death fueled the men's rage at work conditions they could no longer tolerate. Guided by T. O. Jones, a sanitation worker fired in 1963 for his union activities, the sanitation men had been asking the city for recognition of their union and for a resolution of their many grievances ever since. But Memphis city government refused to recognize the union or meet with workers to discuss their grievances.

A larger context of failed race relations set the stage for a racially polarized confrontation. In the early 1960s, in response to the civil rights protests described by Leroy Clark in chapter 5, the city had desegregated most of the downtown, and black voters had helped place a relative moderate, Mayor William Ingram, in office. Whites congratulated themselves for solving racial problems at a time when other southern cities like Birmingham, Alabama, were in turmoil. Blacks also hoped a new form of government would give them more political power. The city previously elected commissioners on an at-large basis, keeping blacks from even running for city government, let alone getting elected, from 1888 to 1951. In 1967 Memphis voters approved a mayor-council form of government, with some offices elected by district, and blacks obtained three out of thirteen seats on the new city council. But the simultaneous election of Republican fiscal conservative Henry Loeb, a hard-line segregationist, signaled a hardening by the city's white residents against further racial change. In a city of 540,000 people, some 40 percent of them black, almost none of the blacks and almost all of the whites voted for Loeb. Loeb "made people proud they were racist" and polarized the community.

White police officers, true to form, touched off the city's powder keg. Police brutality had escalated with urban disorders in the summer of 1967. Now, when sanitation workers and their supporters marched to city hall only a few days into the strike, the police maced and clubbed them. They continued to exacerbate conflict during the rest of the strike. The white community, prodded on by one-sided reporting in the commercial news media, closed ranks behind the mayor, who refused to bargain with any union representing city workers. Displaying his "plantation mentality" in all its nakedness, Loeb told blacks they should come to him as their "friend," leave the union out of it, and he would take care of their problems. His solutions would not include collective bargaining rights or union maintenance agreements. As to discussions with union representatives, he would have none of it.

As with previous labor conflicts, gaining union recognition, including checkoff of union dues from paychecks, provided the crucial precondition for collective bargaining over other grievances. To obtain recognition and dues checkoff, workers continued picketing and engaging in daily marches and mass meetings for over eight weeks. Black ministers, members of the United Rubber Workers and other union locals, schoolteachers and community activists organized impressive support activities including a boycott of Memphis businesses and commercial newspapers, and fund-raising at factory gates and in churches. Most whites, however, carried their own garbage to the curb, and some even took jobs as strikebreakers. Not only the Loeb administration but almost the entire white community seemed intransigently opposed to any expansion of black power or union power.

As the spirits of the strikers began to flag, James Lawson managed to convince Martin Luther King, in the midst of his whirlwind organizing for the Poor People's Campaign,[7] to speak in Memphis. King's March 18 speech to a crowd of ten to fifteen thousand jubilant Memphians in some ways turned the tide for the strikers. In that speech, King denounced "starvation wages" and explained that the civil rights movement, which had won equal rights and the vote through legislation in 1964 and 1965, had now moved to the point where "our struggle is for genuine equality which means economic equality." Most African Americans lived in an economic depression unrecognized by the government or by most whites, he said, and he urged a one-day general strike in support of the sanitation workers. According to King, the strike had moved beyond the question of civil rights to a question of human rights. He concluded, "We are saying now is the time to make real the promises of democracy."

King's speech put national media attention on the strike, revived flagging spirits in Memphis, and led to major financial support and attention by national and local trade unions. But events turned in a tragic direction. By March 28, when King returned to Memphis for a mass march, tensions, exacerbated by police violence, had burst out of control. Window breaking by black youths set off attacks by the police and a complete breakdown of march discipline. Further incidents, including a po-

---

7. This campaign sought to mobilize poor people of all races to camp in the nation's capital, demanding jobs or income and a transfer of federal funds from the military to rebuilding the inner cities.

lice shotgun slaying of unarmed sixteen-year-old Larry Payne in a housing project, led to widespread disorder and occupation of the city by four thousand national guardsmen. The courts enjoined King from leading further marches, and the disorder threatened to discredit his campaign for a nonviolent poor people's march on Washington. Determined to lead a nonviolent march in Memphis despite the injunction, King gave an emotional speech at a church rally on April 3, prophesying that "I may not get there with you, but I want you to know tonight that we as a people will get to the promised land." The next day he was dead.

King's assassination on April 4 led to massive riots all over the United States but, as Clarence Coe comments, a relatively subdued response in Memphis. On April 7 some eight thousand Memphians, most of them white, expressed their concern in a memorial, followed by a completely silent mass march of between twenty thousand and forty thousand people from all over the country through the streets of Memphis on April 8. National labor leaders, President Lyndon Johnson, and Tennessee Governor Buford Ellington all finally pressured the city into recognizing Local 1733 and allowing checkoff of union dues. A signed contract ended the strike sixty-four days after it had begun.

This victory came at a great cost, and ever since April 4, 1968, the city and the nation have attempted to draw meaning out of the events surrounding the sanitation strike in Memphis. For Dr. King, the uprising of the working poor in Memphis illustrated his belief that the civil rights movement must move toward economic demands for human dignity for workers and the poor. Speaking many times to unions in the 1960s, King called for a kind of civil rights unionism, which he thought could begin to address America's intertwined racial and economic problems. Many black workers, as the voices in this chapter illustrate, had the same belief.

Taylor Rogers Relives the Memphis Sanitation Strike

You keep your back bent over, somebody's gonna ride it.

Twenty-seven years after Martin Luther King, Jr.'s death, I spoke with Taylor Rogers about the traumatic events of 1968. He and his wife lived in a pleasant home in a north Memphis neighborhood where the respectable working poor and the "underclass," without employment, skills, or prospects for change, lived almost side by side. Rogers had barely escaped abject poverty himself through unionization, which he felt gave dignity to a life of hard work and little pay.

I was born here in Memphis. I attended Manassas High. I went through about the tenth grade. I went in the service in '42, in the navy. When I got back from the navy I worked in the army depot for a while. I worked there for three or four years. When I came out from the depot I started doin' odd jobs, just little things. I finally got a job with the city in 1958, at the Sanitation Department. There wasn't too much opportunity for a black man at that time. Really wasn't no other jobs hardly to be found. I was at a point I had to take what I could get. That was the situation with most of the men.

At that time working conditions were terrible. We had all kinds of things to go through with the boss. Whatever the boss said was right. You didn't have no rights to speak up for nothin'. We'd go out in the morning, we'd stay out until they'd tell us we could come in. Had roll call in the morning. If the guy didn't like the way you answered your name, he'd send you home. We had no grievance proceedings, there was nothing you could do about those things. It was just awful. But we were all poor black men, not too well educated. We were trying to figure out what to do to try to get some decency.

We started off with T. O. Jones, who was the founder of the thing [the sanitation workers union]. We started tryin' to organize. We would meet, we'd hide out in different places. If the boss'd find out we was doing these meetings we'd probably get suspended or fired. We'd meet upstairs over a cafe called Robillio's. I'm trying to think of the union that let us use their place up there. [Leon] Shepard was one of the leaders in that union. We kept meeting and meeting.[8]

I was workin' on the trucks. Now you see all these garbage cans on the street. Back then, everybody had a 50-gallon drum in the backyard. We had to go in those backyards with tubs. You carried those tubs on your head and shoulders. Most of those tubs were leakin' and that stuff was fallin' all over you. You got home you had to take your clothes off at the

---

8. Leon Shepard later became the president of Local 1529 of the United Food and Commercial Workers.

door 'cause you didn't want to bring all that filth in the house. We didn't have no decent place to eat your lunch. You didn't have no place to use the restroom. Conditions was just terrible. We didn't have no say about nothin'. Whatever they said, that's what you had to do: right, wrong, indifferent. Anything that you did that the supervisor didn't like, he'd fire you, whatever. You didn't have no recourse, no way of gettin' back at him. We just got tired of all that.

Most of the supervisors was white people. All the better jobs the whites had, bulldozer drivers, heavy-equipment people, supervisors, and stuff like that. They didn't have to do too much of nothin'. They would send us home when it was rainin' and we didn't get no pay. But the white guys could sit around and they would get their full day. The men working was 99 percent black. About 1966, I believe it was, we pulled a work stoppage. But we was on the picket line for about an hour, and T. O. Jones came around and told us we had to go in because they put out an injunction on us. Once they found out that we was out there, that's when they got the injunction.[9] So we all went back to work the next day. We kept on. We took things and took things. I was just beginning to buy a home, this house I'm in right now, and had eight kids I was trying to educate. It was kind of hard just to pull off your job but we knowed we didn't have nothin' else we could do. We was making about $1.04 an hour. You could work a forty-hour week and be eligible for welfare. We didn't have no benefits, no safety. People didn't get anything. So we kept meeting, and we kept talking.

Most people was afraid, but we were gainin' momentum as we'd go. We'd get more and more each time we met. We started off with people like myself, Joe Warren, and [Robert] Beasley, and we'd get other guys to come to the meetings. The first time we walked out [1966] they put an injunction on us and we had to go back to work. We just grew from there.

T. O. Jones, at one time he was a sanitation worker. He got fired, him and some other guys. The rest of them went off to [find other] work but T. O. stayed around to help get us organized. He was just a guy that believed in seein' things done right and in people being treated fair. By him being a worker, he knowed what we was going through. He was the one who got the international union to come in.

9. City courts in Memphis had long used injunctions to prohibit strike activity or demonstrations and to stop union organizing, particularly in the public sector.

We finally got to a point where we had lots of followers. We had talked with the city, we had tried to get organized, get some recognition, get some things done that we needed done, and we always got turned down. We just finally got tired of it.

We had some guys that worked over on a kind of a packer where you put your garbage. One rainy day they were up in there and something triggered that thing off, and it just crushed them. We just got tired. Thirteen hundred men decided they was tired and wasn't gonna take no more.

It was gonna happen anyway. It was gonna happen because we had just got to the point that we had to do something. You didn't have no benefits. You didn't have no say so about what you did or how you did it. You did it like they said to do it. That's why we wanted a union, we wanted somebody to represent us, so that we could have some say about our hours and working conditions.

I guess that 1,300 black men decided they was tired and wasn't gonna take no more and withdrew their service from the city. That was hard for us to do. All of us had families. We didn't know what we were gonna do or what was gonna happen. Mayor Loeb kept threatening, sayin' you won't have no jobs no more, and all this kind of stuff. But we hung in there.

With the help of the community and the black leaders and black ministers, that's when we started to pull everything together. Rev. Ralph Jackson, Reverend James Lawson, a number of other preachers, Reverend Henry Starks, marched with us every day for sixty-eight days.[10] And the black community came more together. You would have been surprised how they came together to support the sanitation workers. Without the help of the community we probably couldn't have stayed out. And then AFSCME and the international union came in and brought us help. All the labor unions across the country were sending money to keep the strikers going.

So none of the strikers really did lose anything, like their houses. I was just moved into this house. When you talk about stopping work you have to think about these things, about what is going to happen. But we had got to the point where we was just tired. I called my family together and talked with them. They said, "Dad, you have to do what you have to do. If you

---

10. The well-respected, kind, and gentle Rev. Henry Starks, pastor of St. James AME Church, supported the strikers and many civil rights and community efforts.

think you can better your condition, better our condition, that's what you
need to do." I just tried to tell them what the situation was and what they
might have to go through by me walking off the job. And they understood.
They said, "Whatever help we can give, we'll work together and try to
make things work." I guess all the other men talked with their families the
same way and we just got together, and we decided to stand up and be
men, and that's what we did.

I had one friend in particular, most anything I needed, he would help
me with it. If my car was broke down he helped me get my car fixed. He
had a shoe shine stand and my boys went up and shined shoes for him. He
wouldn't take any money from them. He let them have all their money to
bring home to help support the family. My church, the Gospel Temple
Baptist Church, helped me out. The churches supported everybody. The
churches, the community, and everybody pooled their resources to see that
we had food and places to stay. People who was rentin' they got money to
pay the rent, their house loans, and that's how we survived. The union
would give us a little something, I think it was twenty-six dollars a week.
It was enough to help keep you surviving with the other help we were
getting.

Henry Loeb, he was just a hard-nosed white man. He had a plantation
mentality. He thought that whatever he said was gonna be all right. He
had a lot of support. Before we got the council form of government we had
a commission form of government.[11] Loeb was the commissioner of sanitation. He wasn't such a bad guy as commissioner. But when we started
talkin' union, that's when he got miffed. We didn't talk union [with him]
as long as he was commissioner because we hadn't gotten strong enough
and the men hadn't gotten tired enough. But when he got to be mayor,
that's when we started talkin' union, tryin' to get organized, and tryin' to
get some decency. But he wouldn't hear it at all. He said we was breakin'
the law.

[The Memphis Labor Council], they were supportive. [T. O. Jones]

11. The city commission form of government consisted of five representatives
chosen at large, which effectively excluded blacks because so few whites would vote
for them. The change to a mayor-council form of government, which included some
offices elected by district, produced a city council of ten whites and three blacks
in 1967.

worked with Bill Ross at the Memphis Labor Council.[12] The night that we struck we was at the Labor Council, on Second Street. That's when we decided we wasn't gonna go back to work the next day. We was meeting there and we voted to strike. All the union people, they were already organized and recognized, they gave us support too. We used the Firestone union hall. In fact, they got bombed over there one time. We'd have all our meetings at the Firestone union hall, and the day of the strike we marched from the Firestone union hall to city hall. Somebody bombed it. Nobody was in there when it happened, so we don't know if it was strike related or what it was. One morning they come in and the whole top had been blowed out. We had a lot of support from other unions. Once we got started, the NAACP got involved, they worked along with us and supported us. We had support from everybody.

[But before that] nobody really had paid no attention but the men. This was a strike that *we* called. Labor didn't call it, *we* called it. I don't think nobody knowed too much about our problems. They see us out there doing this dirty work, but I don't think they paid no attention. But we were the men who did it, we got together and decided it. But you keep your back bent over, somebody's gonna ride it. We decided we gotta do what we have to do and we withdrew our services from the city.

[Mayor] Loeb went all off the wall and everything. He did a lot of things. He had strikebreakers. They had police and fire trucks there every day. Some of the men was goin' back in [as strikebreakers] and we'd have a "prayer meetin'" with them, and they didn't go back no more. We'd talk to them and tell them, "It's our job y'all are trying to take out there." We'd talk to them wherever we'd meet them. Right on the spot we'd tell them so, trying to tell them not to go back. The ones that the city was hiring at the time, we didn't bother with them too much. Everywhere they'd go they had to have a police squad car escorting them. We wasn't trying to be violent or anything. We just wanted decent working conditions. But we had to do whatever we had to do to try to keep things goin'. Some of them wouldn't go back the next day. Some of them wouldn't go. We never resorted to violence, to do anything to nobody.

Every Sunday, churches was taking up money for the strikers. We'd

12. W. T. Ross was the AFL-CIO Memphis Labor Council secretary and organized some of the strike support among white trade unionists.

go out to Firestone or International Harvester on Friday and stand outside the gate when the men were coming out, and they gave us a lot of money. We'd just stand there with a bucket and they'd come by and drop the money in. We'd have mass meetings out at Mason Temple[13] and then we'd pass garbage cans around. Those garbage cans were just filled with money. It brought the black community together more so than anything I've seen. That's how we survived.

In the white neighborhoods they'd put the garbage out where people [strikebreakers] could get it. In the white community they would put it in the can and put it out on the street, and somebody could come along and pick it up. Like out in Frayser.[14] All they had to do was drive by, dump it in the truck, and keep on going. But in the black neighborhoods, they'd dump it in the street. It would be such a mess they couldn't get to it, they couldn't pick it up. That would put pressure on the city, too, because then the health department started getting down because of the uncleanness. The streets were filled with garbage. People would just go out the door and dump their garbage in the street, pile it up on the curb.

Everybody wanted to do something. You just felt good about what you was trying to do. You wanted to see things happen. You wanted to have some say about our hours and working conditions. Like now, they got uniforms and everything. It's real good. It was just a great spirit.

You were determined. But sometimes you got weary and things looked bad, it looked like we wasn't making no progress. It dragged out so long some of the men started going back. Some of them were losing spirit, losing confidence. It got a little rough. That's when Reverend Lawson got Dr. King involved. When Dr. King came in, he made some speeches and things, and that built the morale back up and the men started comin' out again. He helped to build the morale of the men up so that the ones that's out would stay out and the ones that's in [working] would come back out.

When Dr. King came the first time and gave his speech, like he was saying, "Don't worry about what would happen to me but [worry] what would happen to the garbagemen if we didn't [win]." It made the community more up and ready and made the men more up and ready to keep on

13. Mason Temple was the largest church meeting space in Black Memphis. Most of the large rallies, including King's last speech on April 3, 1968, occurred there.

14. As noted previously, the International Harvester plant was located in Frayser, a stronghold of white working-class backlash against civil rights.

pushing to get something done. His speech brought people out, brought poor people together.

All those marches were kind of crucial. Right after the first march, we marched with the national guard with fixed bayonets and tanks, but we kept marchin'. There was a lot of crucial moments, you can't pick out just one. We marched every day from Clayborn Temple to the city hall and back.[15] The black ministers were leading this.

After King was killed, all over the country everybody was puttin' pressure, the president, everybody else was puttin' pressure on Henry Loeb for lettin' this kind of thing happen. So he signed it. We finally got a contract, an agreement signed.

Loeb was such a hardnose, I don't know what would have happened if King hadn't got killed. I don't know whether he would have gave in or what. He had support from the white people here in Memphis. That's what kept him so strong. Everywhere he'd go the whites would tell him, "Hang on in there, Henry." It was bad for him. When you get that kind of support, it's hard for you to pull out. He had so much pressure on him then. If he didn't have that support he probably would have gave in. All this wouldn't have happened. [City council member] J. O. Patterson, he came up with a plan that probably would have ended the whole strike. But when he got back to the mayor that was killed. The city council had three blacks, but they were always overruled.[16]

I think after King was killed they [whites] saw that if they hadn't a gave him that support and let him give in, all this wouldn't have happened. So when King got killed, I think that's when the pressure came down on Memphis, and Loeb had to move. Because people from all over the country started comin' in, and unions from all over the country. Walter Reuther

15. Clayborn Temple provided space for mass meetings and a starting place for marches to city hall, which occurred daily during the strike. Rev. Ralph Jackson's minimum-salary office for the AME Church was in a building next to it.

16. On March 5, sanitation workers and their supporters packed a city council meeting, surrounded by two hundred police and a hundred sheriff's deputies. At that meeting, Patterson presented a proposal to allow union dues to be paid through the credit union, so the mayor did not have to directly acknowledge the union by deducting dues from paychecks. Nine white council members voted to table the face-saving proposal, with three blacks and one white in favor. The council's action scuttled possible settlement of the strike and further escalated the tension.

brought fifty thousand dollars from the auto workers. So Loeb had to give in.[17]

Even if it had been poor white workers, King would have done the same thing. That's just the kind of person he was. He stopped what he was doin'. He was plannin' this big march to Washington. All his staff thought it was outrageous of him to stop and come to Memphis. But he went where he was needed, where he could help poor people. That's why he dropped everything, regardless of what all his staff people told him. He said, "Well, Lawson's been around a long time and he just wants me to come in and march and give a speech."

And that's what he did, he dropped all that and come and dealt with it. That's when the first march was. Then he had to continue on. He had to let people know that he could come back to Memphis and have a nonviolent march. But before that nonviolent march, that's when they assassinated him, before that second march. After his death we did have that nonviolent march, we had a silent march, all you could hear was people's footsteps hittin' the pavement. It was a silent march.

He didn't get all accomplished he wanted accomplished, but I don't think he died in vain. Because what he came here to do, that was settled. There was a lot of other things he wanted done, things that needed to be done, and a lot of things have got done.

What a lot of people in Memphis don't realize, white folks and people with good jobs, is that black folks wouldn't be in the position they're in now if it had not been for King comin' here and dyin'. All the banks have got colored tellers, and school principals. Before that, we didn't have that. [Today] city hall is full of blacks, even to the mayor. From the top all the way through. So some of the things he was about happened. And things are still happening. But it's a slow process. I think there's been a big change in Memphis.

The Local AFSCME 1733 grew from 1,300 workers to about 7,000. We organized a number of others after we got that all settled. We got [workers at the] fire commission, city court clerks, auto inspection stations,

17. UAW President Walter Reuther had supported King in numerous civil rights struggles, and made this contribution to signal the Loeb administration that the sanitation workers could hold out for much longer if necessary.

both city and county school boards, Liberty Land [amusement park]. Sanitation had their chapter, park commissioner has their chapter. Each chapter had a chairperson, and those people made up the executive board of the whole Local 1733. All of them come under the umbrella of 1733. I started off as a steward, then I went to chief steward. From chief steward to chapter chairperson for sanitation, from that to president of the local in 1972. And I stayed there until 1992. I was president twenty years. James Robinson was chapter chairperson of the sanitation workers.

Sanitation workers had strength because of their unity. We'd have lots of things going on in city hall, we'd ask all the other chapters to show up. Even if it was for their chapter, the sanitation workers would always be there. There would be more of the sanitation people there than [other] workers, because we was the backbone and we was the strength.

James Robinson Describes the Worst Job He Ever Had

We didn't have no job, we just had somewhere to get up and go every mornin'.

Like many sanitation workers, James Robinson came from the plantation districts around Memphis. Unlike most of his cohort, he had union experience, having worked for ten years in Michigan as a member of the United Auto Workers. He became the leader of the sanitation workers unit of AFSCME Local 1733 following its victory in the 1968 strike. I found him in 1996, in a tiny brick house on the outskirts of Memphis, in a neighborhood of modest homes occupying an area once undoubtedly a cotton field. In Robinson I found a wary and weary man who warmed to his subject as he denounced the new breed of politicians then dissolving welfare and other social programs (see chapter 8) that had been the mainstay for the working poor, of whom Robinson remained one.

I was born in Earle, Arkansas, June 27, 1937. We lived out in the country. When my father was a sharecropper, the five of us boys together, we could pick a bale of cotton a day. Five boys, five bales a week, thirty or forty bales of cotton. But always come out in the hole. Didn't make enough to get nothin'. I went to tenth grade, it was somethin' like a one-room schoolhouse, forty, fifty students, one teacher. I left when I got sixteen. I got a job workin' for [the Army] Corps of Engineers, they worked fixin' the rivers up. I worked there about five years.

About '54, that's when I left for Michigan. I had an auntie who lived in Michigan, in Benton Harbor. [I] worked for a factory, Auto Specialist, in St. Joseph, Michigan. They made jeep housings, Ford parts, this was back during the Korean War. I was a grinder when I first started, and run the sandblaster. I was there about ten years.

But Michigan was just too cold. I didn't like all that snow. I left in '57 and came back to Memphis. I got here in '57, did marble work, marble tiles, we put floors in bathrooms. But it wasn't a steady job. My father was livin' in Arkansas, that was one reason why I came back, on account of he got sick. I started a family when I came back to Memphis. My uncle got me on at the Sanitation Department, he'd been there about fourteen years. That was in '59.

It was a rough job. Rougher than it is now. We had to pick up trash out of the backyard. You had to tote it on your head in a tub. The tub's full of water, rain, garbage, maggots, everything else running out. Back then you had to supply your own clothes, own gloves, they didn't give you anything but the tubs. If you'd get a hole in it the water'd run all out the tub down on ya. Boss would sit around drinkin' coffee, come around once or twice a day to check on the truck.

Back when I first started we had thirteen men on the truck. Ain't like the trucks they got now, it was an open-bed truck, a trailer truck. Two men to load it. That left eleven men on the ground to tote the garbage to the truck, and then you had the driver. When I first went there they had some white drivers. When Mayor Loeb got in there all the whites left Sanitation and found other jobs. They quit because the mayor wanted them to get out and pick up the trash on the street. They wouldn't do it.

When I first went there, everybody made different. They offered me ninety-six cents an hour. They guy in charge, the guy drivin' the truck, he made about $1.65. He wasn't the boss, he'd go where the man told him to go. He couldn't tell you what to do. [And workers], they'd get to fightin' out there. It wasn't black and white, it was black and black. They'd get to fightin' out there.

The job I [had been] working on up north was a union job. After thirty days they gave you a paper and said, "Sign this." You'd sign it and give it back to them and you belonged to the union. You didn't sign, you didn't

work. That was the United Auto Workers. You didn't have to worry about
the boss, he wasn't gonna mess with you or you'd put the union on him.
He's messin' with somebody and they blow the whistle. Everybody stopped
workin'. You didn't take no stuff from the boss.

Sanitation was the worst job I ever had. The job wasn't really as bad as
the folks you were workin' for. They'd never do no work. They had some
attitude ain't nobody else got, retarded or somethin'. I tell you what happened to me, I had been there about two years. In summertime you might
stop under a tree and eat lunch. A lady called in and said we were havin'
a picnic out there. Here comes the supervisor. We had to get out of the
shade and eat out there on the side of the truck. Truck had maggots and
things all fallin' out of it. He said you gotta get out from under the shade
tree and sit under the truck to get some shade. And there was nowhere
to use the bathroom. Had to go down in the ditch, or in the sewer. No
breaks, nothin' but lunch. Lunch depended on the driver. You was supposed to get a hour, but you might not get but fifteen minutes if you
was behind.

When I first started to work, I started out in east Memphis. Our route
was from Sumner, back across to Poplar, everything north of White Station. Depends on how much territory you had to cover. You had to cover
that in a week. You had to stay out there as long as it would take you.
You'd work ten, twelve hours a day. But you didn't get paid but for eight.
You stayed out there until you'd get through. We were out there sometimes
'til dark. You'd start at seven o'clock in the morning, no extra for overtime.
The guy out there now makes about as much in one day as I made in two
weeks. They're makin' eighty-nine dollars a day now. I got too old to work,
now that they're makin' the money. [laughs] You had to work thirteen days
to bring home two hundred dollars. We were workin' every day then for
welfare wages.

[Loeb] was the one that started vacations and sick leave. I give Loeb
credit for that. At first we didn't have none of that. For five years of
work you'd get one week off, ten years you'd get two, fifteen years you'd
get three. That's how it went back then. But now you can get four or
five weeks. I was gettin' five weeks when I left there. They started sick
leave, you'd earn a day and a half a month. After the union, you'd get
two days a month. When I left there I was earnin' two and a half days
a month.

Before the union, it was whatever they decided they wanted to pay you. If they wanted to pay you they did, if they didn't want to they wouldn't. Rules were you were supposed to live in Memphis if you worked for the city. It was cheaper in west Memphis so that's where I lived. I wasn't makin' a damn thing. You can't pay the light bill on no ninety-six cents an hour. When you make cheap wages, you gotta try to get cheap other things. At the time of the strike, I'd been there fifteen years and I made $1.65 an hour.

They were sayin' we gotta get organized. They was gonna go on strike once. A guy named Ferris come in from somewhere, I believe he was with Teamsters. Those guys was gonna strike then but he left town, and they never did see him no more. He run off and left 'em. Good they didn't go on strike, hell, they'd have been up the creek. After things got started, this guy called T. O. Jones, he was gonna try to get somethin' from them [management]. If we don't do no better, we're still gonna strike. Somehow or another AFSCME came in, but we didn't have no union backin' or nothin', we just went out on our strike. T. O. Jones organized it. We paid dues to him, whatever dues we could, three dollars or somethin'.

We had a meeting out there in the church, out there on Broad and Scott, we had a meetin' there that Sunday night. That's when he [Jones] got fired. The next day they fired thirty-three. That's why they named the local 1733, 'cause they fired thirty-three men. After then every morning you'd come to work, they'd fire two or three. This was back in '66.

There was a big fence all around [the sanitation garages where] they called roll every mornin'. This guy was runnin', tryin' to get there before the man called his name. When the man was callin' his name he was just comin' through the gate down the hill, he hollered, "Yeah, I'm here." He heard him, but the man didn't see him. After he got through callin' roll, he went up to tell him he was here. You know what he told him? "Go on back home. Be on time in the mornin'." You just got tired of it.

We didn't have no local backin'. Then Leon Shepard and his brother, they went to their local and donated money and stuff. They had an office down on Vance. The Shepard boys, they knowed all about the unions and organizin'. We didn't know nothin' about all that kind of stuff.

What really kicked off the strike was when them guys got killed in that truck, they got mashed up in that garbage truck. There was gonna be a strike anyway, but that just pushed 'em all out. Folks were just gettin' tired of workin' for nothin', and gettin' all that different kind of treatment.

You'd go on vacation and you might not get no check. You'd be gone for two weeks, you come back lookin' for your check—you might get one you might not. Who wants to work at a place like that?

Well, when they first went out, some of the guys went on back to work. Loeb got up and threatened about what he was gonna do, he was gonna fire 'em all if they didn't show up in a certain amount of days. Some of them went back. A few, but not too many. We were meetin' over at the Firestone union hall then, they raised a lot of money for us. I think T. O. Jones got in touch with somebody over there.

At the early meetings they'd have a snitch who'd tell who went. You'd go to the meetin's and somebody would write down your name and people'd get fired. We found out about that. Somebody snitched on the snitcher. They had police detectives and everything at the meeting, to see what was goin' on. Had one at the meetin', the only way we knowed he was police, his radio went off while he was there. He about got beat to death.

T. O. went to the preachers and all those folks. They were donatin' some of the money from Sunday. Some guy, he was from New York or somewhere, he come in and brought a whole duffel bag of money. Other unions offered support. They'd help out with your light bill or whatever. After then, money was comin' from everywhere. All the locals supported us. Each member'd get so much per week, each member'd get I think thirty-five dollars a week. That was about as much as you were gonna make anyway. We only made about forty dollars anyway.

T. O. Jones, the first president, he kept things rollin'. He kept the men together. He called the meetin's, whatever. His problem was he wasn't educated, he didn't have no good education. That's how he got in trouble. He agreed to some shit, and he didn't even know what he agreed to. That was after the strike. When the union come in they transferred him to somewhere else to organize.

The men was ready to fight. [Bosses], they'd say, "Somebody's gonna lose their job." Well, hell, we ain't got no job! The job's been lost. You ain't gonna lose what you ain't never had. We didn't have no job, we just had somewhere to get up and go every mornin'. You work all week and get paid off and can't buy groceries, you don't call that no job. They'd rather stick with the strike. We stayed out there sixty-five days. I marched every day. And I was young, my kids was young. But we couldn't do no worse, we got to do better. So we stuck with it. Now it's payin' on off for the young folks now workin' in sanitation, they're makin' a decent livin'. If you work every day you should make a decent livin'.

I was livin' in the projects, LeMoyne Gardens, when we were on strike. At that time I didn't pay but thirty dollars a month, that's includin' the light bill. Quite a few were livin' there. We couldn't live nowhere else, we weren't makin' enough money to live nowhere else. At that time I had three children.

[Across from the projects], they had those half-track tanks runnin' up and down the street. Riotin' goin' on, sure there was riotin' goin' on [after the assassination of Dr. King]. But whose doin' all the stealin'? The damn police and the national guard was taking all the stuff, putting it in them trucks and goin' about their business. Where I was livin' there, I could sit up there and look down and see what they were doin'. There was some vandalism by other folks, like, kids would go in break out the windows. They probably had burglar alarms and all that, [and] they sent 'em there to check to see what the hell was goin' on. The vandals might not have gotten much, but when they [police and national guard] went in there they got everything, cigarettes, they cleaned it out. They'd say the rioters got it. That was in the daytime.

And they shot tear gas in the church, I was there that time, down in the basement.[18] When you were marchin', they'd run up and shoot that stuff right in your eyes. Lot of folks had trouble with their eyes for a long time afterwards.

One thing I ain't never figured out about the city: at the time we was tryin' to organize, they already had organized departments in the city. They had unions back then. Why'd they raise so much hell when we wanted to join a union? Shouldn't never have been a strike. Shouldn't never have been a strike. The only thing they was askin' for was recognition. They wasn't askin' for money when they went on strike. They wasn't askin' for a damn nickel. They just wanted 'em to recognize the union. . . .

Reverend Albert Hibbler come up with that "I Am a Man" sign. He's dead now. He was a preacher. He worked at the Sanitation Department. "I Am a Man" [meant] that they weren't gonna take that shit no more. Just like, you'd go in there, you know how much you're supposed to be makin',

---

18. In one of the police department's acts that escalated the conflict over the strike, officers shot tear gas into a meeting at Clayborn Temple.

how much your paycheck is supposed to be. You work two weeks, and payday your money ain't right. You go in there and tell the man, "Look, I worked eighty hours this payday [period], how come I ain't got but sixty?" [He'd say], "Get out of here, You don't know what you're talkin' about." That's the kind of treatment you got. You worked eighty hours, why couldn't they pay you that? You were only supposed to get ninety-six cents an hour, hell, pay you the ninety-six cents. Hell, you work eighty hours, he likely to pay you for sixty. You didn't have no job, you just had a place to go.

We had all kind of folks workin' in sanitation back then, there was some educated folks out there too. I worked on a truck with a guy that had two years of college, but he couldn't find no job. This was the only job he could get. He knowed what they was doin' to him, he knowed damn well if his paycheck wasn't right. But he better not go in there and say nothin' to nobody about it. Hell, they'd fire you.

In sanitation you got about five different installations—north, south, east, and west, and one downtown. And every one got two or three differ-ent preachers. In my installation there was a preacher. You'd go to work early, go to work at seven. You'd might get there and be in the bunkhouse around 7:30 or so. They'd have prayers, the preachers'd say a few words, then you go on to work. Boss didn't want them gettin' together. He would say, "Y'all ain't got time for that stuff." They were doin' it when I was in charge of the chapter. I would go to the mayor when they [supervisors] tried to stop it, say, "Tell the mayor we want to have a prayer service every mornin'." He agreed with it, he said, "Yeah, I think that's good for the men." You work out there you needed some kind of prayer or somethin'. My uncle, he used to work for the Sanitation Department. He's retired now. He was an ordained minister.

[The strike], it changed the city a lot. The whole world has changed since back in the '50s. Back in the '50s, the police would see you walkin' down the street, they'd pick you up and carry you to jail. I don't know if it changed for the better or worse, it just changed. A lot of things changed for the worse. But I think the sanitation strike made a lot of difference for a lot of folks. Not just sanitation workers, all the workers. [It] made a lot of difference for the whole city. There are blacks in different places, like the bank and stuff like that. Before they'd just sweep the floor, now they're tellers. It's changin'. And somethin' I never would have thought would happen: a black mayor of Memphis.

I think Dr. King changed a lot of people's minds. I heard King speak every time he was here. I went to that last speech. I went to the poor folks' march, all the way to Washington. I took my vacation then. Didn't have money for a hotel, stayed in a church. King was like Moses. A lot of that stuff he was talkin' about was true. A lot of that stuff was gonna come to pass. You can't keep treatin' people wrong, you gotta do right some time. They work for you, you gotta pay 'em a decent wage.

If I had a good education, I coulda been a better person. If I coulda went to school and got a better education, I coulda did more. I left [work the] last time I got sick. I'd been there thirty-three years.[19] If they didn't have the union, I'd feel sorry for the sanitation men, the fire commission, the public works, they'd be in big trouble. If they hadn't got the union they'd still be makin' minimum wages.

Leroy Boyd and Clarence Coe Recall a Strike and the Death of Martin Luther King

You had grown men working every day, going to bed hungry.

The momentous struggle of the sanitation strikers involved people throughout the community, but it especially engaged the concern of black trade unionists, who saw it as a merging of labor and civil rights battles they had fought for years. Its outcome also convinced long-timers such as Clarence Coe and Leroy Boyd that the power structure in Memphis, and perhaps higher authorities as well, had something to do with the murder of Martin Luther King, Jr. Few black Memphians at the time would have disagreed with this conclusion.

19. Robinson had a bad auto accident and discovered that the health insurance that he thought the city was paying had been canceled. "I thought they were supposed to take care of their workers. Hell, they don't take care of nothing." He ended up paying over forty thousand dollars in medical expenses. Most of the original group of workers seem to have lost their health insurance in the same way. The later generation of unionized workers apparently did not have this problem, and Robinson felt they were the ones that benefited most from unionization.

LEROY BOYD

The King march [in 1968], some of my kids was involved in that. We was
on the street there when they broke up the parade because some of the
guys started looting. Man, I'm telling you, they [the police] were shooting
after we even went on down to Clayborn Temple. And they were shooting
them tear gas. Boom! Like bombs, man. On Beale Street, that's when some
of them started looting those stores. I seen them. I was going down the
street, but I didn't take no part in it. Shoot, some of the police were running, beating them. So I just continued to march, it didn't scare me. One
thing, I didn't never get hit. I didn't run and none of the police never did
attack me. I held my ground, I just continued on. I didn't stop.

Well, what it [the sanitation strike] meant to black Memphis, they
helped black workers to get a decent salary. See, they didn't want to respect black workers at all. At that time, we had the mayor, Henry Loeb,
and he wouldn't give in. He said they wasn't going to organize. They
was trying to break the strike. So that was the reason King come in and
helped them.

And so that's the reason they got together and killed him. And tried to
cover it up and say it was James Earl Ray acted alone. Well, you never will
get me to believe that. How can one little person do that? The national
guard's on every corner [and] policemen. And he got out of town! Did that
and just got on out of town? And they say it wasn't two minutes before a
squad car was there, after the shooting.

Shoot! They're trying to get people to believe that. No. I have my own
belief about it. I think they used James Earl Ray. He might of did it. They
was telling me they were going to get him out of the country and put him
up, give him a rifle to do it. In fact, he did get out. He had top connec-
tions. All this was figured out in the beginning.

CLARENCE COE

I tried to get the rubber workers union convention to Memphis in 1973,
and they just told me straight up that "no, we're not coming to Memphis,
King was assassinated in Memphis." But local whites were so sure that that
wasn't going to have any impact, they went and built a convention center
here, for the a purpose of entertaining conventions. I mean, they never

had thought seriously about what happened. The local people never really thought seriously about it. And that [King's assassination] was so unnecessary. So unnecessary!

The root of it was, they had organized this union, what we call the sanitation union, they done spread to the hospitals and things like that. You had grown men working every day, going to bed hungry. I mean grown men working every day, qualifying for food stamps. And they just kind of got tired of it, and just finally said, the heck with it, what have we got to lose, and went out on strike. And Loeb was mayor at the time, and he got on the air and rose to the part: "This is not New York" and "We're not going to have it," and so forth.

So over a period of time the black churches moved in, and we had a liberal [union] president at the time that would allow them to meet [at] our union hall. Some of these religious leaders would come in to give a pep talk. The preachers had to take the forefront, because they were so tight on everybody else. It got so bad, some people [later] lost their jobs for going to King's funeral. But our preachers were being paid by us, so they could stick their necks out. A preacher wouldn't lose his job.

So they would bring in people and talk to those folks. They kept 'em busy listening through that strike. They would bring in somebody, and go from church to church raising funds, and so forth, and they weathered that storm. The rubber workers, we allowed them to use our hall for their mass meetings, and they had mass meetings every day. Every day. That's how they got so much solidarity. Every day.

And the union, they met their immediate problems. They didn't allow them to suffer. So later on King came in, and a little radical group we had here at the time called the Invaders really destroyed that thing.[20] I asked them at our church the night before. I said, "I can see what you're trying to do." I said, "If you want to do it, go on and do it, but this is not our

20. The Invaders were a group of young African American men who, using the rhetoric of Black Power and the right to armed self-defense, tried to organize a militant youth movement in the black community. As might be expected, they had tense relations with the black ministers and others organizing demonstrations on the basis of disciplined nonviolence. The Invaders received the blame, rightly or wrongly, for a window-breaking incident that prompted the police attack on the March 28 march led by Dr. King. The failure of this march was instrumental in compelling King's return to Memphis, where he was murdered.

program. Go out there and do whatever you want to do, but stay out of this program. This is nonviolent," and so forth. But the next day, the mass rally came here. We got about halfway through to our destination in the march when all hell broke loose, and police beat up a lot of folks, and just destroyed everything and maced a lot of folks and gassed a lot of folks.

King was discouraged and said, "Well, I never lost a march in this fashion. So, I'll come back later." And on the next time around, he was assassinated. He really should not have had to come back.

This wasn't accidental. No no, it was planned, it was a conspiracy. It was well organized. I mean, if you listen to King's last speech, he could see it, but he had just gone to the point that he couldn't turn around. And he knew it was going to happen. He knew it was going to happen. That was too well organized.

There's some things I would like to say about that but, nobody has ever listened to anybody on it. If he was shot out of a window on Main Street, why the hell did every police in that area run to the Lorraine [Motel, the place where King fell]? You've fired a gun, you've heard a gun, seen it fired. The noise is where the cap burst, you know. If somebody shoots a gun here, why would you run five or six hundred yards away? The gun wasn't fired there. Somebody knew what the target was. You know, everybody knew what the target was. That was just so simple. The police were all spotted around in places. But everybody knew, everybody knew. My wife had a cousin at the time, and she said that the discussions were open on the switchboard where she worked of what was going to happen. I had a friend that got stopped with a speeding ticket that night and [various officials] and Loeb were both on the expressway. From what he told me, they were just kind of waiting for the news on the radio, and everybody knew what was going to happen. But even the FBI won't listen. They've got some sharpshooters, too.

I was working second shift, and the crew I worked with that was predominantly white, they would go in one direction to eat, and I went in another one. Not that we couldn't have gone the same place at that time, but we didn't. And when we came back from lunch, they knew that King had been shot. And you know, nobody told me? And at seven o'clock the foreman came around, said, "We're closing down at seven o'clock, a curfew's going on at eight," or seven-thirty, or something. And I said, for what? That King had been assassinated. And I looked over at Nickles and Fortune and all that bunch, and I swear that did something to you, because they had already got the word, you know. I said, "Why in the world didn't you guys . . ." They said, "We thought you already knew it."

And then I was ready for the worst, I was ready for whatever. I drove from the plant, I told the guy that was riding with me, I said, "We'll probably get stopped." I said, "But if anybody comes to this car, between here and home, this is going to be the end of it." And I told some of the other guys out there that we'd probably never see each other again. Now that's what I was expecting, you know. They shined a light on me at Chelsea Street, but nobody approached the car.

Now they had the national guard and everything on the streets by that time. They shined on me again at Manassas and Union, and again at Mississippi and McLemore. And again at Parkway and Mississippi. And they had stopped some fellows and roughed 'em up and all that stuff. But I was driving a new car with drive-out tags on it, a new Buick, and I guess that's why nobody ever stopped me. They just say he's somebody, he's not out making trouble, he's just probably trying to get out of the street. There were cops all of the way home, and it just wasn't my time. It just wasn't my time.

And I had my plan. Here where I live I got a pretty good little arsenal. I'd planned to go over to the cemetery across the street and get behind that concrete wall, take me a can of gasoline and burn the bridge down in the cemetery, which is a wooden bridge, and that was going to hem up a lot of certain folk in that, you know. That's what I thought everybody else was going to do.[21]

And then, when I found out they [blacks] weren't going to do nothin', I'm tellin' you, it took a lot out of me. It took a lot out of me. I just expected to go to war. I mean, that's what I came home for, that's what I was planning on. And I thought that would just happen all over the world.

But when they had the next march after King was assassinated, we saw people from all over the world right here in Memphis, in line with us. And then Walter Reuther, and some of those guys came in and some of our senators and congressmen, labor people from all over everywhere, and really

21. Coe's fear of armed conflict was far from delusional; some whites had been stockpiling arms ever since a mini-riot took place in the Memphis ghetto in the summer of 1967, almost a year before the sanitation strike began.

financed the strike to such an extent that it was the end of it. So they went on and reached some kind of agreement. But it was encouraging to see the support labor got in Memphis after that. I'll never forget in the lines, I ran into people that I know now, Bill Cosby and all those people. They just came in from around the world, from around the world to join in that march.

But yet Memphis thinks that they can build a convention center and entertain labor and so forth. People haven't forgotten. It will never die. Memphis is just anti-labor. Anti-labor.

William Lucy Reflects on the Strike's Meaning and Outcome

Dr. King recognized that Memphis really highlighted the great contradiction.

William Lucy came to Memphis as an organizer for AFSCME and continued to service workers there long after the 1968 strike. He later became an international vice president of AFSCME and president of the Coalition of Black Trade Unionists. I interviewed him at a coffee shop in Memphis on April 3, 1993, the eve of a celebration of King's life twenty-five years after his assassination at the Lorraine Motel.

Dr. King believed very strongly in the alliance between organized labor, working people, and the civil rights community, and that civil rights obviously had to translate into economic gains and economic rights. As he saw it, the civil rights movement was not able on its own to make that transition. That had to come through the established right to represent workers with employers. So he saw that connection very clearly and spoke about it on several occasions.

There were tremendous gains made from the strike, not just in monetary gains for the strikers but gains in the social and economic and political system here in Memphis. And gains in the political system outside of Memphis. Let me spend a minute on Memphis first. The strike, in effect, galvanized the community. And while the immediate issues may have been a contract and recognition for the union and one more nickel or dime an hour for the workers, the strike really reflected all of the pent-up emotions and aspirations of the community. The strike gave a lot of folks a way of expressing their anger and seeing a vehicle they could organize around.

So there was some institution-building taking place at that point. The workers gained the right to sit down and discuss promotions and the grievance procedures, and vacations and retirements. They had the absolute right by agreement to do that. The new dimension was that you had an institution that had an economic base that reached beyond the workplace, really into the community itself. All the strikers were relatives of somebody and members of something. And because there was a clear understanding of the value of collective action, it took on a political context.

The union and the workers were so credible at that point, their assessment of a political leader [the union's endorsement] was really a powerful statement to people across the city who might not have time to look at the voting record or judge the role that this person had played in community life. So as a political instrument, the union was unmatched. And it served really to be a rallying point in the early days for a lot of other groups who had no resources or who were looking for a stronger ally.

So I think that the political life of the city was changed. Even though you had three black councilmen on the council at the time of the strike, the [black] community broadened its sights and began to think much larger in terms of the role that it would play. People would begin to look at the political life of the county, you know, how do we play a role in the major public policy questions that are going to affect the quality of life in the city, and what's the view of the union. Clearly the fact that there are black judges, black citywide officeholders, females, all of these I think are offshoots of the political gains that flowed from the strike.

The one other area in which I think the union in those days took a very active role, and it was by design, was a program we called the community affairs or the community activities programs of the unions. Recognizing that there are any number of unmet needs at the community level, we set up a fund where a portion of the union dues would go into this fund that would be used for issues that the union thought were important to the community. By focusing on the social problems, economic problems, political problems, the union became a major force for change.

If you look at the wages just of the strikers, and I think probably the wages of other areas of the city, they're substantially higher now than they were twenty-five years ago, although that's not to say that they're in great shape now. In '68, most of the workers were just a hair above the minimum wage or a hair below: $1.65 to $1.75 an hour, somewhere in that area. Although I don't know exactly what they are right now [1993], I think they're probably in excess of $10 to $12 an hour for basic sanitation workers. But a lot of those jobs now promote into other areas, truck driver, crew chief, equipment operators, where [back] then it wasn't a sure promotion into anything.[22]

[Wages went up] in the other direct personal service industries, whether it be hotel or restaurant employees, retail sales, or other industries that were almost like duplicates, for instance, in the waste management industry or what you'd call the commercial solid-waste removal area. Those wages had to almost match what was happening in the city service in order for those private haulers to remain competitive in terms of getting people with the skills to do this. There [was] the assumption that it really doesn't require any skills to pick up garbage, it's just like the more uneducated you are the better worker you are. Well, it really does require some understanding of what you're dealing with to keep you from killing yourself and others around you.

So I think that these tangential effects were there. If people earned more, they could buy more. The fact that they could buy more meant that the economy of the city was improving. So I think that there were a lot of side benefits that flowed from [the strike].

In a city like Memphis you've got families, one worker works in public works and the other works in the city hall. Or one works in public works and the other works at the city hospital or the school board. I mean, while we were dealing with the husband, the wife or the daughter or another relative works somewhere else, and they said, "We want to be organized too." And while it wasn't by design, it was simply a natural follow-through, we began to get inquiries from all over. "We want to be a part of this new thing. We want to join the union. We want to be organized too. When's our turn?" And we organized the hospital, the board of education, the housing authority, parks and recreation, the city zoo.[23] And even though

22. According to AFSCME Local 1733 President Dorothy Crook, a starting sanitation worker at the end of probation made $11.46 an hour, and six grades above that brought a wage of $12.59. Drivers and equipment operators made nearly fifteen dollars an hour, and all had vacations, benefits, and health coverage. Interview with Dorothy Crook, April 1, 1998, Memphis.

23. AFSCME organized workers at John Gaston Hospital in the fall of 1968, led by Jesse Epps. City workers in a variety of departments joined, and the American Federation of Teachers also began organizing city teachers, some of whom were already represented by the Memphis Education Association. In the early 1970s, household workers and welfare recipients also began organizing in Memphis.

it wasn't us [AFSCME], we had other activities taking place—the police department, the fire department. All these things naturally followed.

The interesting thing is that the early perception of the union was that it was this black civil rights organization that was designed to rabble-rouse. And it wasn't long before the other areas of the city recognized that if they were going to get what they were rightfully entitled to, they too had to be organized. So they had a right to sit down with their employer and partici- pate in these decisions. In the early days, in '68 or — 69, the union was overwhelmingly blue-collar, simply because of how the first organizing took place. [But] as we began to organize in the hospital and the schools, we got more females, more technical jobs, a higher-educated workforce, and the union became much more diverse.

Of course, by the time we got fully organized, it was to the advantage of the city to at least allow other organizing to take place, to counterbalance what was happening in the other areas. It was a play-one-off-against-the- other mentality that was beginning to develop. [But] the city simply could not be in the position, in my opinion, of doing business only with one group of employees. The police and fire had always been perceived by the taxpayers as the key important services. And so they organized. I mean the workers took advantage of a situation they saw was important. The city, while they protested mightily, allowed it to take place because it was in their interest. And in the long run, it was in everybody's collective interest that trade union organizing took place.

We tried to make the argument all along that if we were to have a stable workforce, that is wholly dependent upon a stable relationship be- tween the workers. And you can't deal with two thousand or three thou- sand independent workers on problems of common concern to everybody. It's much better that the union play a role. And I think while Henry Loeb never visualized it, people around him and succeeding administrations understood that. Even Mayor [Wyeth] Chandler [Loeb's successor, elected in 1972], while he was certainly by no means pro-union, understood that if you're going to run a successful city, it's dependent upon having a sen- sible relationship with the workforce.

What Memphis and the spirit of Memphis did was gave a new kind of recognition to some workers that had been there all along but never recog- nized. We used to say that people would put their garbage outside and as- sume that by magic it disappeared. There was never much thought given to the fact that some guy got up at 5:00 in the morning and it was his job to take it away. And a new kind of respect and a new kind of recognition and a new enthusiasm to organize really went across sanitation workers across the country.

Dr. King recognized that Memphis really highlighted the great contradiction. Theoretically, if you work hard and play by the rules, you will succeed. But here, you had folks that worked every single day, yet there was no opportunity whatsoever to succeed, by virtue of the social structure and the exploitation that they experienced on the job. [Dr. King] could see the folks in Marks, Mississippi, in poverty and that could be described as the condition of no work. But in Memphis, you got folks who work and are still in poverty.

Clearly something [is] wrong with the order. And if you relieve the civil rights shackles or barriers, that does not necessarily guarantee that your economic station will change. There is something wrong with the social structure. There is something wrong with the economic structure.

The sanitation strike created a level of black unity and mass mobilization not seen before or since, giving vent to decades of accumulated grievances by a community disproportionately filled with poor people and workers who were tired of being dominated by a paternalistic white power structure. The strike hit a nerve not only in Memphis but across the country, for it touched on systemic problems that underlay black urban rebellions going on almost everywhere in the 1960s. Police brutality and racial violence on one hand and a growing crisis among the black working class on the other provided the subtext for those rebellions.

By 1968, both the labor and the civil rights movements had come to a crossroads. The latter had focused on breaking down segregation's barriers to public accommodations, education, and the right to vote, but it lacked a platform to challenge deep-seated economic inequalities. Most unions, on the other hand, had stopped organizing the unorganized and the poor, and the upper-echelon of white workers had largely turned against black demands for integration of housing, schools, jobs, and for economic redistribution. King's Poor People's Campaign offered one possible way to unite the poor and take their demands to the seat of national government. The momentous strike by the Memphis sanitation workers also offered a promising vehicle to focus on the problems besetting the urban working poor across black America. King's last crusade offered the possibility of bringing parallel struggles for economic and racial justice into a powerful movement for fundamental change, something many black labor activists had always hoped for.

His death and the subsequent failure of the Poor People's Campaign blasted these hopes. The Vietnam War, the polarization of the civil rights movement over Black Power demands, continued urban rebellions, the split between white working-class and black constituencies in the Democratic Party, and the growth of the right wing all undercut movements for change, and things only got worse after King's death. Riots spread across the country, the Poor People's Campaign achieved little, and Robert Kennedy was assassinated. Within a year of King's death, Richard Nixon had gained the White House and began his efforts, as his Attorney General John Mitchell later put it, to "take this country so far to the right you won't recognize it." King himself had feared that the country teetered on the brink of a kind of racial fascism, an apocalyptic vision similar to the one that prompted Clarence Coe to arm himself for a race war. King's death left bitterness and despair in its wake.

On the other hand, the workers interviewed here also felt that King's sacrifice was not in vain. His presence in Memphis did bring about change and left a special imprint upon the history of the black labor struggle. The fact that one of the most renowned human rights leaders of the twentieth century died on behalf of poor, working-class people would forever give this history a special meaning. "I'm sure a lot of things have been written about why he came," AFSCME Local 1733 President Dorothy Crook reflected in 1998, thirty years after King's death. "But to these 1,300 guys, it meant a voice speaking for them."

In a real sense, as Taylor Rogers and William Lucy both emphasize, King's ultimate sacrifice in Memphis did turn the tide for the sanitation workers. King's participation and the huge national pressures his death put on the obstinate and blinkered mayor of Memphis forced a strike settlement. Unionized sanitation workers ultimately gained decent wages, working conditions, pensions, and some power at the workplace. In the strike's aftermath, AFSCME became the largest union local in the city, police and firefighters joined public employee unions, and black workers organized in local hospitals (with limited success) and in other city jobs. A protest by the poorest of black workers to some degree had revived a dormant labor movement in Memphis. AFSCME's success also paved the way to public employee union organizing in other parts of the South and the country. Indeed, public employee unionism became the main area of growth for the American labor movement in the 1970s.

The crisis of 1968 and the struggles that came after it also undermined the white "plantation mentality" and forced some degree of change politically. Memphis developed a combative civil rights leadership through an energized NAACP during the 1970s, which opened up the school board to black leadership, while continuing pressure from the African American community opened up more jobs in the previously forbidden zones of white-collar and professional employment. In line with national trends, blacks became increasingly active as politicians, and the growth of the black middle class accelerated. After much internal division and many failed attempts to coalesce politically in the 1980s, the black community in Memphis achieved an extraordinary degree of unity in 1991 when it provided the core of support to elect Willie Herrenton as the first African American mayor of Memphis.

In addition to King's sacrifice, black workers' long struggles played a key role in these victories. Many of those who formerly had unionized— Leroy Boyd, George Holloway, Matthew Davis, Alzada and Leroy Clark, and Clarence Coe among them—joined in the marches and rallies for the sanitation workers. Local 189 of the United Rubber Workers provided a union hall for sanitation workers to meet and raised more funds for the strike than any other union local. Even the relatively conservative Memphis Labor Council provided funds and moral support (white building-trades unionists, predictably, took the side of Mayor Loeb). In one sense, King's martyrdom represented but one more step in the freedom movement that generations of black workers had already initiated. Like King, they demanded not only the right to eat a hamburger at a public place but the money to pay for it. They sought not just a job but dignity, not just better wages but justice.

At the same time, the historic split between white and black remained much in evidence in Memphis. And if the sanitation strike came to symbolize concern for the working poor, America largely failed to move beyond civil rights to the economic justice agenda initiated by Dr. King. The chain of events in Memphis seemed to close one segment of the freedom struggle and to open up a new one, but would the future be worse or better than the past? If King and the civil rights and labor movements of which he was a part left a legacy of activism and protest, they also left an unfinished agenda. Organizing African Americans and other minorities and women became even more imperative and yet more imperiled after King's death. As Ortha B. Strong Jones told interviewer Laurie Green, it "looked like we was going forward for awhile and then all at once it stopped and it seems like we are going backwards."

8 THE FATE OF THE BLACK WORKING CLASS

THE GLOBAL ECONOMY, RACISM, AND UNION ORGANIZING

> At eighty years, I've had experience from a little boy up, and I
> know what I'm talking about. Things are worse now than they've
> ever been.
>
> Hillie Pride

> Billions of dollars have gone from over here to over there, from the
> black community to the white.
>
> Clarence Coe

> Race is always there, always.
>
> Ida Leachman

By the mid-1970s, black workers in a core of unionized factory jobs had torn down most Jim Crow barriers within their workplaces and unions, after decades of painful effort. Just as their labors began to really bear fruit in the form of family-wage jobs distributed on an equal basis, factory closings began to undercut all they had fought to achieve. The dawning progress of black industrial workers made the deindustrialization of parts of North America seem all the more disastrous. While public sector unions expanded, the shut down of factories, many of them still profitable, ripped industrial unions to shreds during and after the 1980s. As companies moved production beyond U.S. borders or simply liquidated holdings to turn higher profits, they tore up the foundation for probably the single largest group of stable wage-earning families in the black community, those with members working in unionized mass-production industries. Political action, community service, church, and family life all suffered as a result.

This turn of events dismayed and angered union veterans. In contrast to their comments about past organizing, in which they spoke proudly of how they helped to make history, speaking in the present tense they felt outraged and sometimes hopeless. From their point of view, capitalism's global reorganization at the end of the twentieth century has had a devastating impact. Under the rubric of a "global economy," business-oriented politicians found numerous ways to turn workers over to the untender mercies of the market, legislate corporate tax breaks, funnel more and more income to the wealthy, and disinvest in government services and social benefits. These measures withered the very support structures Martin Luther King had sought to expand in order to offset generations of racism and black disadvantage. The federal government, once an uncertain ally, now undercut civil rights and labor law enforcement, putting the interests of the wealthy above those of workers, the poor, and minorities. Hillie Pride and others, interviewed during the devastating economic dislocations of the 1980s, elaborate on the deadly results of what people at the time called "Reaganomics." They placed the blame for the plight of their community squarely on Republicans.

Of course, new areas of employment continued to expand throughout the 1980s and 1990s, but they provided little relief for most people in inner-city black communities. Better paid information- or service-oriented jobs often required the higher education that many lacked, and the worst jobs did not provide wages adequate to sustain families. Increasing numbers of women at the bottom of the job and wage hierarchy became the sole support for their families. At the same time, the possibilities for labor organizing waned. In place of Henry Ford's industrial mass-production model where workers turned out millions of products, the model within which the CIO unions had been able to organize so effectively, decentralized production became the norm. More often than not, black factory workers, many of them women, ended up in small non-union shops, fighting battles with employers who could easily become tyrants without the countervailing power of strong unions. Ida Leachman describes how in some ways the struggle of black workers had come full circle; as Alzada Clark comments, "It's back to like it was in the latter part of the '30s and the early '40s." The decline of unions partially closed one of the few avenues blacks had found to exercise some degree of power at work and in the society.

In this chapter, black workers in their final reflections underscore the tragic dimensions of their experience in America. In interviews conducted during the 1980s, Evelyn Bates, Hillie Pride, and others emphasized the shock effect factory closings had on their community of north Memphis in the 1980s. And while the economy produced more jobs in the 1990s, from his vantage point James Robinson still saw little advancement for the working poor, who lost welfare benefits and continued to receive part-time wages for marginal jobs. Leroy Boyd felt amazed and disgusted as foremen bought out or intimidated workers at his old place of employment. Indeed, Federal Compress finally broke the union Boyd had worked so hard to build. It seemed to most of these veterans that younger workers knew little about prior struggles and had few clues about how to fight back; discouragement with the individualistic mind-set of the young became a consistent refrain. Ida Leachman, one of a new cohort of black women organizers, saw the problems of young workers more as the result of their increasing fear of losing their jobs. As she, Alzada Clark, Clarence Coe, and others point out, that fear continued to fan the fires of racial division and conflict, which made organizing all the more difficult.

These workers spent lifetimes resisting racial and economic injustice through unionization, at great cost to themselves, and now they feared their legacy would be lost. "The terrible thing about labor," Edward Lindsey observed, is that "many times the history dies with its membership." Once memory is lost, he felt, workers would be forced to relearn the fundamentals of unionism through hard experience and suffer disasters that might have been avoided. Sustaining memory itself thus became a goal of the earlier generation of black workers. And modern conditions of labor exploitation, black union veterans stress, make it more important than ever to exercise solidarity across the boundaries of race and gender.

Confronting Deindustrialization

Once they got most of this stuff [segregation] straightened out,
they shut the factory down.

After all they had achieved, black workers from earlier generations felt particularly anguished as factories shut down and unions collapsed during a return to an increasingly unregulated "free market" economy. Their long-term perspective provides insight into some of the sources of the poverty, drug abuse, and other social dislocations that struck black communities in the 1980s, during which these interviews took place, and in the 1990s. They believed more than ever in the need to organize.

EVELYN BATES

I don't know about the other cities, but it hasn't completely changed here. And once they got most of this stuff [segregation] straightened out, they shut the factory down, in fact, all of the factories in the South. Every time you looked, there was a factory going out of business. I mean, good-paying jobs. There's no good-paying jobs here now. It's now come to the place that it's not what you know, it's who you know.

I just don't see how people can live off of $3.35 an hour now [1989]. I can't see it, I really can't see it. There's got to be something to change this. I don't know what it's going to be, but there's got to be something. I wouldn't say it needs to be another war, but something needs to be done. This is pitiful how you can go by all of these factories, and the windows are all broke out. The building just sitting there, just going to waste. *No jobs.* Nothing to look forward to.

There's no jobs out there for young people today. You have as many college students walking around as you have children that haven't been to college, 'cause they can't find nothing to do. *Blacks cannot find nothing to do here.* So what good is an education if you can't get a job? It's just a lot of money spent. If you go to college, and then you come home and can't get a job, what's the use of going? And I guess that's the way the youngsters is looking at it. If the youngsters would just realize that this dope and stuff that's going on is nothing but killing them and keeping them from getting good jobs and a good education. But they don't seem to realize. Young people get trapped in that.

So now there's crime, that's what it's doing. Youngsters breaking into your house, killing, selling dope. You're afraid to let your windows up or your door stay open. There's lots of blacks in prison.

I've seen the time I could leave my windows and doors open all night long. Now it's dangerous just sitting in the house without it being all locked up. And sometimes they break in on you when you're locked up in the house! It wasn't always like that. I'd say crime conditions and things like that were much better in the '40s and '50s. I could leave my children at 11 P.M. and walk up the street to catch the bus to Firestone. Now, I'm almost scared to drive in the car to go anyplace. That's right. I never used to feel like that.

But you can't say that I don't want to work when you don't have no job to put me on. You don't know what I want until you try to give me a job. And then if I don't want to work, I'll say, "I don't want to work." But first, give me something to do before you say I don't want to work.

HILLIE PRIDE

After the [Firestone] plant went down [in 1983], the union had nothing. There was nothing the union could do. Mostly all of the blacks are out of work now, and quite a few whites, and there ain't nobody doing nothing about it. This world is going around and around right now, people starving. People ain't got nothing, no job, no nothing, just sitting outdoors. No gas or lights, can't pay for 'em. Use a flashlight to get in the house, if they have a house at all right now! Things just can't continue like this. It's such a tough situation for people. People are dying, that's all there's to it.

Poverty and people's situations are worse now [1983] than they were in the Depression. Back then they could pick cotton and make a little something. But now, all of that's gone. Ain't no work for people now. The Republicans cut all of the jobs out and ran all of the best plants away. We ain't got nothing here in Memphis! It's Reagan and the money, Reagan and the money. Clean across the nation. The jobs people do have, they can't hardly live on them, the cost of living is so high.

It's the most pitiful thing I've ever seen in my life. There's nothing coming into Memphis at all. People are desperate since they cut out all of the plants like Firestone. No women's work, nothing for them to do. They cut out bingo and the horse track, too. There's nothing here anymore. We're just sitting here. You can't make a dime, no kind of way. It can't continue like this! Some of them are going to be dead. There's dope now messing up people, and killing and shooting. It's tough.

A lot of people can't see it, but I've been here long enough to know what I'm talking about! At eighty years, I've had experience from a little boy up, and I know what I'm talking about. Things are worse now than they've ever been. The Lord picked a way for me, so I know. Anybody around here will tell you the same thing.

China and Japan and different countries are buying up the United States. There would have to be a wall between the nations to stop it. What are they going to do? They'll come here and then starve to death here. There ain't nothing here, pitiful situation. The big fish eating up the little ones, that's all.

So many people suffering, don't know what's happening. No job, no nothing. Someone in the government ought to start up some big farms and give people jobs harvesting and planting, and make some decent food to eat. That stuff we buy in the store don't count as food. Can't hardly taste it, and meat is so tough you can hardly get it down. We used to raise our own food, and we had good, pure food. Now it's all chemicals. We used to have much better food, good, pure food that we'd raised in the family.

Anything to help this country, it's in bad shape. Children by the thousands coming in. What are they going to do? They can't all work in the city here, there aren't any jobs here. The government cut all the supports. All the people run from the country to the city. They've got to spread these people out and start making work for people to make a living at. It's going to be just like in Africa here.

People today will break into your house and kill you and take everything you've got. Robbery is so rampant here, you can hardly go anywhere at night, and you can't hardly stay at home. They'll take everything you've got. In the years to come you won't be able to stay at home.

You ain't got nothing to hold on to. This isn't going to bring progress. We have to go back and make some change in this country. This nation has got to start doing something for the people that aren't working to get them some work. They're all in a pile now, one can't help the other, because none of them have jobs. Who's going to help you? We're really being ripped up by the moral structure of this country.

LEROY BOYD

All this dope is being pushed in this country. And this is my personal feeling: I don't feel like all of this is being done by the little person. We got some *top* peoples involved in that that will never be touched. If you notice, only ones that they bust is going to be the little person. But the top person, he'll never be touched. I mean they ain't never going to do anything about it because it's a money-making thing. And after they're pushing all this dope, you're poisoning the mind of the people. White America is just getting back out of the way, and they [young African Americans] just destroying themselves.

All these companies pretend they going out of business, getting rid of all the employees. No jobs, people got to survive. When they put all this stuff out on the street, a guy can make him a thousand dollars a day. Why he going to go get a little job and make him thirty or forty dollars with a five dollar [an hour] job? What he going to do with forty dollars, shoot! That's what happen. When they catch him, regardless of what kind of education he got, he won't never be able to hold a good decent job.

All of them going to have a record. All of them going to be on dope. I think that's the purpose of it. I had one guy to tell me that. He was white. He was working for the railroad. He'd come around checking them box-cars. He used to come my desk, and he used to tell me he believed I was a member of the NAACP. I said, "Well, could be." You know, we'd talk about different things, [and] I said, "Really, I believe you a member of the Klan." And he said, "Well . . ." I said, "Well, you don't have to give no statement." I say, "Used to be a time that y'all put that hood on, we were scared of you." I say, "You put your hood on now, we'll pull it off of you."

So he laughed. We just cracking at each other. So I said, "Well, I tell you. The only thing about you guys, y'all just don't want our black boys going to school with y'all white girls." I say, "It don't matter what your white boys do to our black girls, y'all ain't concerned about that. But the only concern that you got is the black boys and your white girls."

And he said, this is what he told me, "Well, we not going to worry about y'all." He said, "As long as we continue to push this dope into you and supply y'all with them Saturday night specials, y'all going to destroy yourself." That's what he told me. And this is what's happening. There's a lot of truth in it. You pick up the paper and see what they doing. Anything that the blacks do, they make a big issue of it. They blow it up. If white do anything, play it down. The company I used to work in used do the same thing. Some of the [white] workers, they be sure and make a big issue out of any little thing you do, they'd blow it up.

As long as I had my people with me, I was helping myself as well as helping the people. And that's one of the things I stressed to the younger workers in the shop. [Today], that's what the younger people don't have.

They don't have the back training. They don't know how we struggled to get where we're at.

If you really want to know how a company stands, you have to ask him for some money out of his pocket during negotiations, and you'll see his true colors. But it's been kind of rough now on all of them, since there ain't no organizing you can do now. We haven't been able to do any organizing since the Republican Party [election of Ronald Reagan as president in 1980], I'll put it that way.

It ain't anything like it was when I come along. I know what they [the company]'re doing. Whatever it took to get to a person, they [supervisors] loan him money, and they started courting the ladies. This is the way they started getting to the workers. Yeah, I see it. See, I give up on what's going on. You know, there's nothing I could do about it. I figure they free. They do what they want, the younger people. The companies is really putting somebody through a change.[1]

Well, on my job, I had to struggle to keep my people with me and behind me because by doing so I'd be helping them and also helping myself. I couldn't earn a decent salary if I didn't have the support of the people behind me. It's simple. When you got strength, you know, you can accomplish your aim.

JAMES ROBINSON

All the workers are in a struggle in this country. Low wages. This country made its own problems. Now they gotta figure out how the hell they're gonna [get] out of it.

They talk about equal this and equal that. How you gonna be equal if your kid goes to school nine months and my kid goes four?[2] How's he gonna be equal to yours? Hell, he can't be. He's got a disadvantage right there. Now they gotta take care of 'em, and they don't wanna do that. Now they're gonna cut out welfare, gonna cut out social security, cut out every damn thing. The problems were created back then. Now they're catchin' up with 'em today.

1. The Federal Compress shop where Boyd worked voted out the union several years after this interview.
2. Robinson grew up in a sharecropping family, where the children spent most of the school year working in the cotton fields.

Now they're talkin' about cuttin' folks off of welfare. They want you to work for welfare, isn't that what they say now? That's what we [sanitation workers] were doin'! Makin' us work and givin' us welfare wages. You'd work thirteen days and wouldn't bring home two hundred dollars. They want you to work, but they don't want to pay you.

You're supposed to work for a livin', but you aren't supposed to be slavin' for a livin'. People back then wanted to work, but they didn't want to pay 'em. They wanted you to work for nothin'. You never would get everything you was askin' for. But give a man a decent livin' if he's workin'. But they didn't want to do that.

When I was out there workin' like hell, I was workin' and not gettin' nothin' for it. Now jobs out there pay nineteen dollars an hour.[3] That's good pay. Now they [sanitation workers] make as much in a day as I was makin' in two weeks. They're getting practically all the benefits now. If a guy works you're supposed to give him a decent wage.

Republicans say, "Folks don't wanna work." Folks don't wanna work for nothin', that's what it is. People want to work, but they wanna be paid. You can't hold one back. Everybody's gotta profit together.

EDWARD LINDSEY

The terrible thing about labor, many times the history dies with its membership and people get the wrong impression about what labor's about. They get negative attitudes about it. It's due to ignorance, 'cause they just don't really know. Like, I've got two boys, one is already out [of school], he's in the navy. The younger kid, I always tell him things about the union. It's really important.

The civil rights struggles have always been parallel to labor movements. If you solve the labor problems, you're gonna solve them in civil rights, and vice versa. People just don't know about what goes on.

It takes money to get involved, to get your voice heard in politics. And when labor began to do that, then people said it's a special interest group. But that isn't the case at all. Labor has just always been interested in the

---

3. A few jobs paid this much, but pay for most sanitation work in Memphis as late as 1998 ranged around twelve dollars an hour, according to Local 1733 President Dorothy Crook.

well-being of people, education, people's rights, freedom. That's what the struggle's about. You find the same thing going on in Beijing, China, now. It's parallel; all over the world, it's the same struggle.

I would say [the corporations], they're the special interest groups, in order to retain all the things that they have. I understand the process and the political wars that go on in order to try to destroy labor. I understand it, but many people don't. I understand the struggle of these people that want to keep power. Once you get power, the more you want, [and] you want to keep it. But I still think the masses of people need to be able to participate in the political process. I think that if we ever wake up the masses, then you will see some drastic changes that I think will be for the better.

We tend to apathy. I think the problems that labor is having today is simply that apathy set in. You could see it coming. You could see it coming. But you were never able to arouse the people of what was coming. No matter what you struggle for, the stroke of a pen could remove it, just like that. You saw some of it in the Reagan administration. It's struggle many people have died for that will be just removed with the stroke of a pen because people let apathy set in. People were satisfied. They were making good benefits, they were making good wages. They didn't see a need to continue to be organized, to continue to be enthusiastic about unions. They weren't cognizant of this trend that was taking place in this country politically.

A good example of that would be what happened to the PATCO workers.[4] To me, what happened to the PATCO workers was the turning point as far as labor was concerned. Every union person in this country should have participated in that process, because once President Reagan got rid of them, that was it. I think when they were able to turn those people around, a trend was set in this country, and the trend is still there.

When you look at history, I guess that's the way it goes. History repeats itself. I can understand the Jewish people that would never let you forget about the Holocaust, because they don't want it to happen again. Because if you become ignorant of the past, then it's obvious the past is going to haunt you, it's going to come back. And I can understand why they'll never

4. The members of PATCO (Professional Air Traffic Controllers Organization) were fired by President Reagan en masse when eleven thousand of them went on strike in 1981.

let you forget the Holocaust. It's just like, as far as blacks are concerned, we should never forget about slavery, never. We can't. Because if you let your guard down, it will come back. That's just the way it is.

Like, I've got an eleven-year-old kid. I don't know if he's going to be able to accomplish the same things, buy a house, buy a car, things like that. I just don't know. No matter how many schools they go to, college or whatever, it doesn't really matter. If it gets down to the fact that the masses can't survive, then everybody's in trouble. You may not think it, but you are. You pay dearly.

Naturally, when you have a plant closure like this [at Firestone], you have some bad things happen. Like, I can remember one guy, he took his own life. It's a guy I thought it would never happen to him. I thought he just had everything together. And you've had a lot of divorces, family break-ups. Some guys and gals just never recover. And I think it's because they continue to dream it's not going to come to this, instead of picking up the pieces and moving on the best you can. Some of them still haven't done anything yet. They've lost their families, lost everything.

They have some testing going on. There are carcinogens in benzene, that was used daily [at the Firestone plant]. I knew of a guy, periodically he would swell up. Probably he worked there a long time, when conditions were just horrible. OSHA [Occupational Safety and Health Administration] hadn't come in yet. I think he had some type of cancer, but they never talked about it. He eventually died. But in my mind, I think that's what happened to him. We had some strange deaths there. People get sick and die and they never find what's wrong with them. A lot of people had rubber rash, but nobody ever viewed the rubber rash as anything terrible, or you know, thought that much about it. When OSHA come through in the late '70s, if a guy had been there twenty-five or thirty years, the damage was already done.

It was tough, but the wages were good. As a result of organized labor, it was a good place to work, the wages were there, the benefits were there. And all this on the backs of people like Hillie Pride. It took some long strikes at times to get those kinds of benefits. I was involved in one 96-day strike myself. That was in '76, and another in '67 too. That one was about 126 days. It was the whole summer, [over] wages, benefits, retirement, cost of living, dental plan.

And you know, many company people saw this. The thing of it is, the more things we got, the better we got, the better for the company people too. They had to make it more advantageous to be a company man than they made it to the guys down on the floor. If we got a dental plan, that meant they would likely get a dental plan, and theirs was probably better than ours. And so, they understood. I know that there were company people that come by the union hall and leave money, coffee, stuff like that, because they tell us, hey, whatever you guys get will certainly make it better for us. They would wish us luck.

I'm glad you're going to write a book, because a lot of things that labor did, people just have no knowledge. They just think it was a bunch of toughs. That was an image that you had earlier, everybody who was in the union was tough, knock everybody around. But in the latter stage, you had people who knew economics, that's what it gets down to when you're negotiating contracts, you've got to know what the potentials are out there. The company always has to be competitive. I wouldn't want to get something that the company really couldn't afford to do, because then your job's not secure at all.

So I say, a guy had to know his economics, he had to understand his politics. I think you'll end up doing more damage to both the company and your membership if you don't. More so than somebody who's just big and tough and doing a lot of rattling off, I think that's more detrimental to you than anything else. Because a lot of people got that impression, we're just a bunch of people out there that didn't want to work, special interest groups. But I think a real good union man or woman, a leader, has to be a person that's responsible. You have to be intelligent. Otherwise, you're just blowing smoke.

Of course, you can be a fighter and be responsible at the same time. Sometimes, people may get that mixed up. But you can be a fighter and be responsible. In fact, I suspect that that's what you gotta have, you'd better be that way. You always have to keep the people in mind, always keep your people in mind. That's the way I was brought up. That's the way I was taught.

ALZADA CLARK

Things are much more difficult for organizing unions since Reagan came in. His message was to the whites to regain power and control, he thought power was getting out of hand via the unions. Affirmative action was one of the first things that he attacked. So many young people, the new skinhead groups, etcetera, have the wrong perception about the meaning of affirmative action. It's not taking anything away from the majority race, but at least it doesn't allow the exclusion of the minority races of people who have been excluded for hundreds of years in this country. There are certain rights that minorities would never have if we weren't made to respect their rights. Reagan sent out the signal that they could take advantage of those rights.

Some of the American people may be saying that Reagan brought this country back around to where it's supposed to be, to respect God and the flag. Well, there was never any disrespect except during the Vietnam War, which was deserved and I can empathize with. Why should people go off and fight for something they didn't believe in? But Reagan had so many people believing in him that we regressed back to having a bunch of white men rule and what they say, goes. It's back to like it was in the latter part of the '30s and the early '40s.

I never got involved in protesting the Vietnam War, though I agreed with the protesters. But at that time, I was busy down in Mississippi trying to organize the union and get people to help themselves. My philosophy was that we didn't have to necessarily like or love each other, but we had a common goal to accomplish. Together we could accomplish a lot, separately we couldn't accomplish much. There was all of this money in those industries, and we weren't making anything. The whites working were making maybe a dime more. So why not get together and get that rich owner to pay us closer to what we were worth?

My philosophy about the trade union movement was that we are all human beings, and each one of us has certain inherited rights of life, liberty, and the pursuit of happiness. All of us are equal, but at times, some are more equal than others in reality. We have to work together to make all of us equal. This is how I talked to the people at the time I was organizing. I think people began to see some of the changes were positive, and they liked them. They began to realize that some changes were inevitable, and that they needed to change their way of thinking and acting in order to survive.

Ida Leachman Tells How Her Union
Continues to Organize Low-Wage Workers

Everybody knows that God is leadin' this local.

In a hard and mean era for unions in the 1980s and 1990s, Ida Leachman became an organizer for Local 282 of the furniture workers union,[5] and later a vice president and executive board member of her international union. Much in the mold of Alzada Clark, who had earlier broken down barriers to black women as union organizers, Mrs. Leachman was fearless, determined, and yet gracious and full of warmth and humor. In her narrative, she reviews the journey that so many made to factory work and recalls the personal turning points that led her to unionism. Looking back to her own family roots as she examined the struggles of black workers in the global labor market of the late twentieth century, she reflected with sadness on the persistence of racism and economic exploitation. But she also applied a spiritual and woman-centered perspective that gave her strength to carry on. We spoke in 1996 at her modest office, which belied any idea that "big labor" is profiting from the dues of low-wage workers.

My birthday is September 29, 1929. I was born in Holly Springs, Mississippi, about fifty miles southeast of Memphis. I grew up on a farm until I was about thirteen or so. We were living out rural, I guess about five miles out of the little town itself. My father didn't own the land, he was a sharecropper—"one for you and two for him." His father was a sharecropper too, so was my mother, all raised up in Mississippi. My family didn't do too much farmin' because my father was a bird-dog trainer. They would have these field trials, then he would travel with these dogs to feed them and do whatever you have to do with a bird dog. I was about thirteen and then my parents moved uptown and no longer did the farmin'.

My grandmother lived here in Memphis. I understood that my great grandmother were an Indian, and my great grandfather was African. I

5. In a 1987 merger, the UFWA became the Furniture Workers Division of the International Union of Electronic, Electrical, Salaried, Machine, and Furniture Workers (IUE).

have photographs of them. On my father's side, I believe it was, we were related to Ida B. Wells. Matter of fact, from generations up to myself, I think I'm about the last one, there has always been a couple of Idas. That's my namesake. Sometimes when I'm showing off, I'll say "I'm related to Ida B. Wells." We do have some of the same spirit. I guess we were fightin' for the same things, and that's other people. So I guess some of that fightin' spirit did come down through the line. [laughs]

I came to Memphis to go to high school. I went to Douglass. My grandmother lived out in the suburb called Hollywood, I don't know how it got its name. I went to school during the day and worked at night. I operated an elevator at the Claridge Hotel, from five in the afternoon until two in the morning, and went to school during the day. I was about fourteen, I wasn't really old enough to work, but they didn't ask for proof of how old you were. This was long about '42, '43. Now you have automatic elevators, you push the floor you want. Then, they told you what floor they wanted, so you pulled the handle and the elevator would go.

It was a whites-only hotel. You didn't participate with the other workers. The blacks had their little nook, where you had your breaks, the whites had theirs. There were white jobs and black jobs. Operatin' the elevator was just about the highest black job. Anything else above operatin' the elevator was white jobs. Of course, the cleaning, and that kind of stuff, that was black jobs. White jobs were desk jobs, bringin' food to people in their rooms. Washin' dishes would be a black job. There was no union there at that time. I don't think there ever was one, that I'm aware.

After comin' out of school I did a little travelin' here and there. I went to Chicago, Gary, Indiana, up in Missouri, seeing things. It was a group of us. We would do seasonal work. Maybe we'd pick cotton in Missouri, then go pick beans somewhere else. That kind of travelin'. In Chicago and Gary we had some relatives so we bummed on our relatives for a while. As for livin', I didn't like either place, so we migrated back down South. I guess we were just restless, tryin' to see what's goin' on somewhere else. In movin' around I decided that Memphis would be where I would want to make my home.

I've been told that I've never been a child. From the time I left home, coming to school, I have been feeling independent. [But] it was better that we come to Memphis because my oldest sister was married and living here in Memphis, and my grandmother and aunts and uncles were all here. So this would be the natural place to come. They all came from the farms. [But] if you go from Mississippi to Memphis, it wasn't gettin' away from the Jim Crow—it was here! I think they were just lookin' for somethin' better, rather than farmin'.

On trains there were segregated train coaches, coaches where the blacks sat. That happened to be, I believe, right behind the engine. The white coaches, they were all in back. And restrooms, they called it colored then—colored and white. What really bothered me most was restaurants. If they sold you a hamburger, they handed it to you out of the window, out of the back. That irked me. It degraded. This is how you feed dogs. There is a famous restaurant in Missouri now, people goes to it because they throw you the rolls. I'm not ready yet, even today, I'm not ready for that restaurant. I don't want nobody throwin' me my food. I'm not goin' to that restaurant. [laughs] I haven't gotten over them handin' you your food out the back door. It's just degrading. You had to eat it outside, wherever you could sit. That was the common practice.

That was one of the worst things that I felt, I felt it was wrong that there was a division. On the greyhound bus there was the black curtain. When we would come from Holly Springs here, you rode the train, you'd have the black curtain. The black person would always have to sit behind the whites. Even on the city buses, the trolleys, there was a colored line, the colored sit in back, the white sit up front. I knew that was wrong. And the different restrooms, colored restrooms, colored water fountains. And I mean they were *colored* [laughs] because they weren't cleaned. They were *colored*. It was dirty lookin' as well as the name colored, because it had not been kept up as the white's had.

In elementary school we got used books, and I often wondered then why we didn't have new books. I didn't have much contact with whites until I was grown. When we were children we went to the black schools. I don't think people liked it, but people for the most part, I guess, become accustomed—"this is how things are."

Even in the workforce today, people are bein' mistreated, but they feel "somethin' is better than nothin'." I was in negotiations a couple of weeks ago up in Somerville, Tennessee, and this guy said his father always taught him that 10 percent of somethin' was better than 100 percent of nothin'. I told him, "Well, your father misled you. Because I'd rather have 100 percent of nothin' than 10 percent of hell." Ten percent of hell is worse than 100 percent of nothin' [laughs], and that is what a lot of people are catchin' on their jobs.

I think it was about '52 when I came back to Memphis to live. I worked in the laundry at the Chisca Hotel for a while, left there. It was segregated then. Blacks was in the laundry doin' the black jobs. Then I went to work for a cleaners. It was segregated there as well. It was called Hurlbert's Laundry. It was a lot of people worked there. But they were all black in the laundry, doin' the laundry work. The seamstress was white, and of course the supervisors was white, and the clerks was white. But the blacks did the pressing, the folding of the linens, and all that kind of work. It was hot.

I applied for a job at the Blue Goose, they made men's work clothes. That was its trade name, the Blue Goose, because the Blue Goose would always be on the pocket. So I applied for a job there, back in the '50s. I was told that they only hired blacks to press and to clean floors. There were not a black person that operated a sewing machine. At that time I didn't get hired because I told 'em I didn't press and the floor in my house was the only floor that I mopped. [laughs] So I did not work at that place at that time. I guess the Ida Wells [in me] had started comin' out in those days.

I then went to work at a cleaners. I guess there were about maybe fifteen, twenty people worked there. And of course, the blacks was doin' certain jobs. I was hired as a bagger, to put the bags over the clothes once they were pressed and all. I was talkin' one day to a couple of the ladies. The boss, who naturally was white, told me, "You can't talk while you work." I told him that as long as I had a mouth I could talk. I wasn't talkin' with my hands, I was workin' with my hands. So he told me, "Well I'm not goin' to warn you again. I'm payin' you to work, not to talk." I kept on workin'. The next day or so there were two other women that were talkin' and he came in and started railin' on these women. I can't stand to see other people bein' abused. And I took it up. Of course, I got fired. [laughs] I said, "These are women. You don't have to talk to them like that." He said, "This is my place. If they don't like the way I talk to them, there's the door. Matter of fact, you go out of it."

Just like I came in it, I'm out of it. I've never been able to endure another person being abused. I guess that's that Ida Wells spirit. You talk to me as a person and we'll get along fine. I think that's why I enjoy the work I do. I can talk for people when they can't talk for themselves.

When I was a little girl, I guess eight or nine, we could go to the movies on Saturday evenings, when we would go to town. I would see these John L. Lewis[6] movies [newsreels]. Then I knew I was on his side when he was takin' up the other people's problems. I don't know if the spirit has always been there or seein' the movies helped bring it out, but I've always looked out for other people. Because I can take care of myself. I often used to say I was afraid of two things: a little worm and a big-mouthed dog. Until one day I said, now, why am I afraid of a little worm? All I've got to do is [mash] this little worm. And this big mouthed dog? I would cut his throat. So now I'm not afraid of the worm nor the dog. [laughs] The man hasn't been born yet that can intimidate me. I guess the spirit just has always been there. Everybody don't have it.

Sitting here in this room, back in, I guess '83, I was negotiating a contract with the Nylon Net Company. They made fishing nets and things. They had an attorney from Louisiana. We set here and he started starin' at me, and we stared at each other for over an hour, neither one of us sayin' a word, the committee sittin' around the table, just starin' at each other. And I said to myself, "I'll die and go to hell before I'll be the first to look off." After over an hour he looked down, and we started negotiatin'. I just can't be intimidated. Once you're intimidated, the person has control over you. They can manipulate you, use you, any kind of way they want. I control me. Nobody else. We got a contract, too.

I don't have too much of a black and white thing. People are people. In any race there's some that don't have what it takes to speak for themselves. Somebody has to speak for them. I'm like Martin Luther King: "If not me, who? If not now, when?"

I got married in '54 and for a long time I didn't work in a public place, I was a housewife. I went back into the workforce in '64, I believe. I was out of the workforce for about ten years. Then the civil rights actions and all had started and companies then had to start hirin' blacks. Believe it or not, I went back to the Blue Goose. They were advertisin' for experienced

6. John L. Lewis was president of the CIO and the United Mine Workers in the 1930s and was the most powerful labor leader of his day.

seamstresses, and I was an experienced seamstress, but not in the factory. I knew how to sew, I did sewin' at home.

There were four or five of us in this waiting room. When the guy came out to interview the applicants, I was the only black there, so naturally, he went to the whites first. Sometimes bein' last is not bad, because he was askin' them what jobs were they seeking, what operations were they experienced in. This was a garment factory, makin' men's work pants and work shirts. So they were sayin', "I know how to set collars," or "I side seam," "I hem." So me, I'm sayin' to myself, "I've never worked in a factory. What am I goin' to say?"

Bein' the last, I knew what he was lookin' for. So I said to myself, "What can I say that I can do?" And I'm lookin' at him, and a spirit says, "A shirt has pockets on it." So when he came to me, he says, "What can you do?" I said, "I put pockets on." I didn't know the proper term for it, to *set* pockets. I said, "I put pockets on, like that shirt you're wearin'." He said, "That's exactly what we need." So I was hired that day. But I knew I had to do better than the whites. So I set out to do better. And I set pockets on shirts from '64 to '69 at the Blue Goose.

When the Blue Goose ceased its manufacturin' and just started warehousin' [in 1969], the supervisors and managers set up a factory of their own that carried on the same work. I had become talkative with the managers, and they asked me to come to their plant. This plant was named United Uniform. Believe it or not there was an organizin' campaign goin' on when I went to United Uniform in 1969, it was the [United] Furniture Workers, Local 282. That was September of '69, the campaign had the election around October or November of '69.

They lost that campaign, [and] a lot of the black quit. There were about ninety workers, at that time it was about 70 percent white and 30 percent black. The company did a pretty good job of puttin' on an anti-union campaign. They just fooled the workers. Whites didn't—most of them even now—feel they necessarily need a union. They have privileges, so they don't necessarily have to have a union. If they're late gettin' to work, it's okay. If they have a telephone call, they'll answer the phone. If they have to leave, it's all right. With blacks, if you're late, you get disciplined. You just didn't have that kind of privilege.

The pay were different between whites and blacks. It could be quite a bit different. The black wage were, like about a $1.60, $1.65. Minimum wage started about then, $1.65 an hour. We weren't doin' incentive work, we were working by the hour. Some of the whites were making, like, $2.00 an hour. For the same jobs. The majority of the workforce was operatin' sewing machines. There would be a pay difference even though they were operatin' the same machines. There weren't nothin' to do about it, nothin' to prevent disparity in pay. United Uniform was non-union.

I think Willie Rudd was elected president of the local in '75. He set out to organize.[7] So we started an organizin' campaign at United Uniform. The company did move to a new building, hired new people. Working conditions was pretty fair, I could get along there. That could have been because people have a tendency to respect those who demand respect. And that I did. And I got respect. But some didn't.

I worked in the church quite a bit. We were getting ready to go to what was known as the Sunday School and Training Union Conference, in San Francisco. I told my supervisor that I wanted a leave of absence. It was for a week in June. Later on she told me they weren't givin' any leave of absence. I said, "Well, I'm sorry, but when that plane leaves on Friday evening, I'm goin' to be on it, with or without a leave of absence." OK, Friday, sure enough, at seven o'clock when that plane left here, I was on it. On Wednesday, they called my home and left a message to tell me that I was suspended. OK, fine. They suspended me for a week. When I went back to work I find out then there were some Greek women that were working there, they had given them a month leave to go to Greece. Then I marches down to the Equal Employment Opportunity Commission's office. So I filed a [EEOC] charge against the company for discrimination.

In the meantime, the union campaign got started. Of course, I got accused of startin' the campaign because I had filed the charges, but I wasn't the one that started it. But shortly after learnin' of it, most certainly I helped carry it. At this time we were a majority black. The local was run by a black. Willie was black, the vice president was black. Back in '69, Carl Scarborough was the president of the local. He was white and the

7. Willie Rudd rose from the ranks as a worker and organizer in the Memphis furniture industry, succeeding Leroy Clark as president of Local 282 in 1975 and as southern vice president of the international in 1975. He is currently president of the Furniture Workers Division of the International Union of Electronic, Electrical, Salaried, Machine, and Furniture Workers (IUE). We tried to meet to do an interview for this book, but never managed to do it.

majority of workers [at United Uniform] was black. The whole makeup now has changed.

The company attempted to play the race card in those captive audiences. It's called captive audience because the workers must come. They're on the clock, they get paid to sit and listen to these anti-union speeches and see anti-union movies. The company says, "Look around. See who is goin' to be leadin' you. Willie Rudd, he's the president, he's goin' to be leadin' you." So my question to management was "What do you mean, look around and see who is goin' to be leadin' you? Who has been leadin' us all these years? What's wrong with him leadin' us? It's about time we're led by somebody else." You know me, I took 'em on in these meetings. That helped strengthen other workers to be supportive of the union.

We had that election around December of '77. Sure enough, come election day, we won by a large majority. So immediately we started organizin' the shop and electin' stewards and things. In my department, I was the first elected as steward. They'd say, "We want Ida because we *know* she's goin' to speak up for us." During the time I had the EEOC charges filed, I knew that management could not say anything to me about filing the charges. I knew this. So I can walk around with my head high because I know you can't say nothin' to me. This really amazed the workers. But I knew—and they [the company] knew I knew—that they couldn't say anything to me about the charges. Therefore, I didn't have anything to be afraid of. So this then made them [workers] want me as their representative because they knew I was gonna speak for them.

I have always been a reader. I read everything I got my hands on. So I knew just from readin' that the '64 civil rights law had been passed and you couldn't be disciplined because you'd filed charges. I just knew that. I'd read it. I read the newspaper every day—literature, pamphlets, anything. During break, and lunch, we'd be sittin' around the lunchroom talkin'. When stuff come up and I knew something about it, they'd start callin' me Miss Einstein. [laughs] I can't help it—I read.

I didn't march [in the civil rights demonstrations] but we did participate in the Black Mondays and other things.[8] My daughter was just ten or eleven at that time, at Hamilton Junior High School, around seventh

8. On Black Mondays in the fall of 1969, students refused to go to school, in support of NAACP demands for black leadership on the school board.

grade. She did get caught up in a situation. Some people came to the school, [and] they ran all the kids out of school, it was sort of like a riot, the kids just ran. That had a frightenin' effect on her. I had a time gettin' her back to school. I didn't agree with that part of it, but the positive part of the civil rights, I most certainly did approve of.

So I was elected steward for that department. Willie Rudd believed that the more people know, the better he can represent them. He started organizin' [union] schools, I think about '78. I've always been a stickler for classes—if there was a class, I'd take it. So I enrolled into the union organizin' class that Willie had put on. The international officers came down and conducted the class: how to organize, how to be a good steward. All of that.

In the early '79, or latter part of '78, the international then were lookin' for a black female to put on an organizin' campaign. It was brought to the class, any female that would take the job? I have not been too much for volunteerin'. And there were other females there, but nobody would accept the job. So I'm the last. Sometimes it's not too bad to be last. So I said, "If nobody else will accept it, I'll take it." I was sent out to the Fort Worh– Dallas area, to organize a factory out there. I worked with a white Hispanic female and a white female and other organizers attemptin' to organize the A-Brant furniture plant. It was made up of all types of people, around five or six hundred—Hispanics, Mexicans, and a few blacks. Therefore they had all different types of organizers. It was a huge place, majority white. They didn't go for it. It never got to an election, didn't get the necessary cards signed.

When that campaign concluded, on January 1 of 1980, I became employed by the local as a representative. In March or April of '80, we went into negotiation with the Memphis Furniture Company. Memphis Furniture was a slavehold, what is known as a sweatshop. When I got involved, this was for a second contract. They did get a first contract, for two years, the second contract was in 1980. The company was bent on not renewin' the agreement [and] they hired a well-known union-bustin' law firm.

I think the company had already decided durin' those first couple of years that when the contract renewal time come up they was gonna bust the union. [They] just attempted to gut the contract, money was not really the main object. The company wanted to take the binding arbitration out of the contract, and the workers would not have any rights. [Binding arbitration] is when an issue comes up that you can't settle—for an instance, if a person is terminated and you believe it to be unjust, if he files a grievance and you couldn't settle it—then the arbitrator would hear the case and then make a final and binding decision. So the company wanted to take away that right. [They] also wanted to take away the dues checkoff.[9]

When a company comes with that kind of proposal to take away the dues checkoff, to take away the binding arbitration, and increase the management rights clause, you know where they comin' from. And also to impose those slavery work rules, work rules that are so demeaning, such as gettin' permission to go to the bathroom and all of that stuff. Those were the issues that were on the table that caused the strike. The first strike was back in 1949 or so. Well, the company won that strike. So they [had] stayed non-union a long time.

To try to keep it lookin' as though it wasn't a racial thing, they went and hired Otis Higgs, a black lawyer [and mayoral candidate]. And, of course, that didn't help the matter because he was only a figurehead at the table, he wasn't the one makin' the decisions. He told us he accepted it in order to gain negotiation experience. At the table he had to get over the company's program which was in opposition of the employees, and so he sort of got caught in the middle, and I don't think that helped his career in the future.[10]

So over the course of the negotiations for the renewal, [we] came to an impasse. And there was a [time to] hit the bricks so to speak. There was about 1,200 workers and the strike started in March or April of '80. I would estimate that maybe 90 percent would have been women, [and] I would say 95 percent black. There were a few white [women] in the plant [and] in the union, a little sewin' they were doin'. [Conditions were] more

9. As Ms. McKinley explained in chapter 3, Memphis Furniture's opposition to dues checkoff had precipitated the 1949 strike. The company had made union security agreements under duress during World War II, but then tried to shed them during the next contract opening. It followed the same pattern again when it made a contract in 1978. Leroy Clark earlier observed how companies would often sign a contract but refuse provisions, such as dues checkoff, that kept the union in their shop.

10. Higgs ran for mayor in 1975, 1979, and 1983, losing each race. Although he presented himself to the white community as a moderate black leader, few whites during that period would vote for a black candidate. His opponents in 1979 claimed he had no negotiating experience, which they felt the mayor needed in order to deal with AFSCME Local 1733, and that had helped defeat him.

like a plantation, you do what you're told and no more. You know, "I'm the father and I knows best, so you don't need nobody else to come talk to you 'cause I'm gonna take care of you." Matter of fact, they even had a sign posted in the plant—"you don't need to have a union to work here." 'Course the labor board made 'em take it down.

I think the history of the family was they were one of the largest slave owners in Mississippi, [named] Leatherman.[11] Well, the majority of the workers, you know, just simply got fed up with this type of situation and that's when we organized. Surely, havin' lived at least two years under a contract, they were not about to go non-union again, so the support of the strike was tremendous.

They attempted to operate durin' the strike, but with I'd say 90 percent of the employees out, they couldn't do it. It's about two, three blocks from my office right now, in midtown. We had a regular schedule of pickets both day and night, on Saturdays and Sundays, and occasionally we would have mass rallies across the street from the plant. They [the company] just simply couldn't operate. And the community support was so great until we had the march for Martin Luther King. Each year we'd have a march, well that march turned into a rally for the Memphis Furniture strike. He was here marchin' for the sanitation workers, you know, and therefore his death is tied to organized labor in Memphis. And not just civil rights, it's labor, because he was marchin' to help get those workers a union. Coretta King came [to speak] during the initial organizin' campaign in 1977.

We had tremendous support from both white and black churches. There were donations comin' in from other local unions and other groups like NAACP and all of the other groups. So everything went well. And the labor board issued a complaint and this then turned into unfair labor practice. And so I guess the company tried to use its tactics that it used before, to burst the union by busing in more scabs.

11. Robert Morrow, a member of what was once one of the largest slave-owning families in west Tennessee, founded Memphis Furniture in 1892. Members of the Leatherman family, which owned thousands of acres of plantaiton lands in Mississippi, joined the company as partners. According to the union, the "plantation mentality" of this company set it on a collision course with its predominantly black workforce. See "The Real Memphis Furniture Story," a booklet issued by the United Furniture Workers of America, n.d., and accessible at Local 282 headquarters in Memphis.

One day we were in negotiations, for some reason I wasn't with him [Willie] that day, and while I was at the office, an idea came to me. And so I picked up the phone and called the plant and I told the receptionist that I wanted to come to work but I was afraid and what should I do? So she said, "Well, you don't have to be afraid, on tomorrow, we're havin' buses over at the fairgrounds, all you have to do is go over, leave your car, get on the bus and ride on to work." And of course immediately I alerted Willie to what was goin' on and he then got into action. I guess two or three hundred of the strikers were over there and they filled that bus and the driver just threw up her hands, called the company and said, "Just come get the bus, I'm not drivin' it." So that took care of that day. [laughs]

So, of course, we kept an eye on the fairground over there. A couple days or so, then the company had a church bus, all the supervisors came and got on it and a couple of the scabs. We had citizen's band radios and walkie-talkies in cars stationed all the way from the fairground to the plant, and so we tracked the bus clean on to the plant. Of course, just before the bus got to the plant, something happened. I don't know what it was, but something happened to the bus. I don't know if it was rainin' bricks that day [laughter], because I'm sure it wasn't the strikers! [more laughter]

Anyway, that bus trip turned into a disaster [for the company]. Of course, a lot of people were arrested that day, no injuries or anything, but there were some arrests. And later on Rudd found out where the company got the bus. It was a church bus and so Rudd talked with the pastor of the church. So the pastor tells Rudd that the bus were parked on a lot someplace and he did not let the company have it. He came on a news conference with Willie, sittin' side by side, and accused the company of stealin' the bus. So that pastor in support of the workers and accusin' the company of stealin' his bus helped a whole lot in the strike settlement.

[We won the strike], yes, yes we did, shortly after that. There were court hearings, some people got fined, but nobody got sent to prison. It was a mean, vicious strike. And it took its toll. We did renew a contract for three years but the company never really fully recovered from that strike because we did boycott, we did leaflets at Sears. And Sears simply do not like to be picketed, so Sears closed their accounts with 'em. And so they just never recovered from that strike. I think 1985, they went ahead and closed. They sold their franchise to another company, they started using the Memphis Furniture name but they haven't gotten anyplace. They'd a done better by using [their old name] Shelby Furniture.

There were about 1,200 people [at Memphis Furniture], and I would say 1,000 of those were dues-payin' members. So it had a tremendous effect on the membership. Some of these people got jobs in other factories, but it had its effect on the union. It brought down the local.

That one strike lasted like ten weeks. That was a big ruckus, there was quite a bits of arrests made, but, you know, no injuries, and that's a blessing. I think a couple of the strikers were shot at, a time or two. They were drivin' through one of the projects, I guess, spyin' on where the scabs lived. And the scabs turned around and shot at them and sort of put the fear of God in them. But, ah, we're thankful they wasn't hit.

[The company got scabs] from wherever. There were a few that came out the housing projects, and some were the regular workers. Now some of the whites supported the strike, but I would say the majority of the whites scabbed. Of course, there were a few blacks that also scabbed. [She points out that it wasn't like what happened in 1949, when busing in strikebreakers really killed the strike.] Now it may have worked, had we not found out about it, then we were able to combat it before it got goin'. And Willie is I guess one of the most effective persons I know in runnin' the strike and boycottin'. Yeah, he's good.

Everybody still remembers it, yeah. And we don't wish to have another one, you know. For that matter, we don't want to have any [strikes] at all. But sometime it's like that. We have to do what we have to do to represent the people. If a company will sit down and negotiate in good faith with this union, there'll never be another strike at all. All we want is a fair and decent contract for workers and the people to be treated with dignity as they deserve. And we can get along with any employer who is willin' to negotiate and deal fairly.

[But] it didn't hinder organizin'. If anything, it helped, because workers knew that [we] are goin' to represent them. And even if there's a possibility that one goes on strike, the union is goin' to be there for them during the strike. So it strengthened, in my opinion, our organizin' efforts. What I see as the hindrance is the labor laws need to be strengthened.

You know, we don't have a hard time in organizin'. But reachin' that first contract is where I see the big problem, and again I say, the laws really need to be strengthened on reachin' a contract. What happens a lot of times is that the company finally will talk some of the workers into de-certification, filin' a petition or something like that, because a union is only certified for a year. So if a company stalls and stalls until after the

certification year is up, then the workers, some will have become discouraged and the employer will have talked some into thinkin' that we can
do better if we vote the union out.

And a lot of times, this is what's happened, that after the year or so, the
company gets a decert.[12] It's the goin' thing, just string the negotiations
along, just comin' to the bargaining table, stallin' around, hopin' that they
can get the union out. And that's really where the labor laws need to be
strengthened.

I see labor and civil rights as intertwined. Because when you got rights
on the job, it encompasses your civil rights, and when your rights on the
job is violated, it also takes [away] your civil rights. The white women
in the workplace, they too have civil rights trampled and even nowadays,
white women catches [hell] pretty good too. I guess it could be termed
human rights. Yes, yes, because white workers have rights, and they have
civil rights.

RELIGION AND UNION SPIRIT

The average woman wouldn't be able to hold down the kind of job that I
have. Sometimes I leave at seven o'clock in the mornin', it might be twelve
at night before I'm back at home again. I guess for some women it would be
impossible. I just had the one daughter (now I have two grandchildren and
one great-grandchild). For about ten years I did not work away from home,
then I went back into the labor market. I was married—still is married.
But we had an understanding that we were not Siamese [twins]. [laughs] I
have a job to do, this is what I chose to do. My family supported me.

So when I had to travel, I had no problems. However long it takes me
to do an assignment, I was away. For some people it would be too demanding, depending on what kind of relationship they had at home. Some
wives don't hardly go to the grocery store. But I had the kind of relationship where I could go when I pleased and come when I was ready—and
still do. My husband, Fred, is retired now. He was employed with Standard
Parts, a warehouse, they shipped and distributed. They were unorganized,
but he supports unions. [They tried to organize but failed.] Of course you

12. Between 1970 and 1984, the UFWA international lost 1,554 members through
sixteen decertification elections at the local level. Figures on the period since then
may be worse.

couldn't live in my house unless you were pro-union. [laughs]. We got married in '53.

I have always been my own person. He has been able to go and do whatever he wants to do, and me likewise. Sometimes I'm gone for days at a time, or a week. I love it. You have to love it. Otherwise, you'd get burned out because it's very demanding, very stressful. You're out of one situation into another, every day. You get this problem settled and another one has cropped up already. It's constantly problem solving. Constantly. I enjoy it because the end result is, when I get a problem solved, I have helped somebody. That's my only goal in life is to help. If it's just one somebody, then I would have accomplished something. So when I can go into a plant and get a worker his job or her job back, it's very rewarding.

I wouldn't really be able to do the things I do without havin' the inner spirit. Without it, you're not goin' to be able to accomplish any goal because you've got to have direction, guidance, in order to carry out whatever goal you attempt to do. Only the spirit of the Lord can guide and direct and even protect you in your mission, whatever your mission is. I was involved in church activities even before I went on staff. I directed the choir at the Progressive Baptist Church and taught Sunday school.

I rely on the Lord directin' and guidin' me, even givin' me what to say. I can be at the negotiatin' table and a situation arises and I depend on the Lord to give me what to say, and it comes. You're thinkin', "How am I goin' to do this?" Within, you can hear a small voice say, "Try such and such a thing." And you try it, and it works. But it's somethin' within. If you follow that direction, it'll work. It'll work.

I was drivin' down the street, gettin' close to my home. I heard a voice say, "Watch for a car runnin' the red light." I'm drivin', and when I got to the cross street, then I looked to my right, 'cause I had the green light and the car was stoppin'. But because I had heard the voice, I then looked to my left—and the car was bearin' down on me. It made me step on the gas and get out from under there just as he went past. Whereas if the Lord had not spoken and said, "Watch for a car runnin' the light," I would not have been payin' any attention and I would have been hit bad. That's just one instance. That's the protection kind. [In a mass meeting], whatever words that you need to say, comes. "What made me think of that? I hadn't even thought of seein' it that way."

As far as the fear, I don't have that kind of fear. Willie [Rudd] and I went down to Coldwater, Mississippi, oh, thirty miles south of Memphis, to pass out leaflets at one of the shops that had run away from Memphis. As we were passin' out the leaflets the owner came. He drove up in his red Porsche, he jumped out: "I want you off of this highway. I want you off of here. That's the reason I moved from Memphis. I didn't own the streets of Memphis, but I own this. I want you off of here. I'm gonna call the sheriff." Then he says, "No, I don't have to call the sheriff." He reached over in his glove compartment and pulled out a pistol. And says, "When the sheriff gets here, he will find two dead niggers." He done got out of the car now and come around to where we were, and I said to him, "You're gonna have to shoot." I looked him dead in his eye. He accused me of havin' a knife. [laughs] But what is a knife against a gun? "You're gonna have to shoot." He says, "Y'all just crazy. You're just crazy." He got back in his car and left. His gun didn't frighten me. I'm not afraid of death. Because I know death is just another step that you take from this life to another. I'm not gonna go out and walk in front of no car. [laughs] But as far as doin' what I have to do, I'll do it. So I'm not afraid of death.

[That feeling came to me after] I was in an accident that was very serious. This was about 1983. I was comin' from Washington, D.C. A girlfriend and I had driven up there for a women's conference. I had driven from Washington, D.C. to Knoxville, she was goin' to drive along to Nashville. I dozed off and this voice said to me, "Stay awake with Sadie." I said, "No, she's all right." And I went back to sleep. When I woke up again we was bangin' up against the bridges. She had went to sleep and hit the bridge abutment, went across the road and hit the other side of the bridge, and back on this side and hit this bridge again. When I woke up I said, "Oh Lord, you have got to save us." Instantly the car rolled up to the edge of the road and stopped. There was a ravine—you couldn't even see the bottom down there. If it had gone over there, we'd have never got out.

From there I knew that there was another door openin' up for me, that there were no need for fear.

Sadie got a broken hand. I got hurt. The left foot was almost torn off. They had to put a bone in the knee, it was broken. I had a broken vertebrae, broken collarbone. Almost done me in. In fact, the doctor was afraid I wouldn't be able to walk. But he were able to save the left foot. It was almost torn off. He was able to patch them bones back together. I can walk almost as good as at first. This was in Lebanon, Tennessee. I stayed in the Humana Hospital there from about the twenty-seventh of March until June. I had to lay flat on my back for two solid months, either that, or a body cast. I told the doctor I could lay flat on my back, and I did, without a body cast.

During [union] meetings we talk about what goes on with our churches. And we always open our meeting with a prayer. We never have a meeting without a prayer first. The stewards, they are more religious [than the average worker]. They understand responsibility better and are able to carry out instructions better. We have a choir within our union. Sometime our choir would come and do songs at our meetings. So everybody knows that God is leadin' this local, there's no doubt about it.

Even sometimes when we go to negotiations we will have a prayer with the committee prior to goin' in to meet management. Because I know that the Lord changes the hearts and minds of men. Inasmuch as He can change directions of the river, what is it to change the hearts and minds of men? We had a strike about four years ago at the Imperial Manufacturing Company in Walls, Mississippi. The strike lasted about six weeks. And we were in negotiations right here in this room. And the owner of the company, after we had settled the contract, he said, "I don't know what it was that happened to me, for I swore within myself that I would never settle a contract, but I did. I had no intentions of settlin' a contract." I said, "I know what happened. I know what happened."

ORGANIZING IN THE GLOBAL ECONOMY

[Today] it is difficult with the jobs leavin' and the plants closin'. There are any number of young men that don't have jobs. I think what has really affected the young black men, and I suppose whites too, is the drugs. I don't know how it's gonna end or what's gonna happen before the end with the drugs. Because, where a young man may be able to see where workin' for $4.25 an hour, and he can make $1,000 an hour sellin' drugs, unless he is sure-enough rooted and grounded, he's gonna take the drugs because it's easy money rather than working for $4.25 and not bein' able to really buy the things the youngsters is buyin', such as Air Jordan shoes. They sell for $175. Where can a young man buy those shoes makin' even $5.00 an hour?

But to sell some drugs in a day they can buy two, three pair. These same Air Jordans are made in China for $3.55 cents an hour and they bring 'em back to America and sell them for $175, $200 a pair.

So the thing with the young men and some of the older people is the drugs. The bad thing about the drugs is, it ruins a person for life, because it affects the brain and the brain don't renew itself. Once the brain has been damaged, it's gone. It's really heartbreakin' to drive down the street and see young people, women and men, some preachin' to the telephone poles, that kind of stuff. My problem is they didn't bring it over here. Somebody way up is bringin' the dope in and leavin' our young people—both black and white—the sense of bein' used to further some high-up business. That is what is ruinin' this country. I don't think there is a place in America where you're free to walk the streets, like it used to be. The dope selling is all over. If you're makin' a livin' at sellin' it, you'll sell it to anybody. That's what's killin' America, is the dope. I don't know how it's gonna end.

What I tell them, it's corporate greed, movin' the jobs out of the country. Like I say, in Mexico, the workers are only bein' paid three dollars and somethin' a day and they can bring the product back here and sell it for four, five times the cost. That's corporate greed. Not payin' the workers in America, because of downsizin', gettin' the same amount of production out with ten people as they did with twenty, and payin' 'em less. It's greed.

The National Labor Relations Act, it doesn't have any teeth in it. What will happen when the company violates the law and is caught in it, they get a slap on a wrist, post a notice, say I won't do it no more. It takes anywhere up to six or seven years to get a contempt on a company and get it enforced, if it's enforced at all.

Even the salaries the workers make now, they don't earn as much now as they did ten years ago. The corporations don't care nothin' about violatin' the workers' rights, even their civil rights. Now companies discriminate against the workers, for whatever reason, age, race. The workers got to prove it, and unless the company is stark ravin' fools, they don't say, "I'm firin' you because you're black. I'm firin' you because you're old. I'm not goin' to hire you because you support the union." No, they have these slick lawyers who try to make a way for them.

So, it's happenin' more and more, and the workers are the ones have to prove that the company did this to them. And sometimes it's almost impossible for a worker to prove it. You know it, but provin' it is a different thing. Now, with the situation as it is in Washington with the budget, we have cases down at the labor board [NLRB] that was filed back in December of '95, that decisions have not been made on 'em yet, because they're so far behind.[13] The agencies cannot go out of town to take affidavits, they have to take phone affidavits. That's the situation down in Winona, Mississippi. The board agent can't go down there to take an affidavit. And this company knows it, so they fire workers. A worker's been fired, the worker files for unemployment, the company fights that, the state upholds that. The worker's just fed up.

[What I see among workers] is fear of losing the job they got. They're makin', some, up to $5.00 [an hour], maybe, $5.20 is good. They say, "I can't lose this job. If I talk union, support the union, I'm gonna be fired. So and so was fired, she was pro-union, and she's fired. I'm just not gonna stick my neck out." [Fear,] it's there.

In Winona at the Richardson Brothers furniture plant, I had an election there, February fifth of this year. The company hired a new plant manager in September of '95, his name is Charlie. I call him Mister Charlie.[14] It's majority black. Right now he has those workers in the same situation that it used to be on the plantation durin' slavery times, the "house" and the "field."[15] The house persons, Mister Charlie has them thinkin' they're worth more than the ones that work in the field. Some of the employees in that plant, the ones you would call the house persons has permission to go into the office, drink coffee during work hours, use the company's truck to go get lunch, just about a free hand. But in order to do this, they must tell him what the others are doin'. In the industry they call it snitchin'. That keeps him informed of everything that the other employees are doin'.

I've never seen the type of fear that those workers have. I've not seen it. They were afraid to go in there and vote yes because Mister Charlie sent word that he knows everybody who'd signed a card [supporting unionization] and everybody that signed a card and voted yes, he's gonna get rid of. You'd think people'd know better. And he said, if you vote the union in, you're gonna have to start paying twenty-five dollars a week and we'll have

13. This interview was in April 1996.

14. "Mister Charlie" is an unflattering name blacks used to denote a segregationist white man.

15. Malcolm X used the allegory of "the house and the field nigger" to make a similar point about the causes of black disunity.

to start takin' that twenty-five dollars a week out of your check. "I can't afford to have twenty-five dollars a week taken out of my check," [so] they went in and voted no. Well, I can't [afford that] either. The reality would be, until they negotiate an agreement, no dues would be paid. Only after you get a contract ratified would those that signed an authorization to have union dues taken out, have it be taken out. And that would only be once a month, twenty-five dollars a month.

You would think in this day and time people would know better. [We talk about] gettin' the people to stand up for their rights, the right to organize. Doesn't do any good to have it if you don't exercise it. You have a federally guaranteed right to organize a union. You don't have to be afraid. It's illegal for companies to fire you simply because you support a union, but it's hard to overcome that fear. The right is there.

I think if people as a whole would stand up for those rights, then it would be more effective. As the sanitation workers did. One worker standin' up for his rights would not have impacted the situation at all. But as a group, then you can accomplish somethin'. Defend your rights. 'Cause one worker don't have a chance standin' against management. One lady that was leadin' the campaign, when they fired her, then, she was out there by herself. But if all the workers had stood up for their right to have representation on the job, he wasn't gonna fire the whole plant. They wouldn't have to be afraid. And she wouldn't have been fired either. [But they] knock 'em off one at a time. . . .

The Somerville Mills workers is a good example. Our union is the only industrial union in Fayette County, [Tennessee], where the stronghold of slaves were.[16] We represented three plants there—Somerville Mills that made ladies' underwear, Victoria's Secret, and Fredericks of Hollywood. Another one is Master Apparel that makes men's and boys' pants [and] an automotive place that makes car seats and automotive accessories. They're all sewing. In each case there has been an attempt to decertify [remove the

16. Slavery had been very strong in Fayette County, west Tennessee, and some of the most bitter civil rights battles occurred there, when employers threw people off the land and forced dozens of families to live in a tent city during the 1960s. Somerville, home of John McFerrin and other leaders of that struggle, remained a hotbed of reaction in the 1990s. See Robert Hamburger, *Our Portion of Hell, Fayette County, Tennessee: An Oral History of the Struggle for Civil Rights* (New York: Links Books, 1973).

union]. In each one of them, it has been the white workers who the company got to pass the petition. So far, we have been able to get all of those attempts thrown out because the courts have found them to be tainted, because management circulated the petition.

For six years we negotiated at Somerville Mills, in Somerville, Tennessee, for the first contract. In November '94, early '95, employees were told that if they didn't get the union out, the mill was goin' to close. They got the white workers to pass the [decertification] petition, along with the supervisors. Naturally the [National Labor Relations] Board threw that petition out. The workers stood up together and the company could not defeat them. So November of '95 we were sent notice that as of January thirtieth, now the company's movin' to Mexico. Still, the workers are proud. The woman who led that battle was named Moranda Wickerson. She's one of the stronger women I've met in the labor movement.

[Leachman explains that under a federal retraining act these workers could go to school or retrain in another occupation, but the governor and state unemployment officials instead sent them to work for another apparel company and threatened to cut off their unemployment compensation if they refused to go, thus saving companies from paying unemployment benefits.] They got the fear of God in some. Fayette County, the powers that be is still tryin' to control the lives of the workers. And the workers that's there, the company keeps their earnin's down around five dollars simply by limitin' the amount of work [or] changin' them to different machines. People are bein' beat into submission, without hope. Like the guy said, "Ten percent of somethin' is better than 100 percent of nothin'." But it's not true.

I find that the poor whites are pretty much in the same boat with the blacks. [But] the whites are treated a little better, not a whole lot, just a little better, to keep the belief that "we're better than they." Say, for instance, in the mattress factory, the contract would spell out what each piece would pay: if you sew this, you get this amount for that. There's always what they call "good work," that was easy work, some pieces that you can make money on. Then the person that's passin' out the work could give all the easy-money pieces to some [white] person. And the other ones [blacks] get the hard work and could not make it. [She also gives the example of a Somerville company that convinced a white woman shop steward to quit the union by giving her a new job.] Somehow, she resigned from the union and passed a petition to decertify the union. As a result of that, she is no longer moved from her machine, therefore she is making much more now than the others. So, even though there is a rate that applies to all operations, there's always a maneuver that can be done.

At Howard Sipes, they make baseball uniforms, right here in Memphis. And the whites and blacks are workin' together [with a majority-black workforce], and the whites are bein' paid more than the blacks for the same jobs. For a year they had a union, [but] the certification only lasts a year. After that year was up, it was a majority of whites had come in, and they got a petition to decertify. Management tells them, "You don't need the union, all they want is your money. I'm here for you. Look what you're makin' now." Our Local 282 is known as the "black union" because both Willie and myself are black, and the majority of our members are black. Of course, there is always a few whites who will support the union because they are union-minded and some [who] will not.

In organizin', [race is] not a big issue. But the attempt to hire whites and decert is always present. It's still goin' on. Every time. Every time. Race is always there, always. It doesn't come out openly as it maybe used to, but it's always there.

George Holloway and Clarence Coe Reflect on the Importance of Unions and the Struggle against Racism

Unlike Ida Leachman, most of the black union veterans in this book had retired by the time of these interviews. Although conditions had changed dramatically since George Holloway and Clarence Coe began organizing in the 1930s, they felt the history they experienced contained lessons that needed to be passed on to younger generations.

GEORGE HOLLOWAY

Today people seem to think that a company is just going to give them things out of kindness. But the company isn't going to give any worker a thing if you don't have a way of obtaining it. We should learn in this country that if a company is making a billion dollars in profits, it should be shared with the workers. Why shouldn't I be able to have a decent home for my family? There has to be unity and strength through a union to get a company to share in the profits that the workers are helping to make.

I read in the paper about some guys who stole maybe six to ten million dollars, and they're still out on parole. But here's a guy who stole a loaf of bread to help himself, and he's been in jail for five years. It seems to be all about money, if you've got money you're OK, but if you don't you go to jail.

When I was young, I wanted to have a nice house for my family, and I wanted to educate my son. So I got into the labor movement. And now, companies like McDonald's don't even pay minimum wage because they say kids have to be trained how to wipe tables! But people just don't see how crazy this is.

I wish all people would truly want to join a union. So many people are opposed to unions, but they don't read enough to know what's really going on. They didn't understand the great help and benefits that a union could do for them. All newspapers in Memphis was against unions, [just like] a problem today is the monopoly of the newspapers by the Republican Party. Most people don't know that they can't do what a union can do.

When I started out in the United Rubber Workers, I read the [union's] constitution and what rights I had. I read some of the rubber workers' contracts, and I saw how they obtained some of these things. People don't understand why a union is needed for grievance procedures. This gives you a right to go to the union to check out a problem when one arises. You must elect leaders in the union who believe in fair play and justice for all workers. So many don't go to union meetings, and leaders get away with things. I didn't do that, I went to every meeting and learned as I went along. I always tried to be fair.

I don't get too discouraged, I always have hope. I never was afraid to vote, even when I had to pay poll taxes. These days, people think they are being independent by not voting! You need to get registered to vote and change conditions that are unfair to workers, like no [health] insurance or benefits. Canadians can manage national health care, why can't we?

Walter Reuther and other labor leaders were the ones who demanded that cost-of-living increases be added to social security checks. The labor movement caused the minimum wage to go up, demanded that there be public schools for the workers. At [one] time, only rich folk's children went to schools. The United Auto Workers and two other labor unions were the ones that contributed the money and the people to make the 1963 civil rights march in Washington, D.C., a success. Most people don't know these things.

UAW has made our family appreciate organized labor unions and made us a happy family. It made us registered voters and helped us obtain a fair day's pay for a fair day's work. Helped us to obtain vacations, holidays, health insurance, and pensions, all paid for by the company. UAW helped us to buy the things we need and a home and helped us to be a loving family for almost fifty years.

The greatest achievements of all was to earn enough money to send our son to college.[17] [Now] my granddaughter has graduated from nursing school, and she's working on her master's degree now. She works in the Children's Hospital in Washington. When she started there, they offered her a union card, and she signed up right away. She said, "My grandaddy's a UAW staff member, and I'm joining now." She wouldn't wait the thirty days they told her she was supposed to. She learned that from her family.

Sometimes you get kicked around when you're trying to help people, regardless of who they might be. People may or may not like you for what you're doing. [But] I'm a living example of UAW justice. I learned about kindness and fairness in the labor movement. I learned about truthfulness and justice in contracts. I have my UAW flag, and I saved it to be put on my casket, just like Walter [Reuther]'s was. I told my wife I just wanted them to sing "Solidarity" when I go. Some people say not to talk about your death, but I figure you're going to go anyway, you might as well make the arrangements!

King said we need economic fairness and justice. If you make a million, pay the people so they can live happy and buy decent shoes and homes and things of that nature. The rich man is getting richer, the government keeps sending all of this money to the contras in Nicaragua, and to Poland,[18] but the people here have nothing. There aren't even jobs for people.

17. Holloway's son went to University of Michigan for one year and graduated from Lincoln University, an historically black college. He served in Vietnam and later worked in the U.S. transportation department.

18. The Reagan administration carried out a long campaign of covert armed support for the counterrevolutionary "contras" against the leftist Sandinista regime in Nicaragua, despite the fact that Congress had prohibited such action, and backed anti-Communist movements in Poland and elsewhere. He nearly tripled the U.S. military budget, while massively cutting social welfare programs during an era of corporate downsizing and economic dislocation for workers.

These are the things I wish I could correct. I told Walter that I would give my life if every kid when he was seventeen would be guaranteed a job when he reached nineteen. That's what I wish would happen.

CLARENCE COE

Every time I can talk to a group of [young people, I tell them] the things that are important. Some of these jobs now will give you a decent wage, but if you're temporary, you're not accumulating any benefits. Now that all of these industrial jobs have been shut down, there's nothing else to go to. There's nothing else.

And it doesn't make too much difference in the white community. I notice that a lot of the white boys that left the plant, they took a little training in medical work, in plumbing, construction, whatever, on to something else. They never lost much. The guy that come around and put up your storms [windows] is making two hundred dollars a day, but he's white. There's no job in there for a black. These small places maybe only have work for twelve or fifteen people, so they don't even need a black floor sweeper, you know what I mean?

I'd like to explain it like this. Millions, billions, billions of dollars have gone from over here to over there, from the black community to the white. See, I mean the black community has just been drained. That's right. From the black community to the white. And it's still like that. I mean, we had a guy come in here from the Democratic caucus up to Nashville, he was the area political education officer. And he had facts and figures, where X number of billions has just moved from one side of the picture to the other.

How does that money get transferred out? Well, with the business world as it exists now in Memphis, with no labor union you can control wages. You don't have any bargaining power anymore on most of these jobs. Some of our major truck lines have closed, those were good jobs for blacks. Firestone left, Harvester left, and some that I can't even think about right now, but most of your strong jobs where the ordinary man could make a decent living are gone. High-tech jobs, guys with certain training can still make a good living. But not your ordinary people—the backbone of this country are the ordinary people.

We're concerned about the food stamps we provide for the people in the black community that can't get a decent job. Some black woman with two or three kids on minimum wage, I don't consider her on welfare, she's just a victim of circumstance. [But] who supports the lifestyle of the rich? That's where your welfare is. We're workin', we do something. But some of the best schools in the world puts out people who never will have a job, they're not looking for a damn job. Now to me, that's welfare.

And anybody that they want to buy out, to put together six, seven, eight, and up to twenty million dollars to buy out [factories], he's got some of my money in his pocket! See, it's no small group of people, got that money. They have got some of *my* money! For not having been fair with me over a period of years, and with all of the new millionaires being made every year, those people have got some of my money in their pocket. Working a guy for three or four dollars an hour, he's got some of the black community's money in his pocket.

They have gotten us to the place that there's not that many of us concentrated on one job. Except in places like hospitals and things like that, you just don't have the kind of numbers any more. Some of the guys from the plant now working part-time jobs on a temporary basis, they won't hire them on a permanent basis. That way, they don't have any benefits, no insurance, no nothing. And for the most part they've been taken care of in such a way that they're told they don't need a union. They just don't need it.

But what are you going to do about it? If we could just try to tell some of the youngsters that there's strength in organization. There's no way any individual can accomplish very much. You've got to have strength. This younger bunch that's come along, [they] just don't seem to think they need a union. But coming out of the Depression, everybody was in the same boat, and realized it. When you're catching hell together, sometimes you see eye to eye a little better.

When I went to Firestone in '41, [racial] disparity grew in wages and treatment and jobs and so forth, [but] we still held strong until that plant closed. Work was so good, wages was so good. And then the school integration came. That allowed a lot of them [the whites] to run from the inner city to the suburbs. The guy that worked with me, I talked with him daily. He had come out of the navy after about twenty years and he was pretty liberal. But as he progressed, and as he mingled with those guys, I could see the change, and finally he moved to the suburbs.

The day before Reagan took over, I backed him in a corner, and he told me what was on his mind. He was going to get his children off of that damn bus! I was trying to tell him about President Carter needin' a chance. [He said] "Carter went down there and gave away the damn Panama Canal," and I said, "Man when you've been out in the street for a couple of years, this Panama Canal won't seem so significant." [19] And he has been out there in the streets [unemployed]. But it's too late now. They [whites] still don't believe it.

Maybe fifteen years ago you could go down here and catch a Greyhound bus, and ride from here to Biloxi, Mississippi, and couldn't buy a damn sandwich. Everything was closed up to keep from serving us [blacks] on the bus. You just think when they closed out all of the fast-food places you cut off the milkman, you cut off the meat man, everybody in those jobs. And now they talk about we're the poorest state in the union, we can't support our education system. We created that to get *me* [keep me down]!

Prior to that they had been serving you, but you had to go to the back door. But when you had to come in the front they just closed down. When they passed the civil rights law they either had to serve or be sued or fined. Thousands of jobs closed in the South to keep from serving us when that law was passed that you had to do it. And now they're crying about the [poor] economy in the state of Mississippi. They created it!

Their attitude should change. [But] you could ride through Mississippi, and somebody tells you that's where Doctor so and so used to live and his grandson lives down there and so on—hell, it hasn't changed. Don't forget it. That area has not changed. Certain places in Mississippi are just like they were forty years ago.

I told Jim, the guy who works with me, a little tale I tell sometimes. These two guys went coon hunting, and the dog treed a coon, and they couldn't get the light on him to shoot him like you do. You know, you shine that light up there, and get his eyes and shoot him. But old coon would turn his eyes away from you, so one of the guys said, "We know he's up there, Jim. I'm going to take the light and go up there and spot him, and you can shoot him."

So when he got about fifty feet off the ground, as they will do, that coon

19. The canal had been under the control of the United States throughout the twentieth century, but under Jimmy Carter provisions were made to turn it over to the Panamanian government.

tied into him, and he was cutting him to shreds. He was hollerin', "shoot him, shoot him!" The dude on the ground said, "I can't shoot the coon without shootin' you!" And he said, "Well God damn it, shoot both of us!" So I told Jim, I said, "You're doing what you're doing to try to hurt me, but when I get in bad shape, you're going to be in bad shape, too. You're going to want somebody to shoot both of us."

Some of the things we are going through now in the South were created, and we're going to have to live with. And there's going to be a lot more suffering here because you have white folks who still believe they can make it without us, they can make it without an organization.

Hell, we are [the] survivors of the race, or we wouldn't even be here. I never had nobody to make any special effort to help me or anything like that, I've always had to think for myself. But I have given my life to every organizing effort that produced anything. If it has any strength for anything as an organization, I support it.

I won't be around to see it, but it's going to take a long pull. You're going to have to go back to basics, get some of these young whites and young blacks together and start organizing, and the races stand together. Unless you are academically superior to handle the high-tech jobs, you might as well organize some union and try to get some organization or strength and get the wages.

I would think that someone could kind of revive the union spirit. It seems that the powers that be now don't ever push you quite far enough to make you take action in that area. They keep you thinking you're going to make it, and they're constantly drowning you. [In my day], we were pushed into it, we just had to do something. But today they haven't quite reached that area yet. But as it has always been, I think when people are badly enough oppressed, they'll find a way and do it. And organizing labor is the only way. It's the only way you can do it.

The workers who tell their stories here offer a unique personal perspective on what was debated in the 1980s as the urban "underclass" crisis. They insist that the cause of inner-city crisis was linked to a decline in responsible, viable employment for members of their communities, not simply to a decline in "family values" or a self-reinforcing culture of poverty. From their perspective on the ground, it was the loss of well-paying (which usually meant unionized) factory jobs that became a prime factor disorganizing black families in American inner cities. The workers in this volume who lived in or near the old industrial section in north Memphis, where once stable and respectable neighborhoods lie almost in ruins following the closure of Firestone and other factories, could easily witness this reality.

Lieutenant Jerry Miller was raised in the north side of Memphis, and remembers how it was:

I remember when I was a kid, I graduated from Manassas [High School], you could walk all through here. The whistles would blow at Firestone every time the shift would change, and everyone would wake up in the north end. This was one of the most vital areas in Memphis. Homes was beautiful. Most of the black guys in this area worked at Firestone. Beautiful homes and cars. When you said you was Firestone, hey, you was a man! Black, white, I don't care who you was. You go into a store for credit, man say, "Where do you work?" Firestone. "Oh," he say, "pick out what you want." That was the magic word, Firestone. Or International Harvester, or Humko. All unionized jobs.

However, with the closing of Firestone in 1983, followed closely by International Harvester and various subsidiary shops and other factories, the area became the festering sore described by Hillie Pride, Irene Branch, and others who lived in north Memphis. Drugs, robbery, and violence replaced steady employment. On top of the loss of factories, a major expressway "come through here and cut the area right in half," said Miller. "They didn't ask us nothin' about that. You wake up one morning and a bulldozer's outside. They just cut up everything, and the area died a slow death." People like Miller and Matthew Davis continued working in a north-side community club, using the old United Rubber Workers union hall as a place to organize programs that they hoped would revive the area as the proud home of a stable black working class.

The loss of unionized factory jobs had a particularly shattering effect on the group that had been most advantaged by increased access to industrial jobs since the 1940s: young black males. Black male workers were increasingly left to fend for themselves in an internationalized economy that seemed to no longer need their labor. Husky young men could no longer line up for heavy manual labor, like Matthew Davis could in the

1930s, and expect to improve their lives. By 1993, of the top forty employers in Memphis only five were manufacturers, and these were not very large. Most of the commercial, service, and informational companies and government agencies that dominated the economy needed not strong young men but educated workers. Clerical, sales, and professional positions continued to open up to whites and to black women far more readily than they did to black men. As in many cities, one industry after another packed up and left, while transportation, health, government, and retail jobs took their place. But few of these jobs were unionized, and many black men remained marginalized in those areas of employment at the same time that they lost their grip on manufacturing jobs.

Countless black families were sundered by the loss of union jobs among black male wage earners. "When you said you was Firestone, hey, you was a man!"—but the loss of well-paying jobs destroyed that self-concept and the ability to deliver the goods for many black men. Increasing numbers of black families were headed by single black women, forcing more and more of them into the workplace. Even though more black women were able to escape from being perpetually cast as household workers and cleaners than in the past, most of them still suffered the triple impact of race, gender, and class discrimination. Low wages and economic insecurity remained a defining feature of life for most black men and women in Memphis, even for most of those who made it into the "middle class."

The thinning ranks of unionized black workers was a blow not only to the black community but to the labor movement as well. Robert Tillman, an early CIO organizer, had observed that in the 1930s black workers were the "most loyal supporters of the union movement you could find." Similarly, Billie Willis, Memphis Labor Council director in the 1980s, observed that "most of the places that are organized, it's because of the black workers. After the first contract, whites are first in line to get benefits, but it's usually the blacks that make organizing easier." Black workers indeed had become the backbone for the union movement in Memphis, but America's deindustrialization threatened to snap it. Black workers did obtain many of the new nonindustrial jobs in Memphis, but without organization these continued to pay far lower wages than places like Firestone or International Harvester once had.

The decline of unions and the accompanying scourge of drugs, youth violence, teenage pregnancy, and incarceration in the 1980s and 1990s evoked despair among black labor veterans, who once knew relatively more stable communities. But the destabilizing effects of the economy, Clarence Coe tells us, cannot be confined to the inner cities. In Memphis, 20 percent of the white population, or 75,000 people, moved out of the city in the 1980s (the city had a total population of 610,337 in 1990), fleeing urban taxation, crime, school integration through court-ordered busing, and growing economic crisis. African Americans also left when they could, knowing full well that most of the new jobs were being created in the suburbs. But people leaving, Coe points out, only further eroded the city's tax base and schools, and further removed white and black workers from contact with each other. Evasion of social problems and of labor solidarity could only push the society in a downward spiral, he believed. If workers did not get together to deal with common problems and instead continued to fight each other, like the man struggling with the raccoon in a tree they might be asking someone to "shoot both of us."

If conditions in places like Memphis demonstrate how corporate America dashed black workers' hopes of retaining the gains of unionization, some hoped to pin the blame somewhere else. Coe told me that "some of those people in east Memphis, when they want to take a lick at the union, they'll say that 'higher wages and unionism ruined Firestone.' That's not right! Firestone never bothered with us too much about the wages we made. You had to work for it; you earned it. They didn't get hurt, they just decided they were going to move out of Memphis." Even the workers themselves thought perhaps plant closings occurred because unionized younger workers got soft and would not produce. In reality, according to Coe (and even businesspeople quoted in the newspapers), closings occurred because of companies' decisions not to reinvest in antiquated plants and because of the availability of cheaper labor elsewhere. The wreckage of industrial plants owed much to a global reorganization of capitalism, in which multinational corporations shifted production from the United States to less advantaged countries, where workers lacked the right to organize.

American workers did have some responsibility for this situation, Edward Lindsey notes, in that apathy and division allowed plant closings and union busting, followed by wage and benefit give-backs, to go largely unchallenged. But the combined forces of government and business made such a challenge almost overwhelming. The National Labor Relations Board, the Equal Employment Opportunities Commission, and the perception of other governmental support for labor and civil rights had once given black workers means and encouragement to win employment disputes. But the federal government itself increasingly sabotaged the enforcement mechanisms the laws had set up and understaffed and underfunded both the EEOC and the NLRB so they could not effectively operate. In place of federal enforcement came assertions that equality had largely been attained and avowals of an almost religious belief in the "free market," which undermined all sense of community or government responsibility for workers.

That such workers as those described by Ida Leachman in Mississippi, Memphis, or Somerville, Tennessee, had to call on their own religious convictions to garner the courage merely to support a union signified how far labor relations had regressed by 1996. Indeed, in this region, only a few of the unions oriented toward organizing low-wage workers had survived into the 1990s. These often did so by drawing on the tactics and spirit exemplified in the 1968 labor and community mobilization in Memphis, but in addition they often drew more black women to the forefront of labor organizing. In this sense, a besieged labor movement had turned in a more positive direction. Gone were the days when an international union could insist upon white male leadership. Unions in low-wage industries had to have blacks and women in leadership or fail to attract and mobilize their core constituency. An example of this shift occurred when United Furniture Workers Local 282, now part of an international merged with several other larger unions, struck Memphis Furniture, a "slavehold" of low wages, in 1980. Here black women dominated the workforce and took a leading role in organizing. The spirit of Ida B. Wells came forth in the form of her namesake Ida Leachman, who combined unionism with a philosophy and sensibility of aiding the less fortunate and nurturing families and communities. In the Memphis Furniture strike, led by Willie Rudd, she helped to merge labor, civil rights and "womanist" perspectives that had shaped her all her life and guided her actions in her union, church, family, and the community.

That strike, however, also exemplified the tragic dilemma of workers. They struck Memphis Furniture to stop it from dismantling union and worker protections obtained in a previous contract. The company sought to break worker solidarity by busing strikebreakers into the plant, just as it had in 1949. This time it did not work. But its efforts to defeat the union and the resultant reaction against it in the community damaged the company beyond repair, and the company closed its doors. On an even more sinister note, Leachman recalls how a New York–owned company in Fayette County, Tennessee, always one of the roughest plantation districts in the state, closed up shop and moved to Mexico rather than accept unionization in the U.S. Her testimony also illustrates how white factory workers, within this frightening and constraining atmosphere, often rejected organizing with blacks when given small privileges or advancements by their employers. White "privilege," as well as the so-called global economy, continued to wreck many organizing drives.

The hard terrain for organizing in the 1990s made it difficult indeed for workers to make any gains. Although the incomes and the number of people in the still vulnerable black middle class grew, many still lived in poverty under steadily worsening conditions. In Memphis, one study suggests, the dynamics of global capitalism and a long history of low-wage jobs for blacks created "arguably the poorest black underclass of any large United States city." Testimony in this book shows some of the ways in which history shaped this result. Most African Americans worked harder and suffered more to make less than their white counterparts. If they remain behind most white families in terms of capital accumulation and household wealth, it is not as part of a cycle of dependency, laziness, or cultural deprivation, as some conservatives suggest. Rather, as Clarence Coe deftly explains, millionaires today "have got some of my money in their pockets." Black workers in many ways have been and continue to be robbed of the greatest share of the wealth they produce through the devaluation of their labor. As James Robinson puts it, "People want to work, but they wanna be paid. You can't hold one back. Everybody's gotta profit together."

As new generations struggle with the difficult tasks of organizing in a global and mobile labor market, the older workers who spoke their minds to me worried most about whether the lessons of the past would be lost. Had they not unionized, they felt blacks would have gained even less than they did from the American experience; they insisted that in the context of new conditions, organization becomes even more important. Although the fight for economic justice and equal rights is perennial, what many of the narrators in this book feared most was that working-class and poor people might lose the values of solidarity and self-organization that unions and the civil rights movement had inculcated. All of them urged a renewed recognition of the value of organization. "It's simple. When you got strength, you know, you can accomplish your aim," Leroy Boyd explains. Alzada Clark puts it another way, stating one of the basic lessons of her life: "Together we could accomplish a lot, separately we couldn't accomplish much."

The stories of these black union pioneers illustrate the importance of both individual and collective action, of the need for an ethic of mutual aid as well as self-help, and for government, community, church, and civic responsibility for the plight of poor and working people. But most of all, they call for workers to organize as a force for change. "Most people don't know that they can't do what a union can do," George Holloway notes, and in terms of making change in the lives of working and poor people, says Clarence Coe, "organizing labor is the only way . . . you can do it." In the context of these workers' lives, however, "labor" encompasses not a narrow interest group, as Edward Lindsey reminds us, but the interests of the larger community, including those who work for wages, those who work in the unpaid economy, and those who are unemployed. In a town like Memphis, with more churches than gas stations, organizing labor also requires a spiritual base grounded deeply in an ethic of helping the less fortunate, as Ida Leachman tells us.

While the life stories of these workers focus on unions and the workplace, their broader message is the same one that Martin Luther King brought to striking sanitation workers, that "we can all get more together than we can apart . . . and this is the way we gain power." It is the message of group salvation sung by Ida Leachman's union choir. "I don't feel noways tired," "if I can help somebody," "my living shall not be in vain"— these lyrics to the African American gospel of hope and striving call on people to struggle together for a better life for everyone and for discrimination against no one. Perhaps this larger message makes the story of black workers one that American political and corporate leaders least want to hear. For it suggests that organization and solidarity by working and poor people, in the present as in the past, is the only way they as a group or we as a society can get even a small share of justice.

EPILOGUE

Clarence Coe

It kind of leaves scars, I use that phrase sometimes. Certain things in life just leave scars that you never quite get over. I haven't been to the zoo since 1937. You [African-Americans] had to wait until Thursday to use it. For various affairs, I have rented ballrooms at the Peabody [Hotel], but you just don't feel comfortable. I never go to [Crump] Stadium either, nor to Memphis State, though I've gone all over this country. There's just something about Memphis, I just can't handle it.

All I wanted to do was to live in a free country. I like California because people just leave you alone. Here, back in the '60s, you still had that "white" and "colored." I mean with some people it didn't really make any difference. Some people go along and they have never thought about it. But there's some kids that it just does something to them. I have a certain makeup, and it made a big imprint on me. And I decided some of this has just got to change.

We did it, but it took a toll on your health, on your income. You had some people willing to sacrifice their lives and their well-being. If I had been one of those selfish people that just used my brain for my personal use, I could have gone anywhere even in spite of what was going on. But I was determined to try to liberate some of these black youth who aren't appreciated. Man, it was tough. When I was a little boy, some of those songs, like "America the Beautiful," my little kinky hair would stand up when I heard them. I wanted to be included. But it just wasn't about me then, it just wasn't about me. If not, just leave me alone.

There's something special about this city. You heard about the poor
white man who would stay in the ditch to keep you there, and that's kind
of the story of Memphis. Many of them are still alive, keeping me down.

My last conversation with Clarence Coe brought me up short. I was rushing about town trying to get photographs of people for this book, in a brief
trip to Memphis in which I had too many obligations and not enough
time. I didn't come to do more recording. But he obviously had more
he wanted to tell me. Unlike our first meeting, when he wasn't sure he
wanted to remember, now he definitely wanted to remember. He wanted
me to remember, and he wanted the reader to know. His steady, calm, serious manner enveloped me. I had to listen.

He spoke of his endurance of racism and segregation and told me
about the many scars the past had left on him, about how painful his encounters with white racism had been to him emotionally. These scars kept
him from going to public facilities he remembers from the segregated past
because he didn't want to relive the hateful treatment that he felt was so
undeserved. The scars of memory included the contorted faces of whites,
how "they'd put that cheap dirty snarl on their face" or literally seem to
jump back when they saw a black person in a social situation, or how common it was in his boyhood days to see a white man kick a black man in
the rear for fun. He told me for the first time in detail of how an older
black worker tried to kill him when he upset the old order of things by
trying to organize a union. He had mentioned to me almost as an aside
several years earlier that he got "cut up" during his first attempt at organizing, and I had wondered did he literally mean "cut up," or was he
speaking figuratively? Oh no, he said, he meant literally, and he raised his
shirt. I was shocked to see a jagged scar in the form of an X that covered
nearly his entire abdomen. This scar, like his memories, kept alive the personal insults and attacks that he endured as the result of racism. It had
dogged him all his days.

It made me think: how would it really feel to be a sensitive human
being like Mr. Coe and to live with Jim Crow most of your life? He had
told me a number of times that, when confronted with racism, "I just
couldn't handle it." I had thought he meant that it made him too angry,
and he could not hide his feelings, which for blacks in the Jim Crow South
became the key to survival (if the reader doubts this, read *Black Boy* by

Richard Wright). Mr. Coe may have meant that he "couldn't handle it" in this way. But I now realized he also meant that the barbs of racism, often coming without warning, caused him immense mental and emotional anguish. Racism scarred his psyche. I could see that now, as his pain turned to real grief in front of me, so many years after the events he described.

Our last conversation brought me up sharply against my own very partial grasp on the lives of the people I had talked with. It set me to thinking and wondering, what did I really know of these people's lives? That day both Mr. Coe and Matthew Davis told me about their religious faith and how it kept them going all these years. It reminded me of the black workers I had first read about in the 1930s, who organized in black churches, held prayer meetings, and sang hymns that they turned into union songs. For them, organizing the union was a life and death freedom struggle, one that required outside support. This could be the federal government, or in some cases the intervention might be divine. Most every person I had talked to probably carried a strong religious faith. But only with Ida Leachman, in my final interview for this book, did I start to learn more about how faith in a personal God could sustain people. In fact, she said, the black activists in her union were the most religious people she knew. They put a lot of thought into what they did, they were dedicated, they had a sense of purpose, and they didn't back down. Religious commitment wasn't necessarily characteristic of union activists, but these characteristics were key to success. Indeed, they were the same characteristics that Communist organizers had exemplified with such success in the early union movement. How did people like Mr. Coe sustain themselves? Had I asked enough questions, or the right questions, about people's families, their beliefs, the other aspects of daily life so fundamental to us all?

These last conversations impressed upon me that the people who tell their stories here also had another kind of faith that sustained them. They were quintessentially American, in the sense that all of them had hopes that democracy consisted of more than words on paper. Mr. Coe thrilled to hear "America the Beautiful" until he realized that its message did not apply to him. "All I wanted to do was to live in a free country," he said. Coe, Holloway, and others whose stories are told here used unions and the movement for civil rights to make that dream real.

There is so much more to say and to learn. As Leroy Clark told me, "We have only scratched the surface." In truth, this book can only partially reveal the power and significance of the lives told about within its covers. It is not the "real thing": it is not the picket lines, the church meetings, the songs, the prayers, the mass meetings, the lonely and fearful moments praying by the bedside. These are among the unknowable elements that make up the experiences of African American workers, from the present back to the era of slavery. There is a depth and significance to their struggle that cannot be captured here, or perhaps anywhere on the printed page.

To learn more, one could turn to many other books, a few of which are listed in the References and Notes section of this one. But more than that, one could turn to the human beings amongst whom we live today. One can never forget, many of these workers told me, that the scars of the past are part of a chain of history still affecting people in the present. What about the people of our present, they wanted to know, who are being shouldered off life's road by the rich? What about the mother who works two jobs or has no job while raising a family of children by herself, the father who cannot be a father because he is in jail or strung out by unemployment, or the mother and the father who, though both are employed, can't make ends meet? What about the people today who are trying to organize the unorganized, to feed the hungry, take care of the homeless, and raise their families in the era of disposable workers?

As Clarence Coe tells us, the problem from his perspective is that so many people think they can make it without these people, and so many whites think they can make it without blacks. Mr. Coe's story about the fellow white worker who focused on school busing for desegregation and turning the Panama Canal back to the Panamanians, rather than on the economic questions that Coe felt should have concerned working people in the 1980 presidential election, represents a reality that came to plague the labor movement. I, too, spoke with a white worker in Memphis just prior to the 1984 presidential election. The man had worked at International Harvester for many years. He was about to be laid off, as the last operations of the company closed down. He told me in great detail how the Republicans under the Reagan administration had changed the tax laws, stacked the labor boards, and encouraged the movement of factories overseas. He understood exactly how the Reagan government altered the economy to the disadvantage of workers in order to profit multinational corporations.

Somewhat jokingly, I said, "Well, I guess I know who you are voting for." Without missing a beat, he told me he was voting for President Reagan. Thunderstruck, I asked him why, and he told me the story of an African American family that lived down the road from him. He didn't know the family, but he frequently saw a young African American man, in good physical shape he believed, walking the road there. And that family was on welfare. Reagan, he believed, would change all that, and get rid of "welfare chiselers."

Clarence Coe, with a note of incredulity in his voice, says whites "still don't believe it," that what happens to blacks can happen to them. This white man, about to be unemployed, still could not believe that he, an intelligent, able-bodied worker, might soon be on welfare or that he or anyone else couldn't make it on their own. As factories closed down and the laws shifted the tax burden from corporations and the well-to-do to the middle and working classes, many such workers voted their racial biases over their pocketbook interests. This man put me in mind of Coe's story of the hunter tangled in a tree with a raccoon, who called on his hunting partner to "shoot both of us" to get him out of his fix. Many white Americans remain tangled in just this way with the problem of race, unwilling to join with their supposed adversaries in order to get out of the fix both are in.

Some think they can make it individually without the less fortunate or the disadvantaged. But the larger truth, as Martin Luther King, Jr., told striking sanitation workers in Memphis shortly before he died, is that "either we go up together, or we go down together." I only hope this history, told mostly by the workers themselves, might help others appreciate just what King meant. Perhaps understanding starts with seeing through the eyes of Clarence Coe as he peels back the scars of memory.

REFERENCES AND NOTES

Preface: Black History as Labor History

I have not attempted to list the many rich texts in labor and African American history relevant to this study, but cite here sources directly quoted or drawn on for this book. For more details and sources, see Michael K. Honey, *Southern Labor and Black Civil Rights: Organizing Memphis Workers* (Urbana: University of Illinois Press, 1993). For an overview of larger issues related to black labor discussed in the preface, see Jacqueline Jones, *American Work: Four Centuries of Black and White Labor* (New York: W. W. Norton, 1998). Other overviews include Philip S. Foner, *Organized Labor and the Black Worker, 1619–1981* (New York: International Publishers, 1981), and William H. Harris, *The Harder We Run: Black Workers since the Civil War* (New York: Oxford University Press, 1982). These books and many local studies show how white supremacy dogged the lives of black workers everywhere in the United States. For a thorough review of studies on black workers and racial discrimination, consult Joe William Trotter, Jr., "African-American Workers: New Directions in U.S. Labor Historiography," *Labor History* 35, no. 4 (Fall 1994): 495–523. Trotter's quote on the black proletariat is in his edited volume, *The Great Migration in Historical Perspective: New Dimensions of Race, Class, and Gender* (Bloomington: Indiana University Press, 1991), 151. See also Bruce Nelson's "Class, Race and Democracy in the CIO: The 'New' Labor History Meets the 'Wages of Whiteness,'" in *International Review of Social History* 41 (1996): 351–74.

Introduction: The Power of Remembering

White union organizers and leaders, particularly the leftists purged from the CIO during 1949–50, provided me with a rich source of information on southern organizing and led me to some of the workers in this book. My personal interviews of white workers included Richard Routon, February 18, 1983; Daniel Powell, February 1, 1983; George Clark, October 30, 1984; H. B. Griffin, October 30, 1984; Forrest Dickenson, February 20, 1983; Carl Moore, August 1, 1983, all in Memphis; W. E. Davis and Morton Davis, January 28, 1983, St. Louis; Ed and Bea McCrea, March 6 and October 17, 1983, Nashville; Karl Korstad, May 20, 1981, Greensboro; Lawrence and Mildred McGurty, January 17, 1983, Hometown, Illinois; and Mike Ross, November 6, 1982, Chapel Hill.

Black workers interviewed for this book (all in Memphis unless otherwise noted) include John Handcox, May 16, 1985, Silver Spring, Maryland; Evelyn Bates, May 25, 1989; Leroy Boyd, February 6, 1983, and a subsequent phone interview in July 1992; Irene Branch, May 25, 1989, and May 27, 1989 (phone interview); Alzada Clark, May 24, 1989; Leroy Clark, March 27, 1983; Clarence Coe, May 27 and 28, 1989; Dorothy Crook, April 1, 1998; Matthew Davis, October 30, 1984; Rozelle Fields, October 29, 1984 (phone interview); Willie Hall, October 29, 1984; Edward Lee Harrel, October 30, 1984, and May 26, 1989; Fred Higgins, October 30, 1984; George Holloway, March 23, 1990 (and written memo, undated, and notes on unrecorded phone conversation, June 16, 1990, in author's possession); Hosea Hudson, May 28, 1985, Takoma Park, Maryland; George Isabell, February 7, 1983; George King, May 24, 1989; Ida Leachman, April 9, 1996, and May 10, 1997 (phone interview); Mose Lewis, February 17, 1983 (phone interview); Edward Lindsey, May 27, 1989; William Lucy, April 3, 1993; Rebecca McKinley, March 27, 1983 (phone interview); Frances Owens, February 2, 1983; Hillie and Laura Pride, May 26, 1983; Cleveland Robinson, October 15, 1983 (phone interview); James Robinson April 10, 1996; Taylor Rogers, April 10, 1996; Lonnie Roland, November 1, 1984; Josh Tools, March 3, 1983 (phone interview); and Susie Wade, May 27, 1987. My roundtable interview at the United Rubber Worker's Local 186 retiree's hall with Danny Davis, Edward Harrel, James Mitchell, Robert Matthews, and Johnny Williamson occurred on May 26, 1989. My search for Tom Watkins led to a telephone interview with his friend Bertha Jilks, August 13, 1989, and a personal interview with Napoleon Jilks, August 26, 1989, Portland, Oregon. I reviewed additional interviews of people in Memphis from Behind the Veil: Documenting African American Life in the Jim Crow South Oral History Project, Center for Documentary Studies, Duke University, quotations used by permission. Behind the Veil helped me to fill in and understand more details about black life in this era. Laurie Green graciously provided copies of interviews to the Behind the Veil project from her own research work, and I also deposited copies of my interviews of Leroy Boyd and George Holloway there. I used the following interviews from the project: Leroy Boyd, interviewed by Paul Ortiz, June 19 and 22, 1995; Lanetha Jewel Branch, interviewed by Doris Dixon, June 16, 1995; Willie Pearl Butler, interviewed by Laurie Green, August 19, 1995; John David Cooper, Barbara Lee Cooper, Edgar Allen Hunt, interviewed by Paul Ortiz, June 29 and July 7, 1995; Arizona Marie Fort, interviewed by Doris Dixon, June 19, 1995; Lovie Mae Griffin, interviewed by Laurie Green, August 15, 1995; Willie Harrell, interviewed by Mansiki Stacey Scales,

June 29, 1995; Ortha B. Strong Jones, interviewed by Laurie Green, August 8, 1995; Robert Spencer, interviewed by Stacey Scales, June 20, 1995; and Paul Thompson, interviewed by Paul Ortiz, July 7, 1995.

My discussion of oral history is based on Michael Frisch, *A Shared Authority: Essays on the Craft and Meaning of Oral and Public History* (State University of New York Press, 1990), 5–13, passim; Paul Thompson, *The Voice of the Past: Oral History*, 2d ed. (New York: Oxford University Press, 1988), 11, 22–28, passim; and Steven Caunce, *Oral History and the Local Historian* (London and New York: Longman Publishers, 1994), 116–17, quoted on 22, 28. For a compilation of recent perspectives on oral history, see Robert Perks and Alistair Thomson, *The Oral History Reader* (London and New York: Routledge, 1998). An earlier valuable collection is David K. Dunaway and Willa K. Baum, *Oral History: An Interdisciplinary Anthology* (American Association for State and Local History in cooperation with the Oral History Association, 1984).

We have few first-hand accounts about the black working-class experience during segregation. Among the most striking accounts are Nell Irvin Painter's *The Narrative of Hosea Hudson: His Life as a Negro Communist in the South* (Cambridge: Harvard University Press, 1979); Theodore Rosengarten's *All God's Dangers: The Life of Nate Shaw* (New York: Avon, 1974); and Robert Hamburger's *Our Portion of Hell, Fayette County, Tennessee: An Oral History of the Struggle for Civil Rights* (New York: Links Books, 1973). The "store it in the bones" and "spirit of strength" comments to Robert Coles are quoted in Susan Tucker, *Telling Memories among Southern Women: Domestic Workers and Their Employers in the Segregated South* (Baton Rouge: Louisiana State University Press, 1988), 196 and 4. Elizabeth Clark-Lewis deftly weaves together oral histories in *Living In, Living Out: African American Domestics in Washington, D.C., 1910–1940* (Washington, D.C.: Smithsonian Institution Press, 1994). A powerful presentation and interpretive reading of black labor history and its relation to civil rights is Rick Halpern and Roger Horowitz, *Meatpackers: An Oral History of Black Packinghouse Workers and Their Struggle for Racial and Economic Equality* (New York: Twayne Publishers, 1996). Tom E. Terrill and Jerrold Hirsch, *Such as Us: Southern Voices of the Thirties* (Chapel Hill: University of North Carolina Press, 1978) suggests how much the study of oral history in the South owes to the University of North Carolina Press, which under the leadership of W. T. Couch in the 1930s sought to let people speak for themselves.

1. Segregation, Racial Violence, and Black Workers

Arizona Marie Fort was interviewed by Doris Dixon on June 19, 1996, for the Behind the Veil Oral History Project, Duke University. The depositions of Fannie Henderson and William Glover are found in the Robert Church Papers, Mississippi Valley Collection, Brister Library, University of Memphis. Thomas Watkins's affidavit is found in File 144-72-0 in the Justice Department, National Archives and Records Administration, Washington, D.C., Record Group 60. To the extent that the FBI investigated, it largely substantiated Watkins's story.

The deep-seated character of the oppression that black people faced clearly goes back to slavery, under which slaveholders passed laws to stop poor whites and blacks from mixing and punished any open opposition to slavery or elite rule. Under such pressures, many poor and working-class whites joined in suppressing slaves, fought for the Confederacy and, after slavery, used violence to carve out and reserve a spot in the labor market and social system for themselves by excluding or subordinating blacks. Slavery and its aftermath has a voluminous literature. See, for example, Eugene G. Genovese, *Roll, Jordan Roll: The World the Slaves Made* (New York: Random House, 1972), or more recently, Ira Berlin, *Many Thousands Gone: The First Two Centuries of Slavery in North America* (Cambridge: Harvard University Press, 1998). For citations relevant to the Memphis area and the Crump regime, see the endnotes to chapter 1 in Michael K. Honey, *Southern Labor and Black Civil Rights: Organizing Memphis Workers* (Urbana: University of Illinois Press, 1993). On segregation in the North, see Leon F. Litwack, *North of Slavery: The Negro in the Free States, 1790–1860* (Chicago: University of Chicago Press, 1961). On sharecropping and peonage, see Pete Daniel, *The Shadow of Slavery: Peonage in the South, 1901–1969* (Urbana: University of Illinois Press, 1972), and "The Metamorphosis of Slavery, 1865–1900," *Journal of American History* 66 (June 1979): 88–99. For an essential work on slavery, race and labor, see W. E. B. DuBois, *Black Reconstruction in America, 1860–1880* (New York: Atheneum, 1935, 1962, 1969). For a penetrating first-hand account of life under segregation in the Memphis area, see Richard Wright, *Black Boy: A Record of Childhood and Youth* (New York: Harper and Brothers, 1945).

Racial violence was always a part of the slavery system, but riots and lynchings escalated when whites no longer had property interest in maintaining the lives of ex-slaves. At the same time, whites always relied on black labor. W. E. B. DuBois evokes the era brilliantly in *The Souls of Black Folk: Essays and Sketches* (Chicago: 1903). So does Leon Litwack, in *Trouble in Mind: Black Southerners in the Age of Jim Crow* (New York: Alfred A. Knopf, 1998). On race riots, gender politics, and white supremacy campaigns, see Glenda Elizabeth Gilmore, *Gender and Jim Crow: Women and the Politics of White Supremacy in North Carolina, 1869–1920* (Chapel Hill: University of North Carolina Press, 1997). See also the collection of essays in David S. Cecelski and Timothy B. Tyson, eds., *Democracy Betrayed: The Wilmington Race Riot and Its Legacy* (Chapel Hill: University of North Carolina Press, 1998), including Michael Honey, "The Delusions of White Supremacy and the Logic of Racial Violence in the New South." For the bizarre sexual dimensions of segregation, see Peggy Pascoe, "Miscegenation Law, Court Cases, and Ideologies of 'Race' in Twentieth-Century America," *Journal of American History* 83, no. 1 (June 1996): 44–69. On the Memphis riot, see Kevin R. Hardwick, "'Your Old Father Abe Lincoln Is Dead and Damned': Black Soldiers and the Memphis Race Riot of 1866," *Journal of Social History* 27, no. 1 (Fall 1993): 109–28. On lynching, see W. Fitzhugh Brundage, *Lynching in the New South, Georgia and Virginia, 1880–1930* (Urbana: University of Illinois Press, 1993), and Brundage, ed., *Under Sentence of Death: Essays on Lynching in the South* (Chapel Hill: University of North Carolina Press, 1997).

For documentation of white hostility against black workers on the railroads, see Philip S. Foner and Ronald L. Lewis, eds., *Black Workers: A Documentary History from Colonial Times to the Present* (Philadelphia: Temple University Press, 1989), 254–61, and see their four-volume documentary history by the same name. For insight on racism among white railroad workers, see Eric Arneson, "'Like Banquo's Ghost, It Will Not Down': The Race Question and the American Railroad Brotherhoods, 1880–1920," *American Historical Review* 99, no. 5 (December 1994): 1601–33. Arneson details the struggle over race and unionism in *Waterfront Workers of New Orleans: Race, Class, and Politics, 1863-1923* (Urbana: University of Illinois Press, 1994). Alex Lichtenstein documents the pernicious role of forced labor in the Jim Crow labor system, in *Twice the Work of Free Labor: The Political Economy of Convict Labor in the New South* (London: Verso, 1996). David Montgomery situates the politics of race deeply within the workplace in *The Fall of the House of Labor: The Workplace, the State, and American Labor Activism, 1865-1925* (New York: Cambridge University Press, 1987). For the classic treatment on various dimensions of the era of disfranchisement and segregation in the South, see C. Vann Woodward, *Origins of the New South, 1877–1913* (Baton Rouge: Louisiana State University Press, 1951). On the ways that white workers used the Jim Crow image to imagine the working class as "white" rather than multiracial, see Eric Lott, *Love and Theft: Blackface Minstrelsy and the American Working Class* (New York: Oxford University Press, 1993), and David Roediger, *The Wages of Whiteness: Race and the Making of the American Working Class* (London: Verso, 1991). For an elaboration of how racism subverted the material interests of unskilled white workers by undercutting their ability to organize, see Honey, *Southern Labor and Black Civil Rights*. For a treatment of the complexity of interracial labor organizing, see Daniel Letwin, *The Challenge of Interracial Unionism: Alabama Coal Miners, 1878–1921* (Chapel Hill: University of North Carolina Press, 1998). African Americans sometimes reincorporated Jim Crow minstrel songs into their folk tales and songs in a more positive vein. On black folk culture, see Lawrence W. Levine, *Black Culture, Black Consciousness: Afro-American Folk Thought from Slavery to Freedom* (New York: Oxford University Press, 1977).

With its influx of rural people fleeing the plantations, Memphis had long experienced racial tension and conflict as whites tried to maintain the racial dominance they had come to expect in the countryside and blacks sought to be rid of it. Whereas in its early years Memphis had an ethnically varied white working class of Germans, Irish, and other immigrants, after yellow fever epidemics in the 1870s and 1880s the city became populated mainly by whites and blacks from the plantation districts. Its homogenous white population was well schooled in the plantation mentality, and the lack of a cosmopolitan population base and the grip of Bible Belt fundamentalism, in which religion came to uphold slavery and white supremacy, contained the city within the cultural mores of the Old South. Among African Americans, a large black working class became the predominant group, while a small black middle class brokered power with the city's white leaders.

Ida B. Wells-Barnett became the most prominent of the nation's great anti-lynching resisters, and her documentation of the racial violence directed particularly at black men remains shocking to this day. Her pamphlets are collected in Trudier Harris, ed., *Selected Works of Ida B. Wells-Barnett* (New York: Oxford University Press, 1991). Her autobiography, edited by Alfreda M. Duster, *Crusade for Justice, The Autobiography of Ida B. Wells* (Chicago: University of Chicago Press, 1970), offers a few details about the early period of her life in Memphis. Due to the adverse publicity Wells-Barnett created, lynching declined in Memphis after the 1890s, with the Ell Persons incident an exception. For more on women and the anti-lynching crusade, see Jacquelyne Dowd Hall, *Revolt against Chivalry: Jessie Daniel Ames and the Women's Campaign against Lynching*, rev. ed. (New York: Columbia University Press, 1993).

The growth of black institutions and a large black population whose labor was much needed by Memphis employers forced the city's whites to treat blacks in a slightly more civilized manner than whites usually did on the plantations. But it did nothing to displace the plantation mentality among whites, which Mayor Henry Loeb would display so disastrously in 1968. Nonetheless, the black community in the Crump years operated from a position of some strength because Crump depended on their votes. His regime certainly looked more benign than the cruel terror that prevailed in his native Mississippi. For Memphis population figures see Honey, *Southern Labor and Black Civil Rights*, 16; Gloria Brown Melton, "Blacks in Memphis, Tennessee, 1920–1955: A Historical Study," (Ph.D. diss., Washington State University, 1982), 22; and Marcus D. Pohlmann and Michael P. Kirby, *Racial Politics at the Crossroads: Memphis Elects Dr. W. W. Herenton* (Knoxville: University of Tennessee Press, 1996), 5–12. On the repression in the late 1930s, see Honey, *Southern Labor and Black Civil Rights*, 166–73, and Boyle quote on 167, and on the Robert Cotton case, 115, 162, 165. See also David M. Tucker, *Memphis since Crump: Bossism, Blacks, and Civic Reformers, 1948–1968* (Knoxville: University of Tennessee Press, 1980).

Because Crump controlled the votes of the state's most populous district, he could throw elections in the state to whomever he supported. As a result he nearly controlled the governor's office, as well as his state's delegation to the national Democratic Party. Even President Franklin Roosevelt feared to cross him, and federal judges and district attorneys were in his power. He could hire or fire city employees, remove practically any elected leader or public official, and allow police or company thugs to beat up labor or civil rights organizers. His regime also did some good, and created much of the city's infrastructure by drawing on New Deal public works projects of the 1930s. Crump tolerated the white craft unions of the American Federation of Labor and even incorporated them into his political machine, but he crushed unions for black and white industrial workers and public employees. See Roger Biles, *Memphis in the Great Depression* (Knoxville: University of Tennessee Press, 1986). See David M. Tucker, "Brown Screws in the Crump Machine," chapter 7 in *Lieutenant Lee of Beale Street* (Nashville: Vanderbilt University Press, 1971), on the paternalistic and terroristic system of Crump; quote of Blair Hunt on 135. Significant differences existed amongst southern NAACP branches, as Adam Fairclough demonstrates in *Race and Democracy: The Civil Rights Struggle in Louisiana, 1915–1972* (Athens: University of Georgia Press, 1995). NAACP Papers, Group I, Series G, Branches, 1913–39, Box 199, Library of Congress Manuscripts Division, includes some detail on the Carlock case and other equally horrific incidents of racial violence.

2. From Country to City: Jim Crow at Work

This version of Broonzy's song is transcribed by William Barlow from *Big Bill Broonzy*, Folkways Records FG 3586, in *"Looking Up at Down": The Emergence of Blues Culture* (Philadelphia: Temple University Press, 1989), 302–3. Interviews with Willie Harrell, June 29, 1995, and with Robert Spencer on June 20, 1995, by Mansiki Scales for the Behind the Veil Oral History Project, Duke University, used by permission. Mr. Harrell worked at Parchman plantation. Joe William Trotter, Jr., has documented the ways in which black workers from rural areas saw urbanization and proletarianization as an improvements in their lives, in *Black Milwaukee: The Making of an Industrial Proletariat, 1915–1945* (Urbana: University of Illinois Press, 1986).

Michael Honey personal interview with John Handcox, May 16, 1985, Silver Spring, Maryland. For the details on how the segregated economy worked, see Honey, *Southern Labor and Black Civil Rights*, chapter 1, and Neil R. McMillan, *Dark Journey: Black Mississippians in the Age of Jim Crow* (Urbana: University of Illinois Press, 1989), chapter 5. The segregated economy existed even in the relatively liberal racial climate of Seattle, according to Quintard Taylor, *The Forging of a Black Community: Seattle's Central District from 1870 through the Civil Rights Era* (Seattle: University of Washington Press, 1994), chapter 2, and led to terrible hardships in northern ghettoes such as in Detroit; see Thomas J. Sugrue, *The Origins of the Urban Crisis: Race and Inequality in Postwar Detroit* (Princeton: Princeton University Press, 1996).

On the repression of the Memphis black community, see Michael K. Honey, *Southern Labor and Black Civil Rights: Organizing Memphis Workers* (Urbana: University of Illinois Press, 1993), chapters 2 and 6. Hosea Hudson, a black steelworker and Communist activist, repeatedly noted the timidity of the black middle class and preachers during the 1930s in Birmingham. See Nell Irvin

Painter, *The Narrative of Hosea Hudson: His Life as a Negro Communist in the South* (Cambridge: Harvard University Press, 1979). A portrait of Memphis participation in the Negro baseball leagues referred to by George Holloway is available on the film *Black Diamonds, Blues City: Stories of the Memphis Red Sox*, by Steve Ross, available at the University of Memphis Theater Department. Some of the comments by Holloway were related by phone on June 16, 1990, unrecorded.

3. Making a Way out of No Way: Black Women Factory Workers

My interview with Irene Branch was supplemented by a phone conversation on May 27, 1989, in which she told me about her father. For a rich treatment of black women, work, and community, and for the relevant literature, see Jacqueline Jones, *Labor of Love, Labor of Sorrow: Black Women, Work, and the Family, from Slavery to the Present* (New York: Random House, 1986). She lists U.S. census figures in 1920, 1930, and 1940, 160–79, 200, 208, 209–16. For an overview on black women, see Darlene Clark Hine and Kathleen Thompson, *A Shining Thread of Hope: The History of Black Women in America* (New York: Broadway Books, 1998). On black women, labor, and domestic work, see Tera Hunter, *To 'Joy My Freedom: Southern Black Women's Lives and Labors after the Civil War* (Cambridge: Harvard University Press, 1997). See also Mary Romero, *Maid in the U.S.A.* (New York: Routledge, 1992). The quotation from Elizabeth Clark-Lewis is in *Living In, Living Out: African American Domestics in Washington, D.C., 1910–1940* (Washington, D.C.: Smithsonian Institution Press, 1994), 14. Black women workers could feel a particular sense of accomplishment, Jacqueline Jones observes, due to the tangible rewards created for the next generation, *Labor of Love, Labor of Sorrow*, 222.

Clark-Lewis points out that from 1900 to 1940, occupations in clerical, sales, and factory jobs opened up for white women, whose work in household service fell by 40 percent. Most of these employment categories remained closed to black women, and their share of domestic work shot up 43 percent. "'This Work Had a End': African-American Domestic Workers in Washington, D.C., 1910–1940," in Carol Groneman and Mary Beth Norton, eds., *"To Toil the Livelong Day": America's Women at Work, 1780–1980* (Ithaca, N.Y.: Cornell University Press, 1987). For a similar national pattern, see Jones, *Labor of Love, Labor of Sorrow*, 232–62. For more statistics on black women workers in Memphis, see Honey, *Southern Labor and Black Civil Rights*, 29–38, 192–98, 225; for information on Memphis Furniture, 191, 252–63; and for the Corrine Smith bus incident, 208.

Interlude: Not What We Seem

Richard Wright, *Twelve Million Black Voices: A Folk History of the Negro in the United States* (New York: Viking Press, 1941). Robin D. G. Kelley demonstrates in his studies of black working-class life how daily resistance created a hidden transcript, or discourse, of opposition and had "a cumulative effect on power relations," in *Race Rebels: Culture, Politics, and the Black Working Class* (New York: The Free Press, 1994), 8, 56. In his chapter on black resistance in public transportation, "Congested Terrain," Kelley calls public conveyances "moving theaters" where blacks and whites acted out new and old scripts in the drama of Jim Crow, 65, 71–72. Kelley draws on James C. Scott, *Domination and the Arts of Resistance: Hidden Transcripts* (New Haven: Yale University Press, 1990), and *Weapons of the Weak: Everyday Forms of Peasant Resistance* (New Haven: Yale University Press, 1985).

Memphis population figures are in Michael K. Honey, *Southern Labor and Black Civil Rights: Organizing Memphis Workers* (Urbana: University of Illinois Press, 1993), 187, 16. The incidents on the Memphis buses are recounted in Gloria Brown-Melton, "Blacks in Memphis," 202–5, and the sailor incident was told to me in a personal interview of Willie Hall, October 29, 1984, Memphis. For some of the details of Pullman porter organizing and related issues, see Jervis Anderson, *A. Philip Randolph: A Biographical Portrait* (New York: Harcourt Brace Jovanovich, 1972). Jesse Jackson made reference to his father's experience with segregated train cars in World War II in a speech at the Democratic National Convention, Chicago, August 1996, played on National Public Radio. See Robert Rogers Korstad's "Daybreak of Freedom: Tobacco Workers and the CIO, Winston-Salem, North Carolina, 1943–1950" (Ph.D. diss., University of North Carolina, 1987) for an expansive portrait of black working-class resistance to Jim Crow in the 1940s.

4. Freedom Struggles at the Point of Production

On the long struggle over equal rights within the labor movement, see Bruce Nelson's *The Logic and Limits of Solidarity: American Workers and the Struggle for Black Equality* (Princetone: Princeton University Press, forthcoming). On the war and the difficulties that followed in Memphis, see Honey, *Southern Labor and Black Civil Rights*, chapters 7 and 8. Alan Draper describes the role of white workers in the White Citizens Councils in *Conflict of Interests: Organized Labor and the Civil Rights Movement in the South, 1954–1968* (Ithaca, N.Y.: Cornell University Press, 1994), and specifically in Memphis, 23, 29. For an example of how CIO union contracts could institutionalize discrimination, see Robert J. Norrell, "Caste in Steel: Jim Crow Careers in Birmingham, Alabama," *Journal of American History* 73, no. 3 (December 1986): 669–94. On Operation Dixie, see Barbara Griffith, *The Crisis of American Labor: Operation Dixie and the Defeat of the CIO* (Philadelphia: Temple University Press, 1988), and Michael Honey, "Operation Dixie: Labor and Civil Rights in the Postwar South," *Mississippi Quarterly* 45, no. 4 (Fall 1992): 439–52. For a detailed view of black workers organizing in the 1940s South, see Robert Rogers Korstad, "Daybreak of Freedom: Tobacco Workers and the CIO, Winston-Salem, North Carolina, 1943–1950" (Ph.D. diss., University of North Carolina, 1987).

The Firestone black workers' suit and related documents from 1956 can be found in Local 186 URW Memphis Firestone Tire and Rubber Company Papers, unprocessed, Mississippi Valley Collection, University of Memphis.

Additional details about Holloway's plight were taken from a written memo he provided, undated, in author's possession, and from an unrecorded phone conversation, June 16, 1990. UAW certification at the Memphis Harvester plant occurred on April 4, 1948. *Fifty Years of Progress, UAW Region 8, Past and Present* (Detroit: United Auto Workers, c. 1985), 91, provides details of Holloway's career. My account of Holloway's battles are drawn mainly from the UAW files. Items include "Report of Harry Ross," 1952; Ben Mincy to Emil Mazey, December 3, 1952, box 19, folder 19, and George Holloway to Walter Reuther, September 15, 1958, box 59, folder 53, Holloway et al. to Pat Greathouse, June 26, 1961, box 194, all in the UAW Fair Practices collection; Holloway to Reuther, November 28, 1955, UAW Office of the President's files, box 811; Malvin Burns and other workers to James Alexander, Memphis, February 13, 1956, and other items in box 15, folder 1C, in the records of the Agricultural Implement Division; Holloway to E. T. Michaels, director of Region 8, March 3, 1958, box 196, folder History of Local 988; Carl Moore to Carroll Hutton and Bill Dobbs, November 10, 1960, on the presidential race, box 43, folder Carl Moore, 1960–61; "To All Members of Local 988, UAW," May 2, 1960, from Greathouse, Robert Johnston, and Douglas Fraser, box 195, History of Local 988; and Holloway's file, "Personal, 1965–1969," all in UAW Region 8 files, Walter Reuther Archives of Labor and Urban Affairs, Wayne State University, Detroit. Harry Alston to Nelson Jackson, on "Intimidation of Negro Welder," July 22, 1953, Southern Regional Office, General Office Files of the National Urban League, box A153, Library of Congress Manuscripts collection, Washington, D.C. See also *Commercial Appeal*, February 10 and 11, 1960, April 6, 1960, and May 31, 1956. My thanks to Paul Ortiz for bringing his interview with Ralph Thompson, July 7, 1995, Memphis, to my attention, used with permission of Behind the Veil: Documenting African American Life in the Jim Crow South Oral History Project, Center for Documentary Studies at Duke University. Carl Moore personal interview, unrecorded, February 7, 1983. Recorded telephone interview with Hattie Holloway, June 15, 1990.

5. Organizing and Surviving in the Cold War

Leroy Boyd's narrative draws on Paul Ortiz's interview with Leroy Boyd, June 19 and 22, 1995, Behind the Veil Oral History Project, Duke University, used by permission, as well as my own interviews with him. A personal interview with George Isabell in Memphis, February 10, 1983, provided details on the Buckeye plant. For more details on the left-led unions and the red scare in Memphis, see Karl Korstad's account, "Black and White Together: Organizing in the South with the Food, Tobacco, Agricultural, and Allied Workers Union (FTA-CIO), 1946–1952," in Steve Rosswurm, ed., *The CIO's Left-Led Unions* (New Brunswick, N.J.: Rutgers University Press, 1992), 69–94. For more details on the red scare and Local 19, see Michael K. Honey, *Southern Labor and Black Civil Rights: Organizing Memphis Workers* (Urbana: University of Illinois Press, 1993), chapters 7 and 8. For another case study of the red scare's effects on black workers, see Robert Rogers Korstad's "Daybreak of Freedom: Tobacco Workers and the CIO, Winston-Salem, North Carolina, 1943–1950" (Ph.D. diss., University of North Carolina, 1987). My personal interview with Daniel Powell, February 1, 1983, Memphis, provided perspective on black indifference to anti-communism. Information on Federal Compress and Warehouse Company comes from a company profile in the files of Local 19.

For particulars on the red scare era, see Ellen Schrecker, *Many Are the Crimes: McCarthyism in America* (Boston: Little, Brown, 1998), and the oral histories in Griffin Fariello, *Red Scare: Memories of the American Inquisition, an Oral History* (New York: Avon Books, 1995); Bud Schultz and Ruth Schultz, *It Did Happen Here, Recollections of Political Repression in America* (Berkeley: University of California Press, 1989). For more specifics on the red scare in Memphis, see Michael K. Honey, "Labor, the Left, and Civil Rights in the South: Memphis during the CIO Era, 1937–1955" and Gerald Horne, "The Case of the Civil Rights Congress: Anti-Communism As an Instrument of Social Repression," both in Judith Joel and Gerald M. Erickson, eds., *Anti-Communism: The Politics of Manipulation* (Minneapolis: MEP Publications, 1987).

The United Packinghouse Workers of America developed a remarkable program for racial equality, detailed by Rick Halpern and Roger Horowitz, *Meatpackers: An Oral History of Black Packinghouse Workers and Their Struggle for Racial and Economic Equality* (New York: Twayne Publishers, 1996); Rick Halpern, *Down on the Killing Floor: Black and White Workers in Chicago's Packinghouses, 1904–1954* (Urbana: University of Illinois Press, 1997); and Roger Horowitz, '*Negro and White, Unite and Fight': A Social History of Industrial Unionism in Meatpacking, 1930–1990* (Urbana: University of Illinois Press, 1997). For case studies of blacks and Communists in the labor movement, see Robin D. G. Kelley, *Hammer and Hoe: Alabama Communists during the Great Depression* (Chapel Hill: University of North Carolina Press, 1990); Nell Irvin Painter, *The Narrative of Hosea Hudson, His Life as a Negro Communist in the South* (Cambridge: Harvard University Press, 1979).

For the larger and contentious literature on the role of Communists in the CIO, see Robert H. Zieger, *The CIO, 1935–1955* (Chapel Hill: University of North Carolina Press, 1995), particularly chapter 9. Zieger is hostile to the Communists but credits their role on advancing the cause of black workers in the South. His footnotes to chapter 9 provide a good overview of the literature on Communists in the labor movement. On the woodworkers union (IWA), I drew on newspapers and personal interview with white business agent Forrest Dickenson, Memphis, February 20, 1983. See also Jerry Lembcke and William M. Tattam, *One Union in Wood: A Political History of the International Woodworkers of America* (British Columbia and New York: Harbour Publishing and International Publishers, 1984). For perspectives on causes of the decline of CIO organizing, see concluding chapters of Nelson Lichtenstein, *The Most Dangerous Man in Detroit: Walter Reuther and the Fate of American Labor* (New York: Basic Books, 1995), and Zieger, *The CIO*, chapters 12 and 13. For a somewhat different perspective on the Taft-Hartley law's effect on labor, see Melvin Dubofsky, *the State and Labor in Modern America* (Chapel Hill: University of North Carolina Press, 1994), 199–208.

My research on the McGee case is based on files in the United Packinghouse Workers of America Papers, Program Department, Subject and Correspondence Files, box 345, folder 3, Wisconsin Historical Society, Madison, and on articles in the *Southern Patriot*, a newspaper published by the Southern Conference Educational Fund, in Louisville, Kentucky. For a secondary account, see Gerald Horne's *Communist Front? The Civil Rights Congress, 1946–1956* (London and Toronto: Associated University Presses, 1988), chapter 3.

Daniel B. Cornfield, *Becoming a Mighty Voice: Conflict and Change in the United Furniture Workers of America* (New York: Russell Sage Foundation, 1989), provides sketches of the union careers of Leroy Clark and Carl Scarborough, 201–4. According to his statistics, the increase in black women at Memphis Furniture was much greater than the general trend in the furniture industry, 211, but the participation of Alzada Clark and other black women did spur a great expansion in organizing women in furniture and related fields in the 1970s, 1980s, and beyond, 212–23. Willie Rudd and Ida Leachman played a major role in this development, 225–27. On Taft-Hartley and the raids against the furniture union, 105–6.

Interlude: Arts of Resistance

On subterfuge and dissembling as resistance, see James C. Scott, *Domination and the Arts of Resistance: Hidden Transcripts* (New Haven: Yale University Press, 1990), and *Weapons of the Weak: Everyday Forms of Peasant Resistance* (New Haven: Yale University Press, 1985). Personal interview with Junius Scales in Philadelphia, April 3, 1987. Junius Irving Scales and Richard Nickson, *Cause at Heart: A Former Communist Remembers* (Athens: University of Georgia Press, 1987) give an account of Scales's was arrest in Memphis on November 18, 1954, 3–15.

6. Civil Rights Unionism

Nelson Lichtenstein and Robert Korstad explain the lost opportunities of the postwar period in "Opportunities Found and Lost: Labor, Radicals, and the Early Civil Rights Movement," *Journal of American History* 75 (October 1988): 786–811. Kevin Boyle, *The UAW and the Heyday of American Liberalism, 1945–1968* (Ithaca, N.Y.: Cornell University Press, 1995), 161–67 and chapter 5, examines the failures of the UAW to challenge white worker racism. Philip S. Foner, *Organized Labor and the Black Worker, 1619–1981* (New York: International Publishers, 1981), chapters 21–22, provides an overview of the split between labor and civil rights forces. Herbert Hill's "The AFL-CIO and the Black Worker: Twenty-five Years after the Merger," *The Journal of Intergroup Relations* 10, no. 1 (Spring 1982), documents the federation's failure to meet the civil rights challenge. Hill documents black labor's use of civil rights laws in the 1960s in *Black Labor and the American Legal System: Race, Work, and the Law* (Madison: University of Wisconsin Press, 1985). Hill's NAACP report was titled "Racism within Organized Labor: A Report of Five Years of the AFL-CIO, 1955–1960," published by the NAACP Labor Department.

For an example of the political orientation of white working-class voters see Kenneth Durr, "When Southern Politics Came North: The Roots of White Working-Class Conservatism in Baltimore, 1940–1964," *Labor History* 37, no. 3 (Summer 1996): 309–31. On the shifting politics of Memphis whites and blacks, see David M. Tucker, *Lieutenant Lee of Beale Street* (Nashville: Vanderbilt University Press, 1971); Tucker, *Memphis since Crump: Bossism, Blacks, and Civic Reformers, 1948–1968* (Knoxville: University of Tennessee Press, 1980), quote on Kuykendall, 150; Marcus D. Pohlmann and Michael P. Kirby, *Racial Politics at the Crossroads: Memphis Elects Dr. W. W. Herenton* (Knoxville: University of Tennessee Press, 1996).

Working-class blacks played a significant role in the NAACP as can be readily seen in Adam Fairclough's *Race and Democracy: The Civil Rights Struggle in Louisiana, 1915–1972* (Athens: University of Georgia Press, 1995). On the role of black labor leaders in the civil rights struggle, see Foner, *Organized Labor and the Black Worker*, chapters 20–23. Martin Luther King appealed heavily to these leaders and to unions with large black memberships for financial support and participation in the civil rights movement. For exceptional portraits of the mix of people who organized the civil rights movement at the grass roots, see Charles M. Payne, *I've Got the Light of Freedom: The Organizing Tradition and the Mississippi Freedom Struggle* (Berkeley: University of California Press, 1995); and John Dittmer, *Local People: The Struggle for Civil Rights in Mississippi* (Urbana: University of Illinois Press, 1994).

7. "I Am a Man": Unionism and the Black Working Poor

Ralph Jackson is quoted in W. Ellison Chalmers et al., *Racial Conflict and Negotiations: Perspectives and First Case Studies* (Ann Arbor, Mich.: Institute of Labor and Industrial Relations, 1971), 170. The first two quotes from Martin Luther King come from the address of March 18, 1968, and the last quote is from his "Mountaintop" speech, April 3, 1968, both given at the Mason Temple in Memphis, both in box 6, folder 29, Sanitation Workers' Strike Papers, Mississippi Valley collection, Brister Library, University of Memphis. For an overview of the sanitation strike with citations to other sources, see Michael Honey, "Martin Luther King, Jr., the Crisis of the Black Working Class, and the Memphis Sanitation Strike," in Robert H. Zieger, ed., *Southern Labor in Transition, 1940–1995* (Knoxville: University of Tennessee Press, 1997). On the "I Am a Man" slogan, see Stephen Sandford Estes, Jr., "Confronting the 'Great White Father': Paternalism, Gender, and the Civil Rights Movements in Memphis and Charleston" (master's thesis, Rice University, 1994). Ortha B. Strong Jones, interviewed by Laurie Green, August 8, 1995, Behind the Veil Oral History project, Duke University, quoted with permission, p. 26 of transcript.

The crisis of the black working class is documented in Arthur M. Ross, "The Negro in the American Economy," and Charles Killingsworth, "Negroes in a Changing Labor Market," in Ross and Herbert Hill, eds., *Employment, Race, and Poverty* (New York: Harcourt, Brace and Worlds, 1967), 18–19, 58–69. See Manning Marable, "The Crisis of the Black Working Class: An Economic and Historical Analysis," *Science and Society* 46, no. 2 (Summer 1982): 130–61. Anne Marie Cavanaugh researched census statistics for this project, from the *Seventeenth Decennial Census of the United States* (Washington, D.C.: U.S. Government Printing Office, 1952), vol. 2, pt. 4, pp. 57, 61; *Eighteenth Decennial Census* (1962), vol. 2 pt. 4, pp. 199, 423–38; *Nineteenth Decennial Census* (1973), vol. 5 pt. 4, pp. 679–84; *Tennessee Data for Affirmative Action Plans, Annual Averages 1980* (Nashville: Tennessee Department of Employment Security, 1982), table 3, p. 21; Equal Employment Opportunity File, Memphis Metropolitan Statistical Area, 1990. Jacqueline Jones, *Labor of Love, Labor of Sorrow: Black Women, Work and the Family, from Slavery to the Present* (New York: Random House, 1986), documents the position of black women in the labor market in chapters 7 and 8, and I have cited one of her statistics on 234. Black community poverty statistics came from Marcus D. Pohlman and Michael P. Kirby, *Racial Politics at the Crossroads: Memphis Elects Dr. W. W. Herenton* (Knoxville: University of Tennessee Press, 1996), 56, and F. Ray Marshall and Arvil Van Adams, "Negro Employment in Memphis," *Industrial Relations, A Journal of Economy and Society* 9, no. 3 (May 1970): 308–23, 320. The "no worst job" quote is from Thomas W. Collins, "An Analysis of the Memphis Garbage Strike of 1968," in Johnetta B. Cole, ed., *Anthropology for the Eighties* (New York: The Free Press, 1982), 355.

For more on mechanization's disastrous effects on black workers and on male and female employment statistics, see William H. Harris, *The Harder We Run: Black Workers since the Civil War* (New York: Oxford University Press, 1982), 130–37; Jones, *Labor of Love, Labor of Sorrow*, chapters 7 and 8. Because of such realities, civil rights groups always had an economic agenda, as Donna Cooper Hamilton and Charles V. Hamilton demonstrate in *The Dual Agenda: Race and Social Welfare Policies of Civil Rights Organizations* (New York: Columbia University Press, 1997).

For more on deindustrialization, black unemployment, and poverty, see Vivian Henderson, "Region, Race, and Jobs," in Arthur M. Ross and Herbert

Hill, eds., *Employment, Race, and Poverty* (New York: Harcourt, Brace and Worlds, 1967); Thomas J. Sugrue, *The Origins of the Urban Crisis: Race and Inequality in Postwar Detroit* (Princeton: Princeton University Press, 1996).

The quote concerning Loeb and racism is in Pohlmann and Kirby, *Racial Politics at the Crossroads*, 19. For details leading up to the strike, see David M. Tucker, *Memphis since Crump: Bossism, Blacks, and Civic Reformers, 1948–1968* (Knoxville: University of Tennessee Press, 1980), and for the city council decision not to settle the strike, see Joan Turner Beifuss, *At the River I Stand: Memphis, the 1968 Strike, and Martin Luther King* (Memphis: B and W Books, 1985), 156–64. The "Memphis spirit" of labor and community alliance traveled to struggles of the working poor in Charleston, South Carolina, Atlanta, and elsewhere. See Leon Fink and Brian Greenberg, *Upheaval in the Quiet Zone: A History of Hospital Workers' Union Local 1199* (Urbana: University of Illinois Press, 1989), chapter 7. For the most recent review of relevant information and sources on the King murder, see Gerald Posner, *Killing the Dream: James Earl Ray and the Assassination of Martin Luther King, Jr.* (New York: Random House, 1998). Posner finds no basis for the conspiracy theory and concludes King was killed by Ray working alone.

8. The Fate of the Black Working Class:
The Global Economy, Racism, and Union Organizing

I interviewed Lt. Jerry Miller at the United Rubber Workers Retirees Hall, April 9, 1996, Memphis, and undertook additional interviews with Matthew Davis and Clarence Coe, made April 10, 1996, and personal interviews with Robert Tillman, February 24, 1983, and Billie Willis, February 3, 1983, Memphis.

Thomas Sugrue explains how the closure of major industrial plants wrecked inner cities and further undercut much of black America's economic possibilities, in *The Origins of the Urban Crisis: Race and Inequality in Postwar Detroit* (Princeton: Princeton University Press, 1996). William Julius Wilson documents how deindustrialization, low educational levels, and a variety of disadvantages have combined to close off opportunities for black working-class people, in *When Work Disappears: The World of the New Urban Poor* (New York: Alfred A. Knopf, 1997). Wilson also documents the shifting of jobs to the suburbs and its impact on unemployment in the inner cities, 37–44, 54, 223–24. Marcus D. Pohlmann and Michael P. Kirby describe the changing economy in Memphis, *Racial Politics at the Crossroads: Memphis Elects Dr. W. W. Herenton* (Knoxville: University of Tennessee Press, 1996), 53–54, 100. My appreciation to Economics Professor David Cicelski at the University of Memphis for his guidance on the state of the Memphis economy, personal interview, May 12, 1996, Memphis.

For the "womanist" (a term popularized by Alice Walker) philosophy in action and a relevant bibliography, see Mary Field Belenky, Lynne A. Bond, and Jacqueline S. Weinstock, *A Tradition That Has No Name: Nurturing the Devel-*

opment of People, Families, and Communities (New York: Basic Books, 1997), and see 168 for a discussion of terms. Decertification statistics come from Daniel Cornfield, *Becoming a Mighty Voice: Conflict and Change in the United Furniture Workers of America* (New York: Russell Sage Foundation, 1989), 162. According to this account, African Americans and women, especially Alzada Clark and Ida Leachman, played a critical role in revitalizing the United Furniture Workers during a period of major setbacks. The concluding King quote is from the address he gave, March 18, 1968, at Mason Temple in Memphis, box 6, folder 29, Sanitation Workers' Strike Papers, Mississippi Valley Collection, Brister Library, University of Memphis.

INDEX

accommodation and resistance, discussed, xvii–xxi, 9, 19, 123–31, 211, 247–48; examples of, 55, 74, 83–85, 90, 95–96, 121, and passim

affidavits, 20–36, editing method, 20

affirmative action, 334

AFL-CIO: and the Cold War, 237–38; racial policies criticized, 238, 265, 282; and voter mobilization, 240

AFL-CIO Labor Council: black workers in, 251–52; and support of sanitation workers, 297–98, 320

African Americans: and deindustrialization, 49–50, 98, 322–34, 362–65, 359–60, 362–68, 387; capital accumulation, loss of, 359–60; families, xix, 9, 322, 364, chapter eight passim: farmers, 45, 48, 54–55, 73, 109; and labor history, preface, xvii, 49, 123; and military service, 59, 124, 133, 136–37, 138, 185, 247, 263, 294; middle classes, 47, 49, 65–66, 86, 139, 320, 379–80; and slavery, xvii; use of terms, xiv; and World War II, 123–31, 132

African American men: declining economic position, 288–89, 294, 363–64. *See also* "I Am A Man" slogan

African American women: alliances with black men, 91, 121, 151, 153, 282; difficulty obtaining industrial jobs, xviii–xix, chapter three passim; as domestic workers, 46, 87, 91, 93–94, 97–98, 316, 375, 380; double duty, 121, chapter three passim; as heads of households, 364; history of, 380; improved jobs for some, 289, 364; independence from men, 97, 109; labor statistics, 87–89, 289; and oral history, 7; post-war layoffs, 120; poverty of, 323; as union organizers, 271–78, 343–47, 348–51, 355, 366, 388; sexual harassment of, 201; welfare rights organizing, 316n

Alexander, Mary, murder witness, 22–23, 38–39

Allen, Ray, Firestone worker, 78, 144

American Federation of Labor (AFL): 34–36, 49, 67, 76, 79, 134, 154, 169, 171, 320; cooperation with Crump, 40–41; exclusionary racial practices, 47, 49, 61, 154, 184, 238; federal labor unions, 61; railroad brotherhoods, 24, 377; segregated union hall, 61

American Federation of State, County, and Municipal Workers (AFSCME Local 1733): 254; effect on labor movement, 302, 314–20; membership, 301–02; origin of Local 1733 name, 305; political power, 315, 320, 344

American Snuff company strike, 267

TEXT	11/13.75 Adobe Garamond
DISPLAY	Bauer Text Initials & Akzidenz Grotesk
DESIGN	Nicole Hayward
COMPOSITION	G & S Typesetters, Inc.
PRINTING AND BINDING	Thomson-Shore, Inc.